MIKE HARGROVE
AND THE CLEVELAND INDIANS

MIKE HARGROVE
AND THE CLEVELAND INDIANS

A Baseball Life

JIM INGRAHAM

Gray & Company, Publishers
Cleveland

Gray & Company, Publishers
www.grayco.com

ISBN: 978-1-59851-110-9
Printed in the United States of America
1

Contents

Acknowledgements

There is no book without the gracious cooperation and contributions of Mike and Sharon Hargrove, who spent countless hours patiently and candidly answering questions about their remarkable baseball journey. Both have a rare gift of recall for detail, dialogue and anecdotes that enriched these pages far beyond the efforts of this mere typist.

Former Indians general manager John Hart formed, with his manager, a baseball Lewis & Clark, leading the game's most moribund organization out of the wilderness and into the greatest era in franchise history. John was a fountain of knowledge on all the behind-the-scenes intrigue that went into building those powerhouse Indians teams. A prolific rhetorician, John takes a back seat to nobody when it comes to turning a phrase. "We loved Kenny from jump street," nearly knocked me out of my chair, and, about another Indians outfielder: "We couldn't be sure he would play nice in the sandbox," made me wish I'd written it first. Thanks John, for being so generous with your time, and colorful with your stories.

Thanks also to longtime baseball executive Dan O'Dowd, who, as Hart's assistant in Cleveland, had a front row seat to the Hargrove-Hart dynamic, and offered many valuable observations about that partnership, as well as some context to the pressures of managing in general, that eventually led to Hargrove's retirement.

Many thanks to Jeff Scott, who preceded Hargrove and Hart to Cleveland, first as scouting director, then as farm director in the mid to late 1980s. Jeff was also a minor league teammate of Hargrove's for two years in the Texas organization, and contributed some great stories from those days about minor league ball and brawls, the inimitable Jimmy Piersall, and Hargrove's early years as both a player and manager.

An additional special thanks to Jeff for sharing all his stories, as the man who scouted, drafted, signed and sensed, before anyone else, the full fury of the approaching hurricane that was Albert Belle. Jeff was ground zero in those days. My chapter on Belle is really Jeff's chapter.

Thanks to former Indians players Jim Thome, Sandy Alomar, and Charles Nagy, three of the core players on Hargrove's power-house Cleveland teams, plus former Indians president and general manager Mark Shapiro. All four were there throughout Hargrove's entire run as Indians manager, and offered valuable insights on those days, and those teams.

One day, a few weeks after the 1995 season, my phone rang. So, I answered it. "Hello?" I said, creatively. "Jim, this is Albert Belle. Do you want to have lunch?"

It was for moments like this that the spit take was invented. In those days Belle rarely talked to the media, and by "rarely," I mean never. He certainly never called a member of the media asking them to lunch. At that time, I was one of the Indians beat writers. For whatever reason he called me and asked me to lunch. I still don't know why, but after my wife revived me, I answered, "Yeah, sure." As though this happened every day.

So Belle and I went to lunch. He couldn't have been more cordial. We talked about his corked bat, the Hannah Storm incident, him chasing kids in his car on Halloween. We talked about his coming free agency, how he got robbed of the MVP Award that year (Mo Vaughn won it). We talked about everything. After word spread in the restaurant—it took roughly eight seconds—that there was a famous customer in the house, we would be periodically interrupted by waiters, waitresses, and cooks coming out of the kitchen to our table, to say hello. Albert greeted them all warmly.

Then we finished lunch and finished our conversation. Albert picked up the tab and we left.

To this day I still don't know how or why any of that happened. But it did, and parts of our conversation appear in the chapter on Belle, and elsewhere in the book.

So, thanks again, Albert. Next time lunch is on me.

On the procurement of photos for the book, thanks to Greg Drezdzon. Thanks also to the Cleveland Indians, especially Curtis

Danburg of the Indians. To Eric Scott of Northwestern Oklahoma State University. To the Hargrove family, particularly daughter Pam Chuna. Thanks also to publisher David Gray, for guiding a rookie author through the publishing forest, and copy editor John Luttermoser, for tidying up the foliage.

Lastly, but actually firstly, thanks to my family. To my wife Bette, who took one for the team for several years by flawlessly raising our children while I was traveling around the country watching baseball games. To my daughter Dana LeRoy, a world-class editor in her own right, who saved her father from countless mistakes by reading the manuscript, making suggestions, and not once rolling her eyes. To my son Austin, who once called me late one night as I was walking to my car in a parking lot outside Fenway Park to tell me he'd hit two triples and thrown a runner out at the plate from right field to end the game, and preserve a win for his college summer league team. It's the only time in my life I remember smiling and tearing up at the same time.

Baseball is great.

— Jim Ingraham

MIKE HARGROVE
AND THE CLEVELAND INDIANS

Introduction

The Kingdome was shaking. Not because of an earthquake, but because of humans—58,489 of them.

It started shaking just after the national anthem on Oct. 17, 1995. Game 6 of the American League Championship Series. Cleveland's crafty Dennis Martinez vs. Seattle's towering, powerful Randy Johnson.

"David vs. Goliath!" a smiling Martinez chirped to reporters the day before the Kingdome shook. Cleveland led the series, 3-2.

Game 6 lived up to the hype. The crowd inside the giant concrete mushroom spent most of the nine innings bouncing waves of sound off the mammoth concrete ceiling, which threw the racket right back into the faces of the racketeers.

It was tense. It was dramatic. It was a relentless, deafening, suffocating assault on the senses.

The Kingdome shook.

The Indians, leading 1-0, scored three runs in the eighth inning off Johnson, two of them coming on a passed ball—thanks to Kenny Lofton's electrifying mad dash home from second base—and won 4-0, clinching their first American League pennant in 41 years. When it was over, Cleveland's manager admitted his team had almost literally taken his breath away.

"It got so I could hardly breathe," Mike Hargrove said. "We had to win that game. I couldn't have taken another one."

It was an utterly human reaction. A genuine response to an achievement that will forever be remembered as one of the most famous moments in Cleveland sports history. It was also a reaction that was shared by millions of Indians fans watching the game on TV in Ohio and holding their breath, while the Indians' manager searched for his.

For the first time since 1954, the Cleveland Indians were going to the World Series. Their manager, who wasn't even alive the last time the Indians won the World Series, and who was born and grew up in a small town in the Texas Panhandle, 1,252 miles from Jacobs Field, grasped and was humbled by the significance of what he and his team had accomplished that night in Seattle, on Oct. 17, 1995. The night the Kingdome shook.

"It got so I could hardly breathe."

In professional sports, then and now, hardly anyone ever lets their guard down. There are expected patterns of behavior and speech that govern any and all situations and outcomes.

Those who violate those norms do so at their own risk. That is, unless it's so personal, so revealing, so *human* that it is celebrated, not castigated.

That was Mike Hargrove on what was to that point, and maybe still to this one, the greatest achievement of his career. Speaking in the visitor's clubhouse, Hargrove admitted that with his team trying to win its first pennant in almost half a century, he was so freaking nervous he couldn't breathe.

I was a Cleveland Indians beat writer at that time, and was part of a small group of Cleveland reporters to whom Hargrove confessed his bout with asphyxiation. It struck me then and now as the words of a man who was man enough to acknowledge what, in the macho, testosterone-driven world of professional sports, is rarely if ever, acknowledged: that sometimes the moment *can* become too big.

But Mike Hargrove, who has spent most of his adult life leading men, is also known as "Grover" to his close friends. It's a moniker hinting at his more folksy, chummy, docile side. Indeed, his reaction to that history-making night in Seattle was Hargrove's quintessential "Grover" moment.

A moment in time when a former small-town Texas kid, respectful, hard-working and humane, but also hard-charging, ruthlessly competitive (he played for Billy Martin), and Texas tough, got caught in the crosshairs of history and was flattered to the point of near-speechlessness by the attention.

It took his breath away—and he admitted it.

For him, it was "Gee whiz" first, and "We win" second.

"It got so I could hardly breathe" was the manager of the 1995 American League champions confessing that during the clinching game he was just as nervous as everyone else. Maybe more. You can't get any more human than that, and Mike Hargrove's humanity has ridden with him, and served him well, throughout a remarkable baseball life. It's an unlikely story, springing from an unlikely outpost. It's a life and career largely under-appreciated—by us, not by him—perhaps because much of it was spent in the shadows of so many big names, big personalities, and big moments. Moments that are both heart-stopping and heartbreaking, and that's not even counting the time he almost became the manager of the New York Yankees.

It began in tiny Perryton, Texas, which if it isn't in the middle of nowhere, is a suburb of the middle of nowhere. How small was it? Hargrove didn't play baseball in high school because his high school didn't have a team. Instead, he played on a softball team with his father. Dudley Hargrove hit fourth in the lineup. His son batted third.

Then it was on to that noted baseball factory Northwestern Oklahoma State University, an NAIA school, where Hargrove earned a scholarship—for basketball. He had to be talked into trying out for the baseball team, as a walk-on, but he's glad he did.

The Texas Rangers drafted him, virtually as an afterthought, in the 25th round of the 1972 June Draft. Almost overnight he became a phenom. In 1974 he made the nearly unheard-of jump from low Class-A ball to the major leagues and not only stuck, but was voted the American League's Rookie of the Year, ahead of future Hall of Famers George Brett and Robin Yount.

It was during Hargrove's rookie year that the Rangers visited Cleveland on a hot, sweltering June night and Indians management decided selling beer for 10 cents per cup was a good idea. The riot that followed—triggered, by some accounts, when Hargrove cold-cocked a drunk who ran onto the field and tried to steal Rangers right fielder Jeff Burroughs' cap and glove—was not a good idea.

At the time, Hargrove had no way of knowing that Cleveland would become the centerpiece of his career, as a player, and, more significantly, as a manager. He replaced John McNamara as Indians manager in the middle of the team's club-record 105-loss 1991 season.

In 1993 Hargrove was faced with a tragedy for which there was no managerial manual. In spring training two of his players were killed, and a third almost killed, in a boating accident that rocked the franchise and tested the leadership skills and character of Hargrove, his staff, the Indians front office, and the players themselves.

Two years later, in 1995, Hargrove managed one of the greatest offensive teams in major league history, the Kenny Lofton, Albert Belle, Carlos Baerga, Eddie Murray, Jim Thome, Manny Ramirez-led juggernaut that bludgeoned its way to a record of 100-44 in that strike-shortened season, winning their division by a record, and ridiculous, 30 games.

Few know that Hargrove was the stormy Belle's first and last manager in professional baseball. It was an at-times explosive relationship, beginning early in Belle's career when Hargrove benched him for loafing during a game, then told two of his coaches to stand guard outside his office door as potential backups for a one-on-one post-game meeting between Hargrove and Belle in which the manager feared that they might come to blows.

Hargrove had a front-row seat for most of the rambunctious Belle's major league career. It was through the ceiling tile in Hargrove's office in the visitor's clubhouse at Comiskey Park in 1994 that Indians pitcher Jason Grimsley entered the crawl space that took him to the umpire's room on a clandestine in-game mission to retrieve Belle's confiscated corked bat.

It was Hargrove who, during the 1995 World Series, personally apologized to NBC's Hannah Storm for Belle's expletive-laced verbal assault the reporter endured for the "crime" of being in the dugout during batting practice, when Belle happened to be passing through.

Hargrove became an expert at apologizing, defusing, explaining, and selectively circumnavigating the many conflagrations created by Belle's combustible personality.

It was in 1997, after the team lost both Belle (to free agency) and Lofton (traded to Atlanta), that the Indians, in the midst of winning five consecutive division titles, came the closest in Hargrove's eight-plus years as manager to winning the World Series. That excruciating, extra-innings Game 7 loss to the Florida Marlins—the Jose Mesa game—was a punch to the gut that Hargrove, the organization and the city of Cleveland still feel to this day.

It was a loss Hargrove would have avoided had he been fired in the middle of the 1997 season—which he almost was. Hargrove felt that '97 team was the grittiest, but least-talented of the five consecutive teams he took to the postseason. But a lackluster second half of the season led to rumors that Hargrove's firing was imminent, which it was, until he was given a last-second reprieve.

There was no reprieve after the 1999 season, especially given the way that it ended. After taking a 2-0 lead over Boston in the best-of-five Division Series, the Indians lost the last three games by a combined score of 44-18—including a 23-7 mauling in Game 4. Shortly after the Indians lost that series, their manager lost his job, fired just eight wins away from passing Lou Boudreau (728) as the winningest manager in Cleveland Indians history.

There followed four years managing bad Baltimore Orioles teams, where Hargrove was witness to the end of Belle's career. Then the confounding, controversial end, after 2½ years in Seattle, of Hargrove's managerial career. On July 1, 2007, with the Mariners on an eight-game winning streak and in postseason contention, Hargrove stunned the baseball world by saying he'd had enough. He stepped down as manager and walked away, knowing he was writing his career epitaph, that his phone would never again ring with an offer to interview for a job as a major league manager.

He and his wife Sharon rode off into the sunset, and away from the game that had governed their lives for the previous 35 years. It was a full baseball life, and the centerpiece was Hargrove's years in Cleveland, first as a player, then as a manager, when he teamed with prescient general manager John Hart and their staffs, bankrolled by owner Dick Jacobs, to revive baseball's most moribund franchise.

From managing a team that lost 105 games, to winning 100 four years later. From no trips to the World Series in nearly half a century to two trips to the World Series in three years. From managing some of the most memorable games and players in major league history, to quieting a shaking Kingdome.

The kid from that tiny Panhandle town has left some Texas-sized tracks. So many, in fact, that it got so he could hardly breathe.

CHAPTER 1

Perryton, Texas

*"You knew everybody. We were related
to 65 to 70 percent of the town."*

They don't mess around in the Texas Panhandle. If it takes moving an entire town to make ends meet, then you move the entire town—lock, stock and tumbleweed. In 1919, when track was laid and the railroad finally came choo-chooing through the Panhandle, it did so through the open grasslands 8 miles north of Ochiltree, Texas. That was bad news for Ochiltree, whose economic development, specifically the farming and ranching communities, was dependent on good transportation.

But good transportation, the newly arrived railroad, was 8 miles away.

"Now many people might have called that their misfortune and watched their town slowly die," Perryton.com, the town's website, points out.

But not those hardscrabble Panhandlers.

With, in this case, necessity being the mother of transportation, the town's leaders, according to Perryton.com, "decided that if the railroad wouldn't come to them, they would go to it . . . by literally picking up their buildings off (their) foundations and moving to the railroad. This was quite a feat in 1919, and attracted national attention."

As well it should.

"Some of those buildings that rode across the prairie, with families inside," the town's website notes, "are still standing in the town that they named Perryton."

Today, all that remains of Ochiltree is one schoolhouse and an historical marker on Highway 70. Perryton, meanwhile, grew up to become Perryton, "Wheatheart of The Nation" according to the town's "Welcome to" signs.

There was nothing welcoming on the afternoon of Sunday, April 14, 1935. There was only blinding, choking, stinging dust. On that April day, smack in the middle of the Great Depression, after surviving 50 dust storms in the previous 104 days, Perryton endured the worst one yet. "The worst in history," according to residents.

They called it "Black Sunday."

"Dawn came clear and rosy all across the plains that day," according to one account cited in the Black Sunday link on Perryton.com. "By noon the skies were so fresh and blue that people could not remain indoors . . . They went on picnics, planted gardens, repaired henhouses, attended funerals, drove to the neighbors for a visit.

"In mid-afternoon the summery air rapidly turned colder, (the temperatures) falling as many as 50 degrees in a few hours, and the people noticed that the yards were full of birds nervously fluttering and chattering . . . Suddenly there appeared on the northern horizon a black blizzard, moving toward them; there was no sound, no wind, nothing but an immense 'boogery' cloud."

Residents knew immediately they were in for a wild ride.

"Blotting out every speck of light," the Associated Press reported, "the worst dust storm in the history of the Panhandle covered the entire region . . . The billowing black cloud struck Amarillo at 7:20 (p.m.) and visibility was zero for 12 minutes."

Kathleen (Allen) Lewis of Perryton lived through the storm. "We were driving home on this beautiful Sunday afternoon," she recalled, in 1985. "We were caught out in the approaching storm . . . Grandfather Carter told everyone to be sure the windows were rolled up tight as possible. Mother poured water from Norman's bottle onto a diaper and held it over the baby's face and gave him his milk bottle so he wouldn't cry and breathe more dust. We could see the cloud roll upon us as one might helplessly watch an approaching avalanche."

The worst of the storm—"When (it) struck it was impossible to see one's hand before his face even two inches away"—hit Perryton at 5 o'clock. "Catching hundreds of people away from their homes, at the theater, on the highways, or on picnic parties . . . In just a few minutes after the first bank appeared in the north, the fury of the black blizzard was upon us, turning the bright sunshine of a perfect day into the murky inkiness of the blackest night. Many hurried to storm cellars, remembering the cyclone of July, two years ago, which followed a similar duster."

The timing of the storm couldn't have been worse. "This storm put the finishing touch of destruction to what faint hopes this area had for a wheat crop. Business houses and homes were literally filled with the fine dirt and silt driven by this 50-mph gale."

Perryton eventually shook off the dust. The town recovered, the people survived—and 14 years later, Dudley Michael Hargrove was born.

Distant relatives on his mother's side of the family came out in a covered wagon from Thomas, Oklahoma, driving about 20 head of cattle ahead of them. This was before "Black Sunday" and before, even, Perryton. After those town-moving trail blazers from Ochiltree physically moved the town north, hard by the railroad tracks, and re-named it Perryton, Hargrove's mother's family settled there, after getting a $100 loan from the bank in Booker, Texas, which is even smaller than Perryton.

On Hargrove's father's side, the family moved from Alabama to Perryton. His great-grandfather Bud Smith got sidetracked into New Mexico and found himself in the middle of the Lincoln County Wars of the 1870s, riding with a gun-for-hire named William Henry Bonney, better known today as Billy the Kid.

"I don't know what that says about our family," Mike Hargrove said, with a chuckle.

Hargrove was born in Perryton on Oct. 26, 1949. He grew up on a farm, but when he was 5 years old his family moved to Houston, and then, shortly thereafter, moved again, to a town that should have had a song written about it: Texico, New Mexico, on the Texas/New Mexico border.

For the next two or three years the family lived in Texico, where Dudley Hargrove, Mike's father, ran a grain elevator. Then it was back to Perryton, where Dudley got into the oil business, not as an oil baron, but as a contract pumper. Those are the guys who go out and check existing wells every day.

Dudley Michael Hargrove was in fifth grade.

"A lot of people's image of small-town Texas is from the movie 'The Last Picture Show,' with tumbleweeds blowing down main street," Hargrove said. "But it was a combination of 'Friday Night Lights' and good, God-fearing people. It's cattle country and wheat farming. A lot of oil and gas, and a lot of farms. My granddad on my Mom's side had a farm, and my granddad on my dad's side also had a farm."

Perryton in those days is a lot like Perryton in these days—at least the weather. It's not the stereotypical notion of Texas climate. In Perryton it can get cold. Very cold. It's located in the high plains, where they average 17 inches of snow per year. But it also gets very hot in the summer—90 to 100 degrees hot. "In the winter you'll have a week of 75-degree weather, and then a week of 25-degree weather, with a foot of snow," said Hargrove.

Overall, though, it's really hot far more often than it's really cold. Texans learn at an early age that if you can't stand the heat, get into the shade. One way to get yourself some shade is to get yourself some trees.

"The only trees there are around water. Or around the houses of people who planted those trees," said Hargrove. "People in Ohio chop down trees to get a better view. In Perryton, you move your house *to* the trees. So, the trees are kind of like gold there."

Just as there is Texas Hot, there is also Texas Cold, and Hargrove learned that concept at a young age. One year he got a summer job working as a roustabout for a company owned by his uncle. Roustabouts spend their days checking oil wells and fixing leaks—no matter how bad the weather.

One day, as part of a three-man crew, Hargrove and two other workers went out to fix a leak in a flow line. The temperature was about 15 degrees, with a wind blowing about 30 miles per hour, which calculates to a wind-chill of -5 degrees. The men would take 15-minute turns. Two of them would sit in the truck and stay warm and the other guy would go out with a pick and try to knock the ice off the well.

"It was like chipping concrete," Hargrove said. "I was feeling really sorry for myself. I was thinking, 'I must really be low on the food chain right now.'"

But, of course, everything is relative.

"Then we pulled up to another well, and there were these three guys working," Hargrove said. "All oil wells produce salt water. And so, when they were fixing the well—they had big coveralls on and hats and beards—every time they broke the joint, salt water would spray everywhere. They had ice from the tip of their chins down to their stomachs. Just a sheet of ice. And I thought, 'Dear Lord, thank you. I am not the lowest one on the food chain anymore. I've got a great job compared to that.'"

Small wonder, then, that Hargrove preferred his summer job— plowing the fields after the wheat harvest on his two grandfathers' farms.

Perryton is in the Texas Panhandle, 7 miles south of the Oklahoma state line, on the other side of which is the Oklahoma Panhandle. Perryton is about as far away from professional sports as a town in Texas can be. Nevertheless, the Dallas Cowboys, predictably, are the Panhandle's preferred professional sports team. College football allegiance is equally divided between the University of Texas and the University of Oklahoma.

The Perryton High School Rangers—Hargrove's high school, college, and first major league team were all nicknamed "Rangers" —represented the one and only high school in Perryton, with an enrollment at the time of about 450 students. None of them, including a future American League Rookie of the Year, played baseball for the school, because the school had no baseball team.

"They had football and basketball in the fall and winter, and in the spring, they had track and golf," Hargrove said. "I was on the golf team because I hated to run."

He also played football and basketball, and excelled at both. As an all-state football player—he played safety and was the backup quarterback—he was recruited by Texas A&M and TCU.

The Perryton Rangers went 9-1 in Hargrove's senior year. High school football in the Panhandle in those days meant long bus rides to play teams from colorfully named high schools.

"One of the schools in our conference was in Muleshoe, Texas," Hargrove said. "Their nickname was the Mules, but they could have been called the donkeys, because they weren't very good at the time. They were 250 miles from Perryton, but they were in our conference."

So, while Hargrove was starring on the gridiron in the fall and on the basketball court in the winter, when spring rolled around and high school baseball players were playing high school baseball everywhere else, Hargrove was golfing. At a younger age he played Little League ball. But that was it. The town had no American Legion team. The high school had no baseball team. So, he golfed.

He did play some organized ball as a teenager. But it wasn't baseball.

"In Perryton we had a men's fast-pitch softball team, sponsored by McGibbon Oil," Hargrove said. "They traveled a lot. My dad was on the team. My dad was a really good player. He was very fast. He was a really good baseball player and softball player."

Dudley Hargrove, Mike's dad, stood about 6-2, 165 pounds, and in the mid-1950s he played on Perryton's traveling hardball team. The team consisted of men, ages 25 to 40, who would play games as far away as Colorado and New Mexico. Dudley got seen by scouts and, legend has it, was invited to go to spring training with the Dodgers one year. But his father wouldn't let him go because it was wheat harvesting time, and he had to help out on the farm. The next year he got invited to the New York Giants' camp, but he had pneumonia and couldn't go.

Time passed, and so did Dudley Hargrove's unfulfilled baseball career. But then came softball, when again he was the star of his team—as was his precocious son.

"When I was 13 or 14, I was too old to play in the YMCA league, and we didn't have an American Legion team," Hargrove said. "So, for a couple of years I played on that fast-pitch softball team with my dad and his buddies. I hit third and Dad hit fourth. That was pretty cool. He was the third baseman and I played first."

Hargrove the Younger became a teammate of his father's one day when the team had a game, but didn't have enough players because the shortstop didn't show up.

"I just came to watch the game, and then my dad says to me, 'Do you want to play?' I said, 'Sure!' So, he said, 'Ok, go get your glove.' So, I played shortstop that day. A left-handed shortstop. My dad was right-handed. The only thing in life he did left-handed was golf. I'm left-handed, and the only thing in life I do right-handed is golf."

So, there's Hargrove the Younger, at age 13 or 14, hitting third in the lineup of a fast-pitch softball team on which all the players were in their late 20s to mid-30s—including his father. And the kid more than held his own.

"I did pretty well," Hargrove said. "One time we were playing in Pampa, Texas, and they had this really good pitcher. I came to the plate and I hit a triple off the right-centerfield wall. I'm standing on third and I heard somebody yell at the pitcher, 'I told you he could hit!' And then Dad came up next and hit the ball out of the ballpark."

At the time, travel fast-pitch softball teams were a thing in Texas.

"We had to travel a lot, because Perryton is up there by itself" in the Panhandle, Hargrove said. "The closest town of any size is Amarillo, which was 120 miles away and at the time had about 110,000 people. Pampa was 60 miles away and there were about 60,000 people there. So, you had to travel."

Hargrove went into the experience as a wide-eyed teenager. He came out of it as a teenager with not-so-wide eyes.

"I learned a lot playing on that team with my dad," he said. "A lot of it I wished I hadn't learned. But he kind of prepared me for the clubhouses in the big leagues. I enjoyed playing with him."

It was about that time that Hargrove, then in the eighth grade, attended a Perryton High School football game as a spectator. Also at the game was Sharon Rupprecht, a seventh grader.

"Somebody came up to me and said, 'Mike Hargrove wants you to sit by him.' And I said, 'Mike Hargrove? Who's that? I wish it was Don Williams, because I *know* he's good looking.' Then I looked down and saw Mike, and he was good looking, too. So, I said, 'He'll do.'"

That marked the founding of the Hargrove/Rupprecht baseball alliance. They married in 1970, when he was 20 and she was 19. To this day, almost half a century later, she'll bust his chops by occasionally, mockingly, calling him, "He'll do."

But it began for both of them in Perryton.

"When Sharon and I lived there, it was a town of 10,000. They're down to 8,000 now," Hargrove said. "Back then, you knew everybody. Between Sharon and me, we were related to 65 to 70 percent of the town."

The same small-town principles applied years later, when they raised their family in Perryton during the off-season, and throughout the many places they lived during Hargrove's career.

"Mike used to say when we lived in Perryton that if the kids don't come home when they're supposed to, he could make three phone calls and find them," Sharon said. "But if they didn't come home in Cleveland, he didn't even know where to start looking for them."

In the 1960s, Hargrove became the big man on a small high school campus, and had a distinguished career in every sport he played, except for the sport at which he would make his living for 35 years as a professional. As a high school senior, with his fast-pitch softball career over and his hardball career, as far as he knew at the time, also over, Hargrove was recruited by Texas A&M and TCU to play football. Instead, he accepted a full scholarship from an NAIA school, Northwestern Oklahoma State University, to play basketball.

"I liked basketball better then, even though my favorite sport, to this day, is football," he said.

"When he was playing for the Rangers," said Sharon, "we would go to Dallas Cowboys games and he'd sit there and say, 'Gosh, I wish I'd made it in football.'"

Another reason Hargrove chose basketball in college was his experience playing for his high school basketball coach, Roy Pennington. "He was one of the most influential persons in my life," Hargrove said. "He was the guy, if I had problems with anything or needed some advice, I'd go to him. And I really enjoyed my basketball experience in high school."

Northwestern Oklahoma State University is located in Alva, Oklahoma, about 150 miles east of Perryton.

"I had a friend from high school who went there, so I had kind of an in there," said Hargrove, who in 1993 was inducted into the Northwestern Oklahoma State Sports Hall of Fame.

"I went there on a full ride to play basketball. I had no thoughts of playing baseball at all," Hargrove said. "My freshman year we started basketball in late August and didn't get through until late February. When we got through, I was tired. And all my buddies were getting to go out and have fun. That's what I wanted to do."

Then Hargrove the Elder contacted Hargrove the Younger.

It was a life-changing conversation:

"Are you going to go out for the baseball team?" his father asked.

"No, probably not."

"Why don't you just try it?"

"Dad, I'm tired, and these guys are good. I can't play with these guys. I can't compete with them."

"How do you know?"

"I guess I don't. But basketball was tough enough."

"Do me a favor. Go out for the team. Walk on, and see how it works. If you don't like it, then let it go. But just give it a shot."

So, Hargrove the Younger did.

"And I'm glad I did," he said. "It almost makes you sick to your stomach, thinking about it now. Because if I hadn't done that, Sharon and I, our goal when we got married was to get our teaching degrees and I was going to coach football and she was going to teach. We would have been retired by now, and it wouldn't have been in Cleveland, Ohio. Looking back on it now, especially in the last couple of years, I've come to the realization about how God's hand has been in my life, without me even being conscious of it."

Nudged by his father, Hargrove walked on to the baseball team as a freshman.

"I don't remember even talking to the coach at all," he said. He does, however, remember being embarrassed almost immediately.

"One of my teammates had to teach me how to blouse my uniform pants. I didn't know how to put my pants on," he said. "At that time, you bloused your pants. I had no clue. It was a little bit humbling."

Because of the weather, Northwestern Oklahoma State was forced to practice indoors in the spring. Part of the workouts included the infielders taking groundballs on a gymnasium floor. On those hardwood floors, the balls got on the infielders very quickly, but the freshman walk-on first baseman handled them flawlessly, and his teammates apparently noticed.

"My first inclination that I might be able to play with these guys was how quickly they accepted me," he said. "You know, usually when somebody can't play, it's obvious they can't play. People aren't nasty to you, but you're not really included. I was included in everything."

Unlike today, college teams back then used wooden bats. Also unlike today, players took bat preservation seriously.

"I had this favorite bat, and I cracked it," Hargrove said. "So, I took glue and glued it back together and nailed it down with carpet tacks. I used it all year. I want to say I hit nine or 10 home runs that year, with a nailed-together bat. I used that bat all year, batting practice, everything. Never broke it. It was kind of amazing."

Like many freshmen athletes in college, learning to balance academics with athletics was a challenge for Hargrove. The baseball team played its games on Tuesdays and Fridays, and Hargrove had a zoology class that met on Tuesday, Thursday and Friday.

"So, I missed a lot of classes," he said.

Still, Hargrove managed to carry almost an "A" average in the course, which evidently raised the eyebrow of the professor, who told Hargrove that if he missed one more class he was going to fail him. The professor said Hargrove hadn't been to class enough to be carrying that kind of an average.

"In one respect he was accusing me of cheating, which I wasn't," Hargrove said.

In the other respect, Hargrove couldn't afford to fail the course. But there was an important game on Friday of that week, and Hargrove, an all-conference selection as a freshman, was an important player.

"It was a tough decision, so I called my coach and said, 'I can't play.' He said, 'Why not?' I said, 'Because my zoology professor told me if I miss one more class he's going to fail me.' My coach said, 'Well Mike, you've got to make your decision. I can't tell you what to do, but you do what you've got to do.' So, he was basically telling me he was glad I chose to go to class."

The coach's name was Cecil Perkins.

"He was also the athletic director," said Hargrove. "He's the other person besides my dad and (high school basketball coach) Roy Pennington who had a huge, huge impact on my life. A lot of coaching philosophies, and how I talked to players and reacted to players, came a lot from him. But he was a tough man."

Hargrove learned that in a game during his freshman season. He was on third base, and a line drive was hit to the left fielder, a play on which Hargrove should have tagged up and scored. But he didn't.

"I came back to the bag and Coach Perkins, who was coaching third, walked up, got right next to me and grabbed the left cheek of my butt and started squeezing," Hargrove said. "He said, 'Michael'—he always called me Michael when he wasn't real pleased with me—'The next time you don't tag up, I'm going to get about five pounds of your butt.' I said, 'Well, you better stop squeezing, because there won't be five pounds left. You've already got about 16 pounds in your hand.'"

Hargrove's ascension as a college baseball player—he would hit .323 with 18 home runs for his career—coincided with his disillusion over being a college basketball player. Both were coach-driven.

In basketball, he started as a freshman and sophomore, and averaged 10 points per game for the two years. But it wasn't fun. In one game, Northwestern Oklahoma State was leading by two points with three minutes left in the game, when Hargrove, inbounding under his own basket, threw a bounce pass to a teammate in the corner. The ball hit the end line, so it was a violation.

Keith Covey, the Northwestern coach, immediately subbed Hargrove out of the game.

"Goddamit, Hargrove! You're off scholarship!" Covey hollered. "You're blowing this game for us! Get on the end of the bench. I don't want to talk to you the rest of the night!"

Hargrove went to the end of the bench, sat down, and less than a minute later heard, "Goddamit, Hargrove! What are you doing at the end of the bench? Get up here so you can keep your head in the game!"

"That," says Hargrove now, "was kind of typical of why it became un-fun."

The breaking point came shortly thereafter, when Hargrove told his father and grandfather that he was thinking about quitting basketball, in order to play football. He was still on the fence with that decision when he learned that his grandfather had gone to coach Covey and said, "You better talk to Mike. He's thinking about quitting basketball."

This was news to Covey. On a bus ride back to campus after an away game, Covey, a former marine who according to Hargrove was very military-minded, shouted to the back of the bus, "Hargrove! Get up here!"

Hargrove dutifully walked to the front of the bus and sat down next to the coach.

"I hear you're thinking about quitting basketball. Is that right?" said Covey.

"I said, 'Well, I, uh, yes sir, I guess that is right.' I was scared to death," Hargrove said. "He said, 'Well what are you going to do?' And I said, 'Well, I guess I'm going to quit.'"

So he did. He quit basketball, and joined the football team—but not as a walk-on.

"The football coach was always talking to me about coming out for the team, and finally I said that I would. They gave me a full scholarship," Hargrove said. "So, I knew if I quit basketball I'd have a full ride in football. I knew I had that football card in my back pocket."

Hargrove played that card, and it worked well. He retained his full scholarship, and in 1970, as a 6-1, 215-pound safety, he intercepted five passes for the Northwestern Oklahoma State football team.

Hargrove, who graduated in 1972, remains the last athlete at the school who lettered in baseball, basketball and football. He played two years of basketball, four years of baseball, but only one year of football.

He didn't play a second year of football because by then he was attracting the attention of baseball scouts. Between his junior and senior years, he played in a college summer baseball league in Great Bend, Kansas, and was being scouted by major league teams.

"A St. Louis scout advised me not to play football my senior year," Hargrove said. "He said, 'You could very easily go to us in the first three rounds (of the June Draft).' So that did it for me. It was adios, football.

"The one sport I was hesitant about playing—baseball—is the one I ended up playing the most."

CHAPTER 2

The Journey Begins

"What does he mean by that?"

Ray Burris was a decent major league pitcher. At times, better than decent. From 1973 to 1987 he carved out a 15-year career, mostly as a starter, for seven major league teams—the Cubs, Yankees, Mets, Expos, A's, Brewers and Cardinals. In 1972, Burris was one of the top college pitchers in the nation, while at Southwestern Oklahoma State University. In 1972 Burris' team played a doubleheader against Hargrove's team. It was a game that must have set a record for most combined syllables for competing teams in a single athletic contest: Northwestern Oklahoma State University vs. Southwestern Oklahoma State University. Or, if you prefer—which probably everyone did—the Rangers vs. the Bulldogs.

Burris started the first game of the doubleheader. "Ray threw the ball 4,000 miles per hour," Hargrove said. "Didn't have much of a breaking ball, but God, he threw the ball hard."

In one of his at-bats against Burris, Hargrove hit three of the longest foul balls of his life. All three were foul, but Hargrove pulled all three. Scalded them. Smoked them. Crushed them. It was the kind of contact that makes scouts sit up in their seats, which, at that game, four of them did.

Between games of the doubleheader, those scouts—from the Cubs, Rangers, Giants and Dodgers—who were there ostensibly to scout Burris, all stampeded to Sharon Hargrove, who was also at the game. The scouts cornered Sharon and conducted a lengthy interrogation about her husband.

"I knew I was on scouts' radar after my freshman year but I never heard from anyone, or saw any scouts until that day against Ray," Hargrove said.

It was around that time that the Cardinals' scout advised Hargrove not to play football as a senior in college, because there was a possibility he could be a high pick in the Major League Baseball draft. So, Hargrove took that advice. He quit football, waited for the baseball draft, then waited *during* the baseball draft. Waited and waited, and then waited some more.

That St. Louis scout was wrong. Hargrove was not a high draft pick.

Not even close.

Five-hundred and seventy-one players were selected before the Texas Rangers selected Hargrove in the 25th round—eight rounds after the Cubs took Ray Burris.

Hurt? Disappointed? Insulted?

None of the above.

"I was just glad I got drafted," Hargrove said.

On the day of the draft, Hargrove was playing for a college summer league team in Liberal, Kansas. He played ball at night and worked at a beef packing plant painting garage doors during the day.

"I knew the draft was going on, and the first day nothing happened," Hargrove recalled. "The next day, me and a buddy were out there painting garage doors. All of a sudden, I saw Sharon drive up on the highway. There was a big fence. You couldn't get in or out. She parked the car on the highway and came running over to the fence yelling. I went over there and she told me I'd been drafted by the Rangers, and I was supposed to call a scout named Lee Anthony."

Hargrove called Anthony, who told him the Rangers had drafted him in the 25th round, and in order to get him to sign they were offering him an $8,500 incentive bonus, which was a progressive bonus. If the player spent 30 days in Class A he'd get a percentage of the bonus, then another percentage if the player spent 30 days in Double-A. Same thing in Triple-A. The total amount came to $8,500. Hargrove told Anthony that wasn't enough. Anthony told Hargrove he would get back to him.

"Ten days later I hadn't heard from him, and I'm sweating bullets, thinking, 'What have I done?'" said Hargrove.

Anthony eventually called again and set up a meeting, at which Anthony offered a $2,000 signing bonus, which Hargrove quickly accepted.

"But like a nut, I forgot to ask for the $8,500 incentive bonus, which they gave to everybody. That was standard," Hargrove said. "So, for the rest of my career, I kept thinking I'm always going to be $8,500 behind what I should have gotten. Lee Anthony probably thought to himself, 'I can't believe he didn't ask for the $8,500. Are we sure we want this guy?'"

The Texas Rangers at that time were not a very good team. But they were a new team to Texas. Brand new. The new Texas Rangers were the old Washington Senators. After the 1971 season the franchise moved from Washington to Arlington, Texas, which is halfway between Dallas and Fort Worth. The Senators lost 96 games their last season in Washington, and they lost 100 games as the Rangers in their first year in Texas. The manager both years was Hall of Famer Ted Williams.

The Rangers were about halfway through that 100-loss 1972 season when they drafted Hargrove in what was a very strong draft by the team. Counting Hargrove, 11 of Texas' first 25 picks reached the big leagues, which is an excellent percentage. Hargrove's 30.5 career WAR is higher than all of them, with the exception of catcher Jim Sundberg (40.5). In the third round that year the Rangers drafted pitcher Jeff Scott. Because of a torn rotator cuff, Scott never made it to the majors, but he became the Cleveland Indians' scouting and farm director in 1987-88, when Hargrove was a minor league manager in the Cleveland system.

In the summer of 1972 the Hargroves packed up their car and drove to Geneva, New York, on the northern tip of Seneca Lake, one of the Finger Lakes. It was there that Hargrove and a clubhouse full of teenagers and first-year pros would go to war together as the Geneva Senators, in the short-season Class-A New York-Penn League.

"Mike was a little older (22), and one of the few guys on the team who was married," Scott said. "When they were negotiating with

Mike after the draft, the scout, Lee Anthony, called Hal Keller, the scouting and farm director. Lee told Hal 'We can't sign him.' Hal said 'Why not?' Lee said, 'He needs a new car. He's married and he has to bring his wife with him. Otherwise, he ain't coming.' Hal said, 'How much is a car?' Lee said, 'I don't know, $2,000?' Hal said, 'OK, give him the $2,000.'"

Unlike today, in 1972 drafted players signed rapid-fire, right after the draft. "There wasn't a lot of holding out," Scott said. "The draft was June 1, and the report date was June 6 or 7. So you wanted to be signed so you would be there on time. There were no agents or anything like that. Nobody knew what the (contract) numbers were. It was unknown."

Also back then, teams bought bulk during the draft, so 50 players showed up in Geneva hoping to become a Geneva Senator. For 10 days prior to the start of the season the team held workouts, and cut down the roster.

"It was a weeding out process. The manager's duty was to weed out the guys who didn't belong there," Scott said.

That was done through wall-to-wall workouts.

"We had a four-day period where we worked out three times a day. Oh, God, it was awful. Utterly awful," Scott said. "Monday through Thursday we worked out at 10 in the morning, 3 in the afternoon, and 7 at night. We ran 20 foul lines, did 100 sit-ups and 100 pickups in all three workouts. On Friday we had only one workout, so a bunch of us went to the movies that night to see 'M*A*S*H'. All I remember is I made it through the opening credits and then fell asleep. I was 17 years old. I should have been wired, but my ass was dragging."

The manager of the Senators was 35-year-old Bill Haywood, a former minor league pitcher, whose major league career consisted of 14 relief appearances with the 1968 Washington Senators.

"Bill was a great guy. A lot like Cecil Perkins," said Hargrove, referring to his college baseball coach.

Before the start of the season Haywood called a team meeting that sounds as if it resembled the famous welcome-to-the-platoon scene from the Bill Murray movie "Stripes."

"We're all sitting in there, wide-eyed and sucking it all in. Scared shitless," Hargrove said. "Bill was talking about how to conduct ourselves, and he said, 'I've seen more guys' careers go out the end of their dick than anything.' I looked at the guy next to me and said, 'What does he mean by that?'"

You can almost see the two players exchanging clueless shrugs.

"Bill told us, 'You need a good baseball wife. That's what you need,'" Hargrove said. "And I thought, 'What's that?' Well I had one all along, and didn't know it. But the dick thing. I didn't know what that meant . . . But I saw it . . . and he was right."

The Geneva Senators weren't very good. Their record that year was 30-40. But minor league baseball isn't about wins and losses. It's about player development, and in Hargrove's first season as a professional, he hit the ground running. In 243 at-bats he hit .267, which was 20 points higher than the league average, and he led the team in on-base percentage (.396), RBI (37) and walks (52).

"Mike got off to a real good start," said Scott. "There were three guys on the team who were married, Mike and two others. One night they went out with us younger guys to this bar in downtown Geneva. It was our place to go."

This was after a game, and the ballplayers were sitting at the end of the bar talking about the game.

"Some guy walked up from the other side of the bar, and for some reason he didn't like Mike's looks. I don't know why," Scott said. "We weren't even talking to these people, but this guy walks up to Mike and told him he didn't like him. Mike, in that soft-spoken voice, apologized to the guy and said, 'Well, I'm sorry, sir.' The guy said, 'You know, if I didn't have these glasses on, I'd hit you right in the nose.' So, Mike reached across and took the guy's glasses off him, set them down on the bar and said, 'You ain't got your glasses on no more.' The guy took a swing at him, and Mike clocked him."

Hargrove landed the punch, but paid the price: a badly-sprained finger.

"He was hitting over .300 at the time, and after he hurt his finger his average went down to the mid-.260s," Scott said.

Hargrove never told anyone about the injury, and, according to Scott, with good reason.

"Here's a guy who's older, who signed for next to nothing, a low draft pick," Scott said. "If he told the manager what happened and how it happened, in his (Hargrove's) mind, he could have gotten released. So, he played with a busted finger, and never missed a game."

Hargrove finished the season, and despite essentially hitting one-handed, his numbers were good enough to earn him a promotion in 1973 to the Rangers' high Class-A affiliate at Gastonia, North Carolina, in the Western Carolinas League, where Hargrove had a spectacular season, leading the league in virtually everything.

He hit a league-leading .351, which was 46 points higher than the next closest player, and 115 points better than the league average. He also led the league in on-base percentage, slugging percentage, OPS, hits, doubles, and total bases. He tied for second in triples and home runs.

"From day one, all the way through, it was a dream come true. Everything that could have gone right went right," Hargrove said.

"Mike may not have been the best prospect in the league. Willie Randolph was in the league that year. So were John Candelaria and Tom Underwood," said Scott. "But as far as production, and playing the game the right way, Mike was far and away the best player in the league."

Another team in the league that year was the Orangeburg (South Carolina) Cardinals, a St. Louis farm team that finished last in the league, but was by no means boring. Not with Jimmy Piersall as manager. Piersall gained fame and infamy during his major league playing career in the 1950s and 60s for his explosive and unpredictable personality. He spent most of the 1950s with the Red Sox, then three years (1959-61) with the Indians, and with three other teams later in the '60s.

Piersall suffered a nervous breakdown early in his career, and was diagnosed as bipolar, resulting in numerous cases of bizarre behavior, such as running the bases backwards after hitting 100th career major league home run. In 1957 his life was made into a movie, "Fear Strikes Out," starring Anthony Perkins.

For whatever reason, Piersall took an interest in Hargrove's career. The two men talked four or five times that year prior to or after an Orangeburg-Gastonia game.

"One night after a game," Hargrove said, "I walked out of the stadium in Gastonia, and ran into Jimmy. And he says to me, 'Mike, you're a good hitter, but you'll never be able to hit like that in the big leagues. People will eat you up.'"

Hargrove at the time was hitting out of the same open stance that he would use throughout his big-league career. But Piersall saw trouble.

On opening day the next year, when Hargrove had made it to the big leagues, using the same open stance he used in the minors, one of the first people he saw was Piersall, who by that time was working in the Rangers' front office.

"He saw me, but he didn't say a word. I wanted to say something to him, but I didn't," said Hargrove. "Jimmy was a good guy. I liked Jimmy."

There seemed to be something about Hargrove's approach to hitting, his stance, his mechanics, whatever, that seemed to prompt comment. At one end of the spectrum was Piersall's doomsday prediction. At the other end was Hall of Famer and seven-time American League batting champion Rod Carew, whom Hargrove spoke to when both were members of the 1975 American League All-Star team: "Rod told me, 'Mike, I love the way you hit, but there are going to be people who are going to try to change you. Don't do it. Stay with what you believe in.'"

During the season in Gastonia, Hargrove's grandfather died.

"We didn't have anything," said Sharon Hargrove. "Mike signed for $2,000. His salary was $500 per month. He went to the manager and said, 'My granddad passed away, I need to go home.' The manager said, 'You can go for one day. The day of the funeral.' So you start checking airline tickets, and to get to Perryton you had to fly into Amarillo. Two-and-a-half-hour drive home. Funeral. Get back. Plus, the expenses. So, Mike opted not to go, and it was hard on him. He never had closure with his granddad, who was Mike's No. 1 fan on the face of the earth."

The Gastonia manager was 26-year-old (only four years older than Hargrove) Rich Donnelly, who in the future would become one of Hargrove's closest friends in baseball.

Through it all, Hargrove continued to dominate pitchers in the Western Carolinas League. When informed that Hargrove led the league in almost every statistical category, Scott laughed and said, "He also led in time of possession."

That was a reference to Hargrove's famous between-pitches fussing and fidgeting routine that, when he got to the big leagues, earned him the nickname "The Human Rain Delay." Reggie Jackson is frequently credited with coining the nickname, but that may or may not be true.

"My recollection is that we were in Toronto and one of the writers there called me The Human Rain Delay. That was the first time I heard it," Hargrove said.

It all began at Gastonia in 1973. Hargrove went 5-for-6 in a game one night, and at the end of the game his left thumb was so sore he couldn't move it. Because he crowded the plate, he got jammed a lot, which was fine with him, because that's where he wanted the ball.

"Hitters will tell you where they want the ball by the way they stand at the plate," Hargrove said. "Hitters that crowd the plate want the ball in and hitters who are off the plate want the ball away. For some reason, pitchers think if you crowd the plate you really want the ball away. But I wanted it in."

That night in Gastonia, he got it in—in all six at-bats. He wound up with five hits, and a bruised nerve in his left thumb, the result of hitting all those inside pitches.

That led to Hargrove inventing a crude version of what many hitters use today: a rubber protector that slides over the thumb and sits down in the base of the thumb, in the webbing of skin between the thumb and the forefinger, to serve as a cushion against the bat handle.

"They make those things now, but at the time I didn't know anyone else who used one, so I made one myself, and it lasted the whole year," said Hargrove. "The first one I made, it sounds stupid, but it took me the better part of a day to make it."

Scott said it was a team effort.

"We didn't have a trainer," he said. "So, we kind of did things makeshift. A handful of us came up with this little gadget he could wear on his thumb. It was made out of a sponge and what not, to help his bone bruise."

Scott chuckled at the memory of all the players trying to be amateur inventors to come up with something that would protect Hargrove's thumb.

"If we would have had a trainer who was competent, it would have been done in 10 minutes," Scott said. "But in those first two years, '72 and '73, we didn't have a trainer. In the Texas organization there wasn't a trainer on the rookie league team or on the Class A team. There was a trainer at Double-A, although I'd put quotation marks around that.

"The Double-A trainer was an old-timer that had been the bus driver of the team in the Florida-Alabama League, in Pensacola, who took a six-week course to learn how to be a trainer. I'm not kidding! That's true. But that wasn't just Texas. None of the other organizations had trainers at the lower levels."

After eight hours of research and development, the Gastonia Boys came up with a thumb protector for the league's best hitter. The finished product had a piece of sponge rubber covered with tape, which had been doused with alcohol in order to get the stickiness off the tape that touched the bat. It wasn't pretty, but it lasted all year. That, in turn, gave Hargrove another device with which to fidget during his interminable between-pitches routine.

"The genesis of the whole thing was that year in Gastonia," Hargrove said. "I played in a game, and a pitcher threw a fastball right in my wheelhouse. And before the pitch was coming, I felt like my shirt was hanging up on my shoulder. I was thinking a little bit about that. He made the pitch, and I just missed it. I should have hit it a long way, but I popped it up.

"When I got back to the bench, I was pissed that I had missed it. And I was thinking, did I overswing? No. I didn't do that. But I figured out that the smallest part of my mind was thinking about my shirt, instead of seeing the ball and concentrating on the ball. So, I vowed to myself right there, sitting on the bench, that I would never swing at another pitch if my mind wasn't completely focused. So, I started with grabbing at my shirt on my shoulder, and pulling up the back of my pants, and all that stuff."

All that "stuff" was done in the same order, after every pitch, for the rest of his career. After every pitch, Hargrove would step out of the batter's box and tediously—all that was missing was the song that was played on the TV game show "Jeopardy," during "Final Jeopardy"—he went through his routine.

"The only thing I did that I probably didn't have to do is I took three practice swings before getting into the box at the start of the at-bat. Three swings felt right," he said. "But I think what really started it all was screwing down that donut thing on my thumb."

Here, from The Human Rain Delay himself, is the complete program, in order of appearance, of all the nonsense:

"I would add and subtract things as I went along, but most of the time I knocked the dirt off my cleats, then I got in the box, pulled my shirt up, pulled my pants up in the back, then tapped my helmet tighter. Then I'd wipe the corners of my mouth. I don't know why. I guess I didn't want to be drooling as I was hitting. Just little things like that. My nose itched one time, so I scratched my nose, and I got a hit, so I added the nose thing to it."

If you can find video of one of Hargrove's at-bats, it's quite a piece of performance art.

"In time," said Scott, "I think he would do it to aggravate the shit out of the pitchers."

Which it did—along with everybody else.

"I know it bothered the catchers," Hargrove said. "They would never say anything, but I'd hear this big loud sigh. Carlton Fisk would be down in his crouch, and then just look up at me. And I'm thinking, 'You're as slow as I am (batting).'"

Keep in mind that this was during the '70s, when baseball games were played at a much faster pace than they are now. A big reason is that, in the '70s, once a hitter stepped into the batter's box, he didn't step out until he either put a ball in play, struck out, or walked.

Then along comes Hargrove, who stepped out of the box *after every pitch*, and went through this 30-second salute to shilly-shally, grabbing, pulling, tugging, adjusting, and scratching anything and everything he could get his hands on.

At one point, Dick Butler, the American League Supervisor of Umpires, complained to Hargrove about his routine.

"He said, 'Mike, you've got to speed it up. You've got to stop these things. This is ridiculous,'" said Hargrove. "I said, 'Is this you asking me?' And he said, 'No, it's the commissioner asking.' So, I stopped doing it for two games, and I didn't get any hits."

Today, of course—proving that Hargrove was decades ahead of his time—all hitters step out of the box after every pitch and go through all types of contortions and adjustments, to the point that Major League Baseball instituted rules prohibiting hitters from leaving the box during at-bats—rules that seem to be only selectively enforced.

But during his career as a player in the '70s and '80s, Hargrove was the only one holding up games while he fussed over his wardrobe and accessories.

"I didn't do all that stuff just because it was habit," he said. "I used that time to try to figure out what the pitcher was going to throw. I think I was a little ahead of my time with my pre-at-bat routine. But I was thinking what the pitcher had thrown, what the count was, and what he might throw."

It started with the thumb protector, invented by some creative baseball players in Gastonia, North Carolina, in 1973.

"Nobody asked me about it at the time. They probably thought I was nuts," Hargrove said. "But I should have patented that son of a bitch. That would be nice to be known for the Hargrove Donut."

On July 1, 1973, Hargrove was hitting .400 and Scott had a record of 12-3.

"We were both going pretty good. In today's world we wouldn't have still been with that club. We would have been moved up," Scott said. "But back then, all the farm teams above us were in first place. We had a lot of prospects on every team. So, there was nowhere to go. Whose place were you going to take?"

That point was driven home by Texas farm director Hal Keller, who came to Gastonia during the season to meet with the hitting and pitching stars of the team.

"He told us we weren't going anywhere, unless someone got hurt," Scott said. "He told Mike that after the season he was going to go to the instructional league, and they would see what happens. Maybe Mike would go to Triple-A next year instead of Double-A."

Hargrove did better than that.

Much better.

CHAPTER 3

Rookie of the Year

"No, I'm serious. I'm going to Arlington."

In the fall of 1973, after the Texas Rangers had lost 205 games in their first two seasons in Arlington, owner Bob Short and manager Billy Martin made a trip to Florida to watch the team's instructional league team play some games. The first day they were there, as they were walking into the ballpark, they saw one of their kids, a left-handed hitter, belt a long home run off a left-handed pitcher.

"They were there for two or three days, and I really did well in those games," Hargrove said.

After the instructional league ended, Hargrove went home to Perryton and got a job selling crop insurance. "He would leave on Monday and come home on Friday," Sharon said. "We wouldn't talk during the week. We didn't have cell phones then, so you'd have to call collect, and I didn't have any money to accept his calls."

A month before the start of spring training, Sharon, who was teaching back home in Perryton, came home and found a note in the mailbox saying there was a certified letter to be picked up at the post office.

"We'd never had anything like that," she said. "It was after school, and the post office was closed. But I knew the postmaster. So, I went to his house and asked if he could go to the post office and get it for me. He said, 'Yeah, let's go. Everybody is dying to know what that letter from the Rangers is.' So, we got it, and I tore it open, and it was a letter from Billy Martin telling Mike he was invited to the big-league spring training camp."

Even though he ran roughshod over the pitchers in the Western Carolinas League the year before, the spring training invite caught

Hargrove off guard. "I mean, I was a non-roster player, who had played in A-ball, had only played a year and a half in the minors, and to get this opportunity . . . Of course, the Rangers weren't very good then. They lost 100 games the year before," he said.

With a month to go before the start of spring training, Hargrove quit his job and started working out all day long, for 30 straight days. Mike and Sharon were renting a house out in the country. In back of the house was a Quonset hut. "A real long thing, made out of corrugated tin," Mike said.

The Hargroves then raided the American Legion post and got a bucket of old baseballs. For the next 30 days Sharon would soft toss balls to her husband, who would rip them the length of the Quonset hut.

"By the time the 30 days were up, I should have replaced all the tin in that Quonset. It was all dented up," said Hargrove of his pre-spring training spring training.

The Rangers' spring training camp was in Pompano Beach, Florida. One of the Rangers' non-roster, spring training invitees lived 1,700 miles away, in Perryton, Texas.

"That was the first time I was ever on a commercial airplane," Hargrove said. "Sharon took me to Amarillo, which was two hours away. I got on the plane, sat down, and the wind was blowing pretty good. I looked out the window and the wings were flapping. And we were sitting on the ground. I said to the guy next to me, 'Are they supposed to do that?'"

When her husband left for spring training, Sharon was teaching school in Perryton. "I had a substitute teacher contract to finish off the year for a teacher who had a nervous breakdown, and after I had her class, I understood why she did," Sharon said.

A couple of weeks later, Sharon got antsy. "I went to the superintendent and said, 'Mike is in the big-league camp. He may never get to go again, and I'm sitting here in Perryton. I've got to have a week off. Is there any way I can go?'"

There was. She went.

"I spent a week with Mike, and he was doing really, really well," she said.

This was not exactly the Golden Era of Texas Rangers baseball. In 1972 the Rangers were 54-100. In 1973 they were 57-105. Going back to their days in Washington, the franchise had lost 100 or more games in six of 13 years. Over that same span, the Senators/Rangers lost 90 or more games in 10 of 13 years.

In 1972, the Rangers' team leader in WAR was—think about this—a middle reliever named Mike Paul. He was a failed starter who had a record of 8-9, led the league in balks, and in August was traded to the Cubs for a player to be named later. The Rangers' two first basemen in 1972 were fading veterans Don Mincher, who would retire at the end of the year, and Frank Howard, who would retire at the end of the following year.

In 1973, the Rangers' two first basemen were Jim Spencer and Mike Epstein, who were so ordinary, yet alike, that they were traded for each other in May, Epstein to the Angels in exchange for Spencer.

In other words, it was a great time to be young and a Ranger.

"It was kind of the perfect storm that year in Texas," said Jeff Scott. "Billy Martin got hired, and Billy was a guy, even though he had a reputation for liking veteran players, his reputation hadn't been cemented yet. He managed Detroit and Minnesota, and he got shitcanned both places, for the obvious reasons. He came over to Texas, and he was a young player's dream, because he went into spring training in 1974 and we had a lot of nice young players in Texas then, and he knew some of them were going to help him win in short order. So, he opened it up. He said, 'If you're the best player, I'm not fucking around. I'm taking you.'"

That didn't ease any of the stress felt by a player trying to make the jump from Class-A ball to the big leagues. "My first spring training game, I'm just a rookie and we've got veterans like Jim Fregosi and Jim Spencer at first base," Hargrove said. "About the fourth inning I'm thinking I'll be glad if I get 10 at-bats this spring. Then one of the coaches came over and said, 'Get your glove. You're going in for Spencer the next inning.' My first reaction was, 'Are you shitting me?' So, I did, and I didn't screw it up."

During camp Hargrove contracted trench mouth. For about a week he couldn't eat anything, and he would wake up in the middle of the night with his bed soaked with sweat. "But I showed up every day," he said.

One day the Rangers were playing the Braves, and before the game, Hargrove, who was feeling weak and sick, was laying down on the bench in the dugout. Martin walked by and said, "Get the fuck up. What the hell are you doing, laying down?"

"I was just letting him know I was sick. But I got through it and ended up hitting .450 that spring," Hargrove said.

The rookie first baseman was a curious combination of consternation and confidence. He was nervous about being there, but confident that he belonged there. "I don't want to sound conceited, but by that time I knew I could hit. I really did," Hargrove said. "And I'd always been a good athlete. So, I knew I could hit. I didn't know if I'd find a level where I couldn't hit. Where I couldn't do it."

In the spring of 1974, he did it. He started the camp hitting, and never stopped. But would it be enough? Could he close the deal? Could he actually make the nearly unheard-of jump from Class A to the big leagues? As the end of camp approached, the tension became unbearable.

Before the Rangers broke camp, they held a team party. All of the players and coaches were there. At one point first-base coach Merrill Combs approached Hargrove and said, "Mike, where do you think you ought to go this year?"

Hargrove tried to be objective. "I think I should get a shot at playing Triple-A," he said. "If I can't do it, then I can't do it. But I think I should get a shot at Triple-A."

Counting Hargrove, there were five young players in camp that year who, as spring training was winding down, hadn't been told where they were going to start the season. The five players, summoning up their courage, decided to go as a group to Billy Martin's hotel room to find out.

"But four of those sorry bastards went without me," Hargrove said. "So, I didn't go. I was pissed. They found out where they were going and I still didn't know."

As the Rangers began to barnstorm their way from Pompano Beach back to Arlington for the start of the season, Hargrove still didn't know if he was going to start the season with the big-league club, or with one of the minor league teams. The uncertainty was consuming him. On April 1, April Fool's Day, the Rangers were playing the Astros in an exhibition game in Houston, in the Astrodome.

"We were walking down the left field line towards the dugout before the game. I was one of the last ones out," Hargrove said. "And I look around and Billy is right next to me, walking. So, I thought, 'This is as good a time as any.'"

"Skip, could I ask you a question?"

"Sure, Mike."

"I was just wondering where I'm going?"

"Well, I thought I'd take you with me to Arlington."

"I thought my heart would stop," Hargrove said. "I said, 'What?' Billy said, 'Well, I can change my mind if you want.' And I said, 'No, no, no. I'll do that. That's fine.'"

After the game, Hargrove called his wife, who was back in Perryton, teaching her sixth-grade class. "I said, 'Sharon, I made the club.' She said, 'Mike, you asshole, I've been teaching these kids all day and dealing with all these April Fool's jokes. I don't have time for this.' I said, 'No, I'm serious. I'm going to Arlington.'"

For a few seconds, neither Hargrove spoke.

"It's hard to describe the feelings that come over you," Hargrove says now, of that moment. "You feel such a sense of accomplishment. But you also feel a big stab of fear. That, 'Hey, look. Here it is. Here's your shot.'"

Over 40 years after achieving that rarely-seen feat of jumping three levels to the big leagues, Hargrove feels there is only one explanation for how it happened.

"Jumping from A-ball to the majors, that doesn't happen. Something like that shouldn't happen," he said. "But it did. And I believe it did because God had his hands on my life. He didn't make me successful. But he gave me the chance to be successful."

There were three players that year that made significant jumps from the minor leagues to the Rangers' major league club. Catcher Jim Sundberg and infielder Mike Cubbage both jumped from Double-A to the Rangers, and Hargrove made the longest jump of all—from Class-A Gastonia to the big leagues.

"All those young guys adored Billy that first year, because he just let them play," said Jeff Scott. "The other thing, Mike being a left-handed hitter, he was never a power hitter. He probably could have been if he'd played in Detroit or New York. He'd have been a 20-home run guy, because those ballparks were built for left-handed hitters. But back in those days, in Arlington Stadium, a left-handed hitter didn't have a chance. The wind blew in, constantly from right field. So, Mike, being kind of a line drive, middle of the field hitter, made contact, took his walks. That was a plus for him, because he didn't even try to challenge the wind."

He was, however, as a high-strung rookie in the major leagues, ready to challenge anyone who said anything to him that was the least bit provocative. Like, for example, "Hello."

"Back then, there were times when I would walk into the ballpark and somebody would say hello to me and I would want to knock them on their ass," Hargrove said. "People I knew. Teammates. I'd walk in and they'd say hello and it took everything I had to just keep walking. But I wanted to turn around and blast them. Billy kept me out of a couple of jams with things like that."

Sharon says she occasionally saw that side of her husband, but only at the beginning of his career. "Maybe at the beginning he was high strung, but I think it was because he was trying to prove himself," Sharon said. "And we had people coming out of the wood-work to come see him play games. I was going back and forth to the airport all the time."

Today, the relaxed, semi-retired Hargrove talks about that hot-headed Hargrove as if he was a distant, disagreeable, unknowable relative.

"I don't know if I was hot-headed," he said. "But it did seem like I was always ready (to fight). I don't know why. I was that way quite a bit during the course of my career. It changed, for whatever reason, when I got to Cleveland. Sharon would always say she could tell when spring training was getting close because I'd put my game face on. But it finally was blunted to the point where I could say hello to people and mean it."

Jeff Scott, who played with Hargrove in the minor leagues and eventually became his boss in Cleveland when Scott was the farm director and Hargrove a minor league manager, saw this testy side of Hargrove, but far from the big-league spotlight.

"Mike was quiet, soft spoken. But if he got mad, you took notice, because the west Texan came out of him," Scott said. "Sharon was his anchor. She would be like, 'Oh, Mr. Tough Guy!' But there were definitely some little time bombs hidden away inside of him some-where."

Scott saw it during a 1973 game between the Gastonia Rangers and Greenwood Braves.

"I was pitching against Frank LaCorte. It was 0-0 or 1-1, midway through it," Scott recalled. "Jimmy Pascarella was on first base with one or two outs. We had a left-handed batter who hit the ball over the right fielder's head. Pascarella was going to try to score from first, but it was too far for his legs. He was just a little guy. Our manager, Rich Donnelly, was going to try to score him. He's waving him and waving him, and Jimmy's out by 10 feet at home plate. Should never have sent him.

"Hargrove is the on-deck hitter. He's standing at home plate, telling Jimmy where to slide. Pascarella had no chance, so he's just going to run into the catcher. The catcher was a big Puerto Rican guy, and Pascarella just ran right into him. All the guy had to do was just tag him. But the catcher forearmed Pascarella right in the kazoos.

"Hargrove saw what happened, and he ran up from behind and grabbed the catcher, spun him around and clocked him. And it was on. We had a donnybrook. Hoyt Wilhelm was Greenwood's manager, and he walks out and says, 'What's goin' on, boys?'

"It was flying all over the place. Believe it or not, nobody got kicked out of the ballgame. After it was over, Donnelly moseyed by me in the dugout and made it clear to me that he wanted that catcher to feel it again. He said, 'You don't have to hit him, but make sure his ass hits the dirt.'

"So, the catcher comes up the next inning, and all of our guys knew what was going to happen. I threw one right under his neck and he goes ass over tea kettle. His helmet goes flying, and he gets up to come after me. Before he took two steps, Mike was between the catcher and me and, looking at the catcher, Mike is like, 'You want to do this again?' And it was over with. We never had a problem with them the rest of the season."

A year later, Hargrove was in the big leagues, and so were his "little time bombs." He still searches for explanations. "I was mostly like that in my first year (in the majors), and I think it had a lot to do with my feeling the need that I had to compete," Hargrove said.

Or perhaps the stress he felt from being a kid jumping from

A-ball to the big leagues, and that every day he felt like he was on trial?

"You would think that, but that's not the way I felt," Hargrove said. "I never consciously felt that. I know Sharon's mother one time said something to Sharon about, 'You can't do that because you can't imagine how much stress Mike is under.' Sharon told me that, and I didn't feel the stress. I really didn't."

Sometimes ignorance is bliss. On opening day during his rookie season with the Rangers, Hargrove and fellow rookie Sundberg were getting dressed for the game when they got a call in the clubhouse that general manager Dan O'Brien wanted them to come up to his office and sign their contracts. The two players were already in their uniforms, so they put their street clothes on over their uniforms and went up to see O'Brien.

The general manager said to Hargrove, "We'll give you $1,200 a month if you go down to Triple-A, otherwise we'll give you $15,000," which was the major league minimum at the time. Hargrove signed the contract then asked O'Brien if he could get that $15,000 paid over 12 months. "Let's see how long you stay up here before we do something like that," said O'Brien.

"To show you how unconscious I was about the stress, that was the first time that I ever thought that I may get sent down," Hargrove said. "I thought, 'I'm here, so I'm here. I'm not going anywhere.' So that was the first time that it made me think this might not be permanent."

But it was, and it was something Sharon never forgot.

"He never yo-yoed," she said of her husband. "Once he made it to the big leagues, he never got sent back down. Most people don't know that. Just like they don't know that he never played high school baseball, because we didn't have a team."

Rookies do a lot of thinking, and in his rookie year Hargrove thought a lot about the years ahead. Specifically, the importance of not only reaching the big leagues, but sticking around for at least four years, which was the amount of service time in the majors necessary for a player to be vested into the major league pension plan.

"I do remember thinking I've got to do everything I can to stick up here for four years. So maybe that was a little bit of the stress poking its head out," Hargrove said.

At the start of the season Hargrove did not look like a rookie, much less one making the jump from Class A. Through his first six games he was hitting .389 (7-for-18), but that was followed by a 0-for-8 slide. However, in back-to-back games in New York against the Yankees on April 27-28, Hargrove went 6-for-6, including his first major league home run, off Doc Medich, and three RBI.

"That was the first time I realized that I could stick up here. That this was something I could do," Hargrove said. "I thought to myself, 'This might be something that's going to be good for me.' That's when I really started believing."

There appeared to be no period of adjustment, no difficulty in transitioning from hitting against Class A pitchers to facing major league pitchers.

"I may have been really stupid at the time, but I don't remember the pitching in the majors being better," Hargrove said. "But the major league pitchers did throw more strikes. In the minors, you always had some doubt in your mind whether they were going to throw it over the plate, or over your head."

There were some instances in which Hargrove sensed animosity or jealousy on the part of other players about this kid jumping from A-ball to the big leagues. "Nothing overt. But I sensed it a little," he said. "Like a 'What the hell are you doing here?' thing."

In July, Hargrove had one of his few slumps of the season, an eight-gamer in which he went 2-for-24 (.083). "Things weren't going very good, and we were on a plane and I was standing in the aisle. Billy walked up to me and said, 'You need to believe in yourself as much as I believe in you. You're going to be OK. You just need to stay with it, and I've got your back.' That really helped me a lot. Then I started hitting again. Billy treated me really well. I was one of his favorites."

Martin was hired by the Rangers near the end of the 1973 season. He was the ballclub's third manager that year, following Whitey Herzog and Del Wilber, who managed just one game between the firing of Herzog and the hiring of Martin. Martin went 9-14 as manager over the remainder of the season, but there was a growing sense that the team was headed in the right direction. Like most of Billy Martin's players, Hargrove enjoyed playing for a manager with one of the most explosive tempers in the game.

"I loved playing for him because he knew I loved playing for him," Hargrove said. "In the first meeting he had with us he said, 'If there's a fight on the field and I look around and see you're not doing something, or you're sitting on the bench, I will release you, trade you, or shoot you,'" Hargrove said.

The Rangers in 1974 spent two weeks in first place in the AL West, from late April into early May. They were a .500 ballclub for the next two months, but finished strong, going 30-23 in August and September. They finished the year with a record of 84-76, which was good for second place in the six-team AL West, five games behind the division champion A's.

As a rookie Hargrove started 72 games at first base, 27 at designated hitter, and three in left field. He hit consistently through most of the season, and Jeff Scott's observation that Arlington Stadium was not typically friendly to left-handed hitters held true. Hargrove hit much better on the road (a .352 batting average) than at home (.291). However, Hargrove didn't hit anywhere in the month of September. Maybe it was fatigue from his first exposure to the long six-month major league season. Maybe it was the stress of trying to compete on a daily basis to prove his jump from A-ball to the big leagues was justified. Or maybe it was simply a slump, and nothing more.

Whatever the cause, it put a dent in Hargrove's final numbers. He entered the month of September with a slash line of .343/.410/.456. But in September he hit just .234, and all of his other numbers were equally dismal. That September slump led to a 20-point drop in his batting average, from .343 to .323. His on-base percentage fell 15 points to a final mark of .395, and his slugging percentage tumbled 32 points, to .424.

But his performance in his first five months of the season is what the baseball writers remembered most when it came time to vote for the Rookie of the Year Award. Hargrove, a 25th round draft choice who made the jump from Class A to the big leagues, was the overwhelming choice. Hargrove got 16 first-place votes. White Sox shortstop Bucky Dent got three votes, Royals third baseman George Brett got two, Red Sox shortstop Rick Burleson got one, as did Hargrove's teammate, catcher Jim Sundberg, who actually finished with a higher WAR (4.0) than any of the five players. Future Hall of

Famer Robin Yount, who was also a rookie that year, received no votes.

"When Yount and Brett were elected to the Hall of Fame," said Hargrove, "a writer from New York called me and said, 'You and George and Robin were all rookies the same year. Can you explain how you got Rookie of the Year and they didn't?' I said, 'Obviously, I had one year better than them, and they had a whole career better than mine.'"

Hargrove is one of just two Texas players to ever win the AL Rookie of the Year Award. The other is pitcher Neftali Perez, who won it in 2010.

CHAPTER 4

Riot!

"Daddy, something's going to happen
to him. This is getting out of hand."

Well, it seemed like a good idea at the time. In the early 1970s the Cleveland Indians had a baseball problem. They were awful. The Indians also had an attendance problem. Nobody came to their games. From 1969 through 1973 the Indians averaged 92 losses per year, including an epic and, at the time, club-record 102 losses in 1971. That was the year the Indians' home attendance at massive Cleveland Stadium was 591,361—an average of 7,301 per game. This in a stadium where, in 1954, a doubleheader between the Indians and Yankees drew a record crowd of 86,563. The 1971 Indians had attendance figures of under 5,000 in 30 of their 73 home dates. The total attendance for the last five home games of the season was 14,647—an average of 2,929 per game.

That was in 1971. Things weren't much better in 1973, when the Indians drew 615,107 fans to watch a team that finished last or second to last in the standings for the fifth consecutive year. So, the Indians in those years were dreadful, and nobody cared. There were periodic rumors that the franchise was going to move. Prior to the 1974 season, at a meeting in the team's executive offices, club officials brainstormed for ideas on how to improve attendance.

Somebody suggested a promotion in which the team would sell unlimited amounts of beer at 10 cents per 12-ounce cup, for a game against the Texas Rangers on June 4. The promotion was called "Ten-Cent Beer Night." What could possibly go wrong, right?

Right. Well, it seemed like a good idea at the time.

On May 29, six days before the booze flowed and the fists flew in Cleveland, the Indians and Rangers played the final game of a three-game series in Texas. With none out in the bottom of the fourth inning, the Rangers had outfielder Tom Grieve on second base and infielder Lenny Randle on first. Jim Fregosi hit a groundball to Indians' third baseman John Lowenstein, who stepped on third for the force out on Grieve, and threw to second baseman Jack Brohamer to retire Randle. Randle slid very hard into second base. Too hard, the Indians thought.

When Randle batted in the eighth inning, Indians pitcher Milt Wilcox retaliated by throwing a pitch behind his head. Randle retaliated by bunting down the first base line. When Wilcox fielded the ball and tagged him, Randle threw a forearm at Wilcox. Indians first baseman John Ellis retaliated for that retaliation by throwing a punch at Randle. Both dugouts emptied, and the brawl was on.

Hargrove, remembering Billy Martin's warning during a team meeting—"If there's a fight on the field and I look around and see you're not doing something, or you're sitting on the bench, I will release you, trade you, or shoot you"—dutifully raced out of the dugout and onto the field, with the intention of doing something.

The first player Hargrove reached on the field was the 5-10, 165-pound Brohamer. "I didn't realize Jack was a short guy, but there's a tape of that game and I was in the center of the picture whaling away on Jack," Hargrove said. "Jack and I later played together on the Indians, and we became good friends. We used to ride to the ballpark together. One day I said to him, 'Jack, do you remember that fight?' And he said, 'Yeah, I remember it.' And I said, 'I am really sorry.'"

After the brawl, the Indians returned to their dugout, where they were pelted by beer and food thrown by Texas fans.

"Dave Duncan was the Indians' catcher and he was going down the dugout steps when a fan poured a beer on his head," Hargrove said. "I thought to myself, 'Some things are right. But that's just not right.'"

After the game, reporters asked Martin if he was worried about retaliation from Indians fans six days later, when the Rangers opened a series in Cleveland. Martin said he wasn't worried because "They don't have enough fans there to worry about."

They did have plenty of beer, however, and that drew plenty of fans to the ballpark on that swelteringly humid June night. That mix of beer, fans and humidity resulted in plenty of trouble.

"That was my first experience in Cleveland. The first time I had ever seen Cleveland in my life was that game," Hargrove said.

The date was June 4. The attendance was 25,134. Most of them came for the beer, and stayed for the riot. The game time temperature was 82 degrees. The time of game was 3 hours 5 minutes—including the riot. The game was never played to its conclusion, a fact noted with marvelously clinical succinctness by the following note found at the top of the box score from that game, on the website Baseball-Reference.com:

"Game was forfeited to the visiting team. Ten-cent beer night went horribly awry as drunken Cleveland fans attacked Texas outfielder Jeff Burroughs and the umpires declared a forfeit win by Texas over Cleveland."

The score of the game when the forfeit was declared was, fittingly enough on 10-cent beer night: 5-5.

"At the start of the game, we were aware of the potential for trouble, with it being 10-cent beer night," said Hargrove, "but I don't think any of us thought things would transpire the way they did."

Boy, did they transpire.

The hijinks began immediately. From the first inning on, the game was constantly interrupted by fans running onto the field, throwing things onto the field, throwing things at players, drinking lots of beer, then running onto the field some more. There were streakers. There were big-breasted women. Fans mooning the players, fans mooning the umpires. Fans mooning each other. Fans stealing bases. Fans trying to steal equipment. It's what baseball would have looked like if baseball had been invented by P.T. Barnum.

It got worse with each passing inning. By the late innings it had turned ugly, with the game being halted multiple times so the fans, with and without clothes, could be chased, captured and dragged off the field.

"It was nuts," said Hargrove. "Somebody threw an empty gallon jug of Thunderbird wine at me. It landed about 20 feet behind me. I was thinking I should probably kick that off the field. But then I figured the grounds crew would come and get it. But then some guy jumped out of the stands, grabbed the bottle, and ran back into the stands."

As a first baseman, Hargrove was closer to the stands—i.e., in more jeopardy—than most of his teammates.

"I must have had 50 pounds of hot dogs thrown at me when I was on the field," he said. "Obviously, stadium security was over-matched that night. They were guys who were in their late 60s, so they had limited mobility. The only person they roughed up was the big-breasted lady that came out to give Nestor Chylak, the home plate umpire, a kiss."

At another point, a father and son jumped onto the field together, ran out to center field, and mooned everyone.

"That was a good one," chuckled Hargrove.

The streaker appeared around the seventh inning. The police chased him all over the field. All he was wearing were two black socks. "He finally ran out to right center and jumped over the fence just as a cop got to him," Hargrove said. "The cop fell down, reached up to grab the guy, but all the cop got was one of the black socks."

During the lulls between the hijinks, the game continued. The Indians trailed 3-0 after the top of the fourth inning and 5-1 after the top of the sixth. But they scored two runs in the bottom of the sixth, and tied it at 5-5 in the ninth on an RBI single by Ed Crosby and a sacrifice fly by Lowenstein.

Then it got ugly. Or, at least, uglier. Definitely, ugliest.

"The Indians were getting ready to beat us," Hargrove said. "In the bottom of the ninth they had the bases loaded with one out and the game was tied. It was lined up for them to score another run and beat us, and then the riot happened, and stopped it all."

Jeff Burroughs was playing right field for Texas, and Hargrove was playing first base.

"By that time there were a lot of people on the field. A steady stream," Hargrove said. "Jeff was out in right. I looked back and saw somebody run out onto the field and try to grab Jeff's hat and his glove. That's when I took off. I was the first one to get there. It was this great big guy. You could tell he was toasted. He walked up to Jeff, and he never saw me coming. I didn't punch him, but I tackled him. Hard. That's when they stopped the game."

That's when all hell broke loose. Fans poured onto the field from all parts of the ballpark, and there was officially a riot going on.

Billy Martin, bat in hand, led the charge out of the Rangers dugout to rescue Burroughs. The rest of the Rangers followed. The Indians also came pouring out of their dugout.

"Our entire team ended up on the pitcher's mound," said Hargrove. "If it hadn't been for the Indians players coming out to help us, we would have been in a lot more trouble than we were. Both teams ended up around the mound. I was standing on the side of the mound and a broken bat hit the ground right in front of me. I thought, 'Where the hell did that come from?' I bent down to pick up the bat, and (Indians outfielder) Rusty Torres jerked it out of my hand. I looked out to center field and there was just a wall of people coming at us. So, we backed our way into the dugout. I got spit on and cursed at. Nestor Chylak got hit by a chair and got his head split open. That's when they said the game was over."

While all that was going on, 1,200 miles away in the Texas Panhandle a pregnant Sharon Hargrove and her father were driving around in a car, listening to the game on the radio. When Hargrove reached the big leagues with the Rangers the Perryton, Texas radio station, KEYE, got enough sponsors to carry all the Rangers games so the people in Perryton could follow hometown boy Hargrove. On June 4, 1974, while there was a riot going on in Cleveland, there was panic going on in Perryton.

"I'm listening to the game and going nuts, thinking, 'He'll never get out of that city alive,'" Sharon said. "I'm not a worrier, but I kept listening to the game, with my dad, and I kept saying, 'Daddy, something's going to happen to him. This is getting out of hand.' I was crying, and my dad kept telling me, 'That's all right. It's going to be OK.' So that was my first exposure to Cleveland. My first impression of Cleveland."

Asked if he hit anyone during the riot, Hargrove smiled and said, "Well, on the mound, I might have hit one or two people."

The Rangers fought their way back to their dugout and then up into the clubhouse, while it was still anarchy on the playing field. There were officially 11 arrests that night.

"It never really got scary until we got into the clubhouse and started to think about what had happened," Hargrove said. "We were kept in the clubhouse for three hours after the game, and then we had a police escort to our hotel. We were ordered to go to our rooms and not to come out until noon the next day. A lot of us went to bed hungry that night."

One of Hargrove's teammates on that 1974 Rangers team was veteran Jim Fregosi, who reached the big leagues at age 19 with the Angels in 1961, and was a six-time All-Star shortstop in the 1960s. In 1974 with the Rangers, Fregosi was 32 years old and no longer a shortstop. He was the Rangers' opening day first baseman. On April 7, in an 8-4 Texas loss to Oakland, Hargrove made his major league debut, pinch hitting for Fregosi in the sixth inning. The pitcher was future Hall of Famer Rollie Fingers.

"The only thing I remember about my first major league at-bat is that I couldn't keep my eyes from blinking," Hargrove said. "I thought to myself, 'I hope this stops, because this isn't right.'"

The blinking Hargrove grounded into a fielder's choice, but he eventually replaced Fregosi as the Rangers' everyday first baseman.

"Fregosi that year was my sounding board," Hargrove said. "I'd go to him all the time. Coming out of A-ball, I knew how to hit the ball, throw the ball and run the bases. But I didn't know anything about the intricacies about big league baseball. So, I talked baseball all the time with Fregosi."

After the Rangers' second-place finish in the AL West in 1974, expectations were high for 1975. The first sign that things weren't going to go well came on a rain-soaked opening day, when a helicopter that was brought in to help dry the Arlington Stadium turf crashed in the outfield. Then Billy Martin crashed in July. But first, on June 13, with Texas sitting in fourth place in the AL West with a record of 29-29, the Rangers made a blockbuster trade. They traded pitchers Jim Bibby, Jackie Brown and Rick Waits to Cleveland, for Gaylord Perry.

Over the previous three seasons Perry had won 21, 19 and 24 games for some bad Cleveland teams, including his Cy Young Award-winning 1972 season in which he went 24-16 with a 1.92 ERA. But in his first 15 starts for the Indians in 1975, the 36-year-old Perry was just 6-9 with a 3.55 ERA. In his first seven starts for the Rangers, Perry was even worse, going 1-5 with a 6.29 ERA. But then he went on a tear. From July 10 to Aug. 16 Perry pitched eight consecutive complete games and had a record of 6-2 with a 0.89 ERA.

In the middle of that run, the Texas owner Brad Corbett fired Billy Martin. The end came on July 21, with the Rangers mired in fourth place with a record of 44-51, and 15½ games out of first place.

"He wants to call the shots," Martin told the Associated Press. "One year in baseball and all of a sudden he's a genius."

Martin's exit in Texas was in stark contrast to his arrival less than two years earlier. In early September 1973 Martin was fired as manager of the Detroit Tigers. Texas' owner at the time was Bob Short, who was a huge Martin fan, to the point that when Martin got fired Short told Rangers manager Whitey Herzog that he would fire his grandmother for the chance to hire Billy Martin.

A few days later Short fired Herzog and hired Martin, after which the good-humored Herzog told reporters, "I'm fired. I'm the grandmother."

Two years later, Rangers third-base coach Frank Lucchesi replaced Martin as manager. "It was a tough day, but you could kind of see it coming," said Hargrove, who actually started 92 games in left field that year and only 31 at first base, as the backup to Jim Spencer. "Billy was always his own worst enemy. Brad Corbett's business was in plastic pipes and Billy said, 'Brad Corbett knows as much about baseball as I know about plastic pipes.'"

For the ballclub itself, the switch in managers didn't change much but the name plate on the door to the manager's office. Under Lucchesi in 1976 the Rangers were even worse than they were in 1975, going 76-86 and finishing in fourth place in the division, 14 games out of first.

After hitting over .300 in his first two years, Hargrove's batting average fell to .287 in 1976, but he did have a career high 30 doubles, and he led the American League with 97 walks. In 1977 Hargrove was back over .300 again, hitting .305, with a career high 18 home runs in one of the more bizarre seasons in Texas history. The Rangers cycled through four managers, which would seem to indicate it was a disastrous season, but it wasn't.

The 1977 Rangers went 94-68, the most wins in a season by the

Texas/Washington franchise in a 65-year span from 1933 to 1999. Not bad for a team that at one point during the season had four different managers in the span of eight days. Lucchesi returned as manager, but after going 31-31 he was fired following a 9-5 loss in Minnesota on June 21. Eddie Stanky came in and managed the Rangers to a 10-8 win over the Twins on June 22, then quit to go home to Alabama.

"After the game, Toby Harrah and I were the last ones to leave the clubhouse," Hargrove said. "We were both in there shaving, and Eddie came up and told us it was a tough decision to come here because he had been taking care of his dad in Alabama."

Later that night Hargrove got a call in his hotel room from Harrah. "Toby said, 'You're not going to believe this, but Eddie just called me and said he was going back home. He said he couldn't do that to his dad, so he was going home,'" Hargrove said.

So Stanky went home. Up next was first-base coach Connie Ryan, who was named interim manager on June 23.

With Corbett on the prowl for a permanent manager to replace Ryan—former Twins slugger Harmon Killebrew was rumored to have been offered the job, but turned it down—the Rangers' trip continued to Anaheim and Oakland. They went 2-4 under Ryan. On June 28, Billy Hunter was named the Rangers' fourth manager not only of the season but of the road trip. Something must have clicked then, because the Rangers took off after that, going 60-33 under Hunter, including a 6-0 no-hitter pitched by Bert Blyleven over the Angels on Sept. 22. The Rangers finished the season with 94 wins. But that was only good for second place, eight games behind the division champion Kansas City Royals.

Asked at the time about what made Hunter an effective manager, Hargrove said, "He came in here and showed a perfect blend of knowing how to handle people, plus knowing the game. If you took a jar, put Billy Martin and Frank Lucchesi in that jar, shook it up, then emptied it, out would come Billy Hunter. He combines the best qualities of both our previous managers."

Corbett was so pleased with Hunter's work that he offered the manager contract extensions of Hunter's choice, either three or five years. Hunter, a Lutherville, Maryland resident, turned down both offers, because his wife Beverly didn't want to move to Texas.

"She said, 'I'm not moving to Texas. I can put up with this for another year, but not three or five,'" Hunter told the Baltimore Business Journal in 2013. Corbett even offered to buy the Hunters a house in Texas, but that still couldn't persuade Beverly Hunter to make the move.

So, Hunter accepted a one-year extension, but never made it to the end of the contract—close, but not quite—as Corbett fired him with one game remaining in the 1978 season. Corbett replaced him with Pat Corrales, who did accept a multi-year deal in becoming the fifth manager in 16 months for the Rangers, who had 13 managers in their first 14 years in Texas. The Rangers, under Corrales, won their final game of 1978, beating the Mariners 9-4 in Seattle. Hargrove hit a career-low .251 but did lead the league in walks for the second time in three years, this time with 107. He did not play in that season-ending game, which turned out to be his last game in a Texas Rangers uniform.

Three weeks later, on Oct. 25, 1978, Hargrove got a phone call from Texas general manager Dan O'Brien, telling him he'd been traded to San Diego.

"It was a shock, because I had been a good player for the Rangers," said Hargrove, a native Texan, who had been drafted and developed by the Rangers. He was the American League Rookie of the Year and an All-Star for Texas. But on Oct. 25, he became a member of the San Diego Padres. The Rangers traded Hargrove, infielder Kurt Bevacqua and catcher Bill Fahey to the Padres for outfielder Oscar Gamble, infielder/catcher Dave Roberts and $300,000.

"It made me real mad. I was bitter," Hargrove said. "It was the first time I got traded. You don't expect it."

You don't expect it, even if there are rumors. In this case, there were plenty of those. Enough of them so that Sharon Hargrove, who had a good relationship with O'Brien, actually called O'Brien and asked him, point blank, "Is Mike going to be traded?"

"I mean, who calls a general manager and says that?—except Sharon," Hargrove said.

O'Brien's reply to the information-seeking wife: "Well Sharon, let me put it to you like this. If I was selling swimming pools, and you came to me to buy one, I'd tell you to hold off on that for a while."

That not-so-veiled warning from O'Brien that a trade was likely didn't make it any easier to handle when it happened.

"I was crushed," Sharon said.

The Padres at that time had only been in existence for 10 years, having entered the National League as an expansion team in 1969. They lost 100 games in four of their first six years, and didn't have a winning season until 1978, when they were 84-78, finishing fourth in the six-team NL West, under manager Roger Craig.

The Padres' first baseman in 1978 was Gene Tenace, who actually split time between first base and catcher, but led the team with a 5.2 WAR even though he only hit .224. Tenace, however, drew 101 walks, almost 40 more than anyone else on the team, which also included four future Hall of Famers: Ozzie Smith, Dave Winfield, Gaylord Perry and Rollie Fingers.

"I enjoyed my teammates. We had Fingers, Smith, Winfield, Randy Jones and Tenace, who I became real good friends with," Hargrove said. "So, I enjoyed my teammates, but I didn't enjoy playing for the Padres—it was like putting a round peg in a square hole."

It showed. In 1979, the round peg appeared in 52 games, but only started 33 of them. In 125 at-bats he hit .192, with no home runs and eight RBI.

"I started off playing every day, and I ended up not playing at all," he said.

The Padres' hitting coach was 69-year-old Hall of Fame infielder Billy Herman, who broke into the big leagues with the Cubs in 1931, and was a 10-time All-Star during his 15-year-major league career.

"I was taking extra batting practice one day before a game," Hargrove said. "I hit for like 45 minutes. Didn't hit a loud foul. I just stunk. Billy sat in the dugout, smoked a cigarette and talked to some guys there, then went over and sat with Russ Nixon in the Reds' dugout and smoked cigarettes over there until I was through. I got progressively madder as the session went on, because I'm searching for something. By the end of it, I'm so mad I can't stand it. So, I walked out and said, 'So Billy, what do you think?' just being a smart ass. And Billy says, 'Looked good to me, kid.' I looked at him and thought, 'You son of a bitch, you.' So, it was that kind of experience for me in San Diego."

Another one of the Padres' coaches was Doug Rader, who had a decent major league career and later was a manager for seven years, with the Rangers, White Sox and Angels. In 1979 with the Padres, in the middle of spring training, the team flew to Hawaii to play a four-game series with a team from Japan.

"One of the days we were there, six of us decided we were going to go snorkeling in Hanauma Bay, and Rader was the ring leader," Hargrove said. "We were on mopeds. After we finished snorkeling, we were on our way back to the hotel, and one of our guys threw a chain on his moped. So, we're working on it, and these two big Samoan guys come by in this low rider, and they flip us off. They go up to the top of this hill.

"We jump on our mopeds, and go flying up the hill after them. We caught up to the guys. Rader jumps off his moped, runs up to the big guy, who's standing there with a brick in one hand and an ice pick in the other. Rader looks at him, looks at the brick and the ice pick, and says, 'You win,' and runs back to his moped, and we go back down the hill."

Once the season started, Hargrove's playing time was sporadic, to the point that in May he requested a meeting with Craig. When Hargrove asked why he wasn't playing more, Craig said, "Mike, when I put you in, get a couple hits and I'll keep playing you." A few days later Hargrove went 3-for-8 in two games against Atlanta, but his playing time remained inconsistent.

Hargrove finally went to general manager Bob Fontaine's office. "I told Bob it wasn't working out, and I'd appreciate it if he could trade me to a place where I could play every day," Hargrove said. "Later, after the trade, he told me that when I came into his office there was no way he was going to trade me, but he said, 'When I heard your voice, and sincerity, I knew it wasn't just, 'Get me the fuck out of here.'"

A few days later, on June 14, Fontaine traded Hargrove to—of all places—Cleveland.

"When Mike told me, I sat on the floor with our three little girls," said Sharon, "and I bawled and bawled and bawled."

CHAPTER 5

Cleveland, of All Places

"We'd have 5,000 people, but it
would sound like 50,000."

It was a straight one-for-one deal. San Diego traded Hargrove to Cleveland for outfielder Paul Dade.

"When I heard it was Cleveland, I said, 'Oh shit!' because the first thing I thought about was 10-cent beer night," said Sharon. "Mike said, 'Sharon, it's the American League. I just want to get back to the American League.'"

But Cleveland?

"I was crushed," Sharon said. "It was just exhausting. We had just gotten to San Diego. I was trying to make friends. I didn't want to go to Cleveland. Here we were in San Diego. We had just gotten our second car out there. Now we had to go all the way to Cleveland, during the season."

Mike felt he was more of an American League-style player. But the bigger issue was his role in San Diego. He had none. He felt he was a bad fit on the Padres. Cleveland was in the American League. He knew the league and he knew the pitchers in the league. The Indians weren't very good, but there was playing time to be had in Cleveland.

"I wasn't surprised by the trade. But when it was to Cleveland, it shocked me," Hargrove said. "I had never thought of playing in Cleveland. I guess from the beer night, and that stuff. But at that point in time, for me, getting traded to Cleveland was like taking a cold shower. It was refreshing."

At that time the Indians were one of the bleakest outposts in

Major League Baseball. The 1979 season was year 25 in a 40-year stretch—from 1955 through 1994—in which the franchise failed to play a single postseason game. In 1978 the Indians went 69-90 and drew just 800,000 fans to their mammoth, drafty, dreary lakefront stadium.

The 1978 season was the first of eight consecutive years in which the Indians finished sixth or seventh in the seven-team AL East. They bottomed out in 1985, Hargrove's last year as a player, when the Indians staggered to a record of 60-102, finishing 39½ games behind division champion Toronto.

"The joke was that if you were in a plane crash, it was better to have it coming into Cleveland, rather than leaving. I heard that one about a thousand times," Hargrove said. "Had I been traded to Cleveland any other time other than when it happened, it would have been a struggle. But then, it wasn't. I was glad to go there, even though it wasn't a great place to play at that time."'

After being informed of the trade, Hargrove collected his thoughts and equipment and flew to Cleveland on June 16. He was picked up at the airport by Indians traveling secretary Mike Seghi, who drove the team's newest player directly to the ballpark. Hargrove made it to the stadium in time for the game that night—but his equipment didn't.

He was in the lineup, at first base, so he used utility man Horace Speed's first baseman's glove. "I was so glad to be there I would have gone out there with a jai alai stick if I had to," Hargrove said.

He batted fifth in the lineup that night, a walkoff 4-3 Indians victory over Seattle. With one out in the bottom of the ninth, the score was tied, and Seattle pitcher Byron McLaughlin intentionally walked Hargrove to load the bases. Ted Cox then singled home the game-winning run.

It was the fifth win in a row for Cleveland, three of them being walkoff wins. However, they lost the next day, the first of what became a 10-game losing streak. In July they had a four-game losing streak that dropped the team's record to 43-52 and resulted in manager Jeff Torborg being fired. Third-base coach Dave Garcia was named manager, and the Indians promptly won their next 10 in a row.

"His first day as manager, Dave had a team meeting," Hargrove said. "We were all sitting around, and he went to each individual player, not privately, but in the team meeting, and said how he was going to use us, and why we were going to be used that way. He let everyone know what their job was going to be. A couple of guys didn't necessarily like it, but I thought it was great."

They finished at 81-80, only the second time in the previous 11 years they won more than they lost, and even that wasn't enough to climb in the standings. They finished sixth in the seven-team AL East, ahead of only the 109-loss Blue Jays.

Hargrove's exhilaration over escaping the National League and returning to the American League—even if it was Cleveland—was reflected in his numbers. In 125 at-bats with the Padres he had a slash line of .192/.325/.232, with no home runs and eight RBI.

In 338 at-bats with the Indians he hit .325/.433/.500, with 10 home runs and 56 RBI.

"I enjoyed playing in Cleveland," he said. "I know there were some teammates that were biding their time until they could get out of there, so that was annoying and irritating. But for the most part, the majority of the guys enjoyed playing the game. We just could never put it together. One year we'd have good pitching and no hitting and the next we'd have good hitting and no pitching."

Cleveland's 81 wins in 1979 would be their most in any of Hargrove's 6½ years as a player in Cleveland. With the exception of the season after the players' strike that interrupted the 1981 season, the Indians' win total decreased in each of Hargrove's years as a player in Cleveland, culminating in that epic 102-loss 1985 season that tied what was then the franchise record for losses in a season. It was Hargrove's last year as a player in the major leagues.

While his team was floundering, however, Hargrove was refining his skills as a hitter. In his first three years in Cleveland he hit .325, .304 and .317, while finishing off his remarkable streak of having more walks than strikeouts in every season of his 12-year career— sometimes ridiculously so.

With Texas in 1976, Hargrove had 33 more walks than strikeouts: an American League-leading 97 walks and 64 strikeouts. In 1977 he was +44: 103 walks, 59 strikeouts. In 1978 he had 60 more walks than strikeouts: an AL-leading 107 walks and just 47 strikeouts.

In 1979 he had 88 walks and 55 strikeouts. In 1981, when he led the AL with a .424 on-base percentage, he had 398 plate appearances, walked 60 times and only struck out 16 times.

In 1980 he had the best ratio of his career. In 720 plate appearances, he had 75 more walks than strikeouts: 111 to 36.

Times have changed. In baseball today, almost everyone strikes out way more than they walk, and nobody cares. In the analytics-driven game of today, strikeouts are the tax that hitters, and their teams, are willing to pay in exchange for home runs.

Today it's rare to see a hitter's walk total be even within 10 of their strikeout total. In 650 plate appearances in 2018, White Sox second baseman Yoan Moncada, who led the majors in striking out, had 150 more strikeouts (217) than walks (67).

Contrast that with Hargrove in 1980, when he had 70 more plate appearances than Moncada in 2018, but struck out 181 fewer times.

In 6,694 plate appearances in his major league career, Hargrove had 415 more walks than strikeouts.

"I never really thought about going up there trying to draw a walk," he said. "But I knew in my heart the deeper into the count that I could get, the better hitter I became. The walks were a byproduct of trying to get deeper into the count, so I could try to out-guess the pitcher on what pitch he was going to throw."

In his 6½ years as a player with the Indians, Hargrove hit .292, with a .396 on-base percentage. Those were two things he was always confident he could do: hit and get on base.

"Right from the start, I remember being real comfortable about the pitching in the big leagues," he said. "I'm not saying I wasn't intimidated when I first started out. But they threw strikes. I felt I hit the good major league pitchers pretty well, because I knew they were always going to be around the plate."

Hargrove did hit well against good major league pitchers, and he hit great against great major league pitchers. His career batting average against selected Hall of Fame pitchers: Dennis Eckersley .338 (77 career at-bats), Jim Palmer .338 (77 AB), Nolan Ryan .300 (40 AB), Gaylord Perry .514 (35 AB), Don Sutton .303 (33 AB), Rollie Fingers .429 (21 AB), Ferguson Jenkins .316 (19 AB).

Hargrove's career average vs. other outstanding pitchers: Dave Stieb .365 (52 AB), Luis Tiant .333 (48 AB), Ron Guidry .333 (39 AB), Frank Tanana .353 (34 AB) and Wilbur Wood .500 (18 AB).

However, against his old college nemesis, Ray Burris—against whom Hargrove hit three of the longest and hardest foul balls of his life, which helped get him on the radar of major league scouts—Hargrove hit just .125 (1-for-8).

With the Indians, Hargrove was getting on base a lot and rarely striking out for mostly mediocre teams that Cleveland fans pretty much ignored. The Indians drew under 1 million fans in four of Hargrove's 6½ years as a player in Cleveland.

The nadir came in 1985, when only 655,181 customers showed up for the team's home games. A three-game series with Baltimore in April drew 13,548. Not per game. Total. The cold April weather had nothing to do with it. A three-game series with Texas in the July heat drew 14,061. Not per game. Total. It was the old Yogi Berra line: "If the people don't want to come out to the ballpark, nobody's going to stop them."

In 58 of their home games the attendance was under 10,000. For the season they averaged 8,089 per game. This in a stadium with a listed capacity at the time of about 79,000. This was also a team that went 60-102. They were not exactly must-see entertainment.

"It wasn't demoralizing for me, because we'd have 5,000 people, but it would sound like 50,000," Hargrove said. "It wasn't hard playing before small crowds because you knew they were all behind you. They were there to cheer you. To tell you the truth, the only time I was ever aware of the size of the crowd was one time when we played the Yankees and it was 'Beat-The-Yankees-Hankee-Night,' when they had 70,000 people there. That was unbelievable. It was almost like you could see the sound waves coming at you, it was so loud."

On the night of May 15, 1981, there were no sound waves in the old ballpark, at least not until the eighth and ninth innings. It was a Friday night, the first game of a three-game series against Toronto. The attendance was only 7,290, but those that came picked a good night to show up. It was a crisp 49 degrees when Len Barker threw the first pitch of the game. Two hours and nine minutes later Barker threw the last pitch of what at the time was only the eighth perfect game in the last 101 years in the major leagues.

The Blue Jays were only in their fifth year of existence, and that year, for the fifth consecutive year, they would finish in last place in the seven-team AL East. But a perfect game is a perfect game, and Barker took the mound in the top of the ninth inning having retired the first 24 batters in a row. In the ninth he retired the first batter, Rick Bosetti, on a popout to third baseman Toby Harrah. The next hitter was Al Woods, pinch hitting for third baseman Danny Ainge, playing in the last year of his three-year major league career. Following the season, Ainge would join the Boston Celtics, and for the next 15 years would prove that he was a far better basketball player than a baseball player.

Woods struck out for the second out.

With Barker one out away from pitching only the second perfect game in Indians history—the first in 73 years—Ernie Whitt, another pinch hitter, walked to the plate. Whitt was a left-handed hitter. A dead pull hitter. Hargrove, playing first base, was right in the line of fire.

"I'm thinking, 'Oh, shit!'" said Hargrove. "I concentrated so hard. It was like if you took a TV set and covered the screen with black paper, and then cut a hole out of the center of it, that's what it looked like to me. I was concentrating so hard, everything was black, except Ernie Whitt in the center of it. It scared the shit out of me. I thought my head was going to explode."

Whitt hit a flyball to center field.

"I was the happiest person in Northeast Ohio," Hargrove said.

Center fielder Rick Manning caught the ball for the final out of the perfect game, one of only two in Indians history. The other was pitched by Addie Joss in 1908. Barker threw 103 pitches, 74 of them strikes, and didn't have a single three-ball count against any of the 27 hitters he faced. He struck out 11, and they all came in the last 17 batters he faced.

The best post-game quote of all came from Barker's 93-year-old grandmother, who said, "I'm very proud of him. I hope he does better the next time."

*   *   *

Hargrove hit .317 in 1981. It was the third time he'd hit .300 in his three years with the Indians. But his average slipped to .271 in 1982. It was during that season that general manager Phil Seghi began to orchestrate a series of excellent trades that brought a group of young, dynamic prospects to Cleveland. That infusion of talent would eventually lead to diminished playing time for Hargrove, who by then was approaching his mid-30s.

In April 1983 Seghi traded for first baseman Pat Tabler. In 1982, playing for the Cubs' Iowa Triple-A team, Tabler hit .342 with 17 home runs and 105 RBI.

Starting in 1983, Hargrove's at-bats decreased for three years in a row. That was mostly because of the need to find a position for Tabler, whose freakish ability to hit in the clutch dictated that he play every day. The question was: where?

In 1983, Tabler split time between left field and third base. In 1984 he was used almost equally between first base, third base and left field. In 1985, the Indians' manager was Pat Corrales, who replaced Mike Ferraro as manager on July 31, 1983, when Ferraro had to step down to undergo treatment for cancer.

Corrales wanted Tabler to play one position only in 1985. In the previous two years, while playing three different positions, Tabler became an outrageously successful hitter with runners on base. In those two seasons he hit a combined .340 with runners in scoring position (87-for-256), with 10 doubles, four triples, five home runs and a staggering 114 RBI in just 256 at bats. Incredibly, in 1984 he had 57 RBI in 128 at-bats.

With the bases loaded Tabler was even more lethal, hitting a combined .571 (16-for-28) with 39 RBI. Clearly this was a bat that needed to be in the lineup every day, preferably at one position. It became Hargrove's position.

At the start of spring training Corrales called Hargrove into his office. "Mike, relax. You're my first baseman. No problem. You'll be playing every day," said Corrales.

"I appreciated that, but that was the first time I even thought that I wasn't going to be the first baseman," Hargrove said.

A week later, Corrales announced that Tabler was his first baseman.

"I was real, real angry about that for a long time," Hargrove said. "The only way I kept my sanity is that Corrales and I had a special relationship. I like Pat. I liked him then. I love him now. But back then, the only way I could stand it is whenever I walked past him,

I'd say, 'Fuck you' to him. Most managers would knock you on your ass for doing that. But I'd say, 'Fuck you,' and Pat would laugh. I meant it. But the way he handled it got me out of that funk."

Hargrove was mad for a couple of reasons. First, because he was no longer going to be the regular first baseman. But also because his contract was up at the end of the year.

"I told Pat, 'This move kills my career. I can still play every day and I can still be a valuable player,'" Hargrove said. "Pat said, 'Yes you can.' So I said, 'Then trade me. Give me a chance to keep playing. Because if not, then at the end of the year, I'm done.'"

Corrales told Hargrove the Indians weren't going to trade him.

"Phil and Gabe both asked me if I wanted them to trade you and I said no," said Corrales, referring to Seghi and Indians president Gabe Paul.

"So we're not going to trade you," Corrales continued. "You're my insurance if one of the kids falls on their face."

"That was probably when the 'Fuck yous' started," said Hargrove.

That was also when Hargrove learned the meaning of the old baseball adage, "What's the truth today may not be the truth two days from now."

But that still didn't make it any easier.

"It was just one of those deals," Hargrove said. "I don't blame Corrales for wanting to go with a younger club. The older club wasn't doing shit, and it wasn't going to. I understood it. But, selfishly, I didn't like it."

Hargrove did start 70 games at first base that year. But Tabler started 83 games at first, 17 more at designated hitter, and four at third base. Designated hitter wasn't a fulltime option for Hargrove, either, because Andre Thornton, at 35, the same age as Hargrove, still had some gas left in his tank. Thornton had led the team in home runs in each of the previous three years, and he would lead it again in 1985.

Hargrove that year hit .285 with one home run and 27 RBI in 284 at-bats. Tabler, who only played in 117 games because of injuries, hit .275 with five home runs and 59 RBI in 404 at-bats. But Tabler was still magical in the clutch. With runners in scoring position he hit .340, with 55 RBI in 106 at-bats, and with the bases loaded he was a ridiculous 6-for-7 (.857) with 15 RBI.

The team overall was a mess, losing 102 of their 162 games. No starting pitcher won more than nine games. "Closer" Tom Waddell had nine saves. Total. For the season.

When it was over, it was over. The season and, effectively, Hargrove's playing career. Three weeks after the end of the season Hargrove turned 36. He still wanted to play, but it was a bad time to be 36 and out of work. Those years, 1985-86, were two of the years the owners were found guilty of colluding to the keep salaries of free agents and other players down. There were almost no free-agent signings.

Hargrove was a free agent. But nobody would sign him.

"I hit .285, and couldn't find a job anywhere, not even in Japan," he said.

Jackie Moore, the manager of the Oakland A's, was a good friend of Hargrove's, and Moore got Hargrove an invitation to Oakland's spring training camp as a non-roster invitee. But Hargrove wasn't there long.

"In the middle of March, they told me it wasn't going to happen," he said.

"That was awful," said Sharon. "The day he got released, Mike called me and said, 'You need to come and get me.' I said, 'What's going on?' He said, 'I just got released.' I said, 'What?'"

Sharon drove to the ballpark to pick up her husband. As Mike was walking towards the car, a young catcher from another team stopped him and said, "I know this is probably the worst day of your life. I admire your career so much that I hope I have a worst day like this one day."

"That really kind of helped Mike," Sharon said.

That was how it ended. A baseball career that started with him playing on a softball team with his father in Perryton, Texas in the early '60s, ended in the parking lot of a ballpark in Phoenix, Arizona in the spring of 1986.

"Getting released like that, he was embarrassed," Sharon said. "He said we'd have to go back to Texas and put the kids in school. He said, 'How embarrassing for our kids. I can't even get a job.' I said, 'Mike, you've played over 10 years in the big leagues. Calm down.' He said, 'No. I'm embarrassed.'"

The Hargroves had an apartment in Mesa, Arizona, so they

decided to hang around the area for a while to see if Mike's agent got a call from another club. This was uncharted territory. For the first time in 14 years, a baseball season was starting, and Mike Hargrove wasn't on a team.

"That was really, really hard," he said. "I didn't leave the apartment for a week. Never left it. I'd go to bed at night, sleep good, then get up in the morning and it was like somebody had put a wet, woolen warm blanket across the top of my chest."

"He was really struggling," said Sharon. "It was a letdown. He worked real hard to make that (Oakland) club, and thought he'd made it."

Nothing happened for a week, except for Hargrove battling depression. As one week turned into two, Jeff Newman, an A's coach and another friend of the Hargroves, came with his wife to their apartment unannounced. Newman brought some steaks with him and said, "Come on, we're cooking out."

Hargrove invited some players that he wanted to say goodbye to.

"That was the beginning of me getting out of my funk," he said.

"I think that he realized then that, 'I'm not going to lose my friends. This is just baseball,'" said Sharon.

But it was also life, and Hargrove realized he had to get on with his. He preferred that it be in baseball. Over the last couple of years, he had periodically broached the subject with Sharon.

"He said he'd like to stay in the game, and would I be up for that?" Sharon said. "We didn't make enough money back then to support five kids, with all we had going on at the time."

In the spring of 1986 Hargrove was already plotting his next move. In a conversation prior to the start of spring training, Indians president Dan O'Brien told Hargrove that he thought Hargrove would be good in the dugout, and that he should think about managing. O'Brien told Hargrove if things didn't work out with the A's, to call him. Hargrove did better than that. He made the two-hour drive from Phoenix to the Indians' training camp in Tucson. He met with O'Brien, and tried to talk O'Brien into hiring him as a coach on the big-league team.

"No, you need to go down to the minors and learn the game. That's the best thing in the world," said O'Brien, who offered Hargrove a job as the hitting coach with the Indians' rookie-league team at Batavia, New York, in the New York-Penn League. Hargrove accepted.

*   *   *

Not many successful major league players choose to pursue a managerial career after their playing days are over. One of the biggest reasons is that, financially, it's like starting their baseball careers over. In order to get managerial experience, many of them must go back to the minor leagues they desperately fought to escape as a player. "Paying your dues" isn't just a figure of speech. The most Hargrove made as a player was $450,000, which is less than the major league minimum today, but is still $450,000. His salary as the hitting coach at Batavia was $6,000.

The plan was for Hargrove to coach for a year, then become a minor league manager the following year. Becoming a manager was something Hargrove had pondered when he realized his career as a player was winding down.

"Like everybody else, I would sit on the bench and watch what the manager does. I would manage along with him and sometimes second guess the manager," he said. "I always got along well with people, and they seemed to respect me for what I'd done, and how I carried myself. So I figured, let's give it a try."

So the Hargroves packed up the car, and the kids, and drove home to Texas, where he would drop off the family in Perryton, then continue on to Batavia.

"On the drive home I said, 'Let's go to the Grand Canyon,'" Sharon said. "We were right there, in Phoenix. We could show the kids the Grand Canyon. So we stopped at the Grand Canyon, got out of the car, and Mike said, 'There it is, kids.' Then we got back in the car and went on."

The Hargroves returned to Perryton, and in June, Mike left for Batavia. For the first time since 1973, he was back in the minor leagues. The 1986 Batavia Trojans, Tom Chandler manager, Mike Hargrove hitting coach, finished with a record of 30-45, despite having eight future major leaguers on the roster: position players

Tom Lampkin, Troy Neel and Tommy Hinzo, and pitchers Jim Bruske, Bruce Egloff, Jeff Shaw, Joe Skalski and Kevin Wickander.

The next year, 1987, Hargrove was named manager of the Kinston Indians in the Class A Carolina League. The person who made that call was the Indians' farm director Jeff Scott, who was Hargrove's old minor league teammate with the Texas Rangers in 1972 and 1973. As a teammate of Hargrove's at Geneva, New York and Gastonia, North Carolina, Scott said he saw qualities in Hargrove that suggested he had the right stuff to eventually become a manager.

"Oh yeah, definitely," Scott said. "Because as a teammate, he was respected. He was knowledgeable. He knew how to play the game right, and that usually translates, if the guy is interested in doing it, in becoming a manager."

Hargrove was, and he began laying the groundwork as his career was winding down.

"He would tell people, 'I want to stay in the game. Remember that,'" Scott said.

Scott recalled a conversation with Hargrove in 1986, when Hargrove traveled with the A's to Tucson for a spring training game against the Indians.

"He was a non-roster player with the A's, but he didn't really have a chance to make the club," Scott said. "That day, he told Danny O'Brien he was going to make the trip to Tucson for the game, which was a clear indication he wasn't going to make the team, because veterans didn't have to make that five-hour round trip bus ride from Phoenix to Tucson. But Mike knew if he had any shot of making the team, he had to do it."

After the A's arrived for the game, Hargrove went looking for Scott on one of the back fields of the Indians' complex.

"He found me and we chatted for a while," Scott said. "Mike said, 'Scotty, I'm not going to make the team. I'm not ready to do anything right away at the end of spring training. But I'd really like to do something this year, if you've got anything.

"I told him, 'If you want to do it, we'll have something. We still haven't hired a hitting coach for our rookie league club. That would be a good way to start out. Go be a coach. You don't have to be responsible for the day-to-day stuff.' So when the A's released him, we worked out an arrangement, and that started his off-the-field career."

Not many big-league players who retire and want to stay in the game as a coach or manager are willing to go back to the minor leagues to learn the nuances of being a coach or manager. They'd prefer to begin in the major leagues. They had gotten their fill of the long bus rides, the bad food and the bad hours as minor league players, and they aren't willing to go back to the bushes in hopes of making the climb to the majors a second time in their career.

Hargrove was willing to do it, but it wasn't easy.

"It was a difficult transition, going from being a major league player to a minor league manager," he said. "Managing in the minors was difficult and different. Different in ways that I never thought of as a player. It was difficult in going from a big-league clubhouse to Batavia, where you dressed in a tin clubhouse that had concrete or dirt floors. It was so dirty you couldn't tell the difference. That was an eye opener."

But Hargrove was a quick study. So much so that in his first year as a manager he led Kinston to a record of 75-65, and a division championship, for which he was named the Manager of the Year in the Carolina League.

"The game is still the game. From rookie ball to the majors, it's the same game, just degrees of goodness," he said. "I never felt like a fish out of water. I enjoyed being in charge. It felt comfortable. It felt right. It was a round peg in a round hole."

Hargrove's Kinston club was both good and wacky. Especially the pitching staff. That staff included brothers Tony and Andy Ghelfi. Tony spent 10 years in the minor leagues and only appeared in three major league games, with the Phillies in 1983. Andy was a second-round pick by the Indians in 1985 out of Indiana State, but in five minor league seasons he never pitched an inning above Double-A.

Also on that staff was Wickander, who was so hyper he would sprint off the mound to back up first base whenever there was a ground ball hit to the infield, and Rod Nichols, who got so upset after one of his minor league starts that he tried to flush his baseball glove down the toilet.

The most eccentric pitcher on the staff, however, was Archie W.

Shamblin, a fifth-round draft pick by Milwaukee in 1982, out of Mohave High School, in Bullhead City, Arizona. His first four years in pro ball were spent in the Brewers' and Texas Rangers' systems. In 1987, he somehow showed up on Hargrove's roster at Kinston.

"Shamblin was goofier than hell," Hargrove said. "He had a tattoo on his arm that said, 'Baseball Love It!' with a big heart. On his other arm he had a tattoo that said, 'Mother.' He and the Ghelfis were like the leaders of a pack of dogs. They would get guys to do stupid stuff, and then stand off to the side and laugh at them.

"One day the game is going on and I'm coaching third base and I look down the left field line to the bullpen, and the entire bullpen is standing at home plate, lined up like bowling pins, and Shamblin is doing somersaults all the way from the pitcher's mound into the pins at home plate, knocking them down. They all fell down.

"I chewed them out after the game, even though I thought it was hilarious. The next day I said to Shamblin, 'So you like to do somersaults, huh?' He said, 'Yeah.' So, I made him meet me in the outfield the next afternoon, and I made him do somersaults from the right field line to the left field line, and back again. Then I told him that was enough, and when he tried to stand up, he crashed back to the ground and said, 'Boy, that was tough, Skip.'"

At Kinston, Hargrove learned that being a manager in the minor leagues means more than just being a manager in the minor leagues.

"I found out, especially in the low minors, that you're the players' manager, their father, their counselor, their priest. You are everything to them," he said. "That was hard to get used to. As a player, I knew what it took for me to get ready for the game. As a manager, I never had that time, because everyone wants 15, 20 minutes. So you better get your work done early, because you don't have time once the players start showing up."

Despite his well-earned reputation for having a short fuse as a player, Hargrove the minor league manager was rather docile. Most of the time, anyway.

"I got into some arguments. Not many," he said. "In Triple-A I was told by the league president that if I got thrown out of one more game, he was going to suspend me. We had two different games where we had 12 players kicked out of the game, including me."

In 1987 at Kinston, Hargrove also got to manage the Indians' second-round draft pick that year, an outfielder from LSU. The player showed up near the end of the season, following a lengthy, contentious negotiation with Jeff Scott to get him signed. Scott personally accompanied the new player to Kinston, and introduced him to his new manager.

That player was Joey Belle, the artist later to be known as Albert Belle.

Hargrove was Belle's first and last manager in professional baseball. It didn't take the manager long to form an opinion of his new outfielder.

"He could hit. He was real quiet, but, God, he could hit," said Hargrove.

Scott actually came to Kinston four days before Belle's arrival, to prep Hargrove on what he was about to experience.

"Jeff gave me the rundown on his history, but I always believed that the past was the past," Hargrove said. "And back then I don't remember him being particularly difficult. I do remember him hitting some balls a long, long way."

Following the season at Kinston, Hargrove managed the Indians' team in the instructional league. Belle was on that team. "He was a little more demonstrative there," Hargrove said.

That, as Hargrove would later find out, was just the tip of the iceberg.

CHAPTER 6

Back to the Big Leagues

"You got the job, didn't you?"

In 1986, Richard Jacobs and his brother David bought the Cleveland Indians from the estate of F.J. "Steve" O'Neill. In October 1987, Hank Peters was fired as general manager of the Baltimore Orioles. A month later, Peters was hired to be the Indians' president and general manager.

It was a seminal moment in the history of the Indians franchise because with the Jacobs' money, the baseball acumen and leadership of Peters, and two top assistants he brought with him from Baltimore, John Hart and Dan O'Dowd, one of Major League Baseball's most moribund franchises lurched to life.

A creative rebuilding plan, portions of which would be mimicked by other franchises for years to come, was put into place. The scouting and farm departments started drafting and developing impact players. A series of excellent trades got the rebuild rolling. Seven years later the Indians got their much-needed new ballpark, which immediately turned into a cash cow that helped grease the wheels for the franchise's remarkable championship run from the mid-to-late 1990s.

In 1987, Mike Hargrove had no idea all that was about to happen in Cleveland, or that he would play a central role in it. Instead, he was busy watching one of his somersaulting pitchers bowling-ball his way to home plate, into 10 human bowling pins, in the bullpen of some godforsaken minor league field in the Carolina League. But events were already taking place that would impact the future of Cleveland, the Indians and especially Mike Hargrove.

In the meantime, Hargrove moved up a level in 1988, managing the Double-A Williamsport Bills to a record of 66-73 and a sixth-place finish in the eight-team Eastern League.

In 1989 it was on to the Pacific Coast League, where Hargrove managed the Indians' Triple-A affiliate, the Colorado Springs Sky Sox, to the first half title and an overall record of 78-64. For the second time in his three years, he was named Manager of the Year in his league. He added an even bigger accolade when Baseball America named him the No. 1 managerial prospect in the minor leagues.

When he started at Batavia in 1986, his goal was to become a major league manager. He had no timetable, but he was moving quickly up the ladder, and people were noticing. He already had the name recognition, and he earned points for being willing to pay his dues, by going down to the low minors to start this phase of his career.

"I didn't have a timetable for getting a big-league managing job," he said. "I just figured my best chance to manage in the big leagues was with the Indians, because the front office knew me."

He also realized he had a lot to learn about being a manager, and by the end of his third year, he felt he'd learned it.

"At Colorado Springs, about halfway through that season, I felt I was ready to manage in the big leagues," he said. "I had no idea if it would be with Cleveland, but I thought I was ready."

Serendipitously for Hargrove, the managerial situation in Cleveland was a mess. Starting in 1987, the Indians had four managers in four years. Pat Corrales was fired halfway through the 1987 season. He was replaced by bullpen coach Doc Edwards, who played for the Indians in 1962 and 1963.

Edwards managed the Indians for the remainder of the 1987 season, and all of 1988. At the press conference to announce that Edwards would be the Indians' manager again in 1989, he received the mother of all lukewarm endorsements from Peters: "I couldn't think of any reason not to bring Doc back."

Edwards, however, was fired with 19 games left in the 1989 season. The interim manager for those remaining games was Hart, a former minor league manager and major league coach under

Peters in Baltimore. In Cleveland, Hart was hired by Peters as a special assignment scout, but was also being groomed to eventually replace Peters as the Indians' general manager.

Following the 1989 season, Peters hired veteran major league manager John McNamara as the Indians' fourth manager in four years. McNamara was 57 when the Indians hired him. He came to Cleveland with 17 years of experience as a major league manager, with five different teams: the A's, Padres, Reds, Angels and Red Sox.

Prior to hiring McNamara, Peters interviewed Hargrove for the job.

"I think it was more of, not a token interview of Grover, but I think Hank felt he needed a little more time. He needed to manage a little more," Hart said. "At the time, Hank wanted more of a veteran guy there. He knew we were going to do a rebuild, and Hank knew Mac from his days in Kansas City."

McNamara was a minor league player and minor league manager for the Kansas City A's in the early 1960s, when Peters was Kansas City's farm director.

When McNamara was hired to manage the Indians, he asked for Hargrove to be on his coaching staff, and Hargrove became the Indians' first-base coach. That led to speculation that McNamara was grooming Hargrove to eventually become the Indians' manager.

"I got that impression too, but nobody ever said anything like that to me. I know John treated me like that was going to happen," Hargrove said.

"Johnny Mac was a good fit because he was an experienced, wise baseball man," said Hart, who was promoted to assistant general manager following the 1987 season. "It wasn't a fait accompli that Grover was going to be the guy to replace Mac when we made the change. But Grover was certainly on our radar."

A month after hiring McNamara, Peters led the Indians' contingent to baseball's winter meetings in Nashville. It was there that Peters made a blockbuster trade with San Diego that brought to Cleveland the first two core players of what would become the foundation of those powerhouse Indians teams of the mid-to-late 1990s. Peters traded outfielder Joe Carter, who over the previous four years averaged 31 home runs, 107 RBI and 25 stolen bases per season, to the Padres for catcher Sandy Alomar Jr., second baseman Carlos Baerga and outfielder Chris James.

Alomar was Baseball America's Minor League Player of the Year in 1989. He would become the American League Rookie of the Year with the Indians in 1990, and would be selected to the American League All-Star team in six of his first nine years with the Indians. He might have gone nine-for-nine, but was hampered by a series of injuries.

Baerga, a switch-hitting second baseman, hit .305 over his first six years in Cleveland, being selected to the AL All-Star team three times. In 1995, he was the No. 3 hitter in an Indians lineup that was one of the most ferocious in major league history.

The addition of Alomar and Baerga to the lineup didn't have an immediate impact in the won-loss column, as the Indians went 77-85 in 1990, an improvement of only four wins over the 1989 team.

Throughout that 1990 season, however, Hargrove took what became a graduate course in managing in the big leagues from Professor John McNamara. That education came before games, during games, after games, and it grew even more intense on the road, where the two men would talk baseball at the park, and at the hotel.

"We would come off the plane," said Hargrove, "and John would say, 'Grover, come up to my room when we get to the hotel.' I'd say, 'OK,' and, whew! Four hours and a bottle and a half of scotch later, I stumbled back to my room."

Hargrove cherished those moments, however, because Mac "gave me some real words of wisdom."

"I felt Grover was going to learn, just through osmosis," Hart said. "He knew the big leagues. Grover had spent 12, 14 years in the big leagues, so he knew how things worked, but not as a coach. I felt Grover was going to learn by watching the moves Mac made, and by watching our competition, and what was going on out there. I felt it was a really good fit. But we never said, 'Look, Johnny, part of what we want you to do is grow Grover.' That wasn't a part of it."

One of the points McNamara stressed to Hargrove was, "Don't let a star fall on you," meaning don't manage a star player in the last year or years of his career, because then he'll crater on you, and the manager takes all the heat.

"He also told me, 'Don't argue with your general manager over the 25th man on the roster,'" said Hargrove. "He said the most important relationship you have as a manager is with your general manager, so always get a good relationship with him. Little snippets like that, which I did remember when I became a manager."

Hargrove was a willing student. Nobody from the front office had told him he was going to be the next manager of the Indians, but Hargrove could connect what seemed to him to be very obvious dots.

"Mac never actually came out and said, 'When you become manager . . .'" Hargrove said. "But it was almost like he was mentoring me. He may not have been, but it came across that way."

Hart said there was never any specifically detailed plan of succession for Hargrove to take over, although it was generally implied that Hargrove's presence on McNamara's coaching staff was not an accident.

"Mac was never told by us that 'You've got a year or two, and then we're going to Grover. That was never brought up,'" Hart said. "But Mac knew, because we had talked about it, that we were going young, and part of what we were trying to do is build stability in the organization, and that we're going to take one of our own guys and bring him up and put him on the coaching staff. That was sort of the deal."

Then came the train wreck that was the 1991 season, the worst season in the history of the Cleveland Indians.

"That was an unbelievable season. If something could go wrong, it did. Two outs in the ninth, a ball would hit the corner of the base, two runs score and you lose the game. Stuff like that," said Hargrove.

Lots of stuff like that. So much stuff, that once the snowball started down the hill, there was no way to stop it. From June 6 through July 5, the Indians went 4-24, dropping their record to 25-52. Although the Indians still had 53 more losses waiting for them in the second half of the season, there was no point in delaying the inevitable.

"I sensed that the way things were going, that a change was going to be made. But I thought Mac did a great job with what he had," Hargrove said. "I admired the man. I respected him. He just got caught in a tough situation. So, I felt like something had a chance to happen."

On July 1, the Indians flew to New York for a three-game series with the Yankees. Hart, who rarely accompanied the team on road trips, was on this one.

After one of the games, Hart called Hargrove up to his suite, and the two men talked for two hours about the ballclub.

"I got a sense from that meeting that something was happening," Hargrove said. "John didn't let on at all that I was being considered. It wasn't an interview or a pre-interview. And Hank Peters had never said to me, 'You're the next guy.' He never intimated that. But after that meeting with John in his hotel room, and when you saw the way the club was playing, it didn't surprise me when it happened. You get a feel for things. It's like when you're a manager and you can get the feeling you're going to get fired. Nobody has to say anything."

The Indians lost all three games in New York, although they were competitive: 6-2, 8-5 and 3-2. They returned home, and on Thursday, the Fourth of July, Charles Nagy tossed a six-hit 3-0 complete game shutout over Milwaukee. Friday, on a warm, 82-degree summer night, the Indians lost to the Brewers 4-2, in front of 13,221 fans. It was the Indians' 24th loss in their last 28 games. At 25-52, they had the worst record in the majors.

After the game, Hart told Hargrove to be at the ballpark the next day at 10:30 a.m., which was odd, since Saturday's game was a night game.

"Then you start putting two and two together," Hargrove said. "Part of you is excited and part of you feels terrible that a friend of yours, and somebody you respect and admire, is losing his job."

When Hargrove got home, he told Sharon, "I've got to go see Hank tomorrow morning."

"What's going on?" asked Sharon.

"They didn't say. They just said, 'Be here at 10:30.'"

Then came the hard part—waiting for 10:30.

"Laying there, and not being able to sleep at all, because 15,000 things are going through your mind," Hargrove said.

He finally fell asleep, woke up at 6:30 in the morning, went out and ran two miles, came back, took a nap, and then left for the ballpark.

"What I was thinking was I know Mac isn't going to be the manager anymore, but I hope they're not firing me with him. Then the other side of it was, if they're getting rid of Mac, I hope they give it to me," Hargrove said. "On the one hand you feel a lot of sadness that a guy you respect is losing his job. But the other part was, I've got a family to feed, I hope I don't get fired with him."

He didn't. At a hastily called news conference he was introduced as the as the 36th manager in Indians history.

"The rest of that day was a blur," Hargrove said.

"John McNamara is not a scapegoat," Hank Peters said at the news conference. "He's not totally to blame for what has happened here. If there was a shortage of talent on this ballclub, that responsibility is on my shoulders and the shoulders of management."

Peters then publicly stated what the organizational approach had been since the start of the season: "This club is very much dedicated to going with a young, talented team, but it's inexperienced. As a result of this, we have a different type of club today than the one we had a year ago, and it was my belief it was the type of club John might not be accustomed to managing."

The first thing Hargrove did after the news conference was to call McNamara, but he got Mac's voicemail. Hargrove then got in his car and drove out to a Cleveland suburb, where his son Andy was playing a Little League game.

"I walked in, dying to tell Sharon, but there were 100 people standing around us, so I didn't say anything. Sharon looked at me and said, 'You got the job, didn't you?' I said, 'Yeah, I did.'"

According to Hart, the way the 1991 season played out accelerated the decision to make the switch at manager.

"The team, obviously, was really struggling," he said. "A big part of it was, in my mind, that Grover was going to be the next manager. So if that's the case, why not go ahead and make the move and let him get a half season under his belt? He'll be that much further along.

"We were a lot better in '92 and '93, and I think a big part of that was because we made the move with Grover in the middle of the

'91 season. It gave him a chance to make the moves, fill out the lineup card, and develop a relationship with the players."

Just as the hiring of Hank Peters was a seminal moment for the franchise, so, too, was the hiring of Hargrove as manager. It signified not only that the rebuild had officially begun, but that this was the guy that was going to be the manager who was going to help facilitate that rebuild, and the hoped-for emergence of the Indians as a relevant team again in the American League.

"It worked," said Hart, of the decision to make Hargrove manager, and the continuation of the long-range plan that resulted in the building of some of the best teams in franchise history.

"It worked, but it was hard. We didn't have a lot of talent," Hart said. "It wasn't like we said, 'OK we've got all these young players ready.' The young players weren't ready. We were still making deals and building the team."

What Peters and Hart did know was that Hargrove was ready. That was a huge, key piece to have in place as the gears in the machinery for the rebuild started turning and meshing.

"When we hired Grover to be a coach, we all knew there was a good chance that he was going to be the guy eventually," Hart said. "But we knew we had a long, long way to go as far as building the ballclub, and getting talent. Watching Grover, and being around him—his patience, he's even-keel, level-headed, smart all of those things became factors in making him the manager. But when he was a coach, we were still evaluating him. If he would have come in and been something else, we wouldn't have (made him manager)."

Amid all the excitement and drama that surrounded her husband being promoted into a high-profile position, Sharon Hargrove changed the message on the family's answering machine. Unbeknownst to her husband, Sharon changed the message to say, "You've reached the home of the new manager of the Cleveland Indians . . . "

That's what McNamara heard when he returned Hargrove's call on the day of the managerial change.

"That's one thing I really, really regret," Hargrove said. "I got a message that John had called me, and I knew he heard Sharon's new message. I thought 'Gosh darn!' that's not how I felt. I did eventually talk to him and he wished me good luck and I told him how much I enjoyed working for him and appreciated all the advice he gave me. We didn't talk again until he became the interim manager of the Angels (in 1996). We sat in the dugout and talked, and there didn't seem to be any animosity."

*   *   *

On July 6, 1991, after three years as a minor league manager, Hargrove, at age 41, was named manager of the Indians. It was one of the highlights of his 35 years in baseball, it was the payoff for going back to the bushes for three years of dues-paying, and it was one of the most exciting days of his life.

Then reality set in.

His team was awful. The worst in the major leagues. But on July 6, 1991, in Hargrove's first game as a major league manager, his team was the best team on the field at Cleveland Stadium. Greg Swindell pitched seven innings and combined with reliever Shawn Hillegas on a four-hit 2-0 shutout of the Milwaukee Brewers before a crowd of 15,461. The Indians' lineup that day:

Alex Cole-CF
Chris James-DH
Carlos Baerga-3B
Reggie Jefferson-1B
Mark Whiten-RF
Albert Belle-LF
Sandy Alomar-C
Felix Fermin-SS
Mark Lewis-2B

Then it was back to the losing. The Indians lost their next three in a row, then won a game, lost three more in a row, then won a game, lost . . . well, you get the picture. Starting on July 23 they lost nine of 11 games. Starting Aug. 6, they lost 13 of 16 games.

Their last home game of the season came on Oct. 3, when they lost 9-3 to Milwaukee. That was loss No. 104. There were only 5,050 witnesses at nearly empty Cleveland Stadium. Then the Indians went to New York to finish the season with three games against the Yankees.

In the first game the Indians were losing 2-1 with two outs in the ninth inning, when 21-year-old rookie third baseman Jim Thome hit the first of his 612 major league home runs, a two-run shot off Yankees reliever, and former Indian, Steve Farr that landed in the upper deck in right field at Yankee Stadium. That gave Cleveland a 3-2 lead, and, three outs later, their 56th victory of the year.

An unheralded 13th round pick by the Indians in the 1989 Draft, Thome was a September callup by the Indians in 1991. At the time he was not considered a power hitter. In a combined 511 plate appearances at Triple-A and Double-A in 1991, he had hit .319, but with only seven home runs. The power came later (along with, eventually, a team record for home runs, a statue outside Progressive Field and induction into the Baseball Hall of Fame). Losing came immediately, though, as the most dreadful season in franchise history staggered toward its finish. A 7-4 loss to the Yankees on Oct. 6 mercifully dropped the tattered curtain on the Indians' 57-105 season.

"Any time you lose that many games, it's difficult," said Thome. "You're getting called to the big leagues for the first time, which you're so excited for," he said, "and then the team is not accomplishing what it wants."

At 57-105 the Indians finished in last place in the seven-team AL East, 10 games out of sixth place, and 34 games behind division champion Toronto. In 1991 the Indians were 25-52 (.325) under McNamara, and 32-53 (.376) under Hargrove.

Hargrove said that his excitement over becoming a major league manager was not tempered by the fact that he was managing a historically bad team.

"That was a foregone conclusion," he said. "Everybody knew we had a bad team. I really didn't dwell on that a lot. But I had been away from managing for a couple of years, and things were so different from managing in the minors to managing in the big leagues.

"In the minors, you might have one or two writers to talk to after the game. In the majors, you've got 10 or 15. In the majors the game is faster, really faster, as far as the way things happen. I felt like that whole half season, I really felt I was a half-step behind the whole way. I was trying to rev my motor up to get up to speed. I felt like I was a little behind in trying to catch up to the speed of the game, and the attention that's drawn to the game. But the biggest thing was I just remember thinking I needed to speed things up."

Indians officials had no illusions about the team Hargrove was inheriting. So, obviously, any evaluations made on the new manager would be ones that weren't based on the won-loss record. There were only a handful of pieces on that 1991 roster that would still be around when the Indians became a steamroller later in the decade: Alomar, Baerga, Belle, Charles Nagy and, in September, Thome. All of them were at the beginning of their careers. So was their manager. So was their general manager.

On Sept. 18, 1991, Hart was promoted to general manager, but he had been Hank Peters' right-hand man for the last couple of years, and was involved in all the big decisions. Hart also knew that whoever replaced McNamara would have to be somebody he could work with, because—what McNamara told Hargrove was true—the most important relationship of all is the one between the general manager and the manager. So, Hart obviously had more than a passing interest in McNamara's successor.

"In looking at what was going to work for me and the organization, it (the next manager) was going to have to be somebody that I could develop a relationship with," Hart said. "I felt Grover was a man of good character. He knew the game. And he had other qualities. He was a really good player. He had been a former Indians player. As it went along, it just worked. We rolled up our sleeves, made decisions on players and sort of developed our own working relationship."

The importance of the relationship between Hart and Hargrove cannot be overstated, because of what it produced: five consecutive trips to the postseason, after none in the previous 40 years, two trips to the World Series, and some of the greatest players in Cleveland Indians history.

It was a relationship that evolved over the years between two men who weren't particularly close personally. But that was fine, perhaps even healthy. However, professionally, they were very close, in many ways a perfect match. Hart was the quicker to react of the two, Hargrove the more patient. They were an ideal counterbalance to one another.

"I like to have a guy you can trust," said Hart. "A guy that has his own opinion, which Grover did. He's a tough Texas guy. But it wasn't like there were battles. We had disagreements. It's the nature of the game. You hate to even classify it as a disagreement. But if we had opposite opinions on a player or a move, there was a level of respect that we could talk it through. And whenever we opened the door and came out, whether one was happy and the other wasn't, there was still that trust, that relationship, and that loyalty that was there."

It didn't begin that way, of course. In 1991, the men were both new to their jobs. But they both seemed to intuitively grasp the importance of the relationship, that each owed it to the other to make it work, and that the investment to the whole must take precedence over all else.

"A lot of it has to do with our personalities. Grover has always been somebody that people gravitate to. He's a good guy. That meant a lot to me. Good family. Good values. Good heart. Fun guy," said Hart.

"John and I had two completely different personalities, but I think the difference in our personalities and demeanors really played well together, to where we made some really good decisions," said Hargrove.

Both men brought different skill sets to the job of trying to resurrect a franchise that had lain dormant for decades. The Indians at the time couldn't afford to sign high-priced free agents. Prior to the last couple of years their draft history was abysmal, and their trades rarely moved the needle. The last time the team was consistently relevant was in the 1950s, when Hart and Hargrove were in grade school. Now they were charged with recharging the long-dead baseball battery of a team that played in a decrepit monstrosity of a stadium, in a football city, for fans who had long since lost interest in the summer game.

"I had spent so many years on the field, I kind of understood a little more of how tough it was for a manager during a rebuild, and what kind of guy we were going to need to relate to that," said Hart, a former minor league manager in the Baltimore organization. "So, our relationship worked from a personal standpoint. From a professional standpoint, we were coming at it with the same objective, but he was coming at it from the field, and in leading the players, and I was coming at it from the front office perspective.

"Early on, we were acquiring, and presenting opportunities to young players, and Grover was a perfect fit for that. He was all in. He was good with the players. He didn't put a lot of pressure on them. There was a lot of teaching. We had good coaches. There were guys out there that I managed against that I thought might be the right guy. But one of the main reasons I wanted Grover was that I thought he was a good guy, and that turned out to be the case in spades. It was the best time of my life as a professional."

Dan O'Dowd was Hart's assistant general manager through most of what was about to unfold, which was the golden era of Indians baseball.

"The one person who doesn't get enough credit for that was Hank Peters," said O'Dowd. "The trade for Alomar and Baerga that got it started, that was Hank's deal. The other thing Hank did, which has gone unnoticed because he didn't stay around long enough to share in the fruits of his labor is this: When you can get an owner to completely buy into a vision, and to stay patient through the process, without taking any shortcuts at all, that is almost impossible to do. But Hank did that. He got Dick and David Jacobs to really understand where we were going to get to, and how painful it was going to be. That we can't take one shortcut to doing it.

"So Hank laid the foundation for us to be able to do things we would not have been able to do under any owner who was impetuous in any way, shape or form. Hank really got Dick to understand the big picture."

That was good, because the little picture was a mess.

*   *   *

Once the wreckage of the 1991 season was swept aside, the mother of all rebuilds began in earnest. It began with a search for a center fielder, because, well . . .

"For God's sake, we were playing Alex Cole out there," said Hart.

But then the Indians started scouting a cocky little ex-basketball player in Houston's minor league system.

Kenny Lofton was a 24-year-old, 6-foot, 180-pound athletic dynamo who was the sixth man on the 1988 University of Arizona basketball team that reached the Final Four. (He was a college teammate of future Golden State Warriors coach Steve Kerr.) Lofton came to baseball as an afterthought. He didn't play in college until his junior year, and played in only five games that year. But that was enough for the Houston Astros, who took a flyer on Lofton's blinding speed and off-the-charts athleticism, selecting him in the 17th round of the 1988 Draft.

In his first year in pro ball he looked like a basketball player trying to play baseball. In the rookie-level New York-Penn League, Lofton hit just .214, although he averaged almost two stolen bases per game. But the next year, at Class-A, his average jumped to .292, with 40 stolen bases. In 1990 he was moved to high Class-A, in the Florida State League, where he hit .331, with 62 stolen bases.

Back in Cleveland, Hart, O'Dowd and the team's pro scouting staff sat down and took inventory of their roster: "Here's what we think we have, what we're pretty sure we have, and what we don't have." The list of what they didn't have was much longer than the list of what they did have. At the top of the "Don't Have" list was a center fielder.

"We put together a whole list of center fielders," Hart said. "We had seven or eight guys on the list, and one of them was Kenny. Then we went out and scouted them all."

That was in 1991. By then Lofton was playing for Houston's Triple-A club in Tucson, which was convenient, not only because it was the Indians' spring training home, but it was also in the Pacific Coast League, which included the Indians' Triple-A affiliate at Colorado Springs, managed by Charlie Manuel.

"I called Charlie and said, 'You guys are going to play Tucson 20 times this year. Just keep an eye on Lofton,'" said Hart, who made a special trip out west to watch some of those Tucson-Colorado Springs games.

"I got to eyeball Lofton for five games and I loved him," Hart said.

Lofton shot to the top of the Indians' center fielder wish list, although Hart continued to talk to all major league clubs about their center fielders.

At the end of spring training, in what at the time seemed like a yawner of a transaction, the Indians claimed catcher Eddie Taubensee off waivers from Oakland. Taubensee, a 22-year-old left-handed hitter, spent most of the 1991 season at Colorado Springs, where he had a great year, hitting .310, with a .924 OPS. That was good news for Hart. Why? Because he knew Houston needed a catcher.

Lofton had a sensational year at Tucson (.308, 40 stolen bases, 17 triples), earning him a September callup to Houston. But there, he appeared overmatched offensively. In 20 games he hit .203, with 15 hits, 14 of them singles, and just two stolen bases.

"He had an awful September," said Hart. "Just terrible. But we didn't blink on it. We loved Kenny from Jump Street. He was at the top of our list the whole way."

"There were four or five guys out there we liked, but we loved Kenny, because we thought he was the prototype leadoff guy, and he had elite speed," Hart said. "We knew there would be growing pains for him in the outfield. We knew he didn't throw real well. He hadn't played a whole lot of baseball. There was still some development to do with Kenny. But we felt that was another cornerstone piece for us, to go with Sandy and Carlos and Albert. So, all of a sudden you add Kenny to those guys and you go, 'Hmmm!'"

Hart also know that in Houston Lofton was blocked in center field by veteran Steve Finley.

Hart began talking trade for Lofton with Houston GM Bill Woods at the general manager's meetings. But the dialogue didn't really start to heat up until the 1991 winter meetings in Miami. Hart was not overly optimistic about coming home with Lofton.

"I didn't think we were going to get him," he said.

"That was my first winter meetings as a manager," said Hargrove. "At that point, when clubs talked trade, it was talent for talent. Player for player. Today, when teams talk trade, they talk contracts, which is just totally backwards."

Woods' assistant GM was former Astros player Bob Watson. O'Dowd and Watson did most of the preliminary work on the negotiations. At one point at the meetings, Hart, O'Dowd and Hargrove were invited to the Astros' suite to continue the trade talk. The Indians were clearly the aggressors.

"We were ready to make the deal, but they were like 'Maybe, maybe not. Maybe, maybe not,'" Hargrove said.

No agreement was reached, but as the Indians' officials left a few hours later, Watson pulled them aside, outside Houston's suite.

"I'll get this done. I'll get Bill to sign off on this," Watson told the Indians' contingent.

"Bob really wanted Taubensee, and (pitcher) Willie Blair, who we had picked up and had a really good year (at Colorado Springs)," Hart said.

The Indians' group—Hart, O'Dowd, Hargrove and the Indians' pro scouts—went back to their suite and waited. "We were all sitting there just crossing our fingers," Hart said.

Finally, at about 2 a.m., the phone rang. Hart picked it up. It was Watson.

"John, you want to come up? I'd like to see if we can finish this deal off," Watson said.

"I almost passed out," Hart said. "I SAILED up to his suite, and we did the deal."

It was Taubensee and Blair for Lofton and infielder Dave Rohde.

"We were really fired up about the trade," Hargrove said.

Immediately after the trade, Hargrove called Lofton to welcome him to the worst team in the major leagues. A team that had just put the finishing blemishes on an epic 105-loss season.

"I remember getting off the phone with him, and thinking, 'This guy is totally disinterested,'" Hargrove said. "It was like this trade was barely a blip on his radar."

Four years later, in the eighth inning of Game 6 of the American League Championship Series in Seattle's Kingdome, Lofton would score one of the most famous runs in Indians history, scoring from second base on a passed ball, accounting for one of the runs in a 4-0 victory that gave Cleveland its first American League pennant in 41 years.

Sixteen years later, near the end of the 2007 season, Lofton would pick up his 452nd and final stolen base for Cleveland. That's 173 more than any other player in franchise history.

In spring training of 1992, Hargrove's first full season as manager, the new center fielder wasted no time in catching the new manager's eye.

"It didn't take long to notice him, once you saw how he could run, his defensive ability," Hargrove said. "At first he wasn't real strong with the bat but with that kind of speed, you didn't need to be. He was more of a slap hitter, hit it on the ground and beat the throw to first, which is a neat deal. But it didn't take him long to develop into a guy who could drive the ball into the gaps."

Prior to spring training, Hargrove had never seen Lofton play, so he was a little slow to the bandwagon—unlike Hart and O'Dowd, who had both scouted him and seen him play in the minors.

"I didn't envision him becoming the kind of player he became, because I had never seen him before," said Hargrove. "But John and Danny thought he'd be a star. Then the more I saw him, I could see this was a guy who has a chance to be a big-time player, and thank goodness he's ours."

When he first joined the Indians, Lofton—who had been mostly a basketball player at the University of Arizona—wasn't so much a baseball player as he was an elite athlete, playing baseball.

"His speed was unbelievable," said Hargrove. "Whenever he would take a bad route to the ball it's like, no problem, he'd realize it, turn on the jets and outrun his mistake. It's a real testament to his athletic ability that he was able to do what he did. Because he didn't play college ball. He played his junior year, so he was still learning the game. He was raw as raw can be. But everyone saw his potential."

In 1992, the Indians continued to add pieces to the core of what would become the team that would win five consecutive division titles. In early April, Hart signed free-agent reliever Eric Plunk, who over the next six years would be an underappreciated but key member of some killer Indians bullpens. From 1992-97 Plunk made 336 relief appearances, mostly as a setup man, but occasionally as a closer, and had a record of 33-22, with a 3.10 ERA, while averaging nine strikeouts per nine innings.

In July 1992 the Indians traded a minor league outfielder to Baltimore for Jose Mesa, who was a starting pitcher at the time but would eventually become the Indians' closer. In 1995 he was the linchpin to Cleveland's elite bullpen, saving a franchise-record 46 games for the American League champions.

In spring training of 1992, Hart traded two minor league pitchers to Minnesota for first baseman Paul Sorrento, who from 1992-95 would average 19 home runs per year, bringing some bottom-of-the-order sock to those powerful Indians lineups. Sorrento was also one of Hargrove's all-time favorites.

"Paulie wasn't going to carry a team, but he was a really good supporting player," Hargrove said. "You just knew he was going to be there, and he was maybe the best 3-0 hitter I've ever seen. If every pitch could be on a 3-0 count there's no telling what he could do. I turned him loose once on a 3-0 pitch, and he hit the ball out of the park. So, I kept giving him the green light on 3-0, and more times than not it would turn out good."

It turned out very good. In his 11-year major league career— he also played for Minnesota, Seattle and Tampa Bay—Sorrento's career average on 3-0 counts was a staggering .688 (22-for-32), with four home runs, 13 RBI, a .930 on-base percentage, 1.188 slugging percentage and 2.117 OPS. In 1992, his first year with the Indians, Sorrento, on 3-0 counts, hit .889 (8-for-9).

So, by the middle of the 1992 season the Indians had in place much of the framework for their eventual powerhouse: Sandy Alomar, Carlos Baerga, Kenny Lofton, Albert Belle, Jim Thome, Charles Nagy, Mesa and Plunk. There were still some important pieces to be added, but it was obvious that Hart and his staff were building a team to be reckoned with.

But first they had to take a few more baby steps. Thome, still just 21 years old, split the 1992 season almost equally between the Indians (40 games), the minor leagues (42 games), and the disabled list (wrist and shoulder). Nagy won 17 games, but no other starting pitcher won more than six, or had a winning record. Still, the Indians reached the finish line with a record of 76-86, an improvement of nearly 20 games over their dreadful 57-105 season the year before.

Following the 1992 season the Indians signed two pitchers who played for the Dodgers, but became free agents after that season: Tim Crews and Bob Ojeda. The Indians' closer was a 26-year-old submarine-style right-hander who in 1992 ranked eighth in the American League in saves with 29. His name was Steve Olin.

CHAPTER 7

Little Lake Nellie

"Grover, we've got problems."

On June 8, 1991, the Cleveland Indians announced they were moving their spring training home from Tucson, Arizona, where they'd trained for the previous 45 years, to the city of Homestead, Florida, about 35 miles south of Miami. Indians officials signed a 20-year lease to play their spring training games in Homestead's brand-new state-of-the-art ballpark. The Indians were scheduled to begin training in Homestead in the spring of 1993.

"I had been to Homestead, and had seen the ballpark. It was gorgeous. Just gorgeous," said Hargrove.

The Indians would never play a game in that gorgeous ballpark.

Only three Category 5 hurricanes have ever hit the United States. The last time it happened was in the early morning hours of Aug. 24, 1992, when Hurricane Andrew slammed into South Florida, destroying about 600,000 homes and businesses, and leaving 150,000 to 200,000 people homeless.

The city of Homestead and that brand-new, state-of-the-art ballpark were wiped out by the hurricane, whose winds, with gusts up to 175 mph, flattened everything in its path. Spring training 1993 was less than six months away, and the Indians were suddenly homeless. Team officials went into full scramble mode, trying to find someplace in Florida to call their spring training home. Fortunately for Cleveland, the Boston Red Sox, at the end of the 1992 spring training season, pulled out of their spring training complex in the Central Florida town of Winter Haven. The Red Sox relocated their spring home to Fort Myers, Florida.

Winter Haven had lost its spring training tenant. The Indians were spring training orphans. It was a perfect fit.

"Homestead would have had its drawbacks," Hargrove said. "We would have had to fly to most of our (spring training) away games. Winter Haven turned out to be a great place for us. It was centrally located, and the city of Winter Haven put a lot of money into that facility for us."

Winter Haven was also in a great location when it came to traveling to other teams' camps for spring training games. Kansas City's camp was 20 minutes away. So was Detroit's. Houston's was 35 minutes away. Atlanta's, about the same. Several others were less than an hour's drive from Winter Haven.

"That was an improvement from Tucson, where you had to miss a day's work when you drove (the two hours each way) to games in Phoenix," Hargrove said.

So, the Indians got unlucky, then they got lucky. Hurricane Andrew blew them out of Homestead, but quaint little Winter Haven, with its cozy little antique ballpark, Chain O' Lakes Park, welcomed them with open arms.

It was a new beginning for a team that was undergoing a new beginning, a rebirth, itself. The rebuild of the Indians' roster by general manager John Hart and his staff was progressing nicely. Team officials, the players and their families were convening in their new spring training home in Winter Haven, and the construction of the Indians' long-awaited, eagerly anticipated new ballpark in Cleveland was underway.

"We all felt we were still a year away. We had a very young team," Hart said. "Going into that spring Grover had said that we were still going to play the kids. We added a couple of veterans along the way, Bobby Ojeda and Tim Crews, who we felt would provide some veteran experience to the ballclub. The core was so young. It was a very promising team, but our feeling was that we were a year away."

Ironically, on Aug. 24, 1992, the day Hurricane Andrew roared ashore in South Florida, the first structural steel beams were erected for the Indians' new ballpark in Cleveland. It would be called Jacobs Field, and would open in time for the start of the 1994 season. Thus, the 1993 season would be the team's last year in drafty, decrepit Cleveland Stadium.

But first, Hart, Hargrove and their staffs had to put together a ballclub for the 1993 season, which would begin on April 5, at home, against the Yankees.

"Everyone was excited about the season, and our growth and development. We really felt like we were sitting on something special," Hart said.

Their spring training schedule began on March 6 and 7, with two games against the Florida Marlins in Homestead, to raise money for the Hurricane Relief Fund. Starting with those two games, the Indians, counting split-squad games, played 19 games in 16 days, with no days off. That took them through March 21.

Monday, March 22, was a scheduled off day. It was the Indians' only off day of the spring, and they almost lost it. A week prior to the off day, Hart got a call from the Dodgers, who also had an off day on March 22. The Dodgers had a couple of games rained out that spring, and they needed some extra work for some of their players. They were interested in playing a "B" game against the Indians, if the Indians were willing, on March 22.

Hart presented the offer to Hargrove, saying, "It's here if you want it. You know what's best for your club."

The Indians at that point in spring training knew what their club was going to be. There were no pitchers who needed to be seen in order to make roster decisions. There were no position players on the bubble. Roster-wise, everything had been decided. Hargrove had no interest in taking up the Dodgers on their offer.

"John, these guys have been busting their butts all spring," Hargrove told Hart. "A day is not going to hurt. Just give them a day. I would rather not play that game. First of all, the players were looking forward to this. They've been making plans. And all of a sudden, we come in and burst their bubble? We're not going to get a lot out of it because they'll all be resentful that they didn't get the day off. So, I think we should keep it a day off, and I feel pretty strongly about that."

Hart called the Dodgers and said, "Thanks, but no thanks." The Indians were keeping March 22 as an off day.

"In January, they give you a schedule that says when spring training starts, and also the spring training schedule of games, and there's one off day in six weeks. You look at it and say, '*That's* the day we're going to do something with our family,'" said Sharon Hargrove.

So, on March 22, the Hargroves did. They entertained friends from Cleveland. It was a complete day off for the Indians' organization. The players, coaches and front office personnel scattered to various locations to enjoy their only off day of the spring.

Pitcher Tim Crews had spent the previous six years with the Dodgers, but after the 1992 season he became a free agent, and he signed with Cleveland. Crews was a Florida native. He was born in Tampa and attended Valencia Community College in Orlando. In February 1993, just prior to the start of spring training, he bought a 45-acre ranch overlooking a lake in Clermont, Florida, where he lived with his wife, Laurie, and their three kids. The Crewses decided to host a picnic for his new teammates on that off day on March 22.

Among those who planned to attend the picnic was 27-year-old Steve Olin, a member of the Indians' bullpen the previous four years. As the team's closer in 1991 and 1992, Olin appeared in 120 games and had 46 saves and a 2.74 ERA.

Olin was from Beaverton, Oregon, which is close to being as far from Clermont, Florida, as you can go and still remain in the continental United States. This was the Indians' first spring training in Winter Haven. Most of the players were unfamiliar with the city and the surrounding communities.

Steve and Patti Olin, with their three young kids, made the 37-mile drive north from Winter Haven to Clermont on the morning of March 22. But they had trouble finding Crews' home. After spending several minutes driving around, they almost gave up. They grew frustrated, and contemplated abandoning the search and going back to their apartment. But Steve felt it important that they keep trying. "It's a new player. They invited us. He's a good guy. We've got to find it," Steve said to Patti. "We'll try one more time. If we don't find it, then we'll go home."

So, on a March day that, but for a hurricane, they would have spent in Homestead, not Clermont, on the Indians' only off day of the spring, an off day that wouldn't have happened had they accepted the offer from the Dodgers to play that day, trying in vain to find a home in an unfamiliar community, one more empty cul-de-sac away from calling off the search, the Olins rolled down one last country road . . . and there it was.

The Crews' ranch house was not much more than a routine fly ball from the shoreline of Little Lake Nellie. A more harmless-looking, bucolic setting would be hard to find in Central Florida.

Steve Olin parked his car. The off day had officially begun.

In Winter Haven, Mike Hargrove, Indians third-base coach Jeff Newman and pitching coach Rick Adair played golf that day. They kept one eye on the fairway and one eye to the east, towards the Kennedy Space Center, where the space shuttle Discovery was scheduled to be launched. The three golfers did see several F-16s flying low over the coast. But they never did see the space shuttle, because the launch was canceled due to weather.

After their round of golf, Hargrove and his two coaches returned to their apartments in Winter Haven. John Hart and his family were staying in a condo just outside Winter Haven.

The phone calls started coming at about 7 p.m.

At their apartment, the Hargroves were entertaining some friends from Cleveland. They had just finished eating a spaghetti dinner prepared by Sharon Hargrove, when the phone in another room rang. Daughter Pam Hargrove answered it, and told her father it was Fernando Montes, the Indians' strength and conditioning coach. He asked for Mike. "I remember thinking to myself, 'What could be so important that it couldn't wait until tomorrow?'" Sharon recalled.

Her husband found out after he picked up the phone and said, "Hello?"

"Grover, we've got problems. Oly's gone."

"What? Gone where?"

"Mike, he's dead."

"What?"

At about that same time, Hart got a phone call, telling him there had been an accident.

"We didn't know the extent of it, but sensed it wasn't good," Hart said. "We heard that there was potentially a death, and a serious injury."

The boat, with Crews, Olin and Bob Ojeda on board, was out on Little Lake Nellie, after dark, ostensibly to do some bass fishing.

It was an overcast night. From the shore, Montes and a friend of Crews had flashed the lights on a truck, indicating they were ready to be picked up so they could join the group on the boat and do some fishing as well. Crews, the driver of the boat, was on his way to pick up his two friends waiting on the shore when the boat slammed into a dock that extended out into the water.

Olin was killed instantly. Crews was mortally wounded, and Ojeda had a major head injury.

That's when the phone calls started, and the nightmare began.

The boat was an 18-foot, 3,500-pound bass boat, with a 150-horsepower motor. The dock extended 171 feet into the lake, but was considered legal. The dock had no lights on it, but none were legally required. The dock was about 4 feet above the water level, and the water was only about 2½ feet deep. The boat was traveling at least 25 mph when it clipped the end of the dock, then went under it. Olin died of head and chest injuries. Crews died the next day from the same type of injuries. Ojeda suffered serious lacerations to his head, but survived, mostly because he was sitting low in his seat at the time of impact.

The Florida Game and Fresh Water Fish Commission later ruled that Crews was legally drunk, with a 0.14 percent blood-alcohol level. Olin and Ojeda were below the legal limit. A spokesman for the commission told the Orlando Sentinel that the length of the dock, Crews' use of alcohol, the boat's speed and the lack of a searchlight on the boat all contributed to the accident. "It was not just one factor that (caused it)," he said.

"That night was just a blur," said Hart, who phoned retired former Indians general manager Hank Peters to ask for some advice on how to handle the unthinkable. Hart also called Indians owner Richard Jacobs. Then Hart got word that Olin was dead, Ojeda was alive, and Crews was being air-lifted to Orange Regional Hospital in Orlando.

"That's when it sank in," Hart said. "Especially for Grover and I. We had known Steve Olin for years. He was one of our young guys. It's coming on your day off, your one day off in the spring. It was Winter Haven, and it was that era, and people sort of got together on an off day. Crews was doing what veteran guys do. 'Let's bring some guys over to the house.' That's what the veteran guys did."

Hargrove got directions to Clermont from Montes. Mike and Sharon Hargrove and Rick Adair jumped in a car and drove to Clermont. Hart did the same, from his condo outside Winter Haven. During the drive to Clermont, Sharon looked down and realized she was wearing a T-shirt that said, "Are we having fun yet?" She quickly turned it inside out.

When the Hargroves and Adair reached the Crews' home, Montes took them inside. Looking out the windows of the house, Hargrove could see several free-standing klieg lights near the dock on the lake. He could see the boat on the shore, but that's all he could see from the house, besides the police and EMT personnel.

The house was a big one, and all the wives and kids were there. The kids were all running around the house playing, screaming and hollering, which was jarring to the frayed senses of all the adults in the house, most of whom were still in shock.

Sharon Hargrove walked in and saw Patti Olin sitting in a window seat just staring off into space. Sharon immediately sat down next to Patti and asked, "Does your mom know?" Patti said her mom knew. "I'm going to call her and tell her I'm with you and I'm going to stay with you until she gets here," said Sharon, who, as a mother, knew that, if she were receiving a phone call in a similar situation, that's what she would want to hear.

The Hargroves had experience in dealing with such tragedy. During the 1992 season, the Indians were in New York when Hargrove got a call in his hotel room telling him that Indians first baseman Paul Sorrento's mother had died. Sharon happened to be on the trip, so Mike and Sharon went to Sorrento's room and had to tell him that he'd lost his mom. In 1989, when Hargrove was managing Triple-A Colorado Springs, and Olin was a member of the team, the Hargroves got a call telling them that Patti Olin's father had died. They had to deliver that heartbreaking message to Patti, who now, four years later, as a widow, with seven-month-old twins and a daughter who celebrated her third birthday just 24 hours earlier, was sitting in a window seat in a house she'd never been in until this horrific night, trying to pick up the pieces of her shattered life.

"I know this sounds terrible," Patti said to Sharon, "but what am I going to do? How am I going to take care of my kids? Will I get Steve's contract? Will I get any money?"

"Patti," said Sharon, "you're not going to do anything alone. Let's just get through this part."

Next, Sharon called Steve Olin's parents in Oregon. His mother Shirley answered the phone. Sharon said, "Shirley, this is Sharon Hargrove."

"Oh my God, Sharon, what's happened?" said Shirley Olin. "Patti called about an hour ago and said Steve's dead, and then hung up. We're getting all our news off ESPN."

The Olins had called the Indians' office in Cleveland, and got a recording. They called the Indians' spring training office in Winter Haven, and got a recording. They didn't have anybody's number in Winter Haven except Patti's, which they kept calling, but didn't get an answer because she wasn't home. The next day, Olin's parents flew to Florida. They arrived about 9 p.m. Sharon and pitcher Kevin Wickander, Olin's best friend on the team, went to the airport to pick up Steve's parents.

"It was awful," said Sharon.

The night of the accident, as Patti Olin and Sharon Hargrove continued to talk, Patti told Sharon she needed diapers for her babies, and there were some in the trunk of her car.

"Where are the keys?" asked Sharon.

"They're in Steve's pocket," said Patti.

Sharon found Mike and told him he had to go get the keys out of Steve's pocket.

"Oh, Sharon, I can't do that!" said Mike. Sharon told Mike he had to because, not only did she have to get into the trunk of the car, but she had to drive Patti and the kids back to her apartment. "She can't keep sitting here, with all this going on," Sharon said.

"OK," said Mike, who walked out to the lake and found a female police officer.

"I need to get the keys. Can you take me over to the accident?" said Hargrove. "I need to get the keys to the car to take Patti and the kids home."

"You really don't want to go over there," said the police officer. "I'll go get the keys for you."

The police officer left and, a few minutes later, returned with the keys, and handed them to Mike.

"I remember how cold and wet and clammy they were," said

Hargrove. "I thought to myself, 'I can't give the keys to Patti this way.' So, I put them under my arm, and in my hands, and I blew on them, trying to warm them up."

Mike handed the keys to Sharon, who went to the car to get the diapers.

"When I opened the trunk, there was everything about Steve. Fishing poles and baseball caps, and kids' stuff," she said.

Sharon took Patti and the kids home, just about the time Hart and O'Dowd arrived at the Crews' house. The three men, Hart, O'Dowd and Hargrove, drove to the hospital in Clermont to see Ojeda. Ojeda's head was heavily bandaged, and he was a little out of it due to his medication, but the doctors assured everyone that he would be OK.

Hargrove, Hart and O'Dowd then drove to the hospital in Orlando, where Crews was in intensive care. His parents and brothers were there.

"I just remember how sad they were," Hargrove said.

"Tim was still alive when we got there," said Hart. "I had known Tim for years. He was a Florida guy. I knew his father and his mother. They were in the waiting room. Then they went in to see Tim, and they came out just devastated. It was just a tragic night. There's so little you can do to comfort them, other than just being there and offer what words you can."

The following morning, Crews died.

"That whole night was just a blur," said Hart. "To have two players that we'd seen the day before, and both are gone."

Nobody slept that night. On the drive back to Winter Haven, Hart, Hargrove and O'Dowd tried to figure out what they were going to do. Cancel practice? Cancel games? How do we handle this?

They handled it by circling the wagons.

Hargrove was aware that the onus was on him to be a leader in this horrific moment.

"Being the manager, you better lead," he said. "So, in that regard, yes, I knew everybody was going to look to me and John for leadership and direction."

Everything was canceled for the next day, including the scheduled game with the Baltimore Orioles. The players were asked to still come to the clubhouse. Hargrove, who hadn't slept in over 24 hours, arrived at about 6 a.m. All of the players were already in the clubhouse. All of them knew what had happened. Hargrove and Rick Adair went around to the back entrance of the clubhouse. Hargrove knew he had to talk to the team, but that was about as far as it went. What do you say? What can you say?

"I had no clue what to say or what to do. I mean, nothing," Hargrove said. "So, I said a little prayer. I said, 'Lord, I have no idea what to say or what to do. Or what these guys need, or what any of us need. Help me. Talk through me. Help me reach these guys.' Knowing you're not going to make things better in one meeting."

Hargrove grabbed the knob of the clubhouse door, and was struck by how cold it felt. He opened the door and saw the entire team was there, each player sitting in front of his locker. Hargrove told all of them to pull their chairs into a circle in the middle of the room. It was a tight circle, and Hargrove placed his chair in the middle of it. He sat down and just started talking.

"I don't know what I said, but the words came out," he said. "It's the first time in my life I was aware of God using me. I'm not trying to be preachy. I'm really not. This was nothing about me. It was everything about Him."

Jim Thome, who was just 22 years old, was in the room that day.

"That's what made Mike so great. In that situation you put baseball aside and realize that this is, 'Oh my gosh, we've lost two family members,'" Thome said. "We all became one, and the driving force is always the leader. Keeping everyone strong. We're going to get through this together. We're going to become one. When you're tested from an emotional side, as we all were, that says a lot about who Mike was, and where we were about to go."

Hargrove talked until he got choked up and couldn't talk anymore. Then veteran reliever Ted Power started talking, and he talked until he got choked up. Then Wickander, Olin's best friend, talked. It went that way all around the room. Most of them talked. Many of them got choked up.

"The thing that stood out to Mike and I," said Hart, "was this was such a young team, so many of them were under 25. So many of these players had never lost any of their family."

And, as is the case with a high percentage of professional athletes, they feel like they are invincible, indestructible, bullet-proof. That can make the reality of experiencing two young athletes dying young, two teammates, a jolting, disorienting wakeup call on how the real world works.

"Other people go out drinking and then feel like they are invincible and bullet-proof and aggressive," said Hargrove. "These guys (professional athletes) are like that, but without the drinking. So, yeah, it's very sobering. To be successful in a very aggressive business, which (professional sports) is, I think you have to have some of that in you. If you don't, you'll get shot down really quick."

But if you do, you do so at your own risk. That theme got thrown into Hargrove's face the following spring, when he, Adair and hitting coach Charlie Manuel drove up to Clermont to see how Laurie Crews was doing.

"She was pissed," said Hargrove. "She was angry at the fact that they died because of the invincible thing. The bullet-proof thing. 'You guys think this. You guys think that,' she said. We were there to pay our respects, but we realized the best thing we could do was sit there and take our beating."

A few days after the accident, a memorial service was held in Winter Haven. All the Indians players, every member of the organization who was in Winter Haven, attended. So did numerous players from other teams, particularly the Dodgers, Crews' former team. Among the speakers at the service were Hargrove and former Indians designated hitter Andre Thornton.

"Andy was really good. I would drive a lot of miles and pay a lot of money to hear Andy talk," Hargrove said.

At the end of the service, Garth Brooks' song, "The Dance" was played, because Steve had told Patti that if anything ever happened to him, that was the song he wanted to be played.

"We played it, and it was just so emotional. So many tears. Everyone took it so personal," Hart said.

The Indians canceled a few spring games, but the players kept working out on a daily basis until the games resumed.

"I think that was real therapeutic for them to do something they were familiar with," Hargrove said. "I don't remember much about spring training after that. We made a concerted effort as a staff to make sure none of us used the accident as an excuse for what was going on. One of the best ways we could honor those guys' memories was to go out and do our jobs, and do them well."

During the season the Indians took Olin's and Crews' uniforms on the road with the team. There was a locker for each player, where his uniform was hung.

"We did that for a while, but it got to the point where it started bothering me," Hargrove said. "I know we were doing it to try to honor those guys. But it got to the point where I felt it was kind of morbid. So, we stopped doing it about halfway through the year."

But there was no getting around it—or, if there was, it was going to take a while for some, a long while for others. There had been a death in the family. Two of them.

"It was shocking," Hart said. "Olin was close with everyone, because he had been there. And the wives were all friends. Even talking about it now, my voice gets a little wavy. Just talking about it now takes the bandage off, and it's still an open wound. I looked at the wives and I looked at the families, and I knew it would never be the same."

The morning after the accident, Sharon Hargrove went to Patti Olin's apartment because somebody told her Steve's mother was there, she was crying uncontrollably, and Sharon needed to talk to her. When Sharon arrived, Shirley Olin was sitting at the kitchen table sobbing. Sharon came in and sat on the floor.

"Shirley, I know you're hurting. I know this is the saddest thing in the world. But what has happened that has made you out of control sad right now?" asked Sharon.

Shirley Olin pulled herself together and said, "I can't take another day of people telling me, 'Steve's in a better place now.' He had a beautiful wife, a beautiful family, a beautiful life. He's not in a better place. How can he be in a better place, looking down and seeing this mess?"

"Well, I can't answer that," said Sharon. "But I can go find somebody who can help you."

Everybody, it seemed, was flying blind after getting blind-sided by a tragedy of such proportion.

"There was no manual for what we were going through," said

Hargrove. "I really believe God had his hand in what I did and what I said. I tried to be real sensitive to the players, not necessarily their physical needs, because you're always there for that. But their emotional needs. I was close to Steve Olin, but I wasn't as close to Kevin Wickander. Kevin never did recover from that. We ended up trading him, and one of the main reasons we traded him was because maybe it would help him to get away from the daily reminder."

A second-round pick by the Indians in the 1986 June Draft, the high-strung Wickander was one of the Indians' better relievers in 1992, appearing in 44 games and going 2-0 with a 3.07 ERA. But after the boating accident, he was a shell of himself. In 1993 he gave up seven runs and 15 hits in eight innings over his first 11 relief appearances. The Indians finally traded him to Cincinnati on May 7, and he was even worse for the Reds: a 6.75 ERA in 33 appearances. He sat out the 1994 season. The Tigers signed him as a free agent in 1995, but they traded him to Milwaukee in the middle of the season. The Brewers released him in August 1996, and he was out of baseball at age 31, forever, it seemed, haunted not just by the fact that he lost his best friend that fateful night on Little Lake Nellie, but by the knowledge that he was supposed to go out on the boat with those three Indians pitchers that night—but didn't.

Hargrove said he didn't get any calls from other big-league managers offering advice following the accident because "I don't think any managers ever had to deal with something like this." When Miami Marlins pitcher Jose Fernandez was killed in a boating accident during the 2016 season, Hargrove called Marlins manager Don Mattingly.

"We talked for about 10 or 20 minutes. I don't think anything I said penetrated, but he was real nice and thanked me," Hargrove said.

Early in the 1993 season, the report came out saying that Tim Crews' blood alcohol level was not good.

"Nobody expected it to be good," said Hargrove. "It was one of those parties where you sit around and cook out and drink beer."

That didn't stop a fan in Cincinnati from sending a nasty letter to Hargrove, saying how dare he defend this. "That really pissed me off," said Hargrove. "But the guy screwed up because he signed his name and gave me his address. So, I called information and got his phone number. I called him, and we spent 30 minutes talking. I did most of the talking. He said, 'I appreciate you calling. I didn't think of it that way.' I said, 'Well, maybe you should have.'"

Alone, and away from outside distractions, Hargrove admits that it was hard to accept the way that Olin and Crews died.

"The senselessness of it, yeah," he said. "You go back and think about things. If I hadn't said no to playing the Dodgers, this wouldn't have happened. If I would have done this instead of that. But you can do that with almost anything. I finally came to the realization that you do what you think is right in the moment, and if you're thoughtful about it, and did it for unselfish reasons, what else is there?"

Opening day in 1993 was in Cleveland, on April 5, when 73,290 fans showed up for the last opening day ever at Cleveland Stadium. Patti Olin and Laurie Crews were honored before the game, "which was another very emotional time," said Hart.

Then Yankees starter Jimmy Key pitched eight innings of a 9-1 New York victory in which the Indians managed just three hits. Not surprisingly, the Indians started the season slow, losing 14 of their last 19 games in the month of April, en route to a record of 76 86 and a sixth-place finish in the seven-team AL East, 19 games behind division-winning Toronto.

"I don't think that year the team ever got over it," said Hart of the boating accident. "It was such a big national story, and it was one that I don't think ever left our players. It took us a long time as an organization to get through that."

Two weeks after the accident, Mike Seghi, the Indians' callous, hard-bitten, long-time director of team travel, who had been a tower of strength for Hargrove following the tragedy and an integral part of the organization's response to it, came to Hargrove's apartment.

"I need to talk to you," Seghi said.

"So, we went into the bedroom, and I shut the door," Hargrove said. "We talked, and he broke down and cried and cried."

Several years later, when Hargrove was managing the Baltimore

Orioles, he was sitting at home one night watching TV after a game. Sharon came in and they started talking, and it got around to a conversation about how Patti Olin was doing. Hargrove suddenly broke down and cried like a baby for 45 minutes.

"This is stupid," he told Sharon. "This happened eight years ago."

"It was the first time I actually let loose, let it go," he said.

Death does have a way of illuminating life. Sharon Hargrove found that out through a conversation she had with her father, on his death bed.

"Some of the worst things that happen in life teach you the most," she said. "For me, it was losing my dad just as Mike was starting out in baseball. You expect people your grandparents' age to die, but not when you're 49. So, I had not experienced that. That kind of opened my eyes that every day is a gift. My dad had a real serious talk with me that night, his last night."

"The only regret I have is I wish all the people I knew understood how I felt about them. Because I can't let them know now. So don't ever do that," GK Rupprecht told his daughter.

"I promise. I won't," Sharon said.

It's been over a quarter of a century since a boat carrying three Cleveland Indians pitchers ran into a dock in the darkness on Little Lake Nellie, killing two of the pitchers and all but ending the career of the third. Those placid turned deadly waters produced uncharted waters for a team simply trying to find its way, following leaders doing the best they could.

The end of that draining, emotional 1993 season was in many ways greeted by the organization with a sense of relief.

"Enough was enough," Hargrove said. "We persevered. Not just one or two guys, but everybody. I mean, somebody's got to drive the bus, so I get a lot of credit when people talk about that. But it was a group effort. Everybody did what they could do. They did their part. From the players to the staff to the front office. Everybody did their part. To this day, I'm very proud of those people. It was a great tragedy, but organizationally it was a shining moment that allowed us to show the world that we are human."

"I think the fans that year got extra close to that team because the fans looked at them a little differently after the accident," said

Sharon Hargrove. "They realized that Steve wasn't just a good pitcher. He had three little kids and a wife. They saw that these players were real people, not robots. I think that helped."

Indeed, for the franchise as a whole, the 1993 season was less about baseball and more about life itself.

"We had really good people who cared," said Hart. "Did we do everything the right way? We certainly tried to. There was no script for this. This was a close group. We had built this group, the staff and the young players. We had gone through a lot of tough stuff to get to this point. Then we get this.

"The people that were there genuinely cared. To this day, everyone was impacted. Looking back on it, I don't know what else we could have done. We just tried to do the right thing and follow our hearts."

Years later, when Hargrove was managing the Seattle Mariners, he and Sharon would occasionally visit Patti Olin and her children, who lived in the Seattle area.

"I reminded Patti about the family room they had at the old stadium in Cleveland," Sharon said. "I remember how I loved to sit in there and watch Steve. He would open the door, look in, and find Alexa, wherever she was playing. He would watch her play with the kids. She wouldn't see him until he'd say, 'Boo!'—that's what he called her—'Boo! Come see me!' And she would run to him. That's a memory I'll always have of Steve. He was a tremendous guy."

CHAPTER 8

All Dressed Up with
No Place to Go

*"We've got this great team, and we may
never be able to get it on the field again."*

As the emotionally draining 1993 season wound down, Hargrove noticed a pattern starting to emerge. It was toward the end of that season when, unsolicited, he started hearing a steady drumbeat from opposing managers, coaches and players: "You guys are going to be really good."

Going into the 1993 season, Hargrove and Indians general manager John Hart both felt that the Indians were a year away from having a breakout season. But it was nice to have that feeling confirmed by the opinions of those on other teams.

First, however, the Indians and their fans had to say goodbye to the old gray lady on the lakefront, Cleveland Stadium. The mammoth structure was, incredibly, built in just over one year—370 days—opening on July 1, 1931. Cleveland had hoped to use the stadium to attract the 1932 Olympic Games. That never happened, but the Indians played there, splitting their home games for a time between Cleveland Stadium and the much-smaller League Park. Later, the Cleveland Rams, and then the Browns shared the big stadium with the Indians, until the Indians moved into Jacobs Field in 1994. By the end of 1993, the stadium was old, dirty, drafty, decrepit and mostly empty for Indians games.

"I knew the history there, with the Browns, and the '48 Indians and all the great players who played there," said Hargrove. "But it's the only place where, when I walked into it—I would step through the door to walk to the clubhouse—and as I walked in, I felt like I had to go take a shower."

Not everyone was depressed by the ancient arena. Charles Nagy, Mr. Roll With The Punches himself, said he didn't find Cleveland Stadium that bad.

"We were young guys, and even though the old place was what it was—big and cavernous and not very many fans—to us it was still the big leagues. It wasn't the greatest place to play, but we learned a lot playing over there."

John Hart was less sentimental.

"There is something to be said for the old ballparks, but (Cleveland Stadium) was not like Wrigley Field or Fenway Park," he said. "There were not a lot of great memories there."

Unlike many other ballparks built in the first half of the 20th century, there was nothing warm and fuzzy about the enormous ballpark on the shores of Lake Erie. It was too big, too cold, too rundown, and frequently too empty for anyone to feel sentimental about the Indians leaving it.

So, everyone faked it.

In 1992 the Indians were last in the American League in both total home attendance (1.2 million), and per-game average attendance (15,112). In 1993, the last year the Indians played in their giant, empty playpen—sometimes there's no accounting for nostalgia—their attendance figures jumped to seventh in the league in both categories.

Nobody was sad to see the last Indians games played there, but lots of people showed up anyway. The last three Indians games at the stadium, all losses to the White Sox, on Oct. 1, 2 and 3, drew crowds of 72,454, 72,060 and 72,390.

There wasn't a wet eye in the house, and certainly not in the Indians' dugout.

"As a player, when I first got to Cleveland, on days I wouldn't play, I'd sit on the top step of the dugout, and you'd play with the dirt, and dig some rocks out," Hargrove said. "One day I picked out this rock about the size of a half dollar. When I dug it out, I got a whiff of this god-awful smell. I smelled the rock, and that's where it was coming from. It was the landfill that the place was built on."

Another time, Hargrove, during a game, came out on the field, and it was in great shape. He came out the next inning, perhaps 10 or 15 minutes later, and there was a hole in the ground, on the outfield grass, in fair territory, behind first base. The hole was about a foot wide and about two feet deep.

"I thought to myself, 'That just happened,'" Hargrove said.

Because they shared the stadium with the Browns, the Indians grew accustomed to playing home games in September with the football yard lines and the outline of the football field still visible on the outfield grass during baseball games. Sometimes the Indians would take the field and there would be an iron rebar sticking out of the ground, where they put the foam rubber markers on the sideline and the goal line for the football games. Somebody forgot to take them out.

The demise of Cleveland Stadium roughly coincided with the birth of the baseball mascot craze. Cleveland's first mascot was called The Baseball Bug. Let's just say the stadium and the mascot deserved one another.

"I was never really very fond of mascots," Hargrove said. "So, we had this baseball bug or something. I never showed a lot of emotion on the field, because I didn't want to hear Sharon jump my ass when I got home. So, I hit a ball, a rocket, to left center one time, and the center fielder dove and caught it. I slammed my helmet down as I crossed first base. I'm sitting in the dugout seething, just seething inside. Then I go out and I'm throwing grounders to the infielders between innings and the baseball bug walks up to me and says, 'Your conscience just said, "Don't throw your helmet!"' I turned and looked at him and said, 'You need to get the fuck away from me.' Sharon tried to talk the baseball bug—I think it was a bug, or a duck, or something—into letting her get into his costume so she could come on the field and jump my ass. She almost had him talked into it, too."

The Indians got shut out 4-0 in their last game in Cleveland Stadium. It was the final game of an exhausting season that began with the tragic deaths of two teammates. The Indians carried that emotional baggage with them for the entire season, and by the end it was no surprise they were worn out mentally. They staggered to the finish line, losing their last four games of the season. In their last five games they scored a total of just nine runs. Amazingly, they managed to hold it together for most of the season, when a complete collapse might have been understandable. Instead, they finished with the same record, 76-86, as they had in 1992.

*   *   *

In Mike Hargrove's first 2½ years as manager, the Indians had a winning percentage of .450. But the end of the 1993 season was also the end of the losing. Over the next six years the Indians would have a winning percentage of .596, win five consecutive division titles, and make two trips to the World Series.

The unofficial launch of that run came on Dec. 2, 1993, when the Indians announced to the world that they were ready to begin the final stage of their rebuild by making two blockbuster free-agent signings on the same day.

Indians officials had decided it was time to pounce. They had built the infrastructure of the roster, a handful of young, impactful core players. Now it was time to finish off the project by bringing in some marquee names, veteran leaders with enough left in the tank to make a difference.

"We had made the statement that we weren't going to trade for any big-time players, or sign any big-name free agents until we felt like we were ready to get over the hump," Hargrove said. "It was a five-year plan and part of it was to stay the course. To this day, whenever I hear the phrase, 'Stay the course,' I get goosebumps, because John repeated it 50 times a day when we started that deal."

As a player, Hargrove had been down this road before, and it always seemed to turn into a dead end.

"In the seven years I played for the Indians we had about 40 five-year plans," he said. "You'd get one year into it, and then you'd get out of it."

Patience was not always a Hart strength, but the general manager did indeed bide his time through those bleak years, until he felt it was time to strike. In the winter of 1993-94, it was time to strike.

"At the end of the 1993 season I talked to all of our players in their exit interviews," Hart said, "and it was almost to the man. All of them said, 'John, get us some free agents. We're ready. We are ready. Don't be messing around.'"

On Dec. 2, 1993, Hart signed two of the biggest free-agent names available: future Hall of Famer Eddie Murray and pitcher Dennis Martinez. Between them they had, at the time, a combined 11 All-Star selections. They were both on the back nine of their careers, but were far from finished. Murray, 37, had hit 27 home runs and knocked in 100 runs for the Dodgers in 1993. Martinez, 39, had been selected to the All-Star team in three of the previous four years, while with Montreal. He won 15 games in 1993, 16 in '92, and 14 in '91, when he tossed a 96-pitch perfect game for the Expos against the Dodgers. Murray and Martinez were teammates on the Orioles from 1977 to 1986.

With the Indians, Martinez signed a two-year $9 million deal, with a $4.25 million club option for the third year. Murray signed a one-year $3 million deal. The Indians didn't normally fish in those pricey free-agent waters. Their highest paid player in 1993 was Albert Belle at $1.6 million. Most of the rest of the players on the roster made less than $1 million. Now here comes Martinez making $4.5 million and Murray at $3 million.

"We were still Cleveland. We knew the new ballpark was going to make a difference (financially), but we didn't know how much of a difference," Hart said. "Danny (O'Dowd) and I had a relationship with Eddie from our Baltimore days. I knew he would be a good one. As a minor league manager, I had Dennis in Baltimore. I knew they were both a little long in the tooth, but they were still warrior guys, so that was a huge deal to bring those guys in."

Especially if you were a manager who in your first 2½ years on the job had a won-loss record that was 41 games under .500 (184-225).

"I give John a lot of credit for not jumping the gun," Hargrove said. "We knew we had a core of good young players, and the only way we were going to do that was to give them the time to develop, and then the addition of a big-time free agent or leader could make a difference. Sure enough, Eddie and Dennis coming in absolutely added the right ingredients to the pie."

Mark Shapiro, who would later go on to become the Indians' general manager and then team president, was the director of minor league operations in 1994.

"That was all part of our plan, to ramp up for when we moved into the new ballpark," Shapiro said of the signings of Martinez and Murray. "Our plan was to win. We intended to make some strategic free-agent signings, and those two guys were marquee players who were leaders and winners."

The players were as enthused as the front office about the signings of the two former Orioles.

"That provided a great boost to our team because we were bringing in players who had a history of winning," Sandy Alomar Jr. said. "Going into a new stadium, and then adding veteran players like that, it was a huge turning point for our team."

The Indians needed a No. 1 starter for their rotation, and even though Martinez's arm had some miles on it, he was about as durable as they come. In his previous 18 years in the big leagues, Martinez averaged about 200 innings per season. Murray, who would hit 504 home runs in his 21-year career, struck out fewer than 100 times in 20 of those 21 years. He also was valued by Hart and Hargrove because of his clubhouse leadership and his presence. Schooled in the fundamentally sound Baltimore system, Murray, whose 128 career sacrifice flies are a major league record, was a stickler for playing the game the right way. During his time with the Indians, it was not uncommon when Murray played first base for him to put his hands on his hips and glare at an outfielder who had just overthrown a cutoff man.

With the additions of Murray and Martinez, the piece of clay Hart and his staff were molding started to take on a more clearly defined shape. The marquee No. 1 starting pitcher and slugging designated hitter/first baseman were now added to the mix.

Already in place were the perennial .300-hitting, All-Star second baseman (Carlos Baerga), the future 600-homer Hall of Famer at third base (Jim Thome), the prototypical left field slugger (Albert Belle), the quintessential center fielder/speedster/leadoff hitter (Kenny Lofton), the former Rookie of the Year/All-Star catcher (Sandy Alomar Jr.), and one of the most outrageously gifted hitting machines ever produced by the Indians'—or any team's—minor league system was ready to burst upon the scene in right field, Manny Ramirez.

There was just one piece missing.

Felix Fermin had been the Indians' shortstop for the last five years, but the front office still considered him a place holder. The 29-year-old veteran was an adequate defender, a good teammate and a smart player, but one who could hit for neither average nor power, nor provide any speed on the bases.

"He was solid, but we weren't going to the promised land (with him)," Hart said.

So, just two years after his detective work identified, pursued and led to him acquiring a center fielder who would become the Indians' all-time leader in stolen bases, Hart went to work again. This time it was Operation Omar.

Omar Vizquel was, at the time, sort of the Seattle Mariners' version of Felix Fermin, but three years younger, and with a lot more flair and fearlessness. The latter trait was extra apparent when Vizquel barehanded a ground ball and threw to first base for the final out of Chris Bosio's no-hitter in 1993.

"Bosio has a no-hitter, two outs in the ninth, it's a hopper behind the mound, and the hitter wasn't a fast runner. Most guys would run in there, catch it and throw it. Not Omar. He comes in, bare-hands it and throws him out. Who does that?" said Hargrove. "Omar had the guts of a burglar. He's like, 'I'm going to try this, and it has a 1% chance of working, but I'm going to go for it.' He'd do stuff like that and I'd get all clinched up thinking, 'What are you doing? . . . Oh, that's good. That's good.'"

Vizquel had been the Mariners' starting shortstop for the previous five years. "He hadn't broken out yet offensively, but he was so magical to watch defensively. I always had him in the back of my mind," Hart said.

The machinations employed by Hart that resulted in Vizquel becoming an Indian were equal parts legwork and luck work. In Seattle, there was a gathering tsunami behind Vizquel in the person of Alex Rodriguez, a Miami high school shortstop, who was selected by the Mariners with the first overall pick in the 1993 June Draft, and would debut in the major leagues a year later, at age 18.

Following the 1993 season Vizquel became eligible for salary arbitration for the first time. There was talk that the Mariners were going to bring Rodriguez up in 1994, so Hart phoned Seattle general manager Woody Woodward to inquire about Vizquel's availability. The two men started working on a deal. In the meantime, Hart flew to Puerto Rico for a Carlos Baerga charity function. Hart was still working on the Vizquel deal with Woodward. Also at the Baerga charity function was Edgar Martinez, the Mariners' third baseman, soon to become their designated hitter. Hart, who as a minor league manager had become friends with Martinez, started talking with the Mariners star. Hart complimented Martinez on the nice young club Seattle was assembling (A-Rod, Ken Griffey Jr., Jay Buhner, etc.) then innocently said, "Tell me about Omar."

"Oh John, oh my! This guy, he's the best. Great makeup. Everything," gushed Martinez.

That was good enough for Hart, who went back to his room, got on the phone with Woodward, and completed the trade: Fermin and designated hitter/first baseman Reggie Jefferson to Seattle for Vizquel.

"I was ecstatic. I went to the Baerga thing the next day and I saw Edgar there. He wouldn't talk to me. He was really pissed," said Hart, who then flew to Caracas, Venezuela, to watch Vizquel play a winter league game.

"He put on a show in the field, got a couple hits, stole a couple bases," Hart said. "We met for breakfast the next day and I fell in love with him. He was such a terrific guy. I was so excited because I thought this was THE missing piece. With Paul Sorrento and Baerga, and we'd just signed Eddie Murray. We had Albert. We had Kenny. We had Manny and Thome. And now we had Omar, who finished off the core of that young club."

Nobody was more thrilled about getting Vizquel than Hargrove, who as the manager of the Indians' Double-A affiliate at Williamsport in 1988 had seen Vizquel play for Vermont, which was Seattle's Double-A team at the time.

"When I saw Omar in Double-A, he really stood out defensively. With the bat, not so much. He wasn't as strong as he would get, and he was very pitchable," Hargrove said. "We'd throw him fastballs up and away and he'd hit little fly balls to left field. When we got him, Charlie (Manuel) and I spent a lot of time talking to him about laying off those high fastballs. When he got the ball down, he had some pop."

In some ways, however, it was a bittersweet trade for Hargrove.

"I was really excited about that trade, even though I was close with Felix," he said. "Felix was one of the leaders on our ballclub at the time. So, it wasn't easy to say goodbye to him, but getting Omar . . ."

The rebuild of that 105-loss 1991 Indians team was nearly complete. Hart and his staff knew it. Hargrove and his coaches knew it. The players themselves knew it. The five-year plan had been nearly completed in three years.

"I give credit for that to Dick Jacobs," said Dan O'Dowd, the Indians' assistant general manager at the time. "It's one thing for baseball executives to lay out a vision, but then when you go out and totally get your butt kicked. I mean, we were terrible in '89, '90, '91, '92. Some progress in '93. But that's a lot of years of losing. But Dick never wavered. Certainly, the best owner in the game that I ever worked for."

Said Hart: "Just because you enter into a rebuild, there are no guarantees. A core of good young players is the secret sauce to make it work. You can add a free agent here and there, but if you don't have the right core of young players, the chances of it working are slim."

The rebuild had worked, but there were still some trimmings that needed to be added.

"We had good young players. We made good trades. We drafted well. Things really aligned," Hart said. "One thing I felt, though, is that we were a position player, star-dominant, offensive-oriented team. And with Alomar, Omar and Lofton, we were going to be a good defensive team. But we were a little light in the rotation."

So just before the start of spring training in 1994, the Indians signed old warhorse Jack Morris as a free agent. Just three months shy of his 39th birthday, Morris was one of the great innings eaters in the five-man rotation era, which began in the mid-1970s. With Detroit in 1984, counting the postseason, Morris pitched 265 innings. In 1987 he pitched 274 innings, and with Minnesota in 1991 he pitched 283 innings. In 1992 with Toronto, Morris led the league in victories with a record of 21-6 and, at age 37, threw 263 innings.

After that, he was on fumes. In 1993 for Toronto, his 17th year in the majors, he was 7-12 with a 6.19 ERA. The Indians decided to take a flyer on him in 1994, and he would start the last 23 games, record the last 10 victories, and pitch the final 141 of his 3,824 career innings in his Hall of Fame career while wearing a Cleveland uniform.

The Indians at that time seemed to have a thing for out-of-gas players from the Tigers' glory days. On May 7, 1993, they signed 37-year-old catcher Lance Parrish. Parrish appeared in 10 games with the Indians, the last of those coming on May 28, in Minnesota. With the game tied 6-6 and no outs in the bottom of the ninth inning, the Twins had runners at second and third and Kirby Puckett at the plate. The Indians decided to intentionally walk Puckett, but Parrish was charged with a passed ball, on a pitchout, no less, allowing the winning run to score. Two days later, the Indians released him.

They hoped to do better with Morris in '94 than they did with Parrish. They did—sort of. In 23 starts he had a record of 10-6, despite a 5.60 ERA. How did he win 10 games with an ERA that high? Because the Indians scored an average of 7.6 runs in Morris' 10 wins.

*   *   *

On April 4, 1994, Jacobs Field officially opened. It's hard to imagine any team that was in greater need of a new ballpark than were the Indians. Jacobs Field had roughly half the capacity of Cleveland Stadium, but 10 times the luxury. The $167 million ballpark had its genesis on May 8, 1990, when Cuyahoga County voters passed a tax on alcohol and cigarettes to finance its construction. The Indians that night were in Minnesota for a game against the Twins. The election results were being closely monitored by the ballclub as the game progressed. The Indians' first-base coach was among those who were nervous about the outcome.

"I don't think people were aware of how serious Mr. Jacobs was about moving the ballclub (if the tax didn't pass)," Hargrove said. "Because at the time, the talk was that the Indians would move to St. Petersburg (Florida). I had heard that, 'If this doesn't pass, we're gone.' It wasn't 100 percent that we were going, but it also wasn't an empty threat."

In the middle of an inning Hargrove was walking from the first-base coach's box back to the dugout when somebody from the dugout yelled, "It passed!"

"The significance of it, we were all aware of how important it was, because we didn't want to move our families. So, we were all excited when we heard it passed. There was a buzz," said Hargrove. Just under four years later, Jacobs Field opened its gates for the first time.

"It was a cultural revolution for our organization," Shapiro said. "We were moving from an antiquated facility, where we were second-class citizens, with our weight room located in the laundry room of a hospital 2 miles away, to a state-of-the-art facility. It elevated the morale of the franchise and was the culmination of a vision Dick and John had for the organization."

The grand opening came on Monday, April 4, 1994. The game between the Indians and the Seattle Mariners was scheduled to begin at 1:05 p.m. But the pre-game pomp and circumstance ran overtime, and the first pitch didn't take place until 1:21 p.m. That was about seven hours after Hargrove got to the park. For day games he normally arrived at the ballpark about 8 a.m. On this day, however, when he entered the ballpark it was still dark. NBC's "Today Show" was broadcasting live from the ballpark that day, and it included a segment with Hargrove at 7:30 a.m., from the roof of the visitor's dugout on the first base side. After his segment was done, Hargrove was walking across the field to the Indians' dugout on the third base side, when he heard somebody screaming at him.

"Get the fuck off my grass! What the fuck are you doing?"

It was head groundskeeper Brandon Koehnke.

"What did you say?" Hargrove shouted.

"I said get the fuck off the grass. Who in the hell do you think you are?"

"And he was serious!" said Hargrove 25 years later. "That lit my fuse real quick. We had a short meeting in right field, and I won."

The move into the new ballpark was a watershed moment for the franchise, and for the front office that tried to synchronize the completion of the roster rebuild with the opening of the shiny new ballyard.

"For a long time, we didn't know if we were going to get the new stadium," Hart said. "We probably would have had a winning club had we stayed in the old one, but we never would have been able to do the things we did that the new ballpark provided. It was very exciting for all of us to be a part of that. Our players loved it, and it was very attractive to free agents, which also helped us. And, of course, the fans really embraced it."

But not as much as the players.

"When we moved into the new ballpark, we could see the light at the end of the tunnel. When we moved into the Jake, it revitalized the whole city and our fans. It made us even better," said Thome.

"There were so many conveniences we didn't have in the old stadium," said Alomar. "At the old place, you'd have to eat your meals with guys lifting weights all around you. At the old ballpark you didn't look forward to going to work each day. The new ballpark, you always went in early. It really helped the morale of the team."

The opening day reviews of the new ballpark from out-of-town writers were wall to wall raves:

"After 61 years at baseball's worst address, at a cavernous old stadium that was dark and cold and utterly depressing, the Indians now have a home that can stand beside any of the game's other showcases . . . Jacobs Field has the cozy feel of Wrigley Field, the urban backdrop of Camden Yards, and the nooks and crannies of Fenway Park" (Richard Justice, Washington Post).

"With flags flying, balloons and buttons bursting, the Indians couldn't help but celebrate. They threw open the doors on a natural grass wonder built in the heart of downtown Cleveland" (Claire Smith, New York Times).

"Never has one mile seemed more like a thousand, as it has in traveling from the old park to the new in Cleveland" (Chris Berman, ESPN).

Even the president showed up. Lefty Bill Clinton, wearing an Indians jacket to shield the old soup bone from the 48-degree temperature that felt worse than that due to a 14-mph wind on an otherwise bright and sunny day, looked for somebody to play catch with prior to throwing out the ceremonial first pitch.

Indians vice president of public relations Bob DiBiasio found Andy Hargrove, the manager's 13-year-old son, and explained that Clinton wanted to play catch.

"No, I can't do that. I won't do that," said Andy Hargrove.

"Why?" said DiBiasio. "It's the president of the United States. Why can't you do it?"

"My dad doesn't like him," said Andy.

Andy's father had his own issue with the president that day. Clinton also wanted to come into the clubhouse and meet the Indians players. Hargrove thought that was a great idea, until Indians vice president of business Dennis Lehman told him the Secret Service was going to have to put up a metal detector for the players to walk through, and they also were going to wand everybody.

"Well, that's not going to happen," said Hargrove. "This is our house. I'm not going to ask my players to be wanded and to walk through the metal detector and all that, to get into their house. We're not going to do that."

So, Clinton didn't come into the Indians' clubhouse.

"I'm almost ashamed, thinking about it now," Hargrove said. "But I'm also kind of glad I did it. Because right is right and wrong is wrong. I understood where the Secret Service was coming from. And I hope they understood where I was coming from. But it was one of those things. Dennis was a little disbelieving that we wouldn't do it."

When the game finally started, reality set in. The opponents were the Seattle Mariners. It was opening day. Guess what that meant?

"I remember, when the schedule came out that year," said Hart. "I said to Dick Jacobs, 'I've got some bad news.' And he said, 'What could possibly be bad about opening day in a new ballpark?' I said, 'We're facing Seattle, and Randy Johnson is going to be the pitcher. We could get no-hit on opening day!'"

Sure enough, Johnson took a no-hitter and a 2-0 lead into the bottom of the eighth inning.

"We realized going in that we were facing one of the nastiest pitchers in the game," said Hargrove. "At that time, Randy was real excitable. It was real easy to get under his skin. So, we tried to be really aggressive on the bases, and get him excited. It didn't work."

The Indians finally broke through in the eighth inning, when Alomar singled, breaking up Johnson's no-hit bid. A two-run double later in the inning by Manny Ramirez tied it at 2-2. Both teams scored runs in the 10th inning, sending it to the 11th tied at 3-3. In the bottom of the 11th, Murray doubled with one out, then scored the winning run on a two-out single to left field by Wayne Kirby off reliever Kevin King.

"There are certain guys you get a special satisfaction when they do well, and Wayne Kirby was always that guy for me, because he worked hard," Hargrove said. "His talent level may not have been at Kenny Lofton's level, but he knew his job, he didn't piss and moan about it. He knew what he was there for, and he did the best he could. I kind of pull for guys like that."

The year before, in 1993, Kirby was a 29-year-old rookie, destined to become the answer to the trivia question, "Who played right field for the Indians before Manny Ramirez?" Kirby's eight-year career in the majors was spent mostly as a backup outfielder. The only year he was a regular was 1993, when he started in right field for the Indians. He did a little bit of everything. He hit .269, drove in 60 runs, stole 17 bases, and only struck out 58 times in 458 at-bats. He was a good teammate, popular in the clubhouse, always had a smile on his face.

But then there was this high school kid Indians scouting director Mickey White found playing for George Washington High School in the Washington Heights section of New York City, not far from Yankee Stadium. "I asked Mickey where Manny was from," said Hargrove, "and Mickey said, 'Washington Heights. It's so far back in the city they have to pipe in sunlight.'" The Indians selected Ramirez with the 13th pick in the first round of the 1991 June Draft, and to this day Hargrove remembers the first time he saw the kid swing a bat.

"Oh God, yes. A real beautiful, fluid, powerful swing," Hargrove said. "I don't think I ever saw him overswing. And the ball jumped off his bat, even when he was a skinny 20-year-old kid."

Manny Ramirez was born to hit. In rookie ball in 1991 he hit .326 with 19 home runs, 63 RBI and a 1.105 OPS in 215 at-bats. The next year in 291 at-bats at advanced Class-A Kinston, he hit 13 home runs with 63 RBI and an .881 OPS.

Then in 1993, while Kirby was patrolling right field in Cleveland and endearing himself to his manager and general manager,

Ramirez had one of the greatest minor league seasons in Indians history. In a combined 489 at bats at Double-A Canton-Akron and Triple-A Charlotte, he hit .333, with 105 runs, 44 doubles, 31 home runs, 115 RBI, a .417 on-base percentage, .613 slugging percentage and 1.031 OPS. That earned him a September callup to the big-league club, where he hit an uninspiring .170. But in his second major league game, Ramirez gave his team a peek at the future. It was Sept. 3, a 7-3 Indians win against the Yankees, at Yankee Stadium. With hundreds of his friends and family and former high school teammates and classmates in attendance and making plenty of noise, Ramirez went 3-for-4, with a double, his first two major league home runs, and three RBI.

Earlier that season, when Ramirez was at Charlotte, Hart and Hargrove made a special trip to see him play.

"That was the first time I ever saw Manny play. John and I went down to Charlotte on an off day, with the express purpose of watching Manny," Hargrove said. "I remember him swinging the bat well, and him in right field being really timid. He would pull up on balls he probably could have caught. He dove for one ball, missed it, and got up real slow and went after it. That struck me why he would do that. Because Manny wasn't a lazy kid.

"I came to the realization that Manny hated to be embarrassed. So, he would play to stay away from being embarrassed. When he dove for a ball and didn't catch it, he felt embarrassed because he thought he was disappointing everyone. I remember having talks with him about that kind of thing. In spring training, Manny didn't go back on balls. He would pull up short of the wall. So, my decision was to play him really deep. Almost on the track. Because he came in on balls pretty well. At that time, he had gotten over his embarrassment, and that helped. He was always a better fielder than people gave him credit for."

But he was a hitter for the ages. And in 1994 he was ready for the big leagues. But he played right field. So did Wayne Kirby, the teacher's pet.

"John and I talked a lot about that," Hargrove said. "Manny had played Triple-A the year before, and really hadn't been in the minor leagues for very long. So, we took a flyer on Manny. But we did that throughout that build-up process. We would take flyers on certain guys like Manny and Jim Thome, guys we felt were going to be really good and didn't think we were pushing them too fast."

Hart said the Indians felt appreciative of what Kirby had done, but that Ramirez was a potential star.

"What I remember clearly," Hart said, "was when we broke Manny in, Kirby was coming off a really good year. I think Grover wanted to start with Kirby and ease Manny in. I think the staff thought the same thing, that maybe Manny needed another six weeks to eight weeks in the minors before he'd be ready. Because Kirby was a popular guy, coming off a great year."

At the end of spring training the Indians held a staff meeting to discuss the final makeup of the roster. One of the longer discussions involved the situation in right field.

"I said to Grover, 'We need to go with this kid if we're going to rebuild,'" Hart said, speaking of Ramirez. "'He might struggle. I realize we might have to send him out. I realize all the negatives that could happen. But I think we need to do it.' And Grover was fine with that. He said, 'Look, John. I love Manny.' It wasn't that Grover didn't like him, but part of it was a manager who was being loyal to a player (Kirby) who did a hell of a job for him the year before."

Despite the decision to commit to Ramirez in right field, Hart signed Kirby, now relegated to the role of a backup outfielder, to a two-year contract, mainly in appreciation for what he'd done the year before.

"We signed Kirby, a fourth outfielder, to a two-year extension, and off we went. Everything was good," said Hart.

Another outfielder on the '94 team was Candy Maldonado, who was 33 years old and winding down his distinguished 15-year career. The Indians had acquired him the previous year from the Cubs in exchange for Glenallen Hill. In '94, Maldonado appeared in 42 games, mostly as a designated hitter and pinch hitter.

"Candy was losing a step, and his bat was slowing down. John and I had been talking on and off for a couple of weeks about whether to release Candy or keep him," Hargrove said. "So, we're in a game and Candy had screwed up a couple times, not because he wasn't talented, but because he was slowing down, especially with his bat.

"John and I were trying to make up our minds what to do, whether or not we should release him. So, Candy's coming to the plate in this game. We're down one or two runs, two men on, two outs, in the sixth or seventh inning. Candy's going to the plate, and I say to myself, 'OK, I've made my mind up. We need to release him.' I had never done this before, and I never did it again, but I grabbed the dugout phone and called John in his suite, turned my back to the field and said, 'John, you know about that decision with Candy?' And as soon as I said those words, I heard a loud crack. Home run. So I said to John, 'Never mind,' and I hung up the phone."

*   *   *

Ignited by their thrilling win on opening day, the Indians broke fast from the gate, winning six of their first seven games, led by Ramirez, who hit .367 with three home runs and 10 RBI. On April 22 they were in first place in the AL Central with a record of 8-5, and they were in Texas for the start of a three-game series against the Rangers. Morris, who had gone 1-1 with a 5.09 ERA in his first three starts, was on the mound.

With the score tied 3-3, Texas catcher Ivan Rodriguez led off the bottom of the seventh. Morris' first pitch to Rodriguez bounced 40 feet in front of home plate. Morris' second pitch hit Rodriguez on the left elbow. Morris' third pitch was bunted in front of home plate by Manny Lee. It was fielded by Alomar, who threw to Vizquel covering second base. Rodriguez, in apparent retaliation for Morris hitting him, slid over the second base bag, slamming into Vizquel's right knee.

"It was a nasty, 'I'm going to take you out, I'm going to hurt you' slide, and he did. He hurt Omar's knee," said Hargrove.

"That was as cheap a shot as I've ever seen. He went after Omar, no question about it," said Hart the next day.

Vizquel suffered a sprained medial collateral ligament and spent six weeks on the disabled list.

Hargrove said there was only one time in his managerial career that he told a pitcher to intentionally hit a batter. That pitcher was Jose Mesa. That batter was Ivan Rodriguez, after that slide into Vizquel. "I told Jose, 'I want you to hit him. Not in the head, but I want you to hit him every time he comes to the plate for the rest of the game,'" said Hargrove.

Rodriguez came up one more time in that game, and Mesa threw at him twice, missing both times, before Rodriguez flied out.

"I had a meeting after the game about it, and (Texas manager) Kevin Kennedy picked up on it and took Rodriguez out of the lineup for the next game, which was probably a smart thing," said Hargrove. "But we played them a week later in Cleveland, and we went right back at trying to hit him, and they basically said, 'Hey, look, we get it.' And they took him out of the lineup again."

On April 29 in Cleveland, in the first game of a three-game series, Rodriguez's first two at-bats came leading off an inning, so Indians pitcher Charles Nagy didn't hit him, for fear of starting a rally. But Rodriguez's third-at bat came with the Indians leading 4-3, two outs, and nobody on base. Nagy drilled him.

"And they never retaliated, so they knew," said Hargrove of the Rangers. "We weren't trying to hurt Ivan. He was a good guy and a great player. But what he did wasn't right. There are times when you have to defend your teammates and say, 'We're not going to sit back and be your punching bag.'"

Hargrove felt that the only time a manager was justified in telling his pitcher to throw at a batter was if the opposing pitcher had hit one of his hitters, "and you knew it was on purpose. Sometimes you can't tell. You're really not sure. But if a guy has been throwing strikes for four innings and all of a sudden he uncorks one that's that far behind the hitter—because you're going to duck into those ones—then you knew. And you have to say, 'You're not going to intimidate us like that.' So, you send a message, as much to your own team as to the other team."

This was the law of the baseball jungle. It's old-school frontier justice that was even more harsh years before that.

"When I was a player," said Hargrove, "if you swung too hard, they would throw at you. My rookie year, I faced Nolan Ryan. I'm at the plate, and I thought to myself, 'I'm going to bunt.' So I bunted the ball down the third base line and it went foul. I got back into the box and the next two pitches were right at my chest. I fell over backwards because I thought the ball was going to hit me in the chin. Two times in a row. I screamed like a little girl going down, because I thought I was dead. I got up after the second one and I looked out at Ryan and I said, 'I got it. No problem. I understand.'"

Morris could throw at some hitters, too. While with the Blue Jays, he would occasionally buzz Lofton, who, after drawing ball four, had a habit of dropping his bat on top of home plate with disdain, almost mockingly showing the pitcher where his target was. Morris never led the league in hit batters, but he led the league in wild pitches six times, including 1987, when his 24 wild pitches were 10 more than any other American League pitcher. Morris led the league with 13 wild pitches with the Indians in the 1994 season, the end of which he never saw.

"The only time I became frustrated with Jack was early in the season he would complain about it being cold and he couldn't get any sweat going to get a grip on the ball. I understood that," said Hargrove. "But then later in the season when it got hot, he said the ball was slipping out of his hand because his fingers were too wet. I'm thinking, 'It's got to be one or the other, Jack.'"

It was a tough time in Morris' life. His fiancee broke up with him during the '94 season, and he was having trouble dealing with that. He also had a 10,000-acre farm in Montana, and at harvest time his foreman quit. Having grown up in a farming community in Perryton, Texas, Hargrove was sensitive to Morris' plight, to the point that the Indians allowed Morris to fly to Montana between starts so he could oversee things on the farm. Then he'd rejoin the Indians to throw his between-starts bullpen session. He'd make his start, then go back to Montana again.

He did that three or four times. Finally, in early August, the Indians were in Boston, where in order to make up two rained out games earlier in the season, they had to play doubleheaders on consecutive days. Prior to the start of the series Morris came to Hargrove and told him he needed to go back to Montana again.

"Jack, you're going to have to stay here now. We've reached the point where you need to stay," said Hargrove.

"Grover, you don't understand," said Morris. "It's crunch time in Montana."

"Jack, it's crunch time in Boston, too," said Hargrove.

Hargrove told Morris he was pitching the second game of the second doubleheader.

"He pitched that game, and then I never saw him again," said Hargrove.

That was on Aug. 7. The Indians beat the Red Sox 15-10. Morris only lasted 3⅓ innings, giving up seven runs on nine hits and four walks. It was Morris' last appearance in a major league game. He left the clubhouse before the game ended, presumably to return to his farm, this time for good.

The Indians split that doubleheader, then moved on to Toronto, where they took two out of three from the Blue Jays to improve their record to 66-47. They were in second place in the AL Central, one game behind the White Sox, who were 67-46. That was on Aug. 10. The Indians were leading the league in hitting, runs scored, runs per game, hits, doubles, home runs and slugging percentage.

Lofton and Belle were having monster years. Lofton was hitting .349 with 105 runs scored, a .412 on-base percentage, and 60 stolen bases in 112 games. Belle had a slash line of .357/.438/.714, with 35 doubles, 36 home runs, and 101 RBI in 106 games. Belle's .714 slugging percentage shattered, by 70 points, Hal Trosky's Indians' record of .644, which had stood for 58 years.

"Albert was doing damage beyond belief, and Kenny was doing athletic things beyond belief," said Shapiro.

That was on Aug. 10.

On Aug. 11, Major League Baseball owners, through Commissioner Bud Selig, cancelled the remainder of the regular season, the playoffs, and the World Series. The owners had set the Aug.11 deadline for the players and owners to agree on a new basic agreement. When no agreement was reached by the deadline, Selig, speaking for the owners, and blaming the players' 34-day strike, cancelled the rest of the regular season, and, unprecedentedly, all of the postseason.

Earlier in the year Hargrove realized the season was in danger of being stopped, so he met with his coaching staff and told them they were going to play the last two weeks leading up to the deadline like it was the last two weeks of the season.

"I remember the last stoppage they had (in 1981), the teams that were ahead at the time they stopped it, they were the teams that went to the postseason," Hargrove said. "So, we made a concerted effort to try to get ahead of the White Sox by the time they pulled the plug on the season. We even explained it to the players that that was the way we were going to treat it."

When the season was stopped, Cleveland (66-47) was one game behind Chicago (67-16) in the Central Division standings. The Indians did have the best record of any second-place team and thus would have qualified for the postseason as the wildcard team. But, with the Indians primed and ready to make their first postseason appearance in 40 years, there was no postseason.

"We felt we were going to win the division. The White Sox were feeling us. We were playing great baseball and we were getting better," said Shapiro.

But then the plug was pulled on the season.

"I don't think any of us knew what to do with ourselves because it was the middle of the summer and we weren't playing baseball," Hargrove said. "I don't think anybody thought that the owners would go that far. In all the labor discussions I had been involved in as a player, threats would be made, but cooler heads prevailed, and you got something done."

This time, hotter heads prevailed.

The cancellation of the remainder of the season was particularly hard on those in the Indians front office who had been there for the hard times, and now could see the good times on the horizon.

"We were confident that we were headed into a unique stretch of our history," Shapiro said. "The window of opportunity was not going to be a short one. At the time of the strike we understood it from the business side of the game, but we just wanted to get that team out on the field and let them play."

Hart was devastated by Selig's announcement.

"I remember it like it was yesterday," he said. "We found out through a conference call in the afternoon. When it was over, I walked out into the ballpark. It was a beautiful fall-like day, and I sat in one of the seats in the park. It was very disappointing. It made you shed a little tear. But then it was, 'All right, there's nothing we can do about it now, but try to come back with a vengeance next year.' But then we had that nuclear winter, when the strike went through the off-season, and then came the lockout in spring training. We were all sitting there saying, 'Here we've got this great team, and we may never be able to get it on the field again.'"

Said Alomar: "I had been with the Indians since 1990, and now we were finally getting good, and we had a nice new stadium. To see us finally having a winning season in Cleveland, and then having it wiped out, that was hard. Who knows? We might have won the World Series that year."

CHAPTER 9

100-44

*"That team was tough, young, hungry,
big and bad. We hit homers, and we had
young players coming out our wazoo."*

Charles Nagy did not look at the cancellation of the last six weeks of the 1994 regular season, and all of the postseason including the World Series, as a lost season for the Indians.

"It wasn't a lost season, but a lost opportunity," he said. "With the team we had, the attitude, the cockiness and the swagger we developed, we knew we were going to be good for a few years. So, the '94 season ended early, but we picked it right back up in 1995."

As summer faded into fall and then into a nuclear baseball winter, with no World Series played, the Indians, as did most major league teams, conducted their winter press tour. At a luncheon that winter in Zanesville, Ohio, a father, with his little boy in his arms, came up to Hargrove. The father told Hargrove he hoped the players would get back to work because he was hoping to see the Indians become good again, because when he was a young boy he would go to games with his father and the Indians were pretty good at the time. He told Hargrove he and his father had that special bond, just through the Indians.

"I really want to have that with my son, and I hope at some time in the near future I can do that," the man said.

Fast forward eight months.

"When Jimmy Thome caught that ball to clinch the division title in 1995, the first thing I thought of was that guy and his kid," Hargrove said. "I thought, 'I hope that guy is here tonight, with his little boy.'"

With the owners and the players still unable to come to terms on a new basic agreement, the owners locked the players out of spring training.

That's when the circus came to town.

After the World Series was canceled, Hargrove's first thought was that the 1995 season wasn't going to start on time. "Because," he said, "they aren't going to do anything over the winter, because they don't have to do anything."

Hargrove was right. The two sides didn't do anything, but eventually the owners did something. A goofy thing. They decided that, if push came to shove, they would start the 1995 season using replacement players.

"I remember one of the owners saying, 'The people will get used to the level of play they are watching,'" Hargrove said. "In other words, if you're watching shitty baseball, then shitty baseball becomes good after a while."

About the middle of December, push came to shove. Major league teams were told to start constructing rosters of replacement players.

"It was the last thing I wanted to do," Hargrove said. "Part of me wanted to be loyal to the owners' point of view, but I was also a player at one time, so part of me wanted to be loyal to the players. In my case, I was kind of caught in the middle. I didn't want to disrespect either side."

Hargrove wasn't directly involved in trying to find players, but once in a while the front office would give him a player's phone number to call. Once spring training started Hargrove would occasionally go down to the minor league camp and try to talk a player into playing with the replacement players. The real minor league players were in camp because they were not yet members of the Major League Players Association. That was a tough sell for Hargrove to make to those minor league players, who knew that if they crossed the picket lines, so to speak, and agreed to go to the major league training camp, they risked being blackballed.

One of the players Hargrove was asked to speak to was Pep Harris, a 22-year-old pitcher of some promise in the Indians' minor league system. In 1994, in a combined 51 relief appearances at

Class A and Double-A in the Indians' system, Harris was 6-1, with a 2.04 ERA.

"I was assigned to go talk to Pep and try to get him to sign this deal," Hargrove said. "So, I went down to the minor league camp, got him in my golf cart, and we drove off to talk about it. I said, 'Now Pep, after all this stuff I've said to you about playing, if you ask me personally, I would tell you not to do it. Because it's not going to be a good thing.' Pep Harris listened to Hargrove, but then signed the contract anyway. Later, however, Harris thought better of it and never showed up to play.

"But just by agreeing to play, and signing the contract," said Hargrove, "he got blackballed by the Players Association. No pension. Didn't participate in the licensing money. I felt bad about that one because Pep was a really good kid."

Harris went 8-4 with a 2.41 ERA between Double-A and Triple-A in the Cleveland system in 1995. The following year the Indians traded him and pitcher Jason Grimsley to the Angels for pitcher Brian Anderson. Harris spent three years with the Angels, going 10-5 with a 3.92 ERA in 121 games, most of them in relief. He was out of baseball following the 1998 season, at age 26.

Most of the leg work for finding the Indians' replacement players was done by Hart, O'Dowd, Shapiro and scouting director Jay Robertson. On the first day of spring training, Hart and O'Dowd called a meeting that included Shapiro, Robertson, Hargrove and his coaching staff. The purpose of the meeting was to go over the replacement players who had already signed contracts, and to discuss how to proceed, and how to procure other replacement players worthy of being procured. Let's just say the bar wasn't real high.

About halfway through the meeting, Hart got a phone call and had to leave the room. O'Dowd, who spear-headed the replacement player recruitment, took over the meeting. "Danny never did anything halfway. So, he was maniacal about getting this done," Hargrove said.

Hart never came back to the meeting, so the rest of the group continued to go over the players. Finally, O'Dowd stood up, holding a huge loose-leaf notebook with rings, containing all the replacement player information, and said, "Is there anything else?"

"Yeah, I got something to say," said bench coach Buddy Bell. "This shit ain't going to work. This is ridiculous."

O'Dowd slammed the notebook down on the table and shouted, "You don't know how much hard work went into this! We busted our ass to get these players, and you say that!"

O'Dowd stormed out of the room.

"Buddy and I almost got into a fight over that, because he kept making fun of it, and I completely lost it on him," says O'Dowd today. "It was miserable for us to have to do that, but nevertheless we were charged with doing it. Grover and the staff hated it, and they hated us for putting them in that position. But they lost perspective, because we didn't want to do it, either."

"After Danny stormed out of the room I looked at Buddy and said to him real softly, 'I think you might need to go apologize to him,'" Hargrove said. "But, God, it was funny."

So was replacement player spring training, once the replacement players started rolling into camp—sometimes literally.

"We had a guy, the first day, who was a catcher," Hargrove said. "I don't remember his name, but he was terribly out of shape. Just terribly out of shape. I thought he was going to die. I'm standing there watching him, and I thought he was going to die. So, I got (strength and conditioning coach) Fernando Montes, and I said, 'Fernando, don't let this guy out of your sight.' Because his face was all beet red. His uniform was all messy, his shirt tail was hanging out. He looked like a beer league softball guy. But to his credit, he wasn't backing off. He was busting his ass. I told Fernando, 'You watch this guy, and if you see him getting a little woozy, get his ass out of there.'"

At the end of the day, Hargrove went to Hart's office.

"John, you've got to release this guy," Hargrove said.

"It's his first day!" Hart said.

"John, this guy has a chance to die on us," said Hargrove.

So, the Indians did release him. After one day of training camp.

"And the guy was pissed! He was pissed! I think he ended up signing with the Reds," Hargrove said.

The Reds were apparently not as maniacal about signing replacement players as were the Indians. The Reds needed players, so about halfway through replacement player training camp, Hart traded five replacement players to the Reds for no players. That's right, a straight five-for-none deal.

"And the Indians got the better of the deal," cracked Reds manager Davey Johnson.

But that roly-poly catcher may have only been the second most interesting player in the Indians' replacement player camp.

"We had another guy named Mel," Hargrove said. "A big, imposing, intimidating guy named Mel. The reason I knew his name was Mel was the first day I met him, he walked into my office and he had cutoff shorts on, with work boots, wearing one of those gas station shirts, with the sleeves cut off, and he had his name 'Mel' on his chest. Mel was a good guy. But he was Mel."

In one of the spring games, Mel was the batter, and the count was 3-0. Hargrove gave him the take sign and Mel took a strike. Hargrove gave him the take sign again and Mel took it for strike two. Hargrove then gave Mel the take sign for the third pitch, but Mel swung and missed for strike three.

"After the game, I'm in my office and he knocks on the door, and I told him to come in," Hargrove said. "He did, and he says to me in this real deep voice, 'Mel don't take pitches.' I said, 'OK, Mel, you need to get the fuck out of my office. And let's start over and see if we can figure out how to talk about this without me being pissed at you.' So, he did. He walked out. Then he knocked on the door, came back in, and we worked it out."

In another game, the Indians were trailing by one run in the ninth inning, with a runner at third and one out. Hargrove just wanted to get the game over, so he sent up a pinch hitter, a Latin guy who hadn't played much that spring.

"He walks by me and says, 'Grover, I know, I know why you want me up there. You want a fly ball,'" Hargrove said. "I thought to myself, 'Well, yeah, but no. Let's just get this game over, so we can move on.'"

The replacement player spring of 1995 was hard on everyone. The teams, the managers, the coaches, the players, the media. Everyone knew it was a sham, yet everyone had to pretend that it wasn't.

"It wasn't hard to be professional, because it was still the game.

It was still baseball. You respect the game. But it was hard to be enthusiastic. You almost felt phony, with the forced enthusiasm," Hargrove said.

Fortunately, there were interludes of humor that helped keep everyone sane. In normal spring training games, sometimes teams will have pitchers who need extra work, so the two managers will agree to play extra innings, regardless of the score, just to get those pitchers the needed work.

During an exhibition game against Cincinnati, Indians pitching coach Mark Wiley asked Hargrove to ask the Reds if they minded playing an extra inning or two, because the Indians had some (replacement) pitchers who needed to throw.

"I said, 'Seriously, Mark?'" Hargrove said.

The Reds agreed to it, so they played the extra innings, the replacement pitchers got their work, and as the Indians' bus was pulling out of the ballpark, it immediately got stopped by a train.

"This train was 14 miles long, barely moving, and we're just sitting there," Hargrove said. "And the longer we sat, the more pissed Buddy is getting. Finally, Buddy says, 'Hey Mark, you got another pitcher you want to see? We've got plenty of time now.' We sat there for 30 or 40 minutes. It was hilarious. On the enthusiasm scale (during the replacement player spring) we were all at about a five. Buddy was at two."

The replacement player folly came dangerously close to actually happening. After the fake training camp, the fake Indians flew to Cleveland, and played the fake Pirates in a final exhibition (in every sense of the word) game at Jacobs Field, the day before the scheduled fake opening day.

"I remember thinking 'Something's got to happen. They can't let this go on,'" Hargrove said. "Nothing against those guys. They played as good as they could play. But they weren't good. They can't put this out there and expect people to pay money, at major league prices, to see a non-major league product."

In the end, they didn't.

Immediately after the fake Indians' game with the fake Pirates, Hart rushed into Hargrove's office and told him that a new labor agreement had been reached. The replacement player quackery was finally over.

"That's it," Hart told Hargrove. "Tell these guys we're done."

So, a relieved Hargrove walked briskly to the clubhouse and did exactly that.

"I had a meeting and told them, 'The strike's been settled. Your checks will be mailed to you. Thanks for everything. Good luck. See ya!'"

That was it? A 30-second meeting?

"Pretty much," said Hargrove. "I could have walked in and waved and said, 'Bye!' But I didn't."

The Indians, and all major league teams, immediately returned to their spring training camps in Florida and Arizona. The real major leaguers wasted no time in getting there as well, for what would turn out to be an abbreviated, accelerated, three-week training camp.

"We went back to Florida for spring training with the real players, and it was really good to see all of them. Really good," said Hargrove. "It was invigorating."

*   *   *

Throughout the player strike/lockout, which paralyzed baseball from Aug. 11, 1994, through April 1, 1995, Hart was busy finishing off a roster which had powerhouse potential if and when the strike was settled. The position player side of the roster was set, with an all-star caliber player at virtually every position. But the pitching staff needed some work.

"We tried to concentrate on building a deep bullpen, with big arms. That was a theme through those years," Hart said. "We spent some money, but we didn't go crazy. We tried to be five or six deep in the bullpen. It was a philosophy. If you have a lot of number three–type starters, with no aces, but you've got a 900 to 1,000-run club that catches the ball, you're never going to be held down. And if you've got a bullpen that, if you're a run down in the sixth or seventh, you can still come back. Or if you've got a two-run lead, you can hold it. And that's how we played it."

Hart began in April 1992, by signing free agent Eric Plunk, whom Hart, as a minor league manager in the Baltimore system, first saw in 1982, when Plunk was an 18-year-old starter, throwing 100 mph for the Yankees' rookie league team in Paintsville, Kentucky. In July 1992 Hart acquired Jose Mesa in a trade with Baltimore. In March 1995 Hart signed free-agent left-hander Jim Poole. On April 10, shortly after the real Indians players reported to Winter Haven for the three-week spring training following the replacement player circus, Hart signed left-hander Paul Assenmacher as a free agent. Gangly right-hander Julian Tavarez (6-2, 165 pounds), who was 15-6 as a starter at Triple-A Charlotte in 1994, was added to the big-league staff as a reliever.

Those five pitchers did most of the heavy lifting in the Indians' bullpen during their historic 1995 season. But none of that would have happened without the crucial decision, following the 1993 season, to convert Mesa, a mediocre starting pitcher, into a reliever in 1994, and a closer in 1995.

The results were immediate and dramatic. In 33 starts for the Indians in 1993 Mesa was 10-12 with a 4.92 ERA. Opposing batters hit .286, with a .753 OPS against him. In 1994 he made 51 relief appearances as a non-closer, and had a record of 7-5, a 3.82 ERA. Opposing batters hit .254, with a .650 OPS against him. In his epic 1995 season, his first as a closer, Mesa was 3-0 with a club-record 1.12 ERA (minimum 60 innings pitched), with a club-record 46 saves in 48 chances. Opposing batters hit .216, with a .541 OPS against him. He finished second in the Cy Young Award voting and fourth in the MVP voting.

So, you could say moving Mesa to the bullpen worked out rather well.

"Jose was a starter for us," said Hargrove, "and my pitching coach Phil Regan came into my office in spring training and said, 'I really think we should convert Mesa into a closer. He's got a tremendous fastball and he throws strikes. As a one-inning guy, I think he'd be dynamite.' Jose did have a great fastball, 95 to 97 mph, so I talked to John and he said, 'Let's give it a try.'"

The first time Hart had seen Mesa was in 1986 and 1987, when Hart was managing in winter ball.

"I watched Jose for two years, watching him go three or four innings and just be electric. Then we'd get to him," Hart said. "So, in the back of my mind I always had the thought, 'This guy can relieve.' So, we gave him a shot at being a starter (in Cleveland) for a couple years, but I knew as soon as we felt we had enough in the rotation, we were going to move him to the bullpen. I didn't know if he would be a closer, but I felt he could be a dominant bullpen piece. Sure enough, after the end of the 1994 season we were desperate for a guy at the end of the game, and Jose became one of the dominant relievers in baseball."

Like most closers back then, and to this day, Mesa was a failed starter who just sort of fell into the job of closer.

"I wasn't sure it was going to work," Hart said. "There were a lot of things I tried that didn't work. That one did. The staff was for it. There were some questions on whether he could do it, but we gave him the shot, and he did the job."

One of the reasons that bullpen was so effective was that Hargrove was able to give each member a clearly defined role, and that's exactly how he used each of them throughout the season.

"Everybody had their roles," Hargrove said. "Jim Poole knew he wasn't going to pitch in the eighth inning, but he was going to pitch in the sixth or seventh. Plunk knew that he might pitch in the seventh or eighth, and Assenmacher knew the same thing. For me, the two big acquisitions were Plunk and Assenmacher, the back end of the pen guys who could get you to Mesa. Mesa had 46 saves that year, so if we could get the ball to him, it worked out. The strength of our club was obviously our bats, but if you look at our bullpen, and the job they did, it absolutely was a big strength."

Plunk pitched for the Indians from 1992 to 1998, when he was traded to Milwaukee. At the time of the trade Plunk ranked seventh on the Indians' all-time list for games pitched with 373. That kind of dependability made him a Hargrove favorite.

"Toward the end of his time here fans were calling him Kerplunk, and things like that, but he was invaluable to us," Hargrove said. "One time I brought him into a tough situation to face Frank Thomas, and as I was coming off the field a guy ran down the aisle right to the dugout, and he's screaming at me. The veins are popping out of his neck, and his face was purple. I'm thinking, 'This guy's going to have a stroke.' He's screaming, 'Bring in Kerplunk? You dumbass! What are you doing?' He was going on and on, so I waved to him, and went into the dugout.

"A lot of people think you make a move because you say, 'Let's try this now,' or 'Let's try this now.' But the numbers we had at that time showed that Frank Thomas was 0-for-11 with nine strikeouts against Plunk. And at the end of that at bat he was 0-for-12 with 10 strikeouts. Sadly, a lot of people remember Eric Plunk as Kerplunk, and not as the guy who was an integral part of our bullpen and the success of our team."

As the real 1995 Cleveland Indians convened in Winter Haven in early April, Hart continued to add pieces. Big pieces. Or, at least, pieces with big names. Like Orel Hershiser.

Hart needed a starter, but he didn't want to spend wildly on one. So, he drew up a list of candidates, and Hershiser was at the top of his list. Hart sent a scout to watch every game Hershiser pitched for the Dodgers in July and August 1994, all the way up to the day the season was halted. By 1995 Hershiser was 36 years old. Seven years earlier, with the Dodgers in 1988, he set a major league record that still stands of 59 consecutive scoreless innings on his way to winning the National League Cy Young Award, and pitching the Dodgers to a World Series victory over Oakland.

But the Hershiser who Indians scouts were watching was not that Hershiser. "He was throwing 87-88, 88-89, 89-90 (mph)," Hart said. "He was coming back from a debilitating injury. A frozen shoulder. We knew the strike was going to end at some point, so we kept him in mind."

When the strike ended in the spring of 1995, the Indians and Hershiser agreed on a one-year deal for $1.5 million, with $2 million in potential bonuses, plus a club option for a second year. As the real spring training started in 1995, Hart called Hershiser, who lived in Winter Park, Florida, which is where Hart lived. Hart informed Hershiser that the press conference announcing the signing was set up for the next day, and Hershiser said he'd be there. Two hours later Hart got a call from Robert Fraley, Hershiser's agent.

"John, you're not going to believe this. We just got an offer from the Giants. Three years, guaranteed, nine million," said Fraley.

"What?" said Hart.

"The Giants," said Fraley. "They hate the Dodgers, and they love Orel."

Hart was dumbfounded. He asked Fraley to put Hershiser on the phone. Fraley did.

"I said, 'Orel, look. We have a deal. We've got a press conference scheduled for tomorrow,' " Hart said.

"John, let me ask you this," Hershiser replied. "We have a relationship. There's no more that you can give?"

"No. This is what we have, and we had reached a deal," said Hart.

"I just want you to promise me you'll take care of me, because I'll do the job for you. I'll walk away from this money and I'll sign with you guys," said Hershiser.

A panicky Hart finally exhaled.

"I realized Orel is Orel," Hart said. "As it came to pass, he went 16-6 and was the MVP in the ALCS and won 20 games, counting the playoffs, on a one-year deal. So, he made all of his bonuses."

Hershiser wound up making more with the Indians than the Giants were going to pay him. He just had to earn it through those bonuses. After the 1995 season the Indians picked up the option year and gave Hershiser a two-year deal, and he wound up making about $10 million, which was more than he would have made with the Giants.

"It's ironic in this world that you had a man like Orel, who would do that," Hart said. "He just said, 'Hey, I'm coming.' The agent was pissed, but he understood. He said, 'I work for my client. You guys have a relationship.' So, we took care of Orel, and he really did the job for us. You talk about a man who stepped up. He did the deal because of a relationship that we had. And, No. 2, he delivered."

Nobody was more thrilled by the Hershiser signing than Hargrove, who knew his rotation needed another skilled workman.

"Orel fit in well. He knew how to win. Not just his game, but he knew what it took team-wise to win, which was what we were looking for," Hargrove said. "We wanted guys who not only had talent, but guys who had been winners, who had been to the World Series, and knew what it took. And Orel could still throw. He was supremely confident in his abilities. Not arrogant. But very, very confident."

Hershiser slotted into the No. 3 spot in the Indians' 1995 rotation, behind Dennis Martinez and Charles Nagy. All three of them won over 70% of their starts. Martinez was 12-5 (.706) and Nagy and Hershiser were both 16-6 (.727). Mark Clark (9-7) was the No. 4 starter, and Chad Ogea and Ken Hill, a mid-season pickup from

St. Louis, were a combined 12-4 with a 3.43 ERA while sharing the No. 5 spot.

Overall, the Indians' pitching staff in 1995 led the league in ERA, ERA+, shutouts, FIP, WHIP, saves and strikeouts per walk—and pitching was supposedly the "weak" link of the team. But it was the Indians' hitters who scared the fungos out of their opponents.

"We beat people over the head with our bats," Hargrove said. "It was fun to watch."

But first, the winningest, most intimidating team in the American League in 1995 convened in Winter Haven for a three-week tune-up before the carnage began. They were equal parts swagger, arrogance, showmanship and charisma. They were baseball's Beatles. During the season it was not unusual, when arriving at their hotel on the road, for the players to ride the freight elevators up to their rooms in order to avoid the mobs of autograph seekers waiting in the lobby—even at 3 a.m.

But most of all, they were a great team, and they knew it.

"It was good to see the players, and they were all happy to be there," Hargrove said. "That was the only year there was not one major fire. We just kind of rocked along. I think it had a lot to do with the leadership we had in the clubhouse, with Murray and Sandy and Orel, guys like that."

Spring training 1995 was the first time all the players had been together since Aug. 10 of the previous year, their last game prior to the cancellation of the remainder of the '94 season. Now they were all gathering in a sleepy little Central Florida town, determined to bring meaning to Hart's ominous vow "to come back with a vengeance next year," which served as a rallying cry for the franchise through those gloomy days that followed the un-played games in that unfinished 1994 season.

"It almost felt like, 'We're a family again,'" said Hargrove.

Meanwhile, Hart kept throwing logs on the fire. Throughout that 1994-95 period it seemed a new high-profile player was walking through the door almost every day. Murray, Martinez, Morris, Hershiser. The parade never seemed to end. Stars who in past years would never have given playing in Cleveland a second thought were seemingly lining up for a chance to sign with the Indians. Then in the spring of 1995, when the real players replaced the replacement players and convened for their quick, three-week training camp, in walked future Hall of Famer Dave Winfield, signed by Hart as a free agent.

This wasn't peak Dave Winfield. This was end-of-the-road Dave Winfield, although it's easy to see why Hart took a flyer on him. Just three years earlier, with Toronto in 1992, Winfield hit .290, with 26 home runs, 108 RBI, and, at age 40, he finished fifth in the MVP voting.

But in 1995, Winfield was 43 years old, playing with a torn rotator cuff in his left shoulder, and, it turned out, just 46 games and 115 forgettable at-bats away from the end of his career. The Indians quickly saw that Winfield's fuel light was on. The tank was empty. In those 115 at bats he hit .191, with only two home runs and four RBI. Prior to the start of the last series of the regular season, Hart and Hargrove met with Winfield to tell him he wasn't going to be on the postseason roster.

"John McNamara always told me, 'Never let a star fall on you,' meaning don't manage a star at the end of his career. Well, it happened with Dave," Hargrove said. "I was always a little suspicious about guys who didn't get at least a little upset about a decision I made that affected them negatively. It bothered Dave, but he didn't become a cancer and start throwing things, or anything like that."

Winfield was the fourth player taken in the first round of the 1973 June Draft. The Padres selected him out of the University of Minnesota, and brought him straight to the majors. He never played an inning of minor league baseball. In Hargrove's brief time with San Diego in 1979, he and Winfield were teammates. Winfield was 27 years old at the time, and in the midst of the best season (8.3 WAR) of his 22-year major league career. He hit .308, with 34 home runs and a National League-leading 118 RBI. "Back then we were friends, but we weren't close," said Hargrove.

During the 1995 season, when the Indians were on the road, Winfield would come to Hargrove's hotel room and ask Hargrove why he wasn't playing.

"It was obvious to everyone that Dave was not the Dave he had been. So that was a tough one. That was really tough, dealing with that," Hargrove said. "Trying to figure out a way to give him the respect he's due, and still do what's best for the ballclub. To Dave's credit, he handled it really well. He wasn't a problem at all. He was a good leader. I think at some level he understood what was happening."

The 1995 Indians were a unique mixture of ruthlessly cold-blooded baseball assassins, cloaked in a cape of cocky, fun-loving, un-restrained showmanship.

The team as a whole came onto the field for each game like a voracious, insatiable animal, determined to feed on, wipe out and beat up the opposing team. They didn't just defeat the other team, they made opposing players question their choice of professions. They were a blend of the worst of the Detroit Pistons "Bad Boys" and the best of the "Showtime" Los Angeles Lakers.

And the long-suffering Cleveland fans ate it up.

Hargrove is convinced that the take-no-prisoners attitude of that larger-than-life '95 team was cast during a team meeting held during the winter of 1993-94. Indians officials brought the whole club to Cleveland for a week, and they practiced in a gym on the west side. Jacobs Field wasn't finished yet, and there was no place in the old ballpark to work out. At the end of the week, a meeting was held with the players. Hargrove and some of his coaches spoke at the meeting, and then they left. But the players did not.

The meeting continued, a players-only meeting led by Kenny Lofton. They talked about the importance of going first to third on the bases, of playing hard and aggressively all the time, and about the need to carry themselves with a certain swagger.

"The players took over the meeting, and that's what we wanted," Hargrove said. "And in 1995, we carried ourselves that way, so there was a certain amount of intimidation there, even though it's real hard to intimidate another big-league player or team."

But not when you have the lineup the '95 Indians ran out there every day.

"Since then, I've talked to a number of guys who either pitched against us or played against us or managed against us at that time," Hargrove said. "They all said there wasn't a breather anywhere in our lineup. What are you going to do? Walk Belle to face Murray? Walk Murray to face Thome? Walk Thome to face Ramirez?"

In the basement of his home, Hargrove has an extensive collection of baseball memorabilia, uniforms, photographs and other artifacts from his career in the game. But he has only two lineup cards displayed. Not because they are from memorable or historic games, but because of the jarring juxtaposition of two names on the cards, and where those names are located. Both are from games in 1994. One has Jim Thome batting eighth and Manny Ramirez batting ninth. The other has Ramirez batting eighth and Thome batting ninth.

It's the ultimate baseball, "What's wrong with this picture?"

During their careers, those two players hit a combined 1,167 home runs. Thome is in the Hall of Fame, and Ramirez would have been had he not chosen to dabble in steroids. In '94 Ramirez hit eighth or ninth in the Indians' lineup 14 times. Thome hit eighth or ninth 44 times. In '95, Thome hit seventh or eighth 22 times, and sixth, seventh or eighth 104 times. Ramirez hit seventh 71 times, and sixth or seventh 118 times.

"Think about that," said Thome. "Think about having a guy hitting seventh who went into the Hall of Fame. So, Grover wrote these guys into his lineup at seventh and eighth, and then later they hit third, fourth and fifth. When you look down our lineup, we had Albert and Kenny and Eddie Murray. Legitimately, there were, across that lineup, maybe seven or eight potential Hall of Famers. You can't get any better than that."

When Hargrove sat down to make out his lineup every day, he was picking from an embarrassment of riches.

"There are certain lineups that really just put themselves together, and most of those lineups in the '90s made themselves out," he said. "If I hadn't hit Albert right in the middle of the lineup, and then Eddie hitting right behind him—for example, if I'd hit Eddie sixth instead of fifth—people would have said I'd lost my mind. Some of the spots were so obvious that you ran the risk of being called an idiot for doing it differently. Sometimes lineups just fall together, and this one did. Kenny was a great leadoff hitter. Omar was a good second hitter, and right on down the line."

In most games, Baerga batted third, Belle fourth, Murray fifth, Thome sixth, Ramirez, who would finish with a higher career batting average (.312) than any of them, hit seventh, Sorrento eighth, and the catcher, Tony Pena or Alomar (who because of injuries only played in 66 games), ninth.

One of the most memorable games came on June 30, in the Metrodome in Minneapolis, when Murray grounded a single to right field off Mike Trombley for the 3,000th hit of his career. Murray became just the second switch-hitter (joining Pete Rose) in history with 3,000 hits. He was the first player in 70 years (Tris Speaker in 1925) to pick up his 3,000th hit wearing an Indians uniform. The third, and only other time it happened, was with Napoleon Lajoie in 1914.

"I enjoyed it. We've had a lot of fun in Cleveland. This is the wildest group of guys I've ever played with," Murray said after the game.

Hargrove enjoyed Murray's production almost as much as he enjoyed Murray's intangibles, on an Indians team that was heavy on the tangibles.

"Eddie was good. He was very opinionated," Hargrove said. "Everything was black and white with Eddie. There was no gray area, and I don't mean that in racial terms. With Eddie, it was either this, or this. He did a good job for us playing, obviously, but he did a great job for us with leadership in the clubhouse. He was old school to the bone. He and Albert had a few battles here and there. Eddie was one of those guys, like Nagy, Lofton and Thome, you didn't have to worry about. But Eddie knew the game as well as anybody."

Hargrove always made it a point to be on the field, and leaning on the batting cage, when Murray took batting practice before a game.

"He never tried to hit balls hard," Hargrove said. "He knew there were things he could do during the game that made him great, and he would practice those things. Like slapping the ball to the opposite field. He didn't care what you thought of him. He didn't try to hit balls out of the park. An uninitiated fan watching Eddie take batting practice would think he was one of the worst hitters in the world. But he wasn't. He was one of the best hitters in the game. Eddie was, 'This is who I am, and I'm not changing.'"

Murray wasn't afraid to voice his opinions on any and all subjects. He could be a very serious conversationalist on any number of topics, but his specialty, obviously, was baseball.

"I never had arguments or confrontations with Eddie," Hargrove said. "We wouldn't butt heads, but we'd have glancing blows at times. Eddie didn't let an awful lot of people in, but if you understood him as well as you could understand him, you could see what it was about him, mentally, that made him great."

*   *   *

The 1995 regular season was a joke. The Indians turned it into their own private 144-game playpen. Because the lockout led to the replacement players farce, which led to a second spring training of three weeks with the real players, the regular season didn't start until April 27. So, the schedule was shortened to 144 games. The Indians lost two of their first three games, then went into full battering ram mode the rest of the season.

Their swagger, arrogance and cockiness not only intimidated opposing teams, but umpires as well. Especially replacement umpires. As if the near-miss of having to use replacement players in the regular season wasn't bad enough, Major League Baseball DID use replacement umpires in the early part of the 1995 season, thanks to a 120-day strike by the Major League Umpires Association.

On May 2, the Indians played in Detroit. It was the Tigers' home opener, played before a huge crowd. It was also the last day for the replacement umpires. The MLB umpires' strike had ended. But the replacement umps went out with a bang. In the bottom of the first inning, the home plate umpire called a pitch thrown by Dennis Martinez to Bobby Higginson a ball. Martinez reacted by brazenly marching off the mound, all the way to home plate, where he held the baseball over the plate, to indicate to the replacement umpire that the pitch should have been called a strike.

"I'm thinking, 'Holy shit!'" said Hargrove. "I couldn't get out there fast enough. I thought, 'He's gone.'"

Martinez stayed. The replacement umpire, clearly intimidated, did not throw Martinez out.

"I told him, 'You should have thrown me out,'" Martinez told reporters. "He just smiled."

Tigers manager Sparky Anderson scowled.

"I wanted to know why the pitcher was still in the game," said Anderson, after the game. "In my 26 years in baseball, I've never seen a pitcher do that. But this is a guy on his last day of work, with a pitcher named Dennis Martinez on the mound, and I'm sure he didn't want to run him."

Such was the bullying nature of that Indians team.

It also wasn't Hargrove's first brush with replacement umpires.

"When I was with San Diego in 1979, we had replacement umps," he said. "We were playing the Giants. Tie game, bases loaded. I could duck a pitch pretty good. I can't remember the pitcher's name, but it was a big-time pitcher. He threw a pitch right down the pipe. If I would have been standing up straight, it would have been waist high. But I ducked, just to see what was going on, and the ump says, 'Ball one.' And I'm like, 'Oh, man. Well, that's pretty good.'

"So, the next pitch, right down the middle, and I ducked again. 'Ball two.' Third pitch, down the middle, I ducked. 'Ball three.' Same thing on the fourth pitch. I ducked, 'Ball four.' I went to first base, and the pitcher got thrown out of the game. I mean I was almost laying on the ground on the last pitch, but, 'Ball four.' Son of a bitch!"

The big, bad, bullish, boisterous '95 Indians finished with a record of 100-44, winning the AL Central by an outrageous 30 games, a major league record that still stands. Kansas City finished second with a record of 70-74. The Indians clinched the division title on Sept. 8, with 15% of their games left in the season. (In a 162-game season, that would be the equivalent of clinching the division on about Sept. 1.)

The '95 Indians played .700 ball or better in three of the five full months of the season. Their worst monthly winning percentage was .667 in July, when they were 18-9. They were 19-7 (.731) in May, 20-8 (.714) in June, 21-9 (.700) in August and 19-9 (.679) in September. In September they outscored their opponents 177-117, and out-hit them .301 to .238.

"That team was tough, young, hungry, big and bad. We hit homers, and we had young players coming out our wazoo," said Hart.

The Indians were 46-21 (.687) in the first half of the season, and 54-23 (.701) in the second half. In extra innings they were 13-0. In one-run games: 28-14 (.667). In blowouts (games decided by five or more runs): 29-11 (.725). Against Baltimore (10-2), Detroit (10-3),

Kansas City (11-1), Oakland (7-0) and Toronto (10-3) they were a combined 48-9 (.842), outscoring those five teams 322-174.

At home they were 54-18 (.750), outscoring their opponents 400-272, and out-homering them 99-60. On the road the Indians were 46-26 (.639). Only New York and Seattle won as many games at home as the Indians did on the road. Against AL Central teams, the Indians were 37-14 (.725). Against right-handed starting pitchers they were 73-30 (.709), against left-handers: 27-14 (.659). They absolutely destroyed the bums: their record against teams with losing records was 74-22 (.771).

On May 9 vs. Kansas City, the Indians were leading 8-0 before they made their first out of the game. Their first inning went like this: home run, walk, home run, single, single, walk, walk, home run. They won that game 10-0, moved into first place in the AL Central, and stayed there for the rest of the season.

On June 4, vs. Toronto, at Jacobs Field, the Indians were trailing 8-0 going into the bottom of the third inning, against reigning Cy Young Award winner David Cone. With two outs in the bottom of the ninth inning, Paul Sorrento hit a two-run walkoff home run, giving Cleveland a 9-8 victory.

"That's the game that sticks out in my mind, where I remember thinking, 'Wow, we have a chance to be really, really good.' We were down 8-0 to Cone, and came back to win it. It was just a magical season. Anything that could go right did go right. Murphy's Law wasn't anywhere close to Cleveland that summer," said Hargrove.

Many of their wins were outrageous blowouts. Some of the scores looked like lopsided scores from a softball league: 11-1, 10-0, 10-5, 11-5, 11-0, 14-5, 13-3, 14-4, 12-2, 12-4, and, on the last day of the regular season: 17-7 over Kansas City.

"From a position player standpoint, I would argue that the '95 team is one of the greatest teams in the history of the game," said O'Dowd. "When I left the Indians (to become general manager of the Colorado Rockies), I said, 'I want to build something like that again.' Well, good luck with that. When you not only win 100 of 144 games, but in the process, you just obliterate people. I wish I knew then what I know now, because I would have enjoyed it a lot more."

*   *   *

With a 3-2 win over Baltimore at Jacobs Field on Sept. 8, the Indians clinched the Central Division title, guaranteeing the franchise's first trip to the postseason in 41 years. The last out of the game came when Mesa got Jeff Huson on a foul popup to Thome at third base.

"The first thing I was thinking was 'Make sure you catch the ball,'" Thome said. "And then it was a very cool moment. In thinking how long it had been since the Indians had won. To catch the ball, and finally accomplish what we wanted to do, which was to win our division and know we were going to the postseason, there's nothing better. That was our first celebration, when it all started to happen for us. It was a special night, when we all knew this is our time, and we realized we had a chance to do something really big for years to come."

But first, they had to finish the regular season. After clinching the division, the Indians, incredibly, still had 21 more games remaining in the regular season.

"It wasn't exactly nail-biting time at the end," Hargrove said. "My biggest concern, after we clinched, was how do we keep this going for 21 more games, and not lose our momentum going into the postseason?"

One of the carrots Hargrove used to try to keep the players interested was trying to reach 100 wins, and then winning their division by as many games as possible.

A 7-0 win over Minnesota on July 2 extended the Indians' division lead to 10 games. On Aug. 29, they beat Toronto 4-1, to lead the division by 20½ games. They clinched on Sept. 8, extending their division lead to 23½ games.

It was like Secretariat at the Belmont, pulling away from the field (track announcer Chic Anderson: "He is moving like a tremendous machine!"). Secretariat won the Belmont by 31 lengths. When the Indians beat the Royals 17-7 for win No. 100, in the final game of the regular season, they had won the Central Division by 30 games, a major league record that might stand forever.

"'95, '96, '98 and even '99, were all great teams. But I thought '95 was the best," Hart said.

"Those guys liked to play. It all comes down to that. Every one of those guys liked to play, and they didn't like to sit," said Hargrove.

Belle, especially, didn't like to sit. With the Indians thrashing their way to win after win in the month of September, leading their division by well over 20 games, the tendency would have been to ease off the gas. None of the Indians did, but none of the Indians accelerated through the month like Belle, who played with an almost maniacal intensity through the last two months of the regular season.

"One thing I'll say about Albert, the eight years I was with him, I never saw him give away an at-bat. Not one time," said Hart. "We could be down 9-0, up 10-1, rainy day, road game, getaway day. Didn't matter. He never gave away an at-bat. He could be a little difficult. But he showed up. He played."

Belle walloped 17 home runs in September, tying Babe Ruth's major league record for most home runs in that month. Belle also set a major league record by hitting 31 home runs in a two-month span (August and September).

In the last 14 games of the regular season, Belle had a slash line of .365/.443/1.173. He was 19-for-52, and 13 of his 19 hits were home runs. Over the last 76 games of the season he hit 36 home runs, a pace that over a 162-game schedule would produce 77 home runs.

"Albert was in the zone, and nobody else could get into Albert's zone," Hargrove said. "Everybody could get into their own zones. But nobody got into Albert's. And he would stay in it."

It was the greatest statistical season of Belle's career, one of the greatest statistical seasons of anyone's career. He hit .317, with a .401 on-base percentage and .690 slugging percentage. He belted 50 home runs and 52 doubles, becoming the first player in major league history to hit 50 homers and 50 doubles in the same season, and Belle did it in a 144-game season, while having the 28th lowest strikeout rate (12.7) in the American League. He also scored 121 runs and drove in 126. Projected over a 162-game schedule, Belle's numbers would be 56 home runs, 58 doubles, 136 runs and 141 RBI.

Belle led the league in home runs, RBI, slugging percentage, runs, doubles, total bases and extra base hits. He had 103 extra base hits, 22 more than any other player in the league. He became the eighth player in major league history with 100 extra base hits, the first to do it since Stan Musial in 1948. He didn't win the Most

Valuable Player Award, mostly because of his irascible personality, which turned off so many voters that Belle finished second to Boston's Mo Vaughn in the MVP race. Vaughn led the league in strikeouts and had a 4.3 WAR compared to Belle's 7.0 WAR. Vaughn had one more first-place vote than Belle, 12-11, and had 308 points in the voting, to Belle's 300.

"Actually, I was surprised I got as many votes as I did," Belle said at the time. "I'm a little upset that they give the baseball writers all this power . . . I don't think the writers should be voting at all. I think it should be managers and coaches, and media members who are former ballplayers, because they know what we're going through."

In 1995, six of the Indians' nine regulars hit over .300: Murray (.323), Belle (.317), Thome and Baerga (.314 each), Lofton (.310) and Ramirez (.308). Lofton led the league in triples (13) and stolen bases (54).

The hitting coach through most of the Indians' glory years in the 1990s was Charlie Manuel, who had a nickname for everyone, including the general manager ("Hartbeat"). Manuel went on to manage the Philadelphia Phillies for nine years, starting in 2005. He took the Phillies to the postseason five consecutive years, 2007-11, including back-to-back trips to the World Series in 2008 and 2009, winning it all in 2008.

After going to the World Series in consecutive years, Manuel phoned Hart.

"Hartbeat, goddamn, son!" said Manuel. "They think we're something special over here in Philly. We can't even play with those Cleveland teams. We're not even in the same ballpark. It ain't even close."

The Indians in 1995 not only finished 30 games ahead of the second-place team in the AL Central, but the Indians finished 10 games ahead of any other team in the majors. The closest team to the Indians in either league was Atlanta, at 90-54.

"In a 144-game schedule I don't think anyone thought winning 100 games was a realistic goal," Hargrove said. "If there's any complaint I have about that team, it has to do with the fact that it is not recognized as being one of the all-time great offensive teams in the history of baseball. You look at the numbers and percentages of the 1927 Yankees, and teams like that, we compare very favorably to those teams, and that ('95 Indians team) never gets the credit."

The 1927 Yankees played 154 games, 10 more than the 1995 Indians. New York leads Cleveland, percentage-wise, but not outrageously so, in most offensive categories, including runs per game (6.3 to 5.8), batting average (.307 to .291), on-base percentage (.384 to .361), slugging (.488 to .479), OPS (.872 to .839) and OPS+ (127 to 116).

The 1995 Indians fare much better in the following comparison. The '27 Yankees finished with a record of 110-44. Through their first 144 games—the number of games the Indians played in 1995—the Yankees were 102-42. The 1961 Yankees went 109-53, but through 144 games they were 99-45. The 1998 Yankees, who some believe are second only to the '27 Yankees, finished 114-48, and through 144 games they were 103-41.

Some other great major league teams, with their records through 144 games in parenthesis: The 1954 Indians, 111-43 overall (104-40), the 1975 Cincinnati Reds, 108-54 overall (96-48), the 2018 Boston Red Sox, 108-54 overall (98-46), the 2001 Seattle Mariners, 116-46 overall (104-40) and the 1906 Chicago Cubs, 116-36 overall (110-34).

*　　*　　*

The 1995 postseason, Cleveland's first taste of postseason ball in 41 years, was a wild, electrifying ride through the first two rounds, followed by a deflating, empty climax on the biggest stage of all, which is probably the biggest reason why the '95 Indians aren't consistently mentioned in best-team-ever discussions.

At some point between the end of the regular season and the start of the postseason, Hargrove, who was about to become the first person in 41 years to manage the Cleveland Indians in a postseason series, phoned Oakland manager Tony La Russa and Minnesota manager Tom Kelly. Hargrove wanted to pick their brains on what a manager should expect in the postseason.

"My conversations with Tony and Tom were only about 15-20 minutes, and they were really helpful," Hargrove said. "They may have thought, 'What's this idiot calling me for?' but they were helpful."

La Russa and Kelly told Hargrove that the biggest mistake first-time managers in the postseason make is not realizing how everything is so much more immediate in the postseason.

"For example, in the regular season, you'd stay with a starter to get him through a rough patch. Let him give up two, three or four runs to get innings out of him," Hargrove said. "If you do that in the postseason, very often it's going to bite you. Because the first round is five games, the next two are seven games, and you don't have the luxury of having a month to make up for things like that."

But the best advice La Russa and Kelly gave Hargrove was advice Hargrove ignored.

"They both said to be sure and enjoy the journey. Don't get so caught up in the day-to-day minutiae that you don't get to enjoy the journey. But I found out that you can't enjoy the journey. Not until it's over, and you can look back on it," Hargrove said.

The first game of the Division Series vs. Boston was in many ways the wildest one of all in that postseason. Thanks to two rain delays, and 13 innings, the game, which started on Oct. 3, didn't end until 1:49 in the morning on Oct. 4. One of the enduring moments and visuals from the game came after Belle hit a game-tying home run in the bottom of the 11th inning, prompting Boston manager Kevin Kennedy to ask the umpires to confiscate Belle's bat. It was a reprise of Belle's corked bat shenanigans in Chicago in 1994, and Belle didn't take it too well. After the the umpires had confiscated the bat, Belle went to the top step of the Indians' dugout, and with the most menacing Belle glare ever, pulled up his uniform sleeve, flexed, and pointed to his bicep, while f-bombing the entire Boston team but Kennedy in particular.

"I know Kennedy didn't do that on his own," Belle said. "I know he was probably instructed to do that by (Boston general manager) Dan Duquette. I was sort of expecting it. In the playoffs, they were trying to find some way to get an advantage on us."

In the 12th, the Red Sox had a leadoff double, and the Indians had the potential winning run on third with none out, but neither team scored. It was 4-4 going into the bottom of the 13th. By this time, it was past 1:30 a.m., and it was raining, but not enough for the umpires to halt the game for a third time. Sitting in the stands with Sharon Hargrove were three of her children, who were in high school and middle school. Sharon told the three of them to go home, because they had school in the morning.

"Mom, please!" said the kids.

"You've got to go," said Sharon.

The kids went home.

Left-hander Zane Smith, Boston's seventh pitcher of the game, was on the mound. Manny Ramirez led off the bottom of the 13th by grounding out. Herbert Perry, pinch-hitting for left-handed-hitting Paul Sorrento, flied out for the second out. Tony Pena, the Indians' backup catcher, stepped to the plate. Smith's first three pitches to Pena were balls.

"Tony got to a 3-0 count, and I couldn't pinch run for him (if he reached base) because we'd already used Sandy (Alomar). So, we didn't have a catcher left," Hargrove said. "It got to 3-0 on Tony, and I turned our guys loose on 3-0 a lot. So, I'm debating whether to give Tony the take sign, or let him swing. I was at the far end of the dugout, trying to make up my mind. I'm thinking if I give him the take sign and he walks, then it's going to take a double and a single to get him in, because Tony didn't run well. If I let him swing, and he makes an out on a 3-0 pitch, that's not good. We need base runners. So, I was just reaching up to give him the take sign, and he swung and hit the ball out of the park."

When the ball landed in the left field bleachers, it was still raining, it was 1:49 a.m. and it was a 5-4 Indians' victory—the franchise's first postseason win since Game 6 of the 1948 World Series against the Boston Braves, which the Indians won, 4-3, to claim what is still their last World Series title.

After the game, the writers asked Hargrove if Pena had the green light to swing.

"I said, 'It was amber,' because I couldn't make up my mind, and by the time I did, it was too late," Hargrove said.

After meeting with the media in the interview room, Hargrove returned to his office, and was greeted by Sharon.

"Where are the kids?" said Mike.

"I sent them home," said Sharon.

"You sent them home?" said her incredulous husband.

"They were in the players' lot, getting into the car when Tony hit the home run—and they've never let me forget it," said Sharon, 23 years later.

After the game was decided, there was still the matter of Belle's confiscated bat. American League president Dr. Bobby Brown was at the game, and after it was over, Brown conducted an examination of the bat—this was around 3 a.m.—that ended with the bat not being X-rayed, but being cut in half.

"I told the umpires, 'Whatever you do, make sure they X-ray the bat. Don't let them saw it in half, because that's my 50-home run bat. I want to keep that bat, whenever it breaks.' They said they would make sure," Belle said.

Instead, Brown instructed Indians head groundskeeper Brandon Koehnke to get a saw, and cut the bat in half. Brown told reporters that the bat was cut in half rather than X-rayed in order to save time.

"I think Bobby Brown was there because he has it out for me, and he wanted to be there when they checked my bat," Belle said. "I don't know why I didn't think about it, but I should have run over there and made sure they would X-ray my bat instead of sawing it in half. That was the bat I hit my last 20 home runs with."

With Pena's home run serving as the exclamation point, the Indians made quick work of the Red Sox. In Game 2, Hershiser and three relievers combined on a three-hit shutout in a 4-0 Indians victory. Then the series shifted to Fenway Park, where the Indians completed the three-game sweep with an 8-2 rout.

Indians pitchers, overshadowed all year by their Muscle Beach lineup of mashers, led the way to the sweep. Boston hit .184 in the three games. Mo Vaughn, who hit .300 with 39 homers and 126 RBI in the regular season, and Jose Canseco (.306-24-81) were a combined 0-for-27 with nine strikeouts in the three games.

"We pitched Mo and Canseco better than we pitched anybody all year. (Pitching coach) Mark Wiley, who is one of the most creative baseball people I've ever been around, he and (bullpen coach) Luis Isaac came up with the plan on how to pitch those guys," said Hargrove.

The other American League Division Series was as long as the Cleveland-Boston series was short. It wasn't until the 11th inning of the deciding Game 5 that Seattle beat the Yankees, 6-5, to advance to the ALCS against Cleveland.

The first inning of Game 1 of the Cleveland-Seattle ALCS is one of the most confounding postseason innings ever. Seattle's starting pitcher was 22-year-old rookie Bob Wolcott, who had spent most of the year in the minor leagues and had only started six games for the Mariners all year. Game 1 of the ALCS was the seventh start of his major league career. Understandably intimidated by Cleveland's lineup, Wolcott in the top of the first inning walked the bases loaded on 13 pitches. But with the bases loaded and nobody out, Wolcott retired the next three batters in order, two of them future Hall of Famers. Wolcott struck out Belle, got Murray on an infield popup, and retired Thome on a ground ball to end the inning. In a game that looked like the Indians would blow it open in the first inning, Wolcott pitched seven innings and beat Cleveland 3-2.

"It was one of those things where you walked away scratching your head," said Hargrove.

"When Seattle beat New York in the final game of their series, we were sitting in our plane, on the tarmac, waiting to see if we were going to go to Seattle or New York," Hart said. "Then when Seattle brought Randy Johnson in to pitch in relief the last three innings of that game, I wanted Seattle to win it, because that meant we would only get Johnson twice (in the ALCS). We weren't going to get him three times, and we probably wouldn't get him until Game 3. But then we faced Wolcott, hit 12 rockets off him, but still lost, and I'm thinking, 'Shit, that just evened it out.'"

The Indians regrouped to win the second game, 5-2. Hershiser was brilliant, pitching eight innings, allowing one run on four hits, and Ramirez went 4-for-4, with two home runs. The series then shifted to Cleveland, and in Game 3, sure enough, Johnson started and did his Johnson thing, allowing one earned run in eight innings. But so did Nagy, and the game went into extra innings. The Mariners scored three runs in the 11th against Cleveland's vaunted bullpen to win, 5-2.

But again, the Indians rallied. In Game 4, Ken Hill and three relievers combined on a six-hit 7-0 shutout. In Game 5, Seattle took a 2-1 lead into the bottom of the sixth, when Thome blasted a two-run home run to make it 3-2. Hershiser was great again—

one earned run in six innings—and Tavarez, Assenmacher, Plunk and Mesa combined for three hitless and scoreless innings in the 3-2 victory that gave Cleveland a 3-2 lead in the series. That set the stage for Game 6 back in Seattle, where it would be Martinez against Johnson.

"David vs. Goliath!" cracked Martinez, in the interview room, after the off-day workout.

Going into that dramatic Game 6, there was also a quiet little subplot involving Kenny Lofton. The Indians' cocky, ultra-competitive center fielder had this thing about facing Johnson, who, said Hargrove, "threw 99 mph, and didn't care if he hit you."

Lofton would never, ever ask for a day off, but every time the Indians played Seattle, Lofton would come into Hargrove's office and would say he was feeling a little tired, and could maybe use a day off on such and such a day. Hargrove would say OK, and then after Lofton left, Hargrove would check the pitching probables, and, sure enough, Johnson was scheduled to pitch that day.

"Kenny would say, 'I can't hit that guy,' but Kenny was the kind of guy who could really rattle Randy," Hargrove said. "So, I told Kenny, 'Kenny, you're golden off this guy. It may not feel like it, but you are. You hit this guy good.' And I went and looked it up and he was hitting .222 against him."

But not on Oct. 17, 1995, Game 6 of the ALCS.

In Lofton's first two at-bats of that game, Johnson struck him out. But in Lofton's third at bat, he singled to left field, driving in Alvaro Espinoza with the first run of the game. Espinoza started that game at third base in place of Thome, who REALLY couldn't hit Johnson, to the point that he almost never faced him. In the 19-year span when they were both active major-league players, Thome only had nine at-bats against Johnson. He had one hit and six strikeouts, although the one hit, naturally, was a home run.

Lofton's RBI single gave Cleveland a 1-0 lead against Goliath, while David (Martinez) was mowing down the Mariners, pitching seven scoreless innings. In the top of the eighth, with Johnson still on the mound, and the Indians still leading 1-0, Pena led off with a double to right field and was replaced by pinch runner Ruben Amaro. Lofton, attempting to bunt Amaro to third, did so, and wound up with a bunt single when he beat Johnson's throw to first. Lofton then stole second, as Amaro held third.

Goliath was starting to wobble.

A 2-0 pitch to Omar Vizquel glanced off the glove of catcher Dan Wilson, and as the ball rolled towards the on-deck circle near the Indians' dugout on the first base side, Amaro raced home with the Indians' second run. Lofton, running like the wind, came blazing around third base and never hesitated. He was halfway between third and home before Amaro touched the plate. With a dejected Johnson standing absent-mindedly near home plate, his back to the third base line, waiting for the toss from Wilson, Lofton came streaking down the line and slid past the unsuspecting Johnson for a second run to make it 3-0. With the American League pennant on the line, in the eighth inning of a one-run game, Lofton had scored from second base on a passed ball.

"When Kenny was rounding third and coming home, I could feel the blood leaving the ends of my fingers," Hargrove said. "Randy was going to get the ball, and he was on his heels. You could tell by his face he was pissed, and he had no idea Kenny was coming. I've never seen a play like that. First of all, who would do that? After Kenny scored, I felt like we had the game won."

They did. Especially when the next batter, Carlos Baerga, hit a line drive over the right field wall off the totally discombobulated Johnson, giving the Indians a 4-0 lead.

Tavarez, in relief of Martinez, retired the side in order in the eighth inning. Then it was Mesa in the ninth, to face the meat of the Mariners' order. He retired the first batter, future Hall of Famer Ken Griffey Jr., on a groundout. He struck out the second batter, future Hall of Famer Edgar Martinez. Tino Martinez walked, but Mesa got Jay Buhner on a groundout to Espinoza at third to end the game, end the series and send the Indians to their first World Series in 41 years.

"In that last game in Seattle, you couldn't hear," Hargrove said. "I remember sitting right next to Buddy Bell, and to hear each other we had to lean over and yell into each other's ears. About the fourth inning I thought to myself, 'We have to win this thing, because I can't take one more game in this place.' It was so loud and tension-filled, and then to win it the way we won it. You finally let your-self think that you were going to the World Series. Every little kid's dream."

Prior to that final game in Seattle, Sharon Hargrove asked her husband if the wives could come into the clubhouse after the game if the Indians won. "He said, 'If you can assure me none of the wives will complain about getting champagne in their hair or on their dresses,'" Sharon said. "So, I told the wives, 'If we get to go in, don't you complain about anything.'"

The celebration went on forever, as any 41-year-drought-de-stroying celebration is wont to do.

"I thought, there's 41 years of frustration down the toilet, and we were fortunate enough to be the ones who did it," Hargrove said.

"The best part of it," said Sharon, "is when everything was over, we had to walk across the playing field of the Kingdome to get to the busses and we're all talking about the same thing: 'We just won a dang game in here to go to the World Series.' That game was so exciting."

The rollicking, celebratory plane ride home to Cleveland, with all the players, front office personnel and support staff, plus their wives, has long ago passed into legend.

"I don't think anyone sat in their seats the whole trip," said Sharon.

"That was a pretty celebratory team," said Hargrove, who stunned everyone by spending a good portion of the flight literally dancing in the aisles.

"I never thought I'd see my manager dancing the macarena in the aisle, in first class, in an airplane," said Hart.

"It was a good time," said Hargrove. "A great time."

*   *   *

While the Indians felt like they had been in a six-game steel cage match with the Mariners, the Atlanta Braves breezed to a sweep of Cincinnati in the NLCS, holding the Reds to a total of five runs in the four games. In reaching the World Series for the third time in the last five years, the Braves went 7-1 against Colorado and Cin-cinnati, outscoring those two teams 46-24. In going to the World

Series for the first time in 41 years, the Indians went 7-2 against Boston and Seattle, outscoring those two teams 40-18.

Counting the postseason, the Indians went into the World Series with a record of 107-46, the Braves 97-55. They were the two best teams in baseball. The Braves won the Series in six games, and five of the six, including three of the Indians' losses, were one-run games. In the regular season the Indians were 28-14 in one-run games, but they lost three one-run games in the World Series, including the first game, a somewhat controversial 3-2 Atlanta win in which Greg Maddux pitched a complete-game two-hitter. Hershiser, the MVP of the ALCS, combined with three relievers to pitch a three-hitter—but lost.

Hershiser took some heat for asking out of the game in the seventh inning. With the score tied at 1-1, Hershiser walked the first two batters in the bottom of the seventh. He threw 10 pitches to the two batters, and eight of them were balls.

"All of a sudden it was just gone," said Hershiser after the game. "Every pitch I threw was high and outside. I tried to make adjustments, but nothing was working."

After the second walk, Hershiser motioned for pitching coach Mark Wiley to come to the mound.

"He told Mark, 'I've lost my release point. I can't find it,'" Hargrove said. "That's kind of unusual for a pitcher who has pitched as long as Orel had. But he recognized that, and didn't want to screw up our chances of winning the ballgame. I really admire and respect him for that."

Wiley signaled to a stunned Hargrove in the dugout that the Indians had to get a reliever into the game.

"I'm thinking, 'Holy shit!' This was the seventh inning. His pitch count was good. He felt strong. And Orel was The Bulldog," said Hargrove. "It caught us all by surprise because there was no indication. You want your players to be honest with you, and, quite honestly, most of them aren't. They have that competitive nature. They'll say, 'I started this, let me finish it,' or 'Let me get out of this.'"

Instead, Hershiser said get me out of this.

"Orel didn't run scared. He was concerned about the team," said Hargrove. "He didn't do this out of fear. It wasn't him trying to beg out."

Following the game, Hargrove told the media that Orel had asked out of the game, which was apparently a bad choice of words.

"The next day, Orel was pissed," said Hargrove. "He asked me, 'Why did you say that?' And I said, 'What did you want me to say? That's what happened. I thought it was admirable.' But he didn't see it that way. He wanted me to protect him more than that, and I didn't know how to. We took Orel out of the game in the middle of an inning, when he'd been cruising."

Paul Assenmacher relieved Hershiser, and walked pinch hitter Mike Devereaux, loading the bases with no outs. Julian Tavarez relieved Assenmacher and Luis Polonia grounded into a force out at second, allowing the runner from third to score, giving Atlanta a 2-1 lead. Rafael Belliard's squeeze bunt scored a second run, to make it 3-1. The Braves scored two runs in the inning without a hit. The Indians scored a run in the ninth, but lost 3-2.

The Braves, behind Tom Glavine, won Game 2, 4-3. The Indians won 7-6 in Game 3 and 5-4 in Game 5, but Atlanta's Series-clinching win was a 1-0 victory in Game 6, in Atlanta. David Justice, leading off the sixth inning, hit a home run off Jim Poole. Glavine nearly pitched a no-hitter. He and closer Mark Wohlers combined on a one-hitter. Cleveland's only hit was a single by Tony Pena, leading off the top of the sixth.

The 1995 World Series was the series, and the postseason, of the ever-widening strike zone, and no team was better equipped to take advantage of that than the Braves, with three future Hall of Famers—Glavine, Maddux and John Smoltz—in their rotation.

"At that time, where the catcher set up, if the pitcher hit his glove, then it was called a strike. (Braves catcher) Javy Lopez set up far off the plate, and they would hit that spot, and get the strike," Hargrove said.

"Game 6 was a perfect example of that, but it was that way through the whole thing. It's easy to point fingers, but you move on," said Hart.

"Our players would come back to the bench and say, 'Grover, we can't reach those balls. We can't get to them,'" Hargrove said. "I would say something to Joe Brinkman, or whoever was umpiring home plate, I'd say, 'You've got to get them *close* to the plate.'"

In Game 6, Glavine, who averaged a modest 5.8 strikeouts per nine innings during the regular season, and 5.3 for his career, struck out eight Indians in eight innings. In his other three postseason starts that year Glavine struck out three, five and three batters.

"The funny thing was, that going into the Series, we felt there was a possibility that would happen," Hart said. "That these guys (Braves starters) are going to nibble. Smoltz was their only power guy. Those were the kind of staffs that we just ate up. But when you're getting balls 3, 4, 5 inches off the plate being called strikes, there's nothing you can do. Our guys started expanding the zone, and off we went."

Indians pitchers presumably would have gotten those same pitches off the plate called strikes, but Indians pitchers were Indians pitchers. Three of the Braves' starters were future Hall of Famers, who could consistently hit the catcher's glove whether it was on or off the plate.

"We made some good adjustments as that series went on, but then we got to Atlanta and Game 6 with Glavine, to their credit they hit the corners," Thome said. "Now the strike zone was a little wide, and we all know that. So, that was a tough one to swallow. Because you think, 'I've got to find a way to hit balls that aren't on the plate. How are we supposed to manufacture runs?'"

"The strike zone was huge, but the advantage was certainly in Atlanta's favor. You've got to give them credit. They had the pitchers who could do it," said Hargrove.

It was a deflating climax to an electrifying season for a franchise tasting postseason play for the first time in almost half a century. It was the best of Hargrove's five consecutive division winners, maybe one of the best teams ever that didn't win the World Series, and certainly the best offensive team in Indians history.

A season that began with Hargrove managing replacement players—"Mel was a good guy, but he was Mel"—ended with the Indians losing 1-0 in Game 6 of the World Series. Nevertheless, a quantum leap had been made in the reconstruction of a once-proud franchise. Four years after losing 105 games, the Indians had won 109, and the American League pennant.

It was almost like Game 6 in Seattle was their World Series.

"We beat Randy Johnson in Game 6. That was the absolute highlight of my career," Hart said. "I remember going down to the locker room after the game, thinking about the five or six years we put into this thing. Thinking about the strike, when we knew we were a post-season team, and looking at our young players, our staff, Grover, his staff, our veteran players, everybody in there celebrating, acting like 18-year-olds.

"I just stood away, off to the side, and for five minutes I just cried. I was so happy. I was so happy for all those kids who bought in. I was happy for the staff, for Mike, all the coaches who had been there through the lean years. I was happy for the veteran players. And I was happy for the organization. I was standing off by myself, and before I went in and joined it, I just stood back, took it all in and said, 'It doesn't get any better than this.'"

1. An all-state safety and backup quarter-back at Perryton High School, Hargrove was recruited in football by Texas A&M and Texas Christian University. *(Leo Shuler)*

2. Hargrove attended Northwestern Oklahoma State University on a football scholarship. His father talked him into trying out for the baseball team as a walk-on. Three years later he was drafted by the Texas Rangers. *(Northwestern Oklahoma State University Athletic Department)*

3. Dudley Michael Hargrove (left) and his father, Dudley Hargrove, who in the 1950s was invited to spring training with the Dodgers and the Giants. When Mike was in his mid-teens, he played on a traveling fast-pitch softball team with his father. "He was the third baseman. I played first. I hit third and Dad hit fourth. That was pretty cool." *(Courtesy of Mike Hargrove)*

4. The infamous 1974 Beer Night riot in Cleveland. Hargrove (in foreground, left fist locked and loaded) and his Texas Rangers teammates prepare to administer some frontier justice to a fan who wandered into the wrong part of town. "That was my first experience in Cleveland," Hargrove said. "The first time I had ever seen Cleveland in my life." *(The Cleveland Press Collection, Michael Schwartz Library, Cleveland State University)*

5. As a player, Hargrove had a 12-year career in the big leagues, seven with the Indians. In all seven he had more walks than strikeouts. In 1981 he led the American League with a .424 on-base percentage. His .396 career on-base percentage ranks ninth on the Indians' all-time list, and his 111 walks in 1980 are the most by any player in Indians history not named Jim Thome or Carlos Santana. *(Cleveland Indians)*

6. Hargrove's tedious between-pitches routine—"The human rain delay," quipped Reggie Jackson—eventually drew the ire of the American League. "Mike, you've got to speed it up," AL supervisor of umpires Dick Butler once told him. "This is ridiculous." *(Cleveland Indians)*

7. Mike and Sharon Hargrove, outside old Cleveland Stadium, probably around 1979, the year he was traded to the Indians. They were a baseball partnership. When it came to her husband's career, Sharon's antenna were always up. "Sharon was his anchor," said one of his baseball bosses. *(Courtesy of Mike and Sharon Hargrove)*

8. After 12 years as a major-league player, Hargrove literally went back to square one in hopes of becoming a major league manager. Here, in 1986, is square one: as the hitting coach for the Indians' minor league team at Batavia, New York. In 1985 Hargrove's salary as a player with the Indians was $458,000. In 1986 his salary at Batavia was $6,000. *(Courtesy of Mike and Sharon Hargrove)*

9. Manager Mike Hargrove and general manager John Hart. One was patient to a fault, the other was impatient to a fault. But they met in the middle and orchestrated the greatest five-year run in Indians history. "It was the best time of my life as a professional," said Hart. *(Akron Beacon Journal)*

10. Opening Day, 1994, at brand-new Jacobs Field. It was hard to decide which was more impressive: the new ballpark or the home team lineup. From Hargrove (far right) that's, in order, Kenny Lofton, Omar Vizquel, Carlos Baerga, Albert Belle, Eddie Murray and (walking) Candy Maldonado. *(Gregory Drezdzon)*

11. While managing those great Indians teams, Hargrove (here congratulating a very young Jim Thome) didn't get enough credit for handling a clubhouse filled with some of the biggest egos, biggest personalities, and biggest names in the sport. "In the clubhouse he was the best I'd ever seen," said John Hart. "I never worried about the clubhouse. Never." *(Gregory Drezdzon)*

12. Hargrove "helps" Kenny Lofton with his stretching during a spring training drill. It was Lofton's electrifying dash, scoring from second base on a passed ball, that iced the Indians' clinching Game 6 victory in the 1995 ALCS in Seattle. "When Kenny was rounding third and coming home," said Hargrove, "I could feel the blood leaving the ends of my fingers." (*Akron Beacon Journal*)

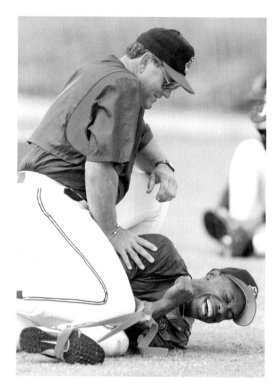

13. The one, the only, Albert Belle. "He was one of those guys who could be OK for eight days, and then for two days you weren't sure what you had going on," said John Hart. Hargrove was Belle's first and last manager in pro ball. "Given the choice of having Albert or not having Albert, the whole package, I would take Albert every time," Hargrove said. "He's a good guy. When he lets himself be, Albert's a good guy." (*Gregory Drezdzon*)

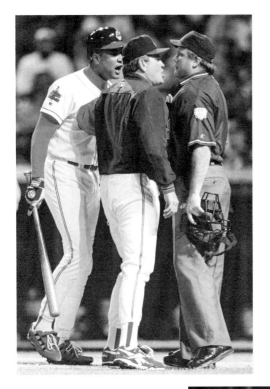

14. Hargrove had a Texas temper that sometimes flared, especially when he sensed one of his players was in danger of being thrown out of a game. "There were a lot of times when I would go out to argue even when I knew the umpire made the right call. But I would go out because the player was arguing, and I wanted to let him know I was there." *(Akron Beacon Journal)*

15. During a 1997 postseason game, Hargrove visits the mound to talk to pitcher Charles Nagy, third baseman Matt Williams and catcher Sandy Alomar Jr. It was Williams' only year with the Indians, but they made it to Game 7 of the World Series, and Hargrove felt a big reason why was "Matt Williams' mental toughness rubbing off on everyone else." *(Akron Beacon Journal)*

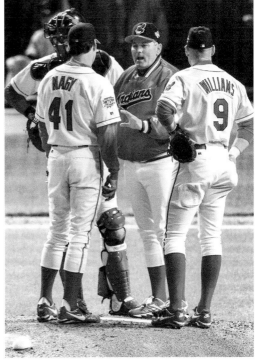

16. A Hargrove team photo at Jacobs Field. Left to right: Pam, Missy, Sharon, Kim, Andy, Mike, Shelly. Talk about a baseball odyssey: From 1970 to 1995 the Hargroves lived in 23 houses in 25 years. *(Courtesy of Mike and Sharon Hargrove)*

17. Back with the Indians as a special advisor, Hargrove throws out the first pitch for game 2 of the ALCS at Progressive Field on Oct. 15, 2016. *(UPI / Alamy Stock Photo)*

18. Reflecting on 49 years of marriage and baseball, Sharon Hargrove said, "We're from a high school in Perryton, Texas that didn't even have a baseball team. How did this happen?" *(Courtesy of Mike and Sharon Hargrove)*

CHAPTER 10

Albert

"We had to learn how to handle this guy."

On May 11, 1991, during the seventh inning of another forget-table Indians' loss, this one 2-1, to the California Angels, in front of 14,720 bored stragglers rattling around baseball's largest mauso-leum, in the summer that would produce a 105-loss Indians season, Angels catcher Ron Tingley hit a sharp foul ball down the left field line. The ball hit off the wall in foul territory and ricocheted towards Indians left fielder Albert Belle.

Belle casually picked up the ball, turned and fired a rocket into the stands, hitting a fan standing in the third row who was heckling Belle. The ball hit the fan square in the chest, leaving a good-sized welt.

In the Indians dugout, first-base coach Mike Hargrove turned toward third-base coach Jeff Newman.

"Did he just do what I think he did?" asked Hargrove.

"I think so," said Newman.

Two months later, Hargrove would become manager of the Indians. For seven of the next 10 years, six in Cleveland and one in Baltimore, Hargrove would be the wild, untamed Belle's manager/wrangler. Hargrove was also Belle's manager in Belle's first two years in the minor leagues. Lucky Hargrove. He had a front row seat for the best and the worst of Belle's explosive career. The best was Belle in the batter's box. The worst was everything else.

"Albert was really lucky that Mike was his guy, so to speak, for most of his career," said Jeff Scott, the Indians' scouting and farm director, who scouted, drafted and signed Belle for the Indians. "Because, not many people would have had the temperament to handle everything with Albert that you had to handle, and still not disrupt what was going on with the rest of the guys in the clubhouse."

Of all the marquee names, high-profile, big-ego, larger-than-life players and personalities on those powerhouse Indians teams in that era, none cast a bigger or more menacing shadow than Albert Jojuan Belle, out of Shreveport, Louisiana, by way of Louisiana State University, until he got kicked off the baseball team in his junior year. A prodigious, intimidating, highly intelligent slugger—he graduated sixth out of 266 in his high school class—Belle would have been the first overall pick in the 1987 Draft if he didn't have the personality of a rattlesnake. Instead, he watched 46 players come off the board before the desperate Indians crossed their fingers and called his name in the second round. Less than a year after signing with the Indians, Belle sour-pussed his way into the Mexican League. He wasted little time in getting thrown out of the league, eliciting a priceless observation by one-time Indians executive Dan O'Brien: "Normally, you get thrown *into* the Mexican League."

Through the years, the longer Hargrove managed Belle, the more he learned how to manage Belle. One of the things Hargrove learned was that he had to pick his battles.

"I had to be more aware of Albert than other players, to make sure he wasn't distracted by things that didn't mean anything," Hargrove said. "That would happen every once in a while. He would be distracted by something, not to the point that he couldn't play, but that he would make a mountain out of a molehill."

With Belle, of course, the whole world was a molehill.

"The fans would bother him a lot," Hargrove said. "After one of the games I told him, 'Don't react and do something stupid. Let me know, and I'll have security take care of it.' In Detroit one day, he came to me and said, 'Grover, there are a couple of guys out there who are getting really personal.' I said, 'OK.' And I had security go check it out. I don't think they threw the fans out. They just told them to calm down a little. With Albert, you would always try to look out in front, and see what was coming."

Scott first saw the Belle locomotive coming almost immediately after the Indians drafted him. He was known then as Joey Belle, and the Indians took him with the 15th pick of the second round, making him the 47th player selected overall in the 1987 Draft. Scott knew he wanted to get someone into the Belle house as soon as possible to make an initial offer, because the Indians knew it was going to be a difficult signing.

"He should have been a first-round pick, but he wasn't," Scott said. "Everybody knew why he wasn't. But at the time, the Belles didn't understand that."

Even though he should have been a first-round pick, there was no way the Indians were going to give Belle first-round money.

Before the Indians' first official meeting with the Belles, Scott began formulating in his mind the approach the team would take. It would go something like this: "We still drafted you. We liked you best. We'll give you more than the going rate, but we're not going to give you the going rate for a first-round pick."

The first step, however, was getting somebody from the Indians down to Shreveport and into the Belle house to make the initial offer. The Indians didn't want the area scout, Red Gaskell, to go in alone and have to deal with Carrie Belle, Joey's mother, because, said Scott, "We heard stories."

So, the Indians sent team president and, in Scott's words, "suave gentleman" Dan O'Brien down to Louisiana to go into the Belle house with Gaskell. The two men went in on a Friday and made the offer. They went back the next day, but came away with no deal. O'Brien went to the airport to fly back to Cleveland, but first he called Indians general manager Joe Klein to give him an update on the negotiations.

"In all my years, nobody like this one," said O'Brien to Klein. "She's all yours now, big boy."

"So, we just let them sit," said Scott, of the Belles. "Our initial offer was $52,500, and the rest of it was paying for Joey's school, which would have been two semesters. So, a package of $60,000, plus school. We let them sit a while."

In the meantime, the Indians flew to Arlington, Texas, for the start of a four-game series on July 9. Klein accompanied the team, with the intention of making the 3½-hour drive to Shreveport to continue the Belle negotiations. Klein did that, and spent a day speaking with the Belles, but they never talked money. They talked baseball, and what the Indians' plans were for Joey.

"We never threw a number out there, and neither did Carrie,"

Scott said. "She always just said, 'He should be treated as a first-rounder.' She was very leery of the NCAA, and didn't understand that we didn't give a rat's ass about the NCAA. But that was her hang-up. She didn't want him to lose his eligibility, so she was as careful as careful could be."

This was strike two for the Indians.

Klein drove back to Arlington with no deal, but not before calling Scott to give him an update on the negotiations.

"Joe called me and said, 'I have to be in the office on Monday, so he's all yours, big boy,' using Danny's line," said Scott. "I said, 'Gee, thanks.'"

By now, it's the end of July, and the Indians are no closer to signing Belle than they were on the day they drafted him. Belle was playing in the Cape Cod League, so Scott decided to drive up there for a weekend, to watch Belle play and to talk to him. Before he left, Scott called Carrie Belle.

"I told her what I was going to do, but promised her I wouldn't talk money with him or anything like that," Scott said. "She said that was fine, and I told her I would call her from my office in Cleveland on Monday and let her know how things went, and to see if we could move this thing along."

So, Scott motored up to the Cape, and, he said, "That was when I got my first clue about the real Joey." The first game Scott saw, the opposing pitcher was Derek Lilliquist, who was a first-round pick by the Braves that year, but he hadn't signed yet, either. In his first at-bat against Lilliquist, Belle hit a home run.

"I think the ball ended up in Nantucket," Scott said. "He just killed it. Then he stood at home plate and watched it. Then he took his sweet time getting around the bases, which didn't go over real well with Lilliquist. Nothing happened. Nothing was said. And I'm sitting there thinking, 'OK, this is interesting. This is what I got us into here.'"

In Belle's next at-bat, he hit a one-hopper back to the mound.

"Lilliquist fields it," said Scott. "Joey starts to run, and when he sees Lilliquist field it, he stops. He was going to be thrown out by 60 feet. He just stopped running. Lilliquist, out of the corner of his eye, sees Joey stop. So, then Lilliquist stops. Joey starts to run, Lilliquist starts to throw, and then Joey stops again, so Lilliquist stops. This went on for like three times. Finally, Lilliquist throws to first, and he's out. I'm sitting there thinking, 'This is just great.'"

Scott talked to Belle after the game and invited him to dinner, but Belle declined because his mother didn't want him to eat with Scott out of fear of breaking an NCAA rule. So, Belle and Scott sat in the house where Belle was living and talked for two hours.

"The more I got to know the family, the more I understood why things were the way they were, and I knew it was going to be a tough task," Scott said. "I knew he wanted to play baseball. That was part of his gig. But it wasn't going to be easy."

Now, it was getting into mid-August, and there was still no deal. Teams could negotiate with a drafted player up until the time the player returned to school. Belle, who had been thrown off the team at LSU, was planning on enrolling at the University of Texas, and that day was fast approaching.

Finally, there was a breakthrough when Scott got a phone call from agent Alan Hendricks, who was representing another player the Indians had taken in the draft. Hendricks wanted to know how the kid was doing.

"But that's not why I'm calling. Do you know Jeff Moorad?" said Hendricks, referring to another player agent.

"Yeah, a little bit," said Scott.

"Well, he's in a quandary. How bad do you want to sign your second-round draft pick?" said Hendricks, referring to Belle.

"There are days right now where I don't want to sign him. Just cut my losses and move on. But I owe it to us to try," Scott said.

"Well," said Hendricks, "Moorad is representing him, but he doesn't want to come out of the closet because it's been a tough deal, getting to talk to the mother, and all that."

"Tell me about it," said Scott, sarcastically.

"Why don't you just say a little birdie told you something, and you can handle it from there," said Hendricks.

So that's what they did. Scott called Moorad and told him exactly where things were at, what the deal was. Moorad told Scott what Carrie wanted. Scott said, "We'll pay more than the going rate that second-rounders are getting, but I'm not giving him a six-figure signing bonus."

"I understand. What will it be?" asked Moorad.

"I'll split the difference with you," said Scott. "I'll give him 80 grand, and three semesters of school, instead of two. I'll soften it for him a little, but it's not going to be the $120,000 or $130,000 she's looking for. That's not going to happen."

"OK," said Moorad.

Scott then set up a conference call for the next day, a drop-dead, "we sign him, or we don't sign him" day of reckoning. The call would include Belle and his mother, Moorad, Scott, Hargrove, who at the time was the manager of the Indians' Class-A team in Kinston, North Carolina, and Hargrove's coaches.

"I called Grover and said, 'This is the deal. You're going to have a new left fielder in a couple of days, or you're not.' I told him what was going on with Belle, and said we're going to have a conference call, and we're either getting him signed tomorrow night, or we're not getting him signed," Scott said.

By this time, it was getting near the end of the minor league season. Kinston only had 10 games left, meaning Scott was willing to burn a whole year of service time just to get a look at Belle in 10 minor league games. At that time, drafted players only had three years to play their way onto the major league team's 40-man roster, or the player could be selected by another team in the Rule 5 draft. Hargrove asked Scott why he was willing to give up a whole year, meaning Belle would only have two years left before another team could draft him from the Indians.

"If he doesn't do what he's supposed to do, in two years we're going to want to get rid of him anyway," Scott said.

"And you're sending him to me?" Hargrove asked.

"Mike, he can hit. If there's anything I know, it's that this kid can hit, and he can hit the ball out of the ballpark. The rest of it, we're going to have to work out together."

So, the next day the conference call took place, with Scott joining Hargrove, all of his coaches, and even the trainer, all of them sitting around a big case of Coors Light in a tub in Hargrove's office.

"I was half tanked by the time we got the thing done," Scott said, with a laugh.

The call came through, and, with Moorad, Belle, Hargrove and his staff all listening, Scott and Carrie Belle are going back and forth, and back and forth.

"She finally agrees to the $80,000, the schooling, and the bonus," Scott said.

"OK, you guys take care of it from here," said Moorad, who hung up.

"So, I'm on the phone with Mrs. Belle and Joey, and I'm going to give her the standard, 'What does he need to bring with him?' talk. I told her, 'Don't even worry about housing. We'll put him up in a hotel for the time he's here. That's a little bit more for you. It's too late in the season to find any housing. He doesn't need to bring any clothing with him. Couple pair of drawers, couple T-shirts. That's all these guys wear, anyway. Don't worry about anything.' So, everything's done. Everything's cool. I'll pick Joey up at the airport. His plane ticket is pre-paid. Everything is good. And then she says to me, in her Southern accent, 'I guess Mr. O'Brien's words to me weren't any good.'"

Scott was stunned.

"What?" he said.

"Well, Mr. O'Brien offered me $52,500 and the bonus, and the bonus would be in cash," said Carrie Belle.

"Really? This is where we're at?" said an incredulous Scott.

"I blew a cork, for the first time since this all began," said Scott, over 30 years later. "She didn't understand that the $52,500 and the bonus were in the past. We had gone way beyond that."

Scott was ready to walk away from the deal and the Belles, once and for all.

"I said, 'That's fine.' I wished Joey well. He was going to go to the University of Texas for his senior year. They didn't want him back at LSU. Then, for the first time on the call, Joey spoke. He said, 'Mom, I'm satisfied with things. I'm going to go play ball tomorrow.'"

"OK," said Carrie Belle.

That was it. A deal had finally, finally been struck.

"He hadn't signed anything yet," said Scott. "But he had just turned 21, so I didn't need to get her signature."

The next day Scott picked up Belle at the airport, drove him to Kinston, signed him to his first professional contract, and then he went out and took batting practice.

"It was one of the most impressive BPs I've ever seen, then or now," said Scott. "Hargrove and I are standing behind the cage, and (coach) Brian Graham is throwing BP. Both teams stopped and watched, in awe. They watched where he was hitting balls, and how hard he was hitting balls. When it was over, Hargrove says to me, 'If you had signed this son of a bitch earlier, we would have won both halves.'"

Belle played in Kinston's last 10 games of the season, hitting .324 (12-for-37), with a .444 on-base percentage, a .622 slugging percentage, three home runs and nine RBI.

Then Belle was sent to the Indians' instructional league team in Florida, where Hargrove would be his manager again.

"There aren't many guys who could have handled Belle as well as Mike did. I know it was difficult," Scott said.

During the 1987 instructional league, Belle struggled, for probably the first time in his baseball career. He hit .200, and he didn't know how to handle it, because he never had to handle failure before. In one of the games it was tied, late in the game, and Belle was up with runners at second and third and two outs. Belle grounded out to third, leaving the runners stranded. Belle ran hard to first, came back to the dugout, put his helmet in his bag, then just started walking.

"The complex was four fields, with a tower in the middle of it, and the back two fields were in orange groves," said Scott. "I'm watching him, and he's walking towards the tower, and I assume it's to get a drink. But he just keeps walking. Walks through the back field and all the way through all the orange groves. He's 500 feet away, and he's still walking."

A friend said to Scott, "What are you going to do?"

"Nothing," said Scott. "I mean, what were we going to do? I ain't going to chase him."

The inning ended, and as the Indians team took the field, the center fielder and right fielder started gesturing wildly towards the bench that there was nobody in left field.

"Where the fuck did he go?" said Hargrove to Scott.

"Just put somebody in for him," said Scott.

"Where the fuck did he go?" Hargrove asked again.

"Just put somebody in for him. We'll talk later," said Scott.

Hargrove put somebody in for Belle, but wasn't done talking with Scott. "Where did he go?" Hargrove said, one more time.

"He just had a meltdown."

"Why? Because he made an out? He's made a lot of outs."

"Let's just wait and see what happens, then we'll deal with it."

Neither man spoke for a short time, then, both men were shocked.

"Joey starts walking back towards us," said Scott. "I'm watching him the whole way. He has his head down, because he knows he screwed up. He gets near the dugout, and Brian Graham was there, and he and Joey developed a little bit of a relationship. I told Brian, 'Go tell the big son of a bitch that we don't want to talk to him today. I'm not going to let him ruin my weekend. Tell him to show up at 7 o'clock Monday morning, and we'll adjudicate this little situation.'"

Belle showed up promptly at 7 o'clock on Monday morning. He met with Scott and Hargrove, who told Belle his behavior was unacceptable, that he had come to the instructional league with baggage, and that he needed to be on his best behavior all the time.

"I told him, 'You don't have to be here for the instructional league, but the last thing I want to do is send you home, because that would be just one more nail in your coffin. But I will,'" said Scott. "I said, 'If anything like this happens again, I'm going to put you on a plane, and you're going home. In the meantime, you've got to go out there and apologize to your teammates for walking out on them in the middle of the ballgame. If you don't do that, you're going home.'"

Belle quickly apologized.

"Yes sir, it won't happen again."

"And he did. He apologized to everybody, and he was a perfect angel the rest of the way," said Scott. "Mike said later, 'That was the easiest bad situation I ever had with him.'"

*   *   *

During spring training in 1988, Indians officials wrestled with the decision over what minor league level they should choose for Belle. Hank Peters, who had replaced the fired Joe Klein as the Indians' general manager, asked Scott where he would start Belle, and Scott told Peters that Belle "thinks he belongs in the big leagues like yesterday." Scott said he felt Belle could handle the big leagues, that he might struggle early, but he'd figure it out in the second half. So, Scott recommended Belle start at Triple-A Colorado Springs.

Instead, the Indians sent Belle to Class-A Waterloo in the Midwest League. That was a level below Kinston, where Belle played 10 games at the end of the '87 season, after finally signing with Cleveland. In 1988 Belle only played nine games at Waterloo before he had a run-in with manager Ken Bolek. That's when the Indians sent Belle to the Mexican League.

He spent a brief time in the Mexican League, which, according to Scott, permanently suspended him following an altercation with an umpire. So Belle returned to the United States, but there was just one problem. Nobody knew where he was. He was still under contract with the Indians, but the Indians couldn't find him.

"Hank Peters called me and said, 'Jeff, Belle's back from Mexico. Do you have any idea where he might be?'" said Scott.

"Offhand, no," said Scott. "But give me two or three days, and I'm sure I can find him."

Scott called a couple of players who he knew were friends of Belle's, or, if not friends, at least as close to Belle as was possible. Scott learned from the players that Belle had hooked up with a woman in Tucson during spring training. The players gave Scott the woman's name and phone number. This was doubly helpful for Scott, who had gotten a call from Carrie Belle, who was "scared to death" because she hadn't heard from her son and didn't know where he was, either.

"Carrie, I'll find him. I have an idea, and when I talk to him, I'll make sure he gets in touch with you," Scott said.

The next day Scott flew to Tucson, where the Indians had their extended spring program. Scott got on a pay phone, and called the number of Belle's friend that the players had given to him.

"A young lady answered and I said, 'Don't hang up on me,'" Scott said. "I told her who I was and said, 'I'm looking for Joey. I heard that you guys are friends. Tell him it's me on the phone and I really need to talk to him.'"

Belle got on the phone—"He was sheepish as all get out," said Scott—and the two men set up a meeting. "Everyone kissed and made up," Scott said. "I think he was embarrassed by the fact that he was sent to low Class A and then to Mexico. But he knew he screwed up with the umpire. Even though he hated umpires, he knew he screwed up."

Scott left the Cleveland organization after the 1988 season. The next time he saw Belle was in 1990. Scott was then scouting for the Oakland A's, who were playing the Indians that day.

"Joey hit a groundball and he didn't run to first base," said Scott. "He wound up in Akron the next day."

After his return from Mexico in 1988, Belle was sent back to Kinston, where in 41 games, 153 at-bats, he hit .301, with eight home runs and 39 RBI. He began the 1989 season at Double-A Canton-Akron, and was leading the Eastern League with 20 home runs and 69 RBI when he was called up by the Indians on July 15. He made his major league debut that day, and in his first at-bat he singled off Nolan Ryan. Belle played 62 games with the Indians that year, hitting .225 with seven home runs and 37 RBI. In 1990, he began the season with the Indians, appeared in nine games, hit .174, was optioned to Triple-A Colorado Springs, and shortly after that he checked himself into the Cleveland Clinic to, according to the Indians, "get treatment for alcoholism."

He went into the Cleveland Clinic as Joey Belle and spent 10 weeks there. When he came out of the Clinic, he was Albert Belle, the name change signifying a fresh start to his life. He did manage to play some baseball after leaving the Clinic. In a combined 33 games at Double-A Canton-Akron and Triple-A Colorado Springs, he hit .320 with five home runs and 22 RBI.

In 1991 he broke camp with the Indians, and in 43 games was hitting .265, with nine homers and 27 RBI. On June 6, the Indians were hosting the White Sox. The score was 1-1 in the bottom of the eighth inning. The Indians had runners at first and second and one out, with Belle at the plate. He swung at the first pitch, hit a ground ball to third, and jogged slowly down the first base line, allowing the White Sox to turn an inning-ending double play.

"He embarrassed himself, he embarrassed his team and he embarrassed this organization. We're not going to tolerate it anymore," said manager John McNamara, who, with Indians president and general manager Hank Peters, met with Belle in McNamara's office immediately after the game and told him he was being sent to Colorado Springs.

"I made the decision to send him down as soon as I saw that play," Peters told reporters.

Belle's demotion lasted 19 days. In 16 games with Colorado Springs, he hit .328, with three doubles, two triples, two home runs and 16 RBI. While Belle was gone, the Indians went 2-15, and were outscored 79-39. At the time Belle was demoted, he was leading the team in home runs. When he returned, he was still leading the team in home runs. He was recalled from Colorado Springs on June 26. The Indians had scored a total of seven runs in their previous four games. In Belle's first game back, the Indians scored nine runs in the first inning of a 10-4 rout of Baltimore. In that first inning Belle went 2-for-2 with three RBI.

"I looked at Albert as a guy who tilts the field," Hart said. "I saw that right away. This guy was an absolute game changer."

But Belle could also be a manager's nightmare. His bat was a manager's best friend, but the rest of him could get managers fired.

"At that time," said Hart, "we didn't have sports psychologists. Your manager handled the players."

*   *   *

Ten days after Belle returned from Colorado Springs, Mike Hargrove became Belle's new manager after replacing the fired McNamara on July 6. Hargrove would be Belle's new handler, and Belle would be Hargrove's new headache.

The suspensions had already started. Belle was suspended for a week for throwing a ball at a fan earlier in the '91 season. In 1992, Belle was suspended for charging Kansas City pitcher Neal Heaton, after Heaton tried on consecutive pitches to hit Belle but failed both times. In 1993, the 6-2, 230-pound Belle was suspended for charging the mound after 6-1, 160-pound Royals pitcher Hipolito Pichardo hit him on the elbow.

"He's a crazy guy," said Pichardo, after Belle chased him all over the field.

Maybe such behavior was partly explained by Belle's traditional pre-game cocktail of Coca-Cola and coffee mixed together in a 16-ounce cup. Whatever it was, the drama, destruction and skirmishes seemingly never ended with the explosive Belle. But that didn't stop Hargrove from trying to nip it in the bud. As a manager, Hargrove hated to confront a player in front of his teammates. He felt it embarrassed the player, and if the player is embarrassed, he isn't going to hear what the manager is saying anyway.

"And when you confront him in front of his teammates, then you're not happy, and you may say things you'll regret," Hargrove said.

During a game at some point in the second half of the 1991 season, after Hargrove became manager, the Indians were leading by one run in the eighth inning, and the opposing team had runners at second and third, with two outs. Belle, playing left field, had just made the last out in the last inning. A batter hit a little looping single down the left field line. Belle trotted after it, allowing the ball to roll past him, all the way into the left field corner. Belle finally tracked it down, picked it up and threw a rainbow back to the infield, over the cutoff man's head. The runner from third scored, and so did the runner from second, on a bang-bang play at the plate, giving the other team the lead.

"Had he gotten to the ball quickly and hit the cutoff man, the runner from second wouldn't have scored, and we would have won the ballgame," said Hargrove, who chose not to confront Belle in the dugout. "His teammates were livid with him when he got back to the dugout. They didn't say a word to him. Nothing. Just livid. They were waiting to see what I would do, because I was a young manager at the time and they were trying to get their gauge on me."

This was in old Cleveland Stadium, where the cramped manager's office emptied right into the clubhouse, which was so small that, "If somebody farted, you could tell who had done it from the office," Hargrove said.

After the game, but before the players filed into the clubhouse, Hargrove sought out Jeff Newman, who not only was the third-base coach but was one of the biggest and strongest members of the team.

"New-New," said Hargrove, employing one of the least creative nicknames in baseball history, "I'm going to have a meeting with Albert in my office, and I'm going to put him in a chair right by that door. I'm going to keep the door closed, but unlocked. I want you and another one of the coaches to stand outside the door. Because if you hear something crash or bang, I can hold Albert off for a little bit, but I'm not sure how long, so get in there and get his ass off me."

Belle finally came into the clubhouse, and Hargrove immediately called him into his office, and closed the door. It was one of Hargrove's first big tests as manager.

"The meeting had a two-fold purpose," he said. "Number one, to let Albert know that was bullshit (loafing on the play in left field). But also, to let the players know that I was taking care of business. I mean, I said things to Albert, screamed and hollered—it wasn't a peaceful conversation—to let Albert know he can't do that. And to let the players know he's not getting away with that."

Hargrove held nothing back.

"I called him things that if I'd said those things to myself, I would have punched myself in the nose," Hargrove said. "But to Albert's credit, he sat there and looked at me and shook his head yes, that he understood. He was listening. And he knew what he'd done wasn't right. From that point on, Albert and I had a pretty decent relationship. I never had to have another meeting like that with him."

Not all the Belle brush fires were raging infernos. But most of them were noisy. Stan Hunter, the Indians' clubhouse manager, was in charge of setting out the postgame spread for the players to eat after each game. Hunter would do so around the eighth inning, using expensive dishes. Belle would frequently make an out in the eighth inning, and come into the clubhouse with his bat and use it to destroy a stack of plates. This went on often enough so that Hunter finally came into Hargrove's office one day.

"Grover, you've got to do something. This is costing me, him breaking up all those plates," Hunter said.

"Stan, stop using the nice plates. Use paper plates. The guys don't care," Hargrove said.

It was pitcher Bud Black who gave Belle the nickname "Snapper," for obvious reasons. But for a time, Belle was known as "Mr. Freeze," which was the product of the fate of one of Belle's mortal enemies: the clubhouse thermostat.

"I didn't see it happen, but I remember it," said Hargrove. "I walked in and saw the thermostat. It wasn't hanging from the wall, or laying on the floor. It was pounded about 3 feet into the wall. He did it during a game. Albert liked it cold, but you could have hung meat in the locker room. I like it cold, too. But he liked it really cold. So, he'd turn it down, and then when he left, one of the players would turn it up. Then when he'd come back in, he'd shut it back down, and stare at everybody. So that day, somebody turned it up, and he came in during the game, I'm sure after he'd made an out. He saw it was turned up, so he smoked it."

On his good days Belle would ignore everyone. On his bad days, everyone tried to ignore him.

"As we moved along, we realized Albert was going to tilt the field in our favor, but we had to learn how to handle this guy," Hart said.

"There were times when I'd just as soon be on the moon than be around Albert," said Hargrove.

Interestingly, for the most part, Belle got along famously with his teammates.

"The players loved him," Hargrove said. "They didn't like some of the things he did at times, but they knew that Albert was there to win and they respected that, and liked that. Albert did things to paint a public picture of a malcontent, but Albert wasn't that. He was a good teammate."

Jim Thome broke into the big leagues in 1991, when Belle, somehow working around a suspension and a demotion to the minor leagues, had his first big year in the majors, hitting .282 with 28 home runs and 95 RBI.

"Albert prepared himself so well, it motivated all of us to try to become better players," Thome said. "He was one of the best clutch hitters I've ever seen. His preparation, I always admired. When he got to the park, he knew exactly what he wanted to do. It's tunnel vision. He knew what he wanted to accomplish to make himself better."

Hargrove frequently said that whenever somebody came to him looking for Belle, he would tell the person, "Go look in the batting cage." Belle spent hours there, before, during and sometimes after games. Charlie Manuel said that when it came to game preparation, from a hitting standpoint, Belle was the hardest worker he knew. Belle kept detailed notebooks on all the pitchers he faced. He was obsessive about batting practice, to the point that he would drive away from the cage with a verbal assault anyone who he thought didn't belong there. Members of the media, mostly.

Belle was popular among his teammates, but it was his unpredictable volatility that from time to time seemed to send everyone's compass spinning.

"He was one of those guys who could be OK for eight days, and then for two days you weren't sure what you had going on," Hart said.

Other times, when a Belle eruption seemed imminent, there was nothing. Such a time occurred before a game during the 1996 season, when Mike Sullivan of the Columbus Dispatch and Andy Call of the Canton Repository came into the clubhouse to interview Damian Jackson, a young infielder who was called up from the minor leagues that day. Sullivan and Call were conducting their joint interview with Jackson, in the partially empty clubhouse. Jackson's locker happened to be next to Belle's, but Belle was not in the room at the time.

During their interview with Jackson, Sullivan, for whatever reason, sat down in Belle's empty chair to continue the interview. Next to him was Call, who was unintentionally and, obviously, unknowingly, standing on Belle's baseball cap, which was on the floor.

It was then that Belle walked into the clubhouse, toward his locker—and that's what he saw. Everyone who witnessed it cringed and waited for the seemingly inevitable conclusion, best described by the NASA phrase: "We have ignition!"

But it never came. Nothing. Without a word, Belle walked out of the clubhouse, down the hall to Hargrove's office, and complained to the manager instead. Go figure.

It was also in 1996 that Belle single-handedly triggered a brawl with the Brewers in Milwaukee. On May 31, after Belle got hit by a pitch in the eighth inning, Murray hit a ground ball to second baseman Fernando Vina, who fielded it in the baseline and attempted to tag Belle, who was advancing from first. Bad idea. The 230-pound Belle threw a forearm at 170-pound Vina, lifting him into the air and slamming him to the ground.

In the ninth inning, Brewers pitcher Terry Burrows hit Belle in the shoulder with a pitch in retaliation. At the end of the inning, as the Indians took the field, Belle yelled toward Indians pitcher Julian Tavarez, apparently reminding Tavarez his job was to hit the first Brewers batter. Tavarez tried, but his first pitch sailed behind the hitter, Mike Matheny, who responded by charging the mound, inciting a brawl that included Tavarez throwing umpire Joe Brinkman to the ground after Brinkman grabbed Tavarez from behind. Tavarez didn't know it was Brinkman. Tavarez and Matheny were suspended for five games.

For Belle, who was suspended for five games but had it reduced to three games after an appeal hearing, it was just another day at the office.

*   *   *

All of that paled in comparison to the 1994 and 1995 seasons, when Belle's fury knew no bounds and when his two most infamous controversies took place. The first came on the night of July 15, 1994, in the top of the first inning of the second game of a four-game series between the Indians and White Sox at Comiskey Park. Belle walked to home plate for his first at-bat of the game. Belle was in the middle of what might have become, absent the players strike that led to the premature end of the season on Aug. 11, the greatest season of his career.

As he strode to home plate in the first inning, Belle was hitting .356, with a .443 on-base percentage, a .696 slugging percentage, 26 home runs and 78 RBI. Belle had barely arrived at home plate before White Sox manager Gene Lamont popped out of the dugout and asked home plate umpire and crew chief Dave Phillips to check Belle's bat.

"I don't know that any of us knew Albert was corking his bats," Hargrove said. "We had our suspicions, and I had a couple of talks with Albert, saying, 'If you're doing this, Albert, you don't need this. If you get caught doing it, it won't be a good thing, and you don't need it.'"

Physically, Belle was one of the greatest specimens to ever wear a baseball uniform. Broad-shouldered, with a heavily muscled upper body, tapering down to a narrow waist and hips. If ever there was a body that looked like it didn't need any illegal assistance in order to hit a ball harder or farther, it was Belle's.

As Lamont talked to the umpires, who were holding and examining Belle's bat, Hart and his wife, Sandy, who had come to Chicago for the series, were sitting in the club seats near the Indians' dugout. White Sox general manager Ron Schueler, a close friend of Hart's, always made sure Hart had those same seats when the Indians played in Chicago. Schueler would even send down dessert to the Harts in the seventh inning of every game.

When the umpires confiscated the bat, "I think everyone in the dugout was a little stunned and shocked, but not a noticeable, 'Oh, shit' moment, because I don't know that we all knew that it was loaded. I certainly didn't," Hargrove said.

But after the bat was taken away by the umpires, Hargrove confronted Belle in the dugout.

"Albert, is that loaded?" Hargrove asked.

"Yeah, it is," Belle replied.

"Oh, this isn't good," said Hargrove.

Two or three innings after the umpires confiscated Belle's bat, Hargrove left the dugout and went into his office in the clubhouse to use the restroom.

"The ceiling tile above my locker was open, and I said, 'What's going on?' And somebody said, 'Grimsley is trying to get over into the umpires' room to get Albert's bat.' I said, 'Are you shitting me?'" Hargrove said, "I went back into the dugout thinking, 'This has a chance to be a serious cluster.'"

Pitcher Jason Grimsley climbed up into the ceiling tiles, and then crawled 30 feet from Hargrove's office to the umpire's room, where he dropped through the tiles into the room to retrieve Belle's bat. According to the Chicago Tribune, Vince Fresso, the umpires' room attendant, had put the bat behind Phillips' equipment suitcase and covered it with Phillips' civilian clothing. The room was locked, but Fresso discovered the heist in the sixth inning when he went back into the umpires' room and noticed clumps of ceiling insulation on the floor, two ceiling tiles out of place, and the metal support strips twisted out of shape.

"I walked into my office the next day, and the Chicago Police are dusting for fingerprints," Hargrove said. "What we couldn't figure out, and I still don't know the answer, is how did the White Sox know that bat was absolutely, 100 percent loaded? I don't know if Albert told somebody, because he never talked to anybody about it."

"I think they knew Albert's bat was corked," Hart said, "because my instincts tell me they X-rayed his bats. They had an X-ray machine. My gut tells me that. So, they knew, and we didn't."

Hart didn't find out until after Belle's bat was confiscated by the umpires. Hart rushed to the Indians clubhouse and was told by some players, "Albert probably has a corked bat."

"I'm like, 'Well *that's* great,'" said Hart.

When Grimsley confiscated the bat the umpires confiscated from Belle, Grimsley left a Paul Sorrento model bat in its place. That seemed to confuse everyone, but the explanation was quite simple. Grimsley couldn't replace it with another one of Belle's bats, because all of Belle's bats were corked.

After the game the next day—"Obviously no dessert coming down from Schueler that night," Hart said—Hart and Hargrove were called to a meeting in the White Sox offices with Schueler and White Sox owner Jerry Reinsdorf.

"They said they wanted the bat back, but all of Albert's bats were loaded, so we didn't know which one it was," Hargrove said. "They pulled out this big panoramic photograph of Albert's bat. It was a closeup of the bat, in the umpire's hands, as they were confiscating it. You could see all the markings, and Albert's name on the bat. And they said, 'This is the bat we want back.' And it was obvious the bat we were trying to give them wasn't the same bat."

The longer the meeting went, the hotter Hart got.

"I'm starting to get pissed, and I say, 'Look, you guys are the same ones that X-rayed this thing. I know you did. You're trying to act holier than thou. You're the guys who used the little scoreboard light to go fastball/breaking ball. We know what's going on here,'" said Hart. "I've got a little Irish in me, and at the meeting we were sitting there listening and taking it, taking it, taking it. I blew up. I opened the quiver and didn't back down. I said, 'Look, there is absolutely no proof here, and on top of it, you guys are as guilty as anybody.'"

"I was really proud of John in that meeting," said Hargrove. "Given the circumstances, and what was going on, most people would have been intimidated, being in front of a powerful owner and general manager. But John was firm, and he wasn't intimidated in the least."

The meeting lasted until 2:30 a.m. On the drive back to their hotel, Hart said to Hargrove, "Grover, I don't think you or I are ever going to have a job with the White Sox."

The White Sox eventually got the bat they wanted, "But I'm not sure how," said Hargrove.

At the time, the White Sox were the Indians' biggest rivals, and that helped fuel that contentious meeting between the four men in Reinsdorf's office.

"Grover and I went at it against Schueler and Reinsdorf," said Hart. "I've stayed good friends with Schueler, and I have great respect for Jerry Reinsdorf, but at that time it was tense. We didn't back off. At the end of it, because of the doubt, the commissioner gave Albert 10 days (suspension), and I trotted myself back to Park Ave. (MLB's offices in New York) to meet with the commissioner, and they reduced it from 10 to seven. So, there was some justice there. But I remember, after the meeting, Grover coming up to me later and saying, 'God! That was impressive!' I said to him, 'Grover, Johnny and Mikey ain't getting jobbed by the White Sox.'"

When all of it was over—the bat confiscation, Grimsley's Operation Bat Retrieval, the blowout meeting between the Indians and White Sox in Reinsdorf's office, the suspension, the appeal by the Indians and the suspension reduction—Hart spoke to Belle about his corked bats.

"I did. I said, 'Albert, look. I don't know whether your bat was corked or not. But I'll tell you this: You don't need a corked bat, number one. Number two, if you have any more, get rid of them. Because you're too good a player. You don't need it. You're going to impact the club,'" Hart said. "He never admitted it to me, and I didn't have any proof. But there were obviously a lot of rumors about it, so I told him to get rid of it, that he didn't need it. Over the course of my time in Cleveland, I told Albert to stop doing a lot of things."

Belle apparently got the message. Either that, or he got better at disguising his corked bats. In an interview following the 1995 season, Belle gave the impression that using corked bats wasn't worth the trouble.

"First of all," he said, "you've got to find someone who can cork them. So, there's one headache. And then you've got to be bold enough to use them in a game, so there's another headache. I feel like I'm big and strong enough where I don't need them."

* * *

Prior to Game 3 of the 1995 World Series between the Indians and Braves, Hart and Hargrove got caught in another Belle maelstrom. Belle unleashed a profanity-laced tirade at NBC's Hannah Storm because Storm and an NBC crew were setting up cameras and lights in the Indians' dugout. They were preparing for an interview with Lofton, two hours before the game.

"That was a mess. Albert was mad because there were too many people in his work space," Hargrove said. "He came in from the field and she was standing in the dugout with about 50 other people, and she just happened to be the first person he came by."

Belle was fined $50,000 by Major League Baseball for that outburst, and Commissioner Bud Selig ordered him to get anger-management counseling. The incident threw a huge wet blanket over an Indians team that was flying high artistically and emotionally after winning their first two postseason series.

"We'd just had that blood-letting in beating Boston, and then the Seattle series, beating Randy Johnson to clinch it," said Hart. "Then we're in the World Series, and not five minutes into our batting practice (at home, before Game 3), and he's got an issue with Hannah Storm. That's all I did for 10 days during that World Series was answer Albert Belle questions."

Maybe Belle was feeling a little edgy after his lackluster performance to that point in the postseason. He was hitting .229, with more strikeouts (nine) than hits (eight). Maybe he was upset by the wide strike zone the umpires were giving Braves pitchers, who were happily taking advantage of it. Or maybe it was nothing more than just Belle being Belle. Whatever it was, prior to Game 3, it quickly came to a head.

"Albert had one of those days. He told her to get out of the dugout, and was impolite. It was horrible," said Hart, who was in Hargrove's office when the incident took place. Both sought out Storm and offered their apologies.

Hart was forced to answer a series of questions from the media in the interview room, one of the first ones being whether the Indians were going to suspend Belle.

"No, we're not going to suspend him," Hart said. "We've apologized. We're sick about this. We're remorseful. We wish it wouldn't have happened, but we're not going to suspend Albert Belle for having a confrontation with a reporter. It wasn't like it was a physical confrontation. It was verbal."

When the Series returned to Atlanta for Game 6, Hart was still answering questions about Belle in the interview room.

"We worked so hard to get there, and all of a sudden we're cast as this bad team. It sort of took the luster, the shine off our club," Hart said. "It certainly took the shine off the World Series for those of us in the front office, and Grover, and everyone who had worked so hard to get there. I mean, here we are, having to answer these kinds of questions."

Belle apologized to Storm the next day, and when Hart relayed that information to reporters in the interview room, the next question was, "Is he going to apologize to everyone he's dropped an F-bomb on?"

Hart quickly left the podium.

In an interview following the 1995 season, Belle gave his side of the incident.

"I came off the field from being in the outfield, to get ready to hit, and there's all these media people hanging out on our bench," he said. "That's the players' bench, not the reporters' bench. I hollered at everybody, not just Hannah Storm. I hollered at everybody that I'd had enough of this stuff. All you media people get out of here. This is our dugout.

"I used some language to tell everyone to get out. I walked the length of the dugout, and Hannah Storm just happened to be sitting there. I didn't even know Hannah Storm. I thought she was Lesley Visser. I don't like her, either.

"They just let people trample all over us, and I don't like that . . . I'm sure during the course of the season there were lots of players shouting at the media worse than I did, and nobody made a big deal about it."

The day after the incident, Storm said Belle apologized to her, not face-to-face, but in writing.

"He took the time to write me a letter," she told WKYC-TV in Cleveland in an interview in 2019. "That night, he must have gone home and the next day he handed me this incredibly thoughtful apology and letter. That meant so much to me."

Three days after the end of the World Series, Belle was still making news. On Halloween night, four teenagers egged Belle's house in Euclid, Ohio, after Belle told them he wasn't giving out any candy. Belle chased the kids in his Ford Explorer.

"I went driving down the street, going the speed limit, and I saw them," Belle said. "They were walking across this open field. So, I drove up on the open field and chased them around. When I caught up to them, I slammed on the brakes, and the truck skidded and bumped this kid, and he fell down. Then he jumped up and kept running."

The teens were charged with delinquency for egging Belle's house, and Belle was charged with reckless operation and fined $100. The guardian for one of the teens later sued Belle for $850,000, but that suit was settled out of court a year later.

"I made a decision five years ago to live in Cleveland, but I never thought people would harass you," Belle said in 1995. "Then after (the Halloween incident) happened, the news media shows up on my doorstep and they put my address all over the screen. Maybe I'll move out to Vegas, where I can at least have some warm weather, and nobody knows you."

Belle would be moving on soon, but it wouldn't be to Vegas. Just over a year after the Halloween incident, Belle would play his last game as a member of the Indians before signing with the White Sox. He was unlike any other player in that he could be equal parts electrifying and infuriating. The specter, the aura of his charismatic yet combustible personality permeated every corner of the organization. Hart said that was one of the reasons why he brought in veteran players like Eddie Murray, Tony Pena and Orel Hershiser. "Guys who understood the team dynamic and would talk to Albert, confront him on certain things. And Grover handled him very well," said Hart.

For all the craziness that could ensue on Belle's bad days, his teammates still enjoyed him and liked having him around. Part of it was because of Belle the ballplayer—the home runs, the doubles, the RBI, and, yes, the terror and intimidation he inflicted on opposing pitchers and teams. But part of it, surely, was Belle the uninhibited, unbridled competitor, the bold recklessness of this baseball desperado, who did and acted as he pleased. That clearly appealed to many of his more cautious, less boisterous teammates, most of whom, to a degree, enjoyed having an outlaw batting fourth in the lineup every day.

"The players liked him," Hart said. "To them, Albert wasn't an issue. They understood he could be moody. That he could tear up a clubhouse, and shatter some lights. In the tunnel at Cleveland Stadium, they had to replace some of the toilets."

"When it was all said and done," said Hargrove. "Albert was a player. I don't mean that in a bad way. He was a player. He played. And he played to win. He demanded excellence from himself, and sometimes he didn't handle not reaching that level of excellence very well. But his teammates liked him. Everyone on the team liked him. The coaches, me, John, everybody liked Albert. We just didn't like some of the things he did."

CHAPTER 11

Never Let a Star Fall On You

"John came into my office and said, 'I'm
thinking we need to trade Baerga.'"

From 1991 through 1995, the Indians' winning percentage steadily improved. From .352 in the 105-loss 1991 debacle, to .694 in the glorious 100-win 1995 season. The textbook rebuild had worked masterfully. The Indians had assembled a roster that featured prototypical players, most of them All-Stars, at every position. The lineup was filled, it seemed, with cleanup hitters in almost every slot. The starting rotation was sturdy, the bullpen elite, the defense exceptional. It was a team with no weaknesses.

But it was a team about to take on a different look. After the 1995 season, first baseman Paul Sorrento, who was third in that monster lineup in home runs with 25, signed with Seattle as a free agent. Pitcher Mark Clark, who was 20-10 the previous two years, was traded to the Mets. Ken Hill, who was outstanding in the second half of the 1995 season, going 4-1 with a 3.98 ERA, left as a free agent and signed with Texas.

To replace Clark and Hill in the rotation, Hart signed three-time All-Star and 1993 Cy Young Award winner Jack McDowell to a two-year, $10.5 million contract. The machine was hitting on all cylinders. The team had stars and a new ballpark in which to showcase them, and the fans were buying in, big time. The 1996 season was the first of four consecutive seasons in which the Indians sold out their entire home schedule before the season even started, a fact not lost on other executives around the league, such as Ron Schueler, the general manager of the White Sox, for whom McDowell played in his first seven years in the majors.

"Every ticket in their park is sold. If you knew your park was going to be sold out every night, wouldn't you go after anyone you could get?" Schueler told the Los Angeles Times' Ross Newhan.

Indeed, they built the new ballpark, and the fans came, and came, and came—and the Indians' payroll went up, and up, and up. So did their win totals. In 1991, when Hargrove took over as manager, the Indians' payroll was $18.2 million, which ranked 22nd out of 26 major league teams. In 1992 their payroll plunged to a major league-low $8.2 million. The Indians' highest-paid player that year was Felix Fermin at $950,000.

But then, with the new ballpark on the horizon, the Indians' payrolls rose quickly. In 1994, the first year in Jacobs Field, the payroll was $28.4 million (19th in the majors). In 1995, $35.1 million (ninth). Starting in 1996, the Indians' payroll ranked fourth in the majors for four consecutive years: $45.3 million in 1996, $54.1 million in 1997, $59 million in 1998, and $73.8 million in 1999.

Payroll is in part tied to attendance, and the Indians' attendance exploded once they moved into the new ballpark. In 1993, their last year in Cleveland Stadium, they drew 2.1 million, which ranked 16th in the majors. In 1994, their first year in Jacobs Field, they were eighth in the majors with a home attendance of 1.9 million in a season cut short by seven weeks due to the players' strike. In 1995 the Indians' attendance jumped to 2.8 million (third in the majors), in 1996, 3.3 million (third), in 1997, 3.4 million (fourth), in 1998, 3.4 million (fourth), and in 1999 they led the American League and were second in the majors in attendance with 3.4 million.

Jacobs Field quickly became baseball's biggest cash cow. On June 12, 1995, the Indians and Orioles drew 41,845 to Jacobs Field. The next time the Indians played a home game that wasn't a sellout was on April 4, 2001. In between, the Indians played before 455 consecutive sellouts, a major league record at the time.

"You'd walk up the runway to get to the dugout, and you could feel the energy the closer you got. It was a real magical time. Something we hadn't seen in Cleveland for a long, long, long time," Hargrove said. "You'd drive around neighborhoods and see Chief Wahoos everywhere. You'd never seen that before."

Tickets to Indians games were so hard to get that the Detroit Tigers started marketing six-game ticket plans to Indians fans for the six games Cleveland played in Detroit, which is about 170 miles from Cleveland. "We had so many Cleveland fans come to Detroit for the games last year that we put an ad in the Plain Dealer thanking them," Tigers marketing director Mike Dietz told the Plain Dealer.

"To be a part of all those sellouts. So many great moments. You look back and cherish them, especially now that I'm retired. We were all very lucky," said Jim Thome.

All those sellouts helped the Indians to afford the salaries of some of baseball's biggest names, and when they signed McDowell it seemed like a case of the rich getting richer.

"We had a chance to sign either Jack, or Kevin Brown," said Hargrove. "We were going after one of the two, and it didn't make any difference to us which one it was, just as long as we got one, a guy who had been an established No. 1 guy. When we got Jack, we were all happy about that."

But instead of the rich getting richer, it was more a case of the rich getting a broken-down jalopy. Two years later the Indians-McDowell marriage ended quietly. In 37 starts, including one postseason start with the Indians, McDowell was 16-12 with a 5.14 ERA. He was 13-9 in 1996, but with a bloated 5.11 ERA. In 1997 he appeared in only eight games due to a strained forearm.

"Jack was at the end of his career," Hargrove said. "If his split finger was working, he would do really well. But if it wasn't, he didn't do very well, so there were a lot of games that I went out and got him early, and I'm sure he wasn't a real fan of that."

"It was kind of bittersweet," McDowell told the New Philadelphia (Ohio) TimesReporter.com in 2017 "It was a great team to play for, but it was the first time I had ever been on the DL." McDowell was only 30 years old when he signed with the Indians, who hoped he could pick up some of the slack for the 42-year-old Dennis Martinez, who was now the No. 5 starter, and in his last year with the team.

Indeed, 1996 was the beginning of a period of transition for the Indians. Starting in late July, in an eight-month span the Indians would part ways with their leadoff hitter and the No. 3, 4 and 5 hitters from their lineup, an exodus that would cripple most major league teams, perhaps even triggering a total rebuild. It's an indication of how well the Indians were built that even with the middle of their lineup gutted, they continued to churn out division championships and a second trip to the World Series. But the winds of change were blowing, and it started in a nine-day span in late July 1996, with the trades of Carlos Baerga and Eddie Murray.

Murray turned 40 years old at the start of spring training in 1996, but he still seemed to have some gas in his tank. He was coming off a 1995 season in which he hit .323, the second-highest mark of his 21-year Hall of Fame career, and he finished strong, slashing .358/.408/.568, with five home runs and 19 RBI in the month of September.

Hargrove loved having Murray on those high-voltage mid-'90s Indians teams. Hargrove valued Murray not just for his production, but for his leadership. Murray had a towering presence and influence on the Indians teams in 1994 and 1995.

But some cracks started to show in the 1995 postseason, when he hit just .232, although with three home runs and nine RBI.

Then Murray started the 1996 season by hitting .211 with no home runs in 24 games in April. April was always Murray's worst month of the season. But when you're 40 years old and hit .211 in April, it can raise some eyebrows.

"Eddie got off to a bad start and it just never came around," said Hargrove.

During that first month of the season Hargrove and Hart met to discuss Murray's situation. Hart was in favor of not playing Murray every day. "And rightfully so," said Hargrove. "But as a manager, my thinking was that you have to look at the well-being of the team. And if I started playing Eddie Murray three or four times a week, you could get some of the other players thinking, 'Gee, if he does that to Eddie Murray, what's he going to do to me, if I start struggling?'"

Hargrove got Hart to agree that they would let the Murray situation play itself out until the All-Star break, and if things were no better than they were in April, Hargrove would concede the point to Hart, and the Indians would look in another direction.

"But I told John that if it comes to that, we need to trade Eddie. No. 1, for Eddie, because he's had too good of a career for him to sit on the bench. If we sat Eddie Murray, who we knew was going to be a Hall of Famer, there will be doubts and questions on the team, and it might derail everything."

Murray did come around somewhat. From May 1 through July 20, the day before the Indians traded him, Murray hit .280, with 12 home runs and 32 RBI in 246 at-bats. But the Indians decided to commit Murray's at-bats to two younger players, outfielders Brian Giles and Jeromy Burnitz. So, on July 21, with Murray just nine home runs away from 500 for his career, the Indians traded him to Baltimore for pitcher Kent Mercker.

"I thought it was entirely the right thing to do, for the ballclub and for Eddie," Hargrove said.

Murray would retire at the end of the 1997 season, so the decision to make that trade was much easier for the Indians than the one they made eight days later, on July 29.

*   *   *

Over the last four years, Carlos Baerga had hit .315, averaged 19 home runs and 97 RBI per season and was selected for the All-Star team in three of the four years. He won two Silver Slugger awards and had one top-10 finish in the MVP voting. He was also just 27 years old and, theoretically, just entering the prime of his career. Plus he was the No. 3 hitter in one of the most powerful lineups ever, not to mention being one of the most popular players on the team.

Over those four years, the switch-hitting Baerga was a hitting machine. In 1992 he became the first second baseman in American League history to hit over .300 with more than 200 hits, 20 home runs and 100 RBI. Then Baerga did it again the next year. In a game against the Yankees on April 8, 1993, he became the first player in history to hit home runs from both sides of the plate in the same inning. "He can get a hit anytime he wants," Montreal manager Felipe Alou told Sports Illustrated in March 1996.

But then, with no warning whatsoever, Baerga's career crumbled. It was like on Monday he was an All-Star and on Tuesday a candidate to be designated for assignment. There was no gradual decline, no sequential loss of skills. No debilitating, career-altering injury. It seemingly happened overnight. From stardom to sad sack. The start of the decline was detected early in the 1996 season.

"John saw the signs first," said Hargrove. "He was a great talent evaluator. Like a really good scout—really good, not the scouts who think they're good. John could see little things, like Carlos was losing a step. It almost started when he had that bad ankle in the '95 World Series. He had a really bad ankle, but, to his credit, he played. But it never seemed like, after that, he ever got back to where he was. John recognized it."

On July 25, the Indians opened a four-game series in Baltimore.

"John came into my office and he said, 'I'm thinking we need to trade Baerga.' That was the first time I thought about it," said Hargrove. "As manager, you're trying to make what you've got as good as it can be. You don't think about things like that. That was John and Danny's job. And they did it at exactly the right time to do it."

In the 1995 regular season, Baerga hit .314, with a career-high .355 on-base percentage, 15 home runs, 90 RBI and only 31 strikeouts in 600 plate appearances. In the first two rounds of the '95 postseason, against Boston and Seattle, he hit .359. But then he hurt his ankle, and only hit .192 in six World Series games against the Braves. In 1996 he started strong, hitting .290 in April, but from May 1 to July 29, the day he was traded, he hit just .259 with a .294 on base percentage.

"I had noticed the year before, 1995, he wasn't the same. The swing wasn't the same," said Hart.

The fun-loving Baerga also had an off-the-field reputation as the first guy to the party and the last one to leave. He was also something less than a workout warrior. He reported to spring training in 1996 weighing 226 pounds, which was about 26 pounds over his playing weight. Following the 1995 season and into the start of spring training in 1996, Indians officials held several meetings with Baerga. They told him that he had to start taking better care of himself, that he didn't have the perfect body, and needed to start working with the strength and conditioning coaches at the workout facilities.

One of those meetings involved Baerga, Hart and owner Dick Jacobs.

"We said, 'Carlos, it's very important that you take good care of yourself.' That kind of thing," said Hart. "So there was some background to (the decision to trade Baerga), and the more I watched it, the more I started tossing it around in my mind. I didn't tell a lot of people. But I remember going to Grover about a week before. I mean, it's not like we went out and shopped Carlos. Like we were talking to clubs about deals. We looked like we were going to win again, and go to the postseason."

But then Mets general manager Joe McIlvaine called Hart and mentioned that he might have some interest in Baerga, before quickly adding, "But you probably won't do anything."

"I low keyed it," Hart said. "But I said to Joe, 'Listen, we're thinking about making some adjustments. It's not going as well as we'd like. Let me get back to you.'"

Hart and Hargrove continued to talk about the possibility of trading Baerga. They both agreed that, although Baerga was only 27, he had become less athletic, and the ball wasn't coming off his bat like it once did.

"But if you do this," Hargrove cautioned Hart about the ramifications of such a deal, "it isn't going to be popular."

"What's it going to mean with the club if we do this?" Hart asked Hargrove. "What's going to happen if we trade one of our most popular, beloved players?"

Hargrove made it clear to Hart that it would be tough for a while, but that the team had enough character that it would survive, and that he was in favor of making the trade.

"And that was what I wanted to hear," Hart said.

Just to be sure, though, Hart consulted with Indians hitting coach Charlie Manuel, one of the most respected and astute judges of talent in the game, and a longtime Hart friend and confidant. Hart basically asked Manuel, point blank, "Is Carlos done?"

"Hartbeat, goddamn, son, it ain't pretty. It ain't pretty at all. He's swinging underwater," said Manuel.

"So Charlie saw it as well," said Hart.

There was also the financial aspect of the trade to be considered. Baerga was making $4.79 million in 1996, and he'd make that same amount in 1997 and 1998, with a $4.5 million club option for 1999.

"He had three or four years left on the deal, and we were on the hook for a significant amount of money," Hart said. "So here we were, with three years left on his deal, and this guy's starting to go south. I'm thinking, 'If I wait any longer, I might have to eat this money.' So that was another part of the motivation to make the deal."

Still, it was an excruciating time to be an Indians decision maker. Before he made the deal, Hart took the virtually unprecedented step of calling the Indians beat writers into his office to ask them how they thought the deal would be received by Indians fans.

"It was the first big one of that core group going away. I was very close to Carlos. We all were," Hart said. "Grover was very close to him. Carlos was an emotional leader. And in his first five years he was an amazing player. But for whatever reason, it had gotten to this point."

Hart also thought back to that advice John McNamara gave both he and Hargrove, to "Never let a star fall on you," meaning don't get caught having to handle a star at the end of his career. That's exactly what the Baerga situation was becoming, and Hart admitted it was a tough trade to sell to owner Dick Jacobs.

"But by that time, Dick trusted that we were going to do the right thing. That we weren't out there on a whim. That we had discussed it," Hart said. "I had brought it up to him when Dick and I had a meeting with Carlos a month before. I said, 'Dick, I might need you in this meeting with Carlos.' And Dick had NEVER been in a meeting with a player. Never went into the locker room. So, Dick was aware that I was concerned about Carlos, and the fact that his skills were deteriorating, and that he wasn't taking as good care of himself as he should be."

The trade was made on July 29, an off day for the Indians, at home. Baerga and infielder Alvaro Espinoza were traded to the Mets for second baseman Jeff Kent and infielder Jose Vizcaino.

McIlvaine was excited to acquire Baerga, warts and all.

"We've been doing background checks for the last three days, and talked to an awful lot of people who have intimate knowledge of Carlos," McIlvaine told the New York Times. "He's not St. Carlos, but at the same time, we are satisfied at what he gives you on the field."

Baerga wasn't at the ballpark the day the trade was made. So Hart was the one who broke the news to him.

"I called and told him," Hart said. "It was a shocking thing for him to hear. There were tears. Carlos loved Cleveland. He loved the Indians. He loved everything about it. He was shocked. It was emotional for him and emotional for me. I was in tears as well. It was tough."

Emotions aside, the Indians nailed it. Charlie Manuel was right. Baerga was swinging underwater. At 27, his career was effectively over. He would spend seven more years in the big leagues, but was only a shadow of his former self. He bounced from the Mets to the Padres, back to the Indians, inexplicably, for 22 games in 1999, then on to the Red Sox, Diamondbacks and, in 2005, at age 36, to the Washington Nationals. On Sept. 30, 2005, as a pinch hitter, in the last plate appearance of his major league career, Baerga lined a single to right field off Cory Lidle, the 1,583rd and last hit of his career.

That was the final chapter of Baerga's major league career. But for all intents and purposes, his career ended on July 29, 1996, when the Indians shocked everyone including themselves by trading a player who at one time in his career could seemingly "get a hit anytime he wants."

"We saw what was happening (to Baerga as a player), but what sealed it was the contract," said Hart. "I might not have done it if the contract wasn't there. So it was that, compounded with what I was seeing. It's one of those instinct moves that you make, and if you can make it before (the player hits rock bottom), you have a chance to make a pretty nice deal, which we did. Quite frankly, we made a nice deal out of it. But unfortunately for Carlos, he never re-captured it. I hated to be proven right on that one, because I loved him and still do. But it is what it is."

*   *   *

Through it all, the Indians never missed a beat, because they became even harder to beat. Their winning percentage at the time of the trade (.610) improved significantly after the trade (.625). They were 64-41 with Baerga, and 35-21 without him. They moved into first place on April 13, nine games into the season, and they stayed there for the rest of the year.

It was the year Charles Nagy won 17 games, was the American League starter in the All-Star Game, and finished fourth in the Cy Young voting. It was the year Hargrove became the first Indians manager to manage the American League All-Star team since Al Lopez in 1955.

"I took my kids to the gala the night before the All-Star Game, in Philadelphia," Hargrove said. "My daughter Shelly, who couldn't have been more than 10 then, danced almost every dance that night with Kenny Lofton. When we traded Kenny later, she wouldn't talk to me for four or five days."

It was the year the Indians lineup was almost obscenely talented. Manny Ramirez hit .309 with 33 home runs and 112 RBI. Jim Thome hit .311 with 38 home runs and 116 RBI. Albert Belle hit .311 with 48 home runs and 148 RBI. Kenny Lofton hit .317, with 75 stolen bases and 132 runs scored. And 37-year-old Julio Franco was the Indians' every day first baseman, which sounds like a bad joke, but even he hit .322. So it wasn't like, with Murray and Baerga gone, the Indians were short on stars.

Five of the Indians' nine everyday players hit over .300, and a sixth, Omar Vizquel, hit .297. Brian Giles, who replaced Murray as the DH, hit .355. Mark Carreon, who backed up Franco at first base, hit .324. On Aug. 31, Hart traded outfielder Jeromy Burnitz, who had no chance of cracking the Indians outfield, to Milwaukee for Kevin Seitzer, and in 22 games, mostly at DH and first base, Seitzer hit .386. The Indians' .293 team batting average is still (through 2018) the highest by any Indians team in the last 82 years.

For the Indians, the 1996 season was a lot like the 1995 season. Once again they had the best record in the majors during the regular season, 99-62, which was seven more wins than any other team in the American League. They led the league in hitting, they led the league in pitching (4.34 ERA) and they led the league in winning.

But it was Franco, a teammate of Hargrove's on the 1985 Indians, who as a first baseman in 1996 was the square peg in a round hole. It was Julio as curio. Franco was a shortstop by trade, a second baseman by necessity, a first baseman by desperation.

"We tried to make Julio a first baseman, and John and I got into it after a game in spring training," said Hargrove. "Julio made three errors at first base, and after the game John came straight out onto the field to the cage—we hit after games back then—and John got real close to me and started chewing me out.

"I thought you said Julio could play first base?"

"He can."

"What's going on with the three errors?"

"It's spring training!"

"It was an important thing to our ballclub that Julio play first, and play it well," Hargrove said. "I told John, 'We're working on it. It's not going to happen overnight. We've got time. It's going to get better,' which it did. I don't blame John. I would have been in a fury, too. John said, 'We gave him all that money, and he can't even catch a groundball.' I said, 'He will.'"

Incredibly, Franco, who was 37 in 1996, would go on to play nine more years in the big leagues. His final year was in 2007, which was 25 years after his rookie season. In a combined 106 at-bats that season for the Mets and Braves, Franco hit .222, but he also hit a home run and stole two bases, which is not bad at all, considering he was 48 years old.

That 1996 Indians team was loaded, but the Orioles unloaded on Cleveland in the American League Division Series, bouncing the Indians out of the playoffs in four games in the best-of-five series. Brady Anderson, who hit 50 home runs that year—26 more than he hit in any of his 14 other big-league seasons—led off the bottom of the first inning of Game 1 with a home run off Nagy, and the rout was on. The Orioles won the first two games, in Baltimore, by a combined score of 17-8. The Indians won Game 3 in Cleveland, 9-4, but Baltimore ended the series with a 4-3 win in Game 4, on a home run by Roberto Alomar off Jose Mesa in the 12th inning.

It almost seemed as if that series may have been a hangover from losing the World Series the previous year, although Hargrove disagrees.

"I don't think there was a hangover," he said. "It did seem, though, like there was hardly any offseason. It was like we just got through with the (1995) World Series, and all of a sudden we're going back to Winter Haven for spring training. But it wasn't a hangover. Baltimore had a good ballclub."

So did the Indians, a 99-win team that lost to the 88-win Orioles in a one-sided Division Series that led into one of the most eventful off-seasons ever for the Indians.

*   *   *

It's not often that an elite team executes such a dramatic and relatively rapid roster makeover that centered around the heart of the team. But that's what Hart and his staff did during an eight-month span that started with the trade of Murray on July 21, 1996, and ended on March 25, 1997. During that period the Indians either traded, or allowed to leave as a free agent, the No. 1, 3, 4 and 5 hitters in their lineup: Lofton, Baerga, Belle and Murray. Name another team that could do that and still go to the World Series for the second time in three years. Name another team that would even want or try, or need to do that.

The Indians did all of that, and still made it work.

But first—or, at least, third in the timeline of enormous trades—was the acquisition of Matt Williams, the slugging third baseman of the San Francisco Giants. Following the 1996 season the Indians knew they needed to add a slugger, because they knew they were going to lose the biggest slugger in the game. Belle was going to become a free agent, and, as most things with Belle, once he decided on a course of action, nobody could stop him. By that point, for a number of reasons, the Indians weren't all that upset about losing him.

That's because Hart was already working on a trade with San Francisco that would bring Williams to Cleveland. "We wanted to replace as much of Albert's bat as we could in the lineup, and Matt sure fit that bill," said Hargrove. "He came in with a reputation as a hard-nosed grinder, and he certainly was that."

In 1994, Williams almost won the National League MVP Award. That was the year he led the NL in home runs with 43 and had 96 RBI in just 112 games. From 1990 to 1996, he averaged 30 home runs and 92 RBI per year, was a four-time All-Star, and won three Silver Slugger and three Gold Glove Awards. He was 31 years old, still in the prime of his career, and the Indians wanted him badly.

They got him on Nov. 13, by trading Jeff Kent, Julian Tavarez and Jose Vizcaino to the Giants.

"The day we made the trade I thought back to the first time I saw Matt Williams, which was in 1989, when I was managing at Colorado Springs, and we went in and played the Phoenix Giants, in Phoenix," Hargrove said. "It had to be 109 degrees. Two o'clock in the afternoon. I put my uniform on and went out and sat on the bench, because all they had in the clubhouse was a fan. Gordie MacKenzie was the manager of that Phoenix team, and he had Matt out there fielding groundballs. He had to be out there, in that heat, for an hour. No let up. I'm thinking, 'Holy shit, I'm dying sitting here watching this, and he's out there doing all this work.'"

In being traded from San Francisco to Cleveland, Williams was going from a last-place, 94-loss Giants team to a first-place, 99-win Indians team. That didn't mean, however, that the trade thrilled him.

"It hurts," he said. "I'm excited about coming to Cleveland, but I'm also saddened to be leaving San Francisco. I've spent 11 years with the Giants. I wanted to spend my whole career in one uniform, but that rarely happens in this day and age."

The trade for Williams meant that Thome's days as a third baseman were over. The Indians had planned to eventually move him to first base, probably in 1997, regardless of whether they traded for Williams. The Franco-at-first experiment ended after one year. Franco started the 1997 season with the Indians. He started 34 games at second base, 42 as the DH, and none as the first baseman. The Indians released him on Aug. 13.

Toward the end of the 1996 season, Indians officials had begun talking internally about moving Thome from third base to first base. When the chance to acquire Williams presented itself, Thome volunteered to make the switch.

"Getting a guy the caliber of Matt Williams, me moving to first base was a no-brainer," Thome said. "Honestly, I needed to move across the diamond anyway. At some point, with my lower back, and how things had progressed through my career, the best move for me was to go to first base, for many reasons. But the main reason was for our club to succeed, and try to go back to the World Series—which we did. The best part of it is, when you do things for your club, and the club gets rewarded for you doing it, which is what happened that year."

The winter of 1996-97 was a very busy off-season for Hart. Among his numerous moves, on Dec. 13, he signed 1989 National League MVP Kevin Mitchell as a free agent. Six days later Hart signed free-agent outfielder Chad Curtis. Neither player made it to the All-Star break.

Before batting practice on May 20, the two players had a brief fight in the clubhouse. It ended when Mitchell slammed Curtis onto the clubhouse ping-pong table. At issue was a song Mitchell was playing on the clubhouse stereo system.

"Chad didn't like the volume, or the song. It was one of those rap songs, with all the language," Hargrove said. "From what I was told, Chad kept going over and turning it down and Kevin would go turn it up. There wasn't a whole lot of back-down in Chad, and there wasn't any back-down in Kevin. So, Chad got to meet the ping-pong table."

Neither Hart nor Hargrove were amused. Mitchell was released two weeks later, and Curtis, who suffered a sprained right thumb in the fight and had to be placed on the disabled list, was traded to the Yankees a couple of days after he came off the DL.

On Dec. 28, the Indians signed free-agent infielder Tony Fernandez, an under-the-radar signing, partly because Fernandez sat out the 1996 season with a broken elbow. But 10 months after signing with Cleveland, Fernandez would hit one of the most dramatic home runs in Indians' history.

On Feb. 20, 1997, 42-year-old Dennis Martinez, who became a free agent after the Indians chose not to re-sign him following the 1996 season, signed with the Seattle Mariners. In 72 starts over his three seasons with Cleveland, Martinez was 32-17 with a 3.58 ERA. In five postseason starts, he was 1-2 with a 2.73 ERA. The one victory, of course, came in the unforgettable Game 6 of the 1995 ALCS, when Martinez pitched the Indians into the World Series by out-pitching Randy Johnson, who that year won the first of his five Cy Young Awards.

On an Indians team loaded with big names and bigger egos, Martinez took a back seat to no one. He could be difficult to handle, but for most of his career his pitching made it worth the effort.

"My relationship with Dennis was good, but contentious at times. But when it was time for Dennis to pitch, he was golden. It was all about the game," Hargrove said.

But the biggest story of the 1996-97 off-season came on Nov. 19, when Albert Belle signed a five-year, $55 million contract with the White Sox. The deal made Belle the highest-paid player in baseball, and he also became the first baseball player ever to earn over $10 million per year.

It was the end game in a drama, the roots of which probably stretched back to when Belle was making one of his many trips to Major League Baseball's offices on Park Ave. in New York, for another hearing in front of the commissioner, to appeal another suspension. Hargrove doesn't remember the year, but it wasn't Belle's free-agent year. Best guess is it was somewhere in 1994, perhaps '95.

"We were in a meeting one time with Dick Jacobs," said Hargrove, "and out of the blue he says to me, 'Mike, can you win without Albert Belle in your lineup?'"

Hargrove was taken aback by the question. "Mr. Jacobs," he replied, "yeah, we can win without him in our lineup, but him in our lineup makes it a whole lot easier."

"Number one, without Albert, we wouldn't have been as dominant as we were in the '90s," Hargrove says today. "We would have been successful, but Albert was a guy you could build a team around. It's nice to have a guy like that."

It's not nice to lose a guy like that, but it's obvious that at some point, well before Belle became a free agent, Indians ownership was trying to gauge whether Belle's production and importance to the lineup was worth all the headaches he caused.

Hart recalls "a very big summit meeting" in Cleveland, following the 1996 season, after the Indians "got whacked" by the clearly-inferior Orioles in four games in the Division Series. Hart felt that the '96 Indians may have been a better team than the '95 team, but they just caught some bad breaks against Baltimore. The big summit meeting included all of the team's chief decision makers, perhaps even Dick Jacobs himself. The owner rarely attended such meetings. But this was a critically important one.

"We realized that we were going to have to start making deci-

sions on players," Hart said. "At that meeting, everyone spoke candidly. We talked about who we are, where are we going, etc. We've
still got this young core. These young guys are growing up. How do
we manage this? And, obviously, Albert was a big topic, because we
were going to look at our economics. He made it very clear he was
going to go after a big contract. We had some money, but we never
envisioned doing with him the big contract he wanted."

As the meeting progressed, Belle's situation—he would become
a free agent five days after the 1996 World Series, which was only a
week or two away—became a bigger and bigger topic of discussion.

"We looked at ourselves the last three years through a prism
of how we got to where we were," Hart said "We were a young,
hard-working team. We did it the right way. We wanted to send
a good message to our fan base. We sort of looked at it like this:
As talented as Albert is, if we sign him, we're not going to be able
to reconnect some dots that we're not going to be able to replace.
We talked about losing Albert's bat. But we felt Thome had gotten
better, Manny had gotten better, and we were trying to emphasize
the team part of everything.

"It wasn't like we were saying good riddance to Albert. It was
a combination of we could afford it (Belle's asking price), but is
this a guy we want to make our flagship player? We just didn't see
that. We didn't see him being that, going forward. The big contract
made it even tougher, for a guy like this, between the lines, that we
couldn't be sure he would play nice in the sandbox."

Dan O'Dowd, Hart's assistant general manager at the time, said
the percentage of payroll the Indians would have to commit to
Belle would have been prohibitive.

"We were very conscious of payroll percentage analysis,"
O'Dowd said. "We were into analytics before analytics were analytics. Nobody realized how analytically-driven we were as an organization back then. One of the models that we had studied, and
come to the conclusion on, was if we invested in Albert, what other
decisions would we not be able to make because of that investment
in him? It would have prohibited us from being aggressive on other
fronts. So we decided to let him walk."

The Belle decision was one of the rare instances that Jacobs
inserted himself into the discussion, mostly because of the mag-

nitude of the player, the magnitude of the decision, and the subsequent repercussions, either way, of whatever the Indians decided to do.

That, says O'Dowd, was another example of Jacobs' astuteness as an owner.

"He never thought with his ego. It was never about him," O'Dowd said. "He never pretended to know the game of baseball. He always knew what he knew, and what he didn't know. He never got in the way of the process. Now, he had a firm belief of wanting to have sustained success, but he never wanted us to go all in in one individual year, because he didn't want to stink in other years. That is the model he espoused and held us accountable to. There were some trades along the way that if we were all in, we probably would have made. But he knew those trades might have prevented us from being competitive somewhere down the road, and he didn't want to do that."

There were reports that, a few days before Belle signed with the White Sox, the Indians had offered him a five-year deal worth $39 million or $40 million. If so, that was likely a cosmetic offer only, one that the Indians knew Belle would turn down. What it came down to, it seems, was that the Indians were willing to offer Belle the most money they could without him actually taking it.

Ironically, at the press conference held by the White Sox to announce Belle's signing, Belle said, "It wasn't about the money," a comment that enraged Indians fans. But Belle didn't realize how true his statement was. It wasn't about the money for the Indians, either. As Hart indicated, talking today about the white-hot emotions that surrounded those negotiations over 20 years ago, the Indians could have afforded the contract Belle got from Chicago. They simply chose not to offer it. Enough had finally become enough. The Indians were willing to pay the going rate for, as Hart called it, a "flagship" player. But in their opinion, Belle wasn't it. The franchise had simply gotten worn out, or worn down by hitching itself to that particular war wagon.

Losing Belle the hitter was a blow, but losing Belle the loose cannon was not. Even at that, it wasn't like the Indians didn't have cleanup hitters waiting in the wings.

"Thankfully, we had Manny Ramirez and Jim Thome, guys who

could fill the spot pretty easily," Hargrove said. "I don't remember thinking, 'Lord, what are we going to do now?' It was just one of those things. It was like I told Dick Jacobs. We can win without him, but it would be a lot easier with him, and that proved to be the case."

Would the Indians have won the 1997 World Series with Belle in the middle of their lineup? We'll never know. We do know what happened to the White Sox after they signed Belle. They went from a winning record (85-77) without Belle in 1996, to two losing records in his two years in Chicago: 1997 (80-81) and 1998 (80-82). The Indians continued to win without Belle, winning their division in four of the next five years after he left.

Belle's contract had a clause stating he could become a free agent after two years if he was no longer among the three highest paid players in the game. After two years, he wasn't, so he became a free agent again.

This time he signed a five-year, $65 million deal with Baltimore, but he only played two full seasons with the Orioles. A degenerative hip condition forced him to retire from the game during spring training in 2001, when his manager at Baltimore was Mike Hargrove.

"I had great respect for Albert Belle," said Hart. "The way he played the game. Not giving up at-bats. What he meant to our club. He was a big part of our (rebuild). I forever will have a soft spot for Albert, even though I know he still chastises me for letting him get away."

Belle's exit from Cleveland in 1996 was undoubtedly a relief for Hargrove, who, for the first time since he became manager of the Indians in 1991, would no longer have to put up with, work around, sort out, apologize for, explain, react to, or shake his head over the many distractions caused by baseball's most explosive slugger.

Right?

Wrong.

"No, I never did think that. Still don't today," said Hargrove. "Given the choice of having Albert or not having Albert, the whole package, I would take Albert every time. Albert's a good guy. When he lets himself be, Albert's a good guy."

CHAPTER 12

True Grit

"There were so many things that went on in our '97 postseason, it almost seemed like it was our destiny to win it all. I had that thought in my mind a lot."

What was perhaps the wildest, most improbable, heart stopping, yet ultimately most heartbreaking season in Indians history began with a thunderclap trade near the end of spring training. It was the final sonic boom of what had been a frenzied, noisy off-season of activity as Cleveland dramatically re-shaped its roster. Albert Belle left as a free agent. So did Dennis Martinez. The team had traded for Matt Williams to play third base, and moved Jim Thome to first base. Cleveland signed former National League MVP Kevin Mitchell, who hit .153 in 20 games before being released. The Indians also signed Tony Fernandez, a 35-year-old four-time All-Star and four-time Gold Glove shortstop—to play second base. In the span of 11 days in October, Fernandez would hit one of the most famous home runs and make one of the most infamous errors in franchise history. It was his only year in Cleveland.

But the ground in Winter Haven, Florida, shook the most on the morning of March 25, 1997, a week before opening day, when the Indians and Atlanta Braves announced a stunning blockbuster trade. Cleveland traded Kenny Lofton and pitcher Alan Embree to Atlanta for outfielders David Justice and Marquis Grissom. With that trade, the Indians, in the span of eight frenetic months, had subtracted the leadoff hitter (Lofton), No. 3 hitter (Carlos Baerga), No. 4 hitter (Belle), and No. 5 hitter (Eddie Murray) in their lineup. A team that had won 199 games over the previous two seasons was throwing its furniture around like a drunken interior designer.

"That was a sobering fact. It changed the whole face of the ball-club in a year," Hargrove said.

During spring training, it was not unusual for Indians owner Dick Jacobs to fly down to Winter Haven in his plane, with some high rollers and friends from Cleveland. In the middle of spring training in 1997, Jacobs and friends flew into Winter Haven, collected Hart, O'Dowd and Hargrove, then flew on to Key West for dinner. The following morning the group would fly back to Winter Haven, "like they were taking a taxi," Hargrove said.

But during that dinner in Key West, Hart took O'Dowd and Hargrove into a separate room and delivered some stunning news.

"He told us the deal we had for Kenny, getting Justice and Grissom," said Hargrove, who was shocked at the news.

"It was totally out of the blue. There were no rumors or anything flying around about it," Hargrove said.

"We traded Kenny because he was going into the last year of his contract, and I couldn't get him to sign an extension. Grissom and Justice were both on long-term deals," said Hart.

Lofton was stunned by the news.

"My head is boggled right now," he said at the press conference. "I can't think too much right now. It's like somebody stabbing you in the back."

Lofton said he and his agent told the Indians they didn't want to negotiate a contract extension until after the season, because he didn't want it to become a distraction. Instead, it created a distraction before the season, resulting in Hart pulling the trigger on a franchise-rocking four-player trade.

"I'm disappointed. I've done everything I could have done for this team. I expected to be rewarded. Maybe that was my reward, going to Atlanta," Lofton said.

"That one broke my heart," said O'Dowd. "I was the one guy in the front office that had a close relationship with Kenny. That one really hurt me. But Kenny was being Kenny, and he put himself in that situation. He wouldn't give us any assurance we could sign him. I told him, 'You're being arrogant, and arrogance leads to stupidity.'"

Between the end of the 1996 postseason and the start of the 1997 regular season, Hargrove's lineup card had lost two-thirds of what was the best outfield in the major leagues. Belle and Lofton were gone. Only right fielder Manny Ramirez remained. But for a variety of reasons, all three could have, and should have, wound up in the Hall of Fame.

"Given the circumstances, as much as I hated to see Kenny leave, I thought it was a pretty good deal for us, because we got back two established major league players" on long-term deals, Hargrove said.

The radical roster reboot was most dramatically revealed by the Indians' opening day lineup in 1997, compared to 1996. There wasn't a single player from the opening day lineup in '96 who was in the same spot in the order in the opening day lineup in '97. Four of the players in the '96 opening day lineup were no longer on the team on opening day in '97. Only three players were in the opening day lineup at the same position both years: Ramirez, Sandy Alomar Jr. and Omar Vizquel. The 3-4-5 hitters in '96 were Baerga, Belle and Murray. The 3-4-5 hitters in '97 were Thome, Williams and Justice.

"That's what I mean when I say John, Danny and Mark (Shapiro) found ways to keep us in the World Series conversation, while losing a Belle, Baerga and Lofton," Hargrove said.

"We re-invented ourselves," said O'Dowd. "A lot of the contracts of those guys came to an end, and we had to reconfigure what we were going to do. John and I were as proud of that as we were about getting the club to where it got in '94, '95 and '96. Because we re-did it, and didn't miss a beat. That was a testimony to the culture we built, and to Grover's adaptive ability to handle all those diverse personalities that we had, and to get the most out of them."

By this time in their relationship, Hart and Hargrove were in lockstep on all the major trades and free-agent signings the Indians executed. "I tell people that all the time, and they think I'm full of shit, but good or bad, there was never a deal done for a free agent or trade that I didn't sign off on," Hargrove said.

"My job was to find the players, acquire the players, but I wasn't going to put guys on the roster that Grover didn't want," Hart said. "He was always consulted on anything we did. Some guys he didn't know. Some guys he did. Some guys he was ambivalent about. But I would always say, 'Mike, heads up. We're sort of looking at a deal involving so-and-so,' and we would hash it out. We were a big meeting group in the early days, trying to make sure we had the right players. It was like baking a cake."

Sometimes the cake would be baked from two different continents. Following the 1998 season, the Indians were in need of a left-handed reliever. Hart was talking to the Pirates, who wanted Brian Giles, and were willing to give Hart his choice between one of two lefty relievers, one of whom was Ricardo Rincon. At the time, Hargrove was in Japan, managing an all-star team. One of the players on the all-star team was Jason Kendall, the Pirates' catcher. Hart called Hargrove and told him about the potential trade with Pittsburgh, in which the Indians would get one of the two lefty relievers. Hart asked Hargrove which of the two relievers he preferred.

Hargrove told Hart he would call him back in an hour. Hargrove then went to talk to Kendall about the two pitchers.

"I went down to Jason's room and I said, 'If you had Rincon, and this other guy, and you're in a tough spot, which one do you want to pitch?'" Hargrove said. "Jason said the other guy, but they were both similar. So I called John back and told him it was six of one, half a dozen of the other. So we did the deal for Rincon."

It was not a good deal for the Indians. Giles hit over 30 home runs four years in a row for Pittsburgh, drove in over 100 runs in three of the four years, and was selected to the All-Star team in two of the four years. Rincon was what he was: a situational left-hander who rarely pitched to more than a batter or two in 207 appearances over 3½ seasons with the Indians, during which he only pitched 154 innings.

"Giles was a good player, and had a good career, but our outfield was loaded. There was no place to play him," Hargrove said. "It was like when we traded Sean Casey. He was a first baseman, but guess what? We've got Jim Thome."

Hart and Hargrove tended to have the same kind of core ideas on players, but there was one major difference between the two of them.

"John was a much better talent evaluator than I was. That's probably one of my biggest weaknesses, talent evaluation, as far as projecting what kind of player a guy can become. Once he got to the big leagues, I was OK," Hargrove said.

The remodeled Indians did not get off to a good start in 1997. They won four of their first six games, but then lost six of their next seven. They were 12-13 in April, snapping a streak of 18 consecutive months without a losing record. It was their first losing April since 1993. They didn't get over .500 for good until May 20. From July 18-30, they lost 10 of 14 games. As late as Aug. 10, they were still only three games over .500 (58-55).

The lackluster beginning to the season begged the obvious question: Was the sputtering start to what became a sputtering season due to the team having so many new players?

"I think so, yeah. Every team tries to get good chemistry, but not all clubs get it. That entire year we were trying to find our identity, who we really were," said Hargrove.

It was a choppy, uneven season, with fits and starts, frustrations and aggravations, and, at times, total discombobulation. The latter reared its ugly head on April 9, in the Indians' eighth game of the season, in Seattle. Indians rookie Bartolo Colon, in the second start of his major league career, never made it out of the first inning. He threw 61 pitches and got two outs. He faced nine batters in the inning, and it went like this: walk, pop-out, single, walk, single, walk, single, flyout, walk. In only two of the 61 pitches Colon threw did a Seattle hitter swing and miss. Colon's pitching line: ⅔ of an inning, three hits, six runs, four walks, no strikeouts. The Indians lost, 11-1.

"They hit a lot of foul balls, and as we're going along, they keep fouling them off and we're at 30 pitches, and it just keeps going on and on, and you think, 'Holy shit, he's not getting through the second. He's done,'" said Hargrove.

It was a shocking performance that could have unnerved a pitcher or unraveled a career before it even got off the ground. But Hargrove said he wasn't worried about the psychological damage such a spectacular meltdown might cause in his 23-year-old right-hander.

"I didn't think it would have an effect on Bartolo. He didn't show a lot of emotion, good or bad. In a young kid, that's a pretty good deal. So, I didn't worry about how it would affect him. But it made you realize he needed to develop a better off-speed pitch to get hitters off his fastball. Because in that game he was just throwing one fastball after another. Even at 98 mph, hitters will foul them off."

Colon in that up-and-down season was sent to Triple-A Buffalo three different times. In 17 starts with the Indians he was 4-7 with a 5.65 ERA. In 10 starts at Buffalo, he was 7-1 with a 2.22 ERA. One of those wins was a no-hitter on June 20, in which Colon faced the minimum 27 batters. He walked the second batter he faced, but that batter was thrown out trying to steal.

Colon eventually had a very good, and extremely long major league career. Despite having one of the worst bodies in professional sports, he still managed to pitch in the majors until he was 45 years old. His career finally ended in 2018, when he was 7-12 for Texas. His was a very substantial career. He won a Cy Young Award, finished in the top six in the voting three other years, and was a four-time All-Star. His 2,535 career strikeouts ranked 35th all-time when he retired, and he was 49th in wins with 247.

"At the end of his career he still threw mostly fastballs, but his command was incredible," Hargrove said. "Before your physical talents diminish, guys will lose their competitive edge. But Bartolo was able to keep that edge."

*   *   *

On May 13, prior to a game against the Texas Rangers, in Texas, the Indians made an announcement that was at best odd, at worst, suspicious. They announced that Hargrove had been awarded a contract extension, through the 1998 and 1999 seasons, with a club option for 2000. It seemed like a curious time to do so, given that the Indians to that point were the picture of mediocrity, with a record of 17-18, which put them in third place in the AL Central. Normally teams would make such an announcement at home, to maximize the media coverage. But instead, the Indians made the announcement on the road.

Making it even more bizarre was that there was no formal announcement or press conference. Hart, the man who would normally be presiding over the press conference that didn't happen, wasn't even there. He had been with the Indians for the first games of the trip, but the day before Hargrove's extension was announced,

Hart left the club to go scout the Indians' Class A team in Kinston, North Carolina. To some it seemed as if Hart was fleeing the club to avoid having to talk about or take part in the announcement.

According to Hargrove, however, Hart's trip to Kinston had been planned for a long time.

So the "announcement" of Hargrove's extension was done through a printed press release distributed to members of the media.

Hart's only comment on the extension came in that statement: "Mike Hargrove has done everything asked of him for this organization as a player, coach and manager over the last 19 years. He has been at the core of our success over the last four seasons and we look forward to him guiding the club into the next century."

It was left to the opposing manager of the team the Indians were playing that night to say a few complimentary words about Hargrove.

"He's done a good job. That's not an easy job, when you're always expected to win," Texas manager Johnny Oates told reporters. "Sometimes that makes it harder. Having the most talent doesn't always guarantee you'll win."

June 3 was the day many Indians fans had circled on their calendar since the day Albert Belle signed with the White Sox the previous winter. June 3 was Belle's first appearance at Jacobs Field as an opposing player. The game that night was more spectacle than game. The sellout crowd of 42,994 produced nine innings of rage directed at Belle, who endured it all. Then, following the last out of the bottom of the ninth inning of a 9-5 Indians loss, Belle, playing left field, turned and faced the fans in the left field bleachers, gave them the finger, and jogged triumphantly to the White Sox dugout. American League president Gene Budig later fined Belle $5,000 for the gesture.

The rage that night was vicious and unceasing. For nine innings the boos, the taunting and the invective rained down on Belle, from the moment he appeared on the field until the moment he left it. It peaked during each Belle at-bat. It reached its most comical when Belle jogged to his left field position in the first inning, and the fans standing against the railing above the left field wall threw hundreds of fake $20 bills onto the field in the direction of Belle.

Taunting chants of "Joey! Joey! Joey!" cascaded down on Belle. Twice during the game, White Sox manager Terry Bevington came onto the field to complain to the umpires about the debris being thrown at Belle.

"You knew that was going to happen. The fans were upset, but baseball is a business," said White Sox third baseman Norberto Martin after the game.

"We knew in the beginning it was going to be loud," said Chicago outfielder Dave Martinez. "But after a while, it gets old. Albert made a career move. I know he has nothing against Cleveland. He's never said anything bad about it to us."

Belle had the last laugh, going 3-for-5, with two doubles, a home run and three RBI.

"This is the first time I've seen a hostile crowd here," Hargrove said after the game. "I understand their frustration, their sense of betrayal. But there is no cause to throw anything out there. Someone can get hurt badly."

The Indians' manager had problems of his own at that point in the season. Two big ones were Marquis Grissom and Matt Williams, two of the Indians' big additions during the off-season. Neither player was hitting. So, on June 4, the day after the Welcome Back Albert trash bash, Hargrove moved Grissom, who was hitting .213 overall and .200 in his last 100 at-bats, from the leadoff spot to the No. 9 spot in the order. Williams, hitting .256, was dropped from the No. 4 spot to the No. 7 spot in the order.

"They're pressing. Maybe this will help them relax," said Hargrove, who moved Vizquel to the leadoff spot and Justice into the cleanup spot. Hargrove's first choice to hit cleanup was Ramirez, who said no thanks.

"Manny doesn't feel comfortable hitting in that spot," said Hargrove at the time. "But I made it clear to him that sometime in his career he is going to be expected to hit there."

Ramirez did eventually hit cleanup in 41 games that year, but he more often hit third (51 games) or sixth (51 games).

The lineup changes didn't help much in the second game of that series with Chicago. The White Sox hammered six Indians' pitchers, including starter Albie Lopez (five runs on six hits and four walks in 4⅔ innings), for nine runs and 13 hits, in a 9-4 rout of the Albert

Belle-less home team. Belle went 1-for-3 with three RBI. So, in his first two games at Jacobs Field since leaving the Indians as a free agent, he was 4-for-8, with three doubles, a home run and six RBI. In the eighth inning, Jose Mesa hit Belle in the left shoulder with a pitch. Belle walked slowly to first base while giving Mesa a death stare. Two batters later, Mesa hit Mike Cameron. "Jose was just trying to throw inside," Hargrove said after the game. "You could tell he was wild, because he hit Cameron later on. Jose is not a headhunter, and Albert knows that. He's played with him."

The White Sox responded when reliever Bill Simas threw a pitch behind Ramirez, leading off the bottom of the ninth. The umpires issued a warning to both benches. Four batters later, Simas threw one inside on Grissom, who took a couple of steps towards the mound, but stopped. The benches and bullpens emptied and the two teams engaged in some shouting and pointing. Simas and Chicago manager Bevington were both ejected.

"We weren't throwing at them, but there's no doubt in my mind they were throwing at us," said Hargrove after the game.

Lost in the blowout loss and near-fight between the Indians and White Sox was still another indication that Jose Mesa was becoming Jose Mess. After saving a franchise record 46 games in 1995 and 39 more in 1996, Mesa blew a tire in the early part of the 1997 season. In his first 19 appearances he was 0-3, with a 7.45 ERA. In 19 innings he allowed 35 hits, including six home runs, 10 walks, and opposing batters were hitting .389 against him.

Mesa was so bad that Hargrove took him out of the closer's role and replaced him with Mike Jackson. From April 26 to Aug. 8, Mesa did not have a single save, as he was moved into a setup or middle relief role. But then, suddenly, from Aug. 9 through the end of the regular season, Mesa, in 24 appearances, was almost untouchable. He was moved back into the closer's role and went 2-0 with a 0.39 ERA, 13 saves, and an opponents' batting average of .157.

By the end of the season, Mesa and Jackson's numbers were very similar. In 66 appearances, Mesa was 4-4, with a 2.40 ERA, and 16 saves. Jackson, in 71 appearances, was 2-5 with a 3.24 ERA, and 15 saves. In the postseason, Jackson, in 13 appearances, was 1-0 with a 0.68 ERA, while averaging 10.8 strikeouts per nine innings, with no saves and no blown saves. Mesa, in 11 postseason appearances, was 1-0 with a 3.95 ERA, four saves and two blown saves, one of which is one of the most infamous blown saves in World Series history.

Pitching was a problem for most of that season. Indians pitchers finished ninth in the league in ERA, and 13th in both complete games and shutouts.

The hitters were much better than the pitchers. Alomar had the best year of his career, hitting .324 with 21 home runs and 83 RBI. He also had a 30-game hitting streak, the second-longest in Indians' history, one short of Napoleon Lajoie's franchise record 31-game streak set in 1906. Alomar's streak ran from May 25 through July 6. During it he hit .422 (49-for-116), with a .455 on-base percentage. In game 10 of the streak, on June 6, Alomar tied a major league record by hitting four consecutive doubles in a 7-3 win over the Red Sox at Fenway Park. On July 10 the streak ended when Alomar went 0-for-4 in an 8-2 loss at Minnesota. Alomar struck out in his first two at bats, grounded out in his third at bat, and then, in the ninth inning, popped out to end the game.

"I've had the attitude during this streak that it could end any day. But tonight I was anxious about it. I wanted to go out and get a hit right away, to make good contact right away. That's not a good game plan to take into something like this," Alomar told reporters after the game. "I feel like a load has been taken off my back. I held nothing back, but it was a bad night for us all the way around."

Ironically, Alomar's streak ended in the first game after the All-Star break, which was another highlight in his dream season. In the All-Star Game, Alomar's two-out, two-run home run in the seventh inning broke a 1-1 tie and gave the American League a 3-1 victory. The fact that the game was played in Jacobs Field made it even sweeter for Alomar, who was named the game's MVP, the first and only Indians player to ever win that award. He also became the only player to be named the All-Star Game MVP while playing in his home park.

"I felt like I was flying. I've never run the bases so fast on a home run," Alomar said. "This is a dream I don't want to wake up from. You probably only get one chance to play an All-Star game in your home stadium."

In the middle of June, in an attempt to strengthen their sagging pitching staff, the Indians called up 21-year-old Jaret Wright, the Anaheim, California, high school pitcher whom the Indians selected with the 10th pick in the first round of the 1994 June Draft. Like his father, Clyde, who enjoyed a colorful 10-year career as a left-handed pitcher, mostly with the Angels, Jaret was a cocky, confident competitor. In a combined 15 starts at Triple-A Buffalo and Double-A Akron that year, Wright was 7-4 with a 2.82 ERA, averaging over nine strikeouts but almost four walks per nine innings.

The Indians' pitching in 1997 was spotty at best, sub-standard at worst. Especially the starting rotation. Only two starters reached double figures in wins, Charles Nagy (15-11) and Orel Hershiser (14-6). The third and fourth starters, Chad Ogea and Colon, were a combined 12-16, with a 5.27 ERA. In addition to those four pitchers, 10 others started games, as Hargrove and pitching coach Mark Wiley spent much of the year looking for ways to bolster the rotation. Among those other 10 pitchers who started games were career relievers Albie Lopez, Jason Jacome and David Weathers, the washed-up Jack McDowell and rookie Steve Kline, who on May 24 started against Baltimore, and lost 8-3, a game in which he never got out of the second inning. It was the only start by Kline in 796 career appearances in the big leagues.

On July 31 Hart traded reliever Danny Graves and three minor leaguers to Cincinnati for 32-year-old lefty John Smiley, an accomplished veteran who in 1991 led the National League in wins when he was 20-8 for the Reds, finishing third in the Cy Young voting. Smiley had reached double figures in wins in each of the previous three seasons, including 1995 when he was 12-5 and was a National League All-Star.

Smiley was expected to be another workhorse starter, plugged into the rotation behind Nagy and Hershiser. But all those plans went out the window on Sept. 20. Smiley was warming up in the bullpen prior to a scheduled start in Kansas City.

"He threw a curveball and you could hear a crack. I've never seen anything like it. It almost made me sick," said Wiley.

Smiley screamed and grabbed his arm. Reliever Jason Jacome ran to the dugout for help.

"You could see the upper part of his arm was sort of deformed," Jacome said after the game. "We all knew something was really wrong. I hope I never have to see something like that again. My stomach turned."

The injury was a spiral fracture of the humerus bone in Smiley's left arm. That's the bone in the upper part of the arm that runs from the shoulder to the elbow.

The injury ended Smiley's career.

It was that kind of year for the Indians, who really only had two dependable starters—Nagy and Hershiser—which led to the mid-June callup of Wright. "We can win with him," Hart said.

Wright made his major league debut against the Twins on June 24. He pitched poorly, but won, 10-5. He pitched five innings, threw 109 pitches and gave up five runs on seven hits, three of them home runs.

Hargrove and Jaret's father, Clyde Wright, were teammates on the Texas Rangers in 1975.

"Clyde was tough as a boot," Hargrove said. "There are a lot of guys I wouldn't want to meet in a dark alley, and Clyde would probably be at the top of the list. Jaret had the same sort of mentality and toughness."

*   *   *

The Indians went into first place for good on June 5. They stayed there for the rest of the season, but never ran away from the pack. Their play was spotty. They appeared bored at times, almost as if they knew no team in the division was capable of passing them. They were right. But that didn't prevent a mid-season malaise, in which they didn't play well, even in games they won. The team really struggled getting any momentum.

"I know," said Hargrove. "John made me very aware of that fact."

Indians assistant general manager Dan O'Dowd, who worked in the Indians front office from 1988 to 1998, had the best view of anyone of the relationship between Hart and Hargrove.

"The most difficult relationship within a front office is the relationship between the general manager and the manager, because they see the game from different perspectives," O'Dowd said. "One sees the game from a box. The other sees it from the dugout. They literally look at the game from two different perspectives. So there's always going to be, in that relationship, creative tensions. I would say John and Mike had a very healthy creative tension. There was a respect between the two of them. They each made the other better. They were a perfect complement to each other's personalities, and their desire for what needed to get done to help the Indians."

"There were times when we butted heads, but not regularly," Hargrove said. "Professionally, I think we meshed pretty well. There were times when I had to slow him down on some things, and there were times when he had to prod me to get me moving."

That symbiotic relationship was the foundation of the two men's partnership. But it wasn't indestructible, and, as the Indians continued to slog their way through the summer of '97, Hargrove's job security became a topic of discussion in the media and on sports talk radio. Such talk seemed odd, given that Hargrove had recently been awarded a two-year contract extension. But that's how bad the team looked at the time.

The somebody's-getting-fired-and-it-might-be-you vibe started swirling around Hargrove, and he was very conscious of it. In early August the Indians lost five in a row and eight out of 11. During that stretch, the annual Cleveland Indians Charities golf tournament was held. All the players and front office personnel traditionally showed up for it. But on this day, the only ones who didn't attend were John Hart and Charlie Manuel.

"I got the feeling, from the people I talked to that day, that something was going on," Hargrove said. "Nobody ever came out and said it. But everyone was kind of reserved in their response to me. At that time, I really had my antenna out, because we had just gone through a really rough patch. We were still in first place, but I knew that managers had been fired before during the season when they were in first place. So, when John and Charlie didn't show up at the golf tournament, and there was no game that day, I thought that was real curious. It didn't give me the warm and fuzzies."

Two years later, when Hargrove did get fired, and Manuel succeeded him as manager, rumors surfaced that Hargrove felt Manuel had been pursuing the job through back channels, which Hargrove now says was never the case.

"I don't want to give the impression that I thought Charlie was going behind my back. But it was just curious to me that the only two guys who weren't at the golf tournament that day were Charlie and John Hart," Hargrove said. "It could have been for any reason in the world. But I never felt Charlie was after my job. I know there were rumors that he was, but I don't think that was the case. It was just my insecurities coming out more than anything."

Around the same time as the golf tournament, the Indians' wives held a food drive, at which Sharon Hargrove was feeling the same ominous vibe as her husband.

"I sat at the same table with Sandy Hart (John Hart's wife) and she didn't say a word to me all day, and I thought, 'Hmm, what's with that?'" Sharon said.

All of it was a sobering reminder to Sharon of the fish bowl that those who make their living in professional sports sign up for. It comes with the territory, a fact that was underscored for Sharon many times, including during the players' strike in 1985. Kim Hargrove, their daughter, came home from school one day and said, "Daddy, one of my friends said that his dad said that you already make too much money, and you won't go to work."

"Mike asked her what she said," said Sharon. "And Kim said, 'I told my friend that my daddy doesn't even work. He just plays baseball.'"

In the summer of 1997, Kim's father's fate was again a topic of public conversation and speculation, to the point that Kim's mother felt certain that Kim's father was about to get fired.

"The day after the golf tournament, Sharon said she was shocked that I didn't get a call that day to go see John," Hargrove said.

In the end, despite he and his wife getting the cold shoulder at two separate team functions, Hargrove survived. He kept his job, and later speculation was that it was owner Dick Jacobs who nixed the idea at the 11th hour.

"We didn't play well for the bulk of the year, but I know Dick really liked and valued continuity in our group," said O'Dowd.

That didn't mean that Hargrove wasn't as tired as the fans, the media, and, obviously, some members of the front office, of the Indians sleepwalking through much of that summer. After a 10-3 loss to Kansas City in the first game of a doubleheader on Sept. 19, Hargrove held a team meeting in which only one voice was heard:

his. Those waiting outside the clubhouse door didn't have to strain to hear it.

"If you don't want to play, if you don't want to pay the price, then tell me. Please tell me . . . the door is right there," Hargrove told his players.

Later, when speaking with reporters, Hargrove explained the reason for the meeting.

"I don't think we played with any intensity. After what we've been through on this road trip, it's understandable, but not acceptable," he said.

The road trip was a mammoth 14-game, four-city trip, of which the doubleheader in Kansas City marked games 11 and 12. The Indians went 7-7 on the journey, which reflected the win-one-lose-one syncopation of much of that season.

Interestingly, Hargrove and most of his players pointed to a bonding pact to which everyone pledged their oath, well before that trip began, as the turning point of their season. The date was Aug. 27, Jim Thome's 27th birthday.

"We were in Anaheim, and it was Jimmy's birthday. He was the only one who wore his uniform socks up," Hargrove said. "So on his birthday, Matt Williams said, 'We're all going to wear our pants up, in honor of Jimmy's birthday.' Just being stupid, we all did. The coaches, me, everybody. And we blew out the Angels that night (10-4), so we said, let's do it tomorrow, and it took off from there."

"I don't know if everyone was for it, but I think most of them were," Thome said. "We won the ballgame that day, and the next thing you know—it's baseball, we're all superstitious—we won another game, and boom! Let's continue to do it. We went on this run, and it was like, 'OK, now we *have* to wear our socks up.' For me, it was pretty cool. It said a lot about our group of guys, that we all came together and did that for the good of the team."

"It was a stupid, silly, unifying factor," said Hargrove. "If we would have known we would win games because we pulled our socks up, we would have done that back in April, because some of us looked really goofy with our socks up."

Technically speaking, it really wasn't much of a "run." At the start of it, the Indians were six games over .500 (67-61), and during the "run" they were seven games over .500 (29-22, counting the postseason). On the other hand, they did make it to Game 7 of the World Series, and you can't get much runnier than that.

But first came one of the most preposterous, outrageous, electrifying runs through the first two rounds of the playoffs that anyone had ever seen.

*   *   *

The Indians went into the playoffs having lost seven of their last 11 games. After winning 100 and 99 games in their previous two seasons, they tumbled to just 86 wins in 1997 (86-75; one rained out game was not made up). The 86 wins were by far the fewest of any AL playoff team, 10 fewer than the Yankees, who finished second to Baltimore in the AL East but reached the playoffs as a wildcard team.

The Division Series between the Indians and the Yankees started in Yankee Stadium, where in Game 1 the Indians bludgeoned David Cone for five runs in the first inning, three coming on a home run by Alomar. After the top of the fourth inning the Indians led 6-1, but then their bullpen let them down. The Yankees scored single runs in the fourth and fifth innings. In the Yankee sixth, Eric Plunk and Paul Assenmacher combined to give up three consecutive home runs, to Tim Raines, Derek Jeter and Paul O'Neill, giving New York an 8-6 lead, and that's the way it ended.

The Indians won Game 2, 7-5. After the Yankees scored three times off Wright in the first inning, the Indians took control with a five-run fourth, thanks to consecutive RBI singles by Justice, Alomar and Thome, and a two-run double by Fernandez off Andy Pettitte. Williams added a home run off Pettitte in the fifth, and the series moved to Cleveland tied at 1-1.

New York blew out Cleveland 6-1 in Game 3 as Nagy never got out of the fourth inning, and David Wells pitched a five-hit, 104-pitch complete game.

The last two games of the series were choked with drama, tense moments, and two one-run victories for the Indians. In Game 4, the Yankees led 2-1 with two outs in the bottom of the eighth inning and Hall of Fame closer Mariano Rivera on the mound. But with New York just four outs from winning the series, Alomar's fairytale season continued. On a 2-0 pitch from Rivera, Alomar hit a line drive to right field that just barely made it over the wall for a game-tying home run.

"Sandy hitting a home run off Rivera was so unexpected, not because Sandy wasn't capable of it, but because Rivera was Rivera. You're sitting there thinking, 'Holy shit!' It was something you didn't see off Rivera. It obviously really gave our team a shot in the arm," Hargrove said.

"I saw the ball letter high, and when I hit it, I thought I hit it pretty good," Alomar said after the game. "Mariano throws very hard. With Mariano, you don't have to swing very hard. Basically, his velocity made the ball go."

"It was a ball. I left it out, a little high. He was hacking. I was surprised he hit it," Rivera said.

Alomar, who called the hit "The biggest home run of my life," was one of the few players who had success against Rivera, who in 2019 became the first player in history to be unanimously voted into the Hall of Fame. Alomar's career batting average against Rivera was .462 (6-for-13).

But Alomar's homer only tied the game. The Indians needed one more run to win it. They got it in the bottom of the ninth inning. Grissom led off with a single off Ramiro Mendoza. Grissom went to second on sacrifice bunt by Bip Roberts. Vizquel dribbled a soft single that just got through the left side of the infield. Grissom, who was running on the pitch, scored from second with the winning run, a thrilling 3-2 victory that forced a deciding Game 5.

In that Game 5, the Indians took a 3-0 lead against Pettitte with a three-run third inning, two of the runs coming on a double by Ramirez. A sacrifice fly by Fernandez in the fourth drove in what became the deciding run. Wright started and gave up three runs (two earned) in 5⅓ innings, and the bullpen took it from there. Jackson, Assenmacher and Mesa combined to pitch 3⅔ scoreless innings to close it out, although Mesa had to survive a harrowing ninth inning.

With two outs and nobody on in the ninth, O'Neill hit a rocket to center field that hit off the top of the wall for a double. It missed by inches from being a game-tying home run. "I thought it was gone. I just wanted it to stay in the park," Mesa said.

"When O'Neill hit that ball it scared the hell out of me," Hargrove said. "He was such a good hitter. He was the last guy you wanted to face in that situation, even though the Yankees had a whole lineup of those kind of guys. But for me, O'Neill was like the Edgar Martinez of the Yankees."

Then Bernie Williams hit another rocket, to left-center, that would have easily scored O'Neill, but Giles ran a long way to catch the ball for the out that ended the game and the series.

The unsung hero for the Indians was Wright, who was the winning pitcher in two of the Indians' three wins in the series. In the deciding Game 5, Wright pitched into the sixth inning, holding the Yankees to two earned runs. In his two starts, Wright was 2-0 with a 3.97 ERA.

"We knew 10 days ago when we picked Jaret to start Game 2 in New York that it could come down to this," said Hart after the game. "We did it because we felt Jaret could win a big game in Yankee Stadium and then come back and do it again if there was a Game 5."

There was, and Wright did.

That Indians win in the Division Series interrupted a relentless stretch of dominance by New York. In the five-year span from 1996 through 2000, the 1997 season was the only one in which the Yankees did not win the World Series.

*   *   *

Victory over the Yankees sent the Indians into the ALCS against Baltimore. The Orioles won 98 games in the regular season, the most in the American League, and they had four future Hall of Famers on their roster: Cal Ripken Jr., Roberto Alomar, Mike Mussina and Harold Baines.

The Orioles won Game 1, 3-0 as Scott Erickson and Randy Myers combined on a four-hit shutout. No surprise there. In their four trips to the postseason from 1995 through 1998, the Indians' combined record in Game 1 was 1-8.

In Game 2, the Indians were trailing, 4-2, with two outs in the top of the eighth inning, and were four outs away from going down 2-0 in the series. But Grissom belted a three-run home run off Armando Benitez, giving Cleveland a 5-4 lead. The bullpen closed it out, with Mesa getting the save. Five Indians relievers combined to pitch 3⅓ hitless and scoreless innings.

Game 3 was in Cleveland, and the Indians took a 1-0 lead into the ninth inning, but Mesa blew the save by giving up a one-out, game-tying RBI double by Brady Anderson, and the game went into extra innings. It ended with one of the most bizarre plays anyone had ever seen.

With one out in the bottom of the 12th inning, Grissom walked and went to third on a single by Fernandez. The batter was Vizquel, facing Randy Myers, who led the American League with 45 saves, and would finish fourth in both the Cy Young and the Most Valuable Player voting. So Hargrove called for a squeeze play.

Myers threw to the plate as Grissom was streaking down the third base line. Vizquel made a stab at a bunt attempt, but he missed the ball. Fortunately for the Indians, so did Orioles catcher Lenny Webster. The ball bounced out of the glove of Webster, who thought the ball had hit Vizquel's bat and was a foul ball—except that it wasn't. It was a live ball. Home plate umpire John Hirschbeck ruled that Vizquel's bat did not make contact with the ball.

Grissom crossed the plate with the winning run. The Indians poured out of the dugout and celebrated at home plate with Grissom, as Webster and Orioles manager Davey Johnson argued that the ball hit Vizquel's bat.

"I missed the ball," Vizquel said after the game. "I never tipped it. You can feel it if you tip it. I looked around to see what the umpire called, and I saw Marquis crossing the plate. All of a sudden we'd won the game, and everybody was jumping up and down."

Webster lost his argument with Hirschbeck.

"He definitely tipped the ball and deflected it off my glove," Webster told reporters. "I saw contact. I heard contact. When Hirschbeck gestured, I thought he meant it was a foul ball. That's why I didn't run after it."

It wasn't a foul ball. It was the end of the game, and the Indians were leading the series 2-1.

"First of all," said Hargrove, speaking more than 20 years later of the game-winning play, "you call for a squeeze in the 12th inning of a postseason game, your palms start sweating and your heart rate goes up about 400 beats per minute. We had our best bunter at the plate. It wasn't that I didn't have confidence in Omar putting the ball in play and hitting a fly ball. Omar could have, and would have done that. But we hardly ever squeezed, and I felt it was the right play at the right time, with the right hitter at the plate."

Incredibly, the Indians got the right result, despite a failure to execute.

"I remember telling the players to get the hell off the field. Let's go to the clubhouse and get out of here," Hargrove said. "If they're going to change the call, they're going to have to call us back from the clubhouse. Webster thought it was a foul ball. I looked at the replay and I couldn't tell if Omar fouled it off. I asked Omar, and he said he didn't. So I guess you could say the play worked. It's all about the outcome, so it worked like a charm."

The Indians won the next night, in a wild Game 4 that was 7-7 going into the bottom of the ninth. Alomar's two-out single off Benitez drove in Ramirez from second base with the winning run in an 8-7 Indians victory.

With a chance to close out the series and win the American League pennant at home in Game 5, the Indians lost 4-2, sending the series back to Baltimore for what became an epic Game 6.

The Game 6 numbers alone don't tell the story. They scream the story. The pitching matchup was Nagy vs. Mussina. Nagy was pitching out of trouble the whole night, while the Indians could barely get anybody on base against Mussina. Nagy somehow managed to pitch 7⅓ scoreless innings, despite allowing 13 base runners: nine hits, three walks and a hit batter. But the Orioles were 0-for-12 with runners in scoring position and left 14 men on base.

"I remember being on the edge of my seat the entire night. We just kept getting out of it," Hargrove said.

Mussina pitched eight scoreless innings, allowing one hit.

He retired the first 12 batters he faced, then gave up a double to Justice leading off the fifth inning. Mussina then retired 12 of the last 14 batters he faced.

The Orioles' best chance came in the bottom of the seventh inning. Mike Bordick and Anderson led off the inning with singles, putting runners at first and second with nobody out.

The next batter was Roberto Alomar, who in attempting a sacrifice bunt to move the runners to second and third, bunted Nagy's first pitch down the third base line. Williams came racing in and fielded the ball, but instead of throwing to first he wheeled and threw to third, where Vizquel, who had out-run Bordick, was standing at the bag. Vizquel caught the ball for the 5-6 out at third. Nagy then got Geronimo Berroa to ground into an inning-ending double play. Stunningly, a rally that looked like it might produce one or two runs for the Orioles was over in the blink of an eye.

It's called the wheel play.

You almost never see it, because it's so hard to execute properly.

"The way you teach it," said Hargrove, "is the shortstop comes behind the runner at second, just off the runner's right hip, taps his glove so the runner knows he's there. Then the shortstop breaks for third, and when the pitcher sees clearance between the shortstop and the baserunner, the pitcher throws a strike to the plate. We tell the pitcher, 'We don't care how hard you throw it, but throw a strike, because we want them to bunt the ball.' The first baseman, pitcher and third baseman all come straight in. So you've got all that covered. It was a good bunt, but Matt Williams was standing 20 feet away, and we got the guy at third. When you put the wheel play on, if they don't bunt, you're in deep shit."

In today's game, it's as extinct as a dinosaur, partly because in this analytics-driven era, teams rarely bunt under any circumstances. But on the night of Oct. 15, 1997, in Baltimore, Maryland, Indians infielders, under the almost unbearable pressure of a scoreless game in the seventh inning of a possible playoff elimination game, executed it flawlessly. It's a play that requires guts for the manager to call for it, infielders with the nerves of a safe cracker, and the timing and skill of a Gold Glove performer, which both Williams and Vizquel were.

"You hardly ever see that play run successfully, because even though everybody practices it, nobody ever uses it, probably because the play has to be run perfectly. There's no room for error," said Hargrove.

In this case, Hargrove said he had no trepidation about calling for the wheel play.

"None," he said. "I was absolutely sure they were going to bunt.

The book called for it. That's what I would have done. Maybe not in the regular season. But in this game—you're trying to go to the World Series—it was a tie ballgame. And it worked.

"I felt certain it was the right thing to do. I was shocked after the game, when (Orioles manager) Davey Johnson said he couldn't believe we ran the wheel play there. For me, it was Baseball 101. Runners at first and second, no outs, tie game in the seventh inning. They have to bunt there."

The sign for the play was not given by Hargrove. He had bench coach Johnny Goryl flash it to Williams at third. Williams gave the sign to the rest of the infielders, then went to the mound and told Nagy, "We've got the wheel play on. You're going straight in (off the mound, prepared to field a bunt)."

"Sandy's job is to call for a fastball right down the pipe, then stand there and direct traffic," Hargrove explained. "If we have no chance at third, then he calls for the throw to first. If the ball is bunted right in front of the plate, Sandy gets it and throws to third. But ideally, you want the third baseman to field it, because Omar will be at third, because he's going to be halfway there before the ball is bunted."

The shortstop's job on the wheel play is to break for third base, and make sure he gets there before the runner advancing from second.

"Even if the bunt goes to the first baseman, you can still get the out at third," Hargrove said. "In that situation the hitter is taught to bunt it to the third baseman, because that means he can't cover third, which is unoccupied. But with the wheel play, the third baseman comes in, but the bag is still occupied, by the shortstop."

In that particular situation, what scared Hargrove the most was Roberto Alomar's baseball IQ. One of the smartest players in the game, seeing a pitch "coming right down the pipe" and, perhaps, as an infielder himself, detecting that the wheel play was on, might swing away instead of bunt.

"The hard part of the wheel play is getting the hitter to bunt," Hargrove said. "Because if they swing the bat, you're screwed. It's one of those either/or plays, because you're selling out. Robbie was the hitter, their best hitter, so maybe it was up for grabs whether he was going to bunt or not. Maybe in their mind, but not in my mine."

Given the stakes, it was an incredibly gutsy play to call.

"Don't get me wrong. I'm not a genius," Hargrove said. "I think I'm a good baseball guy and I think I was a good manager. But I'm not a genius. I would rather have lived with the results had he swung the bat than live with the results if he didn't swing the bat.

"The stake to my heart would have been they bunted, and we didn't get the out at third because we didn't have the wheel play on. You roll the dice sometimes. I think a lot of people thought I was robotic as a manager. If 'A' happens, 'B' is going to follow. But there were a lot of times when you go with your gut instinct. And that was one of them."

The second-worst outcome for the manager is if he puts on the wheel play, but the batter takes the pitch. Because it makes it almost impossible to run the play again on the next pitch.

"You can, but they probably aren't going to bunt. That's why the pitcher has to throw a strike," Hargrove said. "You want him to bunt the ball. You don't want to go 0-1 or 1-0. If he's going to bunt, you want him to put the ball in play right away, so you throw a batting practice fastball."

Even with Robbie Alomar's matchless baseball acumen, Hargrove said he didn't think Alomar, given a fat pitch like that, would swing away.

"I don't know of very many hitters that can have in their mind, 'OK, I'm bunting here' and be able to change their mind in the middle of it. Although if anyone could do it, it would have been Robbie. But thank goodness he didn't," Hargrove said.

That one play produced a huge momentum swing. What looked like a potential huge inning for the Orioles in a scoreless game turned out to be no inning at all. The rally was wiped out by the Indians' execution of a borderline obsolete defensive maneuver.

"I think it turned the whole game and series around. I know it shocked Davey," said Hargrove. "It's one of the few times in my career I saw that play be successful."

While there was a huge momentum swing in the Indians' favor, when the dust had settled, it was still a scoreless game.

"It surprises me that more people don't remember that play, in that game," Hargrove said. "George Will, who I got to know when I was in Baltimore because he would always come to the games with his son, wrote a book that included that play. He's the only guy I ever saw nationally that paid a lot of attention to that play."

It remained scoreless through the eighth inning, the ninth inning and the 10th inning. In the 11th inning, Benitez came on in relief of Myers, who pitched two scoreless innings in relief of the brilliant Mussina. Benitez retired the first two batters in the top of the 11th.

But then Fernandez hit the first pitch Benitez threw him over the wall in right field for a stunning home run, the first and only run of the game. That elicited the priceless mid-course correction description by Indians radio voice Herb Score, who after making his home run call, told his listeners, "And the Indians are going to the World Series! . . . maybe."

Score forgot the Orioles still had to bat in the bottom of the 11th inning, and Hargrove brought Mesa in to get those last three outs.

Trying to protect a 1-0 lead, on the road, in extra innings, Mesa struck out the first batter, Chris Hoiles. Webster, the second hitter, hit a bouncer back to the mound for out number two. But Brady Anderson singled, bringing Robbie Alomar to the plate again. Everybody knew he wasn't bunting this time.

Alomar worked the count to 3-2. Then, as Mesa prepared to deliver his seventh pitch of the at bat and 18th of the inning, Hargrove had seen enough.

"I couldn't watch the last pitch. I couldn't watch it," he said. "I just leaned back where the wall of the dugout comes out. I leaned back so I couldn't see the plate. And then everybody started screaming, and I'm like, 'Oh, good!' But I couldn't watch. It didn't matter if I saw it or not. It was going to be what it was going to be. That was one of the few times where I gave in to, 'I can't watch this.'"

What Hargrove missed was strike three.

The Indians were going to the World Series . . . for sure.

They had managed just three hits in 11 innings, but they won 1-0. Baltimore had 10 hits, left 14 runners on base, and was 0-for-12 with runners in scoring position. "It seemed like every inning they were going to score, but they never did," said Hargrove. Cleveland had three hits, left five runners on base and was 0-for-5 with runners in scoring position.

The Indians won their second American League pennant in

three years, even though for the series they were out-scored by the Orioles (19-18), out-hit by the Orioles (.248 to .193), out-homered by the Orioles (7-5), and the Orioles' pitchers had a better ERA (2.64 to 2.95).

Fernandez, who hit the pennant-winning home run in the 11th inning, wasn't even in Hargrove's original lineup for Game 6. Bip Roberts had started four of the first five games at second base, but hit just .150 in those games. Shortly before the start of Game 6, Roberts came to Hargrove and said he was sick.

"He told me, 'Grover, I think I have symptoms of the flu,'" Hargrove said. "I always encouraged my players to be honest with me, so I appreciated his honesty. And I've got Tony Fernandez sitting there, who is healthy and a really good player. And another player comes in and says he's sick. For the sixth game of the ALCS, if you want to play, don't come in and tell me that. So we made the change."

And, of course, Fernandez turned out to be the hero of the game.

"There were so many things that went on in our '97 postseason, it almost seemed like it was our destiny to win it all. I had that thought in my mind a lot," Hargrove said.

The one constant in the ALCS was that every time the Orioles brought in Benitez, the Indians did some damage, the biggest blow being Fernandez's pennant-winning home run in Game 6. Baltimore's team ERA in the ALCS was 2.64, but if you remove Benitez, their ERA was 2.29. Benitez appeared in four of the six games and had an ERA of 12.00. He was the losing pitcher in two of Baltimore's four losses. In a total of three innings he gave up four runs on three hits, two of them home runs, both of them killers: Grissom's three-run homer in the eighth inning of Game 2 and Fernandez's game-winning blast in Game 6.

During the regular season Benitez was a dominating reliever for the Orioles. In 71 appearances he had a 2.45 ERA, with nine saves, as the backup closer to Myers, while averaging 13 strikeouts per nine innings and holding opposing batters to a .191 batting average. But in the ALCS the Indians wore him out.

"He tipped his pitches," Hargrove revealed. "We didn't catch it until the end of the season. He would come set and if his glove was straight up and down, he would throw his fastball. When his glove was over top, laying over top, he'd throw his splitter. So we had his pitches through the whole series."

Hargrove wasn't sure how or who on the Indians deciphered the fact that Benitez tipped his pitches.

"I don't know if someone from another club told one of our players, or what," he said. "The clubs I had in the '90s were real good about picking up pitches. Maybe a guy, when he came set, the finger out of his glove would wiggle, and he'd throw one pitch, or if the finger was still, he would throw another. Stuff like that.

"Eddie Murray was really good at that, and he taught Kenny Lofton, who was in Eddie's hip pocket all the time anyway. So, Kenny got to where he was pretty decent at it. We didn't spend a lot of time on it. It's not like we all sat there saying, 'OK, let's get this guy's pitches.' But they would notice things. They really paid attention to detail, and it made a huge difference in the Baltimore series."

Normally it's the players in the dugout, not the hitters in the batter's box, who figure out if pitchers are tipping their pitches.

"It takes a little bit of a verification process to make sure you're right," Hargrove said. "Because you don't want to get fooled. There would be times when a guy would say, 'I think I've got his pitches,' and then you'd watch it for two or three hitters and say, 'Ahh, maybe not.' There are probably more times when you thought you had a guy's pitches, but you didn't."

Sometimes a team will think they have an opposing pitcher's pitches, but a player on that pitcher's team will beat them to the punch and tell the pitcher he is tipping his pitches.

"There was a time when Charlie Nagy was having a tough run for a while, four or five starts. People were having really good swings on Charlie, where they hadn't been having them before," Hargrove said. "We looked at hours and hours of tape to see if he was tipping his pitches. We really thought that he was. But we never could find it, and I never heard anything. Usually, you'll hear something later on if a guy has been tipping his pitches. But I didn't hear anything. It was just one of those things. Charlie was just going through a rough spot."

What reveals that a pitcher might be tipping his pitches?

"When hitters take good swings at pitches that there shouldn't be good swings at," Hargrove said. "Or you take close pitches. Like Charlie had a good split, and they'd take a borderline split. Most of the time a guy would be hacking at that thing. Because a split comes in waist high, but that's not a good pitch for you to hit, because it's going to go down. When a pitcher of Charlie's caliber is not getting goofy-looking swings from hitters who historically have had goofy-looking swings off him, you say to yourself, 'Hey, wait a minute. Something's going on here.'"

After the strikeout that Hargrove couldn't watch that ended the 1997 ALCS, with the Indians winning their second pennant in three years, there was the usual clubhouse champagne celebration. It carried over, after hours, to an impromptu party in a nearby restaurant that stayed open so the Indians could enjoy their accomplishment a little longer. The team stayed overnight in Baltimore, because it had to leave for Florida the next day to begin preparation for the World Series.

But after the party in the restaurant, Hargrove, his wife Sharon, Indians third-base coach Jeff Newman and his wife Diane walked to a cigar bar for a quieter celebration. Just the four of them. It was the first time Sharon had ever had a chocolate martini.

"Her and Diane had a chocolate martini, and Jeff and I sat up there and had a scotch and smoked a cigar," Hargrove said. "Then we walked back to the hotel, went to bed, and I woke up the next morning feeling like I had been run over by a truck."

CHAPTER 13

I'll Let You Know
When It Happens

"I just remember how quiet it was.
How deathly quiet it was."

As the Indians flew to Florida for the first two games of the World
Series, Hargrove reflected on the difference between his 1997 World
Series team and the Indians' 1995 World Series team. The '95 team
just overwhelmed opponents. The '97 team wasn't bursting at the
seams with off-the-charts talent like the '95 team. The shadow of
the '95 team easily eclipsed that of the '97 team. The '95 team was a
big team, with big names, and big personalities that did big things.
The '95 team was over-talented. The '97 team was overachieving.

"Getting to the World Series in '97 was more a feeling of accomplishment than '95, because in '97 our team was so different. They
were such grinders," said Hargrove. "Of all the clubs that I had in
that run (of five consecutive division titles in Cleveland), the '97
club was probably the least-talented. It was still awfully good. But
offensively it wasn't to the level of the '95 club. I think a large part
of the success we had in '97, to get to the World Series and damn
near win it, was due to Matt Williams' mental toughness rubbing
off on everyone else. I really believe that. I never talked to Matt
about whether he enjoyed playing here or not, but I do know I sure
enjoyed having him on the ballclub. He was another guy you never
had to worry about."

Williams was professional to a fault. He seemed to have no
lighter side, on or off the field. He had only two known facial expres-
sions: a grimace and a slight grimace. His lips seemed perpetually

pursed. In his one year with the Indians, the closest Williams came to being whimsical may have been on the night of Sept. 19, in the first inning of the Indians' 6-2 win in the second game of a doubleheader at Kansas City. Royals rookie Jed Hansen had just stolen third base. After Hansen slid into third, Williams, who still had the ball in his glove, innocently asked Hansen to step off the base so Williams could kick the dirt off the bag. Hansen, the rookie, obliged Williams, the veteran—and Williams tagged him for the third out of the inning.

When Williams came to bat in the top of the second inning, Kansas City pitcher Ricky Bones hit him in the hip with a pitch. Williams was not amused. He took several steps toward the mound and shook his finger at Bones. When asked by reporters after the game if Bones hit Williams as retaliation for the hidden ball trick, Royals manager Tony Muser said, "Yes, it probably was."

Williams took the game serious. He took life serious. He was always serious.

"Oh yeah," said Hargrove. "You'd say hello to him and you worried he would punch you in the nose or bite your head off. But he would loosen up every now and again."

Carrying himself with an almost regal bearing, Williams, who hit 32 home runs with 105 RBI and won Gold Glove and Silver Slugger awards in his one year in Cleveland, was the unquestioned nobleman of Hargrove's band of grinders.

"It always bothered John (Hart) a lot that we only won 86 games. I understood that. But these guys were grinders," Hargrove said. "You look at all those one-run games." Six of the Indians' 10 wins in the postseason in '97 were by one run. "You don't win all those games—I mean you get three hits in 11 innings and win 1-0 (in the ALCS Game 6 clincher in Baltimore), you don't do that unless everybody has sold out for it. I mean everybody is all in. And our guys were really good at that. As the season went along, it was more and more and more that way."

According to Hargrove, the '97 team was built that way because of the presence of Williams.

"One of the reasons that team made it to the World Series was Matt. I give full credit to him for that," said Hargrove. "When it was time to play, Matt played. I mean he played. Never made any excuses. Never tried to show anybody up. Didn't hot dog it or anything like that. He was a solid professional player, and he was awfully, awfully good."

Unbeknownst to many, Williams was going through a divorce during that 1997 season, a fact that wouldn't be made public until after the season. That made what he did statistically and as one of the Indians' leaders on and off the field even more impressive.

"This has probably been the toughest year I've ever been through. Inconsistent professionally, tough personally. It hasn't been good," said Williams during the World Series.

After the Indians' heart-pounding, pennant-clinching 1-0 victory over Baltimore in the ALCS, Hargrove felt that so many wild things had happened and gone in the Indians' favor during the postseason that it was their destiny to win it all. His players felt the same way.

"We peaked at the right time, and started playing our best base-ball at the end of the year," said Jim Thome. "Like the wheel play in Baltimore, and the way we manufactured runs. That whole year, that club did so many of the little things that helped us win. Those are the type of teams that you think are going to win a World Series."

The 1997 Florida Marlins didn't even win their division. They won 92 games, but finished in second place in the NL East, nine games behind the Atlanta Braves. At that time just one wild-card team qualified for the postseason. The Marlins' 92 wins allowed them to claim the wildcard spot by four games over the Dodgers, who finished second in the AL West with 88 wins.

Florida swept the Giants in three games in the Division Series, then upset Atlanta in six games in the NLCS, even though Florida hit just .199 as a team against that tough Braves pitching staff.

"I knew they were a good ballclub," Hargrove said of the Marlins. "They had Gary Sheffield and Bobby Bonilla and Kevin Brown, Al Leiter, Charles Johnson, Jeff Conine, Darren Daulton. They had some big-time players. We knew we had our work cut out for us. But at no point in the postseason that year did we ever think, 'We're lucky to be here.' We knew we'd worked for it, and that we had as good a chance to win it all as anybody else did."

The Marlins, who were only in their fifth year of existence, had a roller coaster season thanks to their owner, Wayne Huizenga. The

Marlins went 80-82 in 1996 and finished third in the NL East, 16 games behind division-winning Atlanta. That was the fifth of 14 consecutive division titles by the Braves, which obviously frustrated Huizenga. So, after the 1996 season he decided to go all out to try to win it all in 1997.

During the off-season between 1996 and 1997 the Marlins signed six free agents, three of them to big money deals: Bonilla, Moises Alou and Alex Fernandez. During the season they traded for Daulton and Cliff Floyd. As a result, the Marlins went from 15th (out of 30 teams) in the majors in payroll in 1996 to seventh in 1997.

Around mid-season, however, when Huizenga became discouraged by poor attendance and his inability to gain any traction in his attempt to secure funding for the building of a new stadium with taxpayer money, he announced he was going to sell the team, a decision that led to the Marlins getting rid of most of their highest-paid players immediately after the World Series.

It was against that backdrop that the Indians and Marlins convened for what became one of the least artistic World Series ever played. The two teams combined for 13 errors, a 5.08 ERA, and a World Series-record 76 walks. The starting pitching matchup in two of the seven games was Cleveland's Chad Ogea vs. Florida's Kevin Brown, an All-Star who pitched the only no-hitter in the majors that year. In the regular season Ogea was 8-9 with a 4.99 ERA, and Brown was 16-8 with a 2.69 ERA. However, in their two World Series matchups, Ogea was 2-0 with a 1.54 ERA and Brown was 0-2 with an 8.18 ERA.

It was a zany World Series all the way around. The last pitch of the Series was thrown by the Indians' No. 1 starter, four hours and 10 minutes after he didn't throw the first pitch of Game 7. The discrepancy of the weather in the two venues matched the dyspepsia the Indians felt following the excruciating result of that final pitch. The average game-time temperature for the four games in Miami was 81 degrees. The average game-time temperature for the three games in Cleveland was 43 degrees. During one of the games it snowed.

"People tell me that it snowed, but I didn't realize it," Hargrove said. "We got home and Sharon said, 'I can't believe it snowed.' And I said, 'It snowed?' I was totally oblivious to the weather."

The World Series began the way most postseason series began for the Indians—with a loss. Manny Ramirez and Jim Thome hit home runs, for Thome his first since Sept. 14, a span of 73 consecutive homerless at-bats. But it didn't matter, because Orel Hershiser gave up seven runs on six hits, two of them home runs, and four walks in just 4⅓ innings. The Indians lost 7-4, the fifth consecutive postseason series in which they lost the first game.

They won the second game, 6-1, the first of the two Ogea-Brown duels. Ogea, who lost his two starts against Baltimore in the ALCS, held the Marlins to one run on seven hits in 6⅔ innings. The Indians rocked Brown for six runs and 10 hits in six innings. One of the home runs was by Sandy Alomar Jr., his fourth of the postseason.

After playing in temperatures of 84 and 78 degrees in the first two games at Pro Player Stadium in Miami, the Series shifted to Cleveland, and was greeted by 47-degree weather for Game 3. For the Indians, this was the great bullpen failure game, worse even than the still-to-come Game 7 meltdown. Had the bullpen done its job in just one of those two games, instead of neither, the outcome of the Series would have been different.

Game 3 was a slugfest in a slop-fest. The Indians usually won slugfests, but they lost this one, and looked awful doing so. Both teams did. The Indians and Marlins combined for 11 runs, seven hits and three errors—and that was just in the ninth inning. For the entire game—a 4-hour, 12-minute, nine-inning monstrosity—they combined for 25 runs, 26 hits, 17 walks and six errors. It was not a baseball Mona Lisa.

The Indians led 2-1 after the first inning, 5-3 after the fourth inning, and 7-3 after five. But going into the ninth inning it was 7-7. It was then that Indians relievers Eric Plunk, Alvin Morman and Jose Mesa combined to throw 57 pitches to 11 batters, giving up seven runs on four hits, all singles. The three walks, three errors and one wild pitch didn't help, either.

When the carnage was cleared, the Marlins had a 14-7 lead. But the Indians weren't done. In the bottom of the ninth, facing Marlins' closer Robb Nen, the Indians—this is what Hargrove meant when he called his '97 team a bunch of grinders—forced Nen to throw 43 pitches to eight batters, as the Indians scored four runs on three hits, but still came up short in an exhausting, demoralizing 14-11 loss.

"We played so poorly, and it was such an ugly game that I don't think we'll have trouble letting go of this game," said Hargrove after the poorly played ugly game.

Had the Indians' relievers allowed zero, one, two or three runs in the top of the ninth inning, the Indians would have won the game and there would have been no Game 7. But they didn't, and there was. Charles Nagy started and gave up five runs, including three home runs and four walks in six innings, an outing of such alarm that it may have influenced Hargrove to make the decision he did when the time came to choose his Game 7 starter. After Nagy's exit, five of the six relievers who followed him to the mound also gave up runs, nine in all by the bullpen, although three of the runs were unearned thanks to errors by Jim Thome, Tony Fernandez and Marquis Grissom.

"We didn't get good starting pitching, good middle relief or good short relief," said Hargrove after the game. "I was really surprised with the way our bullpen pitched. That's the one thing our pitching has done all this postseason. It's kept us in the ballgame."

Bud Selig, who at the time was Major League Baseball's acting commissioner, was neither thrilled nor impressed by the poorly played, poorly pitched marathon Game 3.

"Mike Hargrove called it ugly, and he was right," said Selig. "Through the whole game I felt the 'Unfinished Symphony' had a better chance of being finished before that game ended."

The Game 3 abomination rekindled complaints nationally that the Cleveland-Florida World Series wasn't nearly as sexy as an Atlanta-Yankees rematch from the 1996 World Series would have been, or, for that matter, if Baltimore or Seattle represented the American League.

"Both teams gave everything they had in Game 3. The thing that offended me was ball one, ball two, ball three. But there has been bad pitching in the World Series before," said Selig, who conceded that the TV ratings would be better if it was a New York-Atlanta World Series.

Hargrove fumed at the notion that the Marlins vs. the Indians made for a stale World Series matchup.

"I know people are saying woe is baseball, because Cleveland and the Marlins are in the World Series instead of New York, Baltimore or Atlanta. But they all had the same chance we did," Hargrove told reporters at the time. "I think it's just built into being Cleveland or Minnesota or Kansas City. You're going to hear these things whenever you don't have a team from a big market like Los Angeles or New York in the World Series."

Prior to Game 5, Marlins manager Jim Leyland also chimed in with a rant against critics who blamed the small-market teams in the World Series for the record-low TV ratings.

"Mike Hargrove said it best. They (big market teams) had the same chance that we did. We won it. We are the teams that are supposed to be here, and it makes me puke when I continue to hear people talking about the Marlins and the Indians," said Leyland. "Aren't our fans entitled? I'm sick of hearing the weak comments about the pitchers, and everybody crying because Atlanta, Baltimore and New York aren't here. People in Florida are happy. People in Cleveland are happy. We don't have to apologize for being here. If everybody wants New York and Atlanta in the Series, why don't we just cancel the season and put them in?"

In Game 4, it snowed.

The game-time temperature was 35 degrees. The wind-chill was 18 degrees. "I heard an announcement that they're switching the fifth-inning (infield) drag to a fifth-inning plow. And they're thinking about bringing in salt trucks," joked Hershiser.

Playing through occasional snow flurries for parts of the game, Alomar had three hits and three RBI and Williams and Ramirez both homered as the Indians led from start to finish in a 10-3 victory that evened the Series at two games apiece. Jaret Wright pitched six solid innings, although he did walk five, to get the win, as the 21-year-old rookie improved his postseason record to 3-0.

For Game 5, the temperature shot all the way up to 46 degrees. The Indians took a 4-2 lead into the sixth inning, three of the Indians' runs coming on Alomar's fifth home run of the postseason. But in the sixth inning Hershiser gave up a two-out, three-run home run to Alou, and later in the inning Plunk walked Devon White with the bases loaded, giving Miami a 6-4 lead. The Marlins scored single runs in the eighth and ninth innings to make it 8-4.

Then, for the second time in three games, the Indians scored multiple runs in the bottom of the ninth inning but lost the game by one run. A two-run single by David Justice and an RBI single by Thome off Nen cut the Miami lead to 8-7. But with a runner at first and two outs, Alomar, who would hit .367 with two home runs and 10 RBI in the World Series, flied out to end the game. The Marlins' 8-7 win gave them a 3-2 lead as the Series shifted back to Miami.

Hershiser's two starts in the '97 World Series were his last two starts in an Indians uniform. He lost both of them, and gave up 13 runs and six walks in 10 innings (an 11.70 ERA).

"I have let the team down in my two starts," he said. "Now my role is to cheerlead, and ask these guys to pick me up, just like they've done all year."

Following that Game 5 loss, Hershiser seemed to sense that it was his final start in a Cleveland uniform.

"I'll remember the fans, the whole experience of Cleveland," he told reporters after the game. "This is an awesome place to play, a great place for my family."

Although Hershiser is best remembered, and rightfully so, for his years pitching for the Dodgers, he actually appeared in more post-season games while with the Indians. In 13 years for the Dodgers, he started seven postseason games and was 4-0 with a 2.02 ERA. In three years with the Indians he started 11 postseason games and was 4-3 with a 3.54 ERA.

As the Series returned to the warm weather of South Florida, Game 6 was a re-match of the Game 2 pitching matchup of Ogea and Brown. With the Indians' backs to the wall, Ogea won again. He not only out-pitched Brown, he out-hit Brown. Ogea held the Marlins to one run in five innings, and with one out in the top of the second inning, he slapped a two-run single to right field to give the Indians all the runs they needed in a clutch 4-1 victory, sending the Series to a deciding seventh game. In the fifth inning, Ogea led off with a double down the right field line off Brown, and later in the inning Ogea scored on Ramirez's second sacrifice fly of the game. So, in the Indians' must-win Game 6, Ogea was the winning pitcher and he was directly responsible for three of their four runs: he drove in two and scored one.

"I haven't gotten a hit since I was in high school," said Ogea after the game.

"When he hit the double down the line, I turned to Jeff Newman and said, 'Are you shitting me?'" said Hargrove. "We've got all those professional hitters going up there and scuffling, and then Ogea goes up and hits a double down the line."

Florida's only run came on a sacrifice fly by Daulton in the bottom of the fifth. Following Ogea to the mound were Mike Jackson, Paul Assenmacher and Mesa, who combined to pitch four scoreless innings.

"The Indians played almost a perfect game. They were flawless," said Leyland.

The Indians had won a must-win Game 6. Their magic carpet ride through the 1997 postseason was alive and well, with just one final chapter to be written. For the first time in six years, the World Series would go the distance. There would be a Game 7, and it would be played on Oct. 26, 1997—Hargrove's 48th birthday. Maybe he was right when, after that preposterous 1-0 pennant-clinching win in 11 innings at Baltimore, he said he felt his team was destined to win it all. The Indians hadn't won a World Series since 1948. They had only won two World Series in their entire 96-year history as charter members of the American League, dating back to 1901, when Roosevelt was in the White House. Not Franklin. Teddy.

In 1920, the Indians won the World Series over Brooklyn, in seven games. But that was when the World Series was a best-of-nine series. The Indians won it five games to two. In 1948, they won the World Series by beating the Boston Braves in six games. But that's it. To this day, that's it. Still. Those are the only two times the Indians have won the World Series.

*   *   *

The first World Series ever played in the state of Florida had wound its way to a Game 7, in the most orderly sequence possible. Miami had won all the odd-numbered games and Cleveland had won all the even-numbered games. Game 7 would break the tie— and millions of hearts.

First, Hargrove had to decide on his starting pitcher. There were two options: 30-year-old Nagy or the 21-year-old rookie, Wright. Nagy, the starter for the American League in the 1996 All-Star Game, was an Indians lifer. He came in on the ground floor, right at the start of the methodical but magnificent rebuild of a franchise that went from being a hapless loser to a hellacious winner. Nagy was there for the entire ride. The Indians' first round pick, out of the University of Connecticut, the 17th player taken overall in the 1988 June Draft, Nagy was in the big leagues two years later.

He was the only pitcher to reach 10 wins on the Indians' 105-loss train wreck in 1991. Over his next seven full seasons—he missed most of 1993 due to injuries—Nagy averaged 15 wins per year. During his 13-year career with Cleveland, he was the Indians' opening day starter four times, an All-Star selection three times, and he finished in the top seven in the Cy Young Award voting three times. He still ranks in the top 10 among all Indians pitchers in career wins, strikeouts and games started. In 1997, through his seniority, production and personality, Nagy was one of the leaders of the team.

Mindful of all that, Hargrove instead chose Wright as his Game 7 starter.

"That was a tough one. One of the hardest decisions I ever had to make," said Hargrove, who consulted with pitching coach Mark Wiley before making it.

"It wasn't a decision I made lightly," Hargrove said. "As a manager, you always struggle. You know you have to make decisions with your head and not your heart. My heart was saying Charlie, because he had been so good for so long. But Jaret in the postseason had been really good, and he threw the ball 96-97 miles per hour. Jaret had pitched in Yankee Stadium and done well, and Jaret was a young kid then, and I'm not sure he understood what was going on around him. He just went out there and competed, and he was a great competitor, who had good stuff. So I went with Jaret. That was a really hard conversation to have with Charlie. He had to be pissed. But he was never visibly upset, or down. He just said, 'OK.'"

"I wasn't happy about it, but it was the best decision for the team," said Nagy, in the MLB Network Documentary "The Dynasty That Almost Was."

"They told me I was starting Game 7. I honestly didn't get nervous. I just said, 'Cool, let's do this,'" said Wright, in the MLB documentary. Wright became the youngest pitcher ever to start

Game 7 of the World Series. Though just 21, Wright, who didn't get called up to the Indians until late June, had a workload in 1997 that was far more than most people realized. Counting his 15 starts in the minors before being summoned to Cleveland, plus his 16 regular season starts and five postseason starts for the Indians, Wright made 36 starts overall. He pitched 216 innings and had a record of 18-7 and a 3.71 ERA.

He was young, cocky, talented, and, to a certain degree, clueless. Too clueless to realize—or, perhaps, too cocky to let it prey on his nerves—the magnitude of what starting Game 7 of the World Series meant to his team, the franchise, and millions of long-suffering Indians fans throughout Ohio and the country. Hargrove liked all those qualities in his starting pitcher for a winner-take-all game.

As she and her family arrived at their seats behind the Indians' dugout on the third-base side in Pro Player Stadium for the most important baseball game in what at that time was her 27-year baseball partnership with her husband, Sharon Hargrove didn't like what she was seeing from Wright's fiancee, who was sitting nearby.

"She was talking to all these people and putting on makeup, and I thought to myself, 'She has no idea what's going on here,'" Sharon said. "Her fiance is pitching the seventh game of the World Series. We spent 22 years in baseball before we even went to a playoff game. So, I went over to her and said, 'I never looked as good as you, but I didn't start out looking like this,' and I pointed to myself. I said, 'This isn't an easy life. But this is the best it gets. This is Game 7 of the World Series. This doesn't happen every year.'"

Florida's Game 7 starter was left-hander Al Leiter. It was his second start of the Series. His first came in that riotous 14-11 Marlins win in Game 3. The Indians in that game took Leiter to the woodshed, roughing him up for seven runs on six hits and six walks in just 4⅔ innings, during which Leiter launched a whopping 114 pitches in the general direction of home plate. But Leiter was a quality major league pitcher, who had a 19-year career, and he pitched like it in Game 7, producing a quality start of six innings and two runs allowed.

Those two Cleveland runs came in a rally in the top of the third inning that was aided, for the second game in a row, by a good at-bat by the Cleveland pitcher. Thome led off the inning with a walk, and he went to second on a single by Grissom. Wright then laid down a perfect sacrifice bunt, moving the runners to second and third, with one out. Fernandez then drove in both base runners with a single to center, giving Cleveland a 2-0 lead.

Meanwhile Wright, presumably with his then-fiancee—they never married—paying attention, was brilliant. Through six innings he held the Marlins scoreless on one hit, and the Indians took that 2-0 lead into the seventh inning, meaning they were just nine outs away from winning the World Series for the first time in 49 years.

Through six innings Wright's pitch count was at 97, and Hargrove decided to let the rookie start the seventh inning. But Bonilla hit Wright's 98th pitch into the seats in right-center field for a home run.

"First-pitch changeup. I never liked first-pitch changeups before that game. I really disliked them after Bonilla hit that home run," said Hargrove, who let Wright face two more batters. Wright struck out Charles Johnson, but Craig Counsell drew a walk, which in turn drew a walk to the mound by Hargrove to change pitchers. Assenmacher relieved Wright and retired the next two batters to end the inning. The game went into the eighth inning, with the Indians leading 2-1.

"The tension is palpable," said Indians pitcher Brian Anderson, in the MLB Network documentary. "You're nine outs away . . . you're eight outs away . . . "

Antonio Alfonseca retired the Indians in order in the top of the eighth inning. In the bottom of the eighth, Hargrove brought in Jackson, who essentially shared the closing duties with Mesa that year. Mesa had 16 saves, Jackson 15. But in the postseason Mesa was Hargrove's closer, while Jackson was sensational as a setup man. Jackson appeared in 13 of the Indians' 18 postseason games and had a 0.68 ERA.

"Before Game 7, (pitching coach) Mark Wiley talked to Jackson, who we had used a lot in that postseason," Hargrove said. "Jackson told Mark, 'I've got one hitter in me.'"

Hargrove brought Jackson in to start the eighth inning and he let Jackson face two batters. Jackson retired them both. He retired Edgar Renteria on a ground ball back to the mound, and he struck out Gary Sheffield. Hargrove brought in Anderson, who got Jeff

Conine to fly out for the third out. The game went to the ninth inning with the Indians leading 2-1.

Alfonseca stayed in to start the ninth for Miami, and Williams led off with a walk. But Alomar grounded to short, where Renteria flipped the ball to second baseman Counsell for the force out on Williams. It could have been a double play, but Williams' hard slide into the bag up-ended Counsell, so the Marlins only got one out, and they were fortunate to get that one. Counsell never touched the base. He straddled it as Williams slid in and was called out. Had there been video review available back then, Cleveland certainly would have challenged the out call, which would have been reversed. That would have given the Indians runners at first and second with no outs, and the rest of that inning could have played out much differently than it did.

Felix Heredia then replaced Alfonseca, and Thome hit Heredia's first pitch to right field for a single, moving the hustling Alomar to third. So the Indians had runners at first and third with one out. Nen relieved Heredia, and got Grissom to hit a grounder to Renteria at short. Renteria, who was playing at medium depth, leaving open the option to go to second and a possible double play, double clutched trying to get the ball out of his glove, and thus threw to the plate, where catcher Charles Johnson put the tag on Alomar, who did not slide. Brian Giles, pinch hitting for Anderson, flied out to end the inning.

As the teams changed sides, preparing for the bottom of the ninth, John Hart was summoned from his seat and told to go to the Indians' clubhouse, in preparation for the postgame celebration and trophy presentation.

"I fought it. I'm not leaving my seat," said Hart, before acquiescing, after being told it was MLB protocol. Hart proceeded to the clubhouse, where much to his horror . . .

"The trophy is in our locker room. Biggest jinx ever," he said in the MLB Network documentary.

Anderson went back to the clubhouse about the same time. "They were building the stage, and putting up the plastic," Anderson told the MLB Network. "I'm like, 'Not yet . . . not yet.'"

Tom Hamilton, who was Herb Score's partner on the Indians' radio broadcast, went down to the clubhouse in the top of the ninth to prepare for live postgame interviews. He was there when they brought the trophy into the clubhouse, which made Hammy clammy. "This doesn't feel right. We're tempting the baseball gods," he said in "The Dynasty That Almost Was."

Then the longest, most nightmarish inning in Cleveland Indians history began to unfold, starting with Mesa jogging in from the bullpen. Alou led off with a single. But Mesa struck out Bonilla for the first out. The next hitter was Johnson, and Mesa got ahead in the count at 1-2. The Indians hardly ever called pitches from the bench, but in this situation, Alomar got a sign from the bench for Mesa to throw a fastball. But Mesa did not want to throw a fastball. He kept shaking off Alomar.

"If you throw a fastball inside to Johnson, he's out," said Hargrove in recounting the inning over 20 years later.

"If you've never called the game on me, why are you going to call the game that night? Let me pitch my game. I know how to do it," Mesa told the MLB Network.

Hargrove was not surprised by Mesa's recalcitrance.

"I've heard Jose say stuff like that before," Hargrove said years later. "Jose had a problem with me. One day he closed a game early in his career in Baltimore, and he threw a curveball to a guy, who almost hit it out of the ballpark. I told Jose, 'You don't need three pitches. Fastball, slider. That's enough. I don't want to see you throw the curveball anymore.' I think he resented that a little bit."

With Johnson down in the count 1-2, Hargrove was convinced a fastball was the correct pitch for Mesa to throw in that situation.

"I felt it then, and I feel it now," said Hargrove, over 20 years later. "If he throws a fastball inside, even it it's a ball, it gives him the outer half of the plate again, because he had thrown a number of sliders to Charles, and it looked like Charles was starting to lean out there. So we gave the sign to Sandy for a fastball and Jose shook it off two or three times. I've always believed that if a pitcher shakes off a pitch, especially like that, three times in a row, that him having the conviction to throw the pitch that he wants is better than throwing the pitch that I want, and not believing in it. So we let it go."

And Johnson hit the pitch Mesa wanted to throw into right field for a single, moving Alou to third.

"I wasn't real pleased. I don't think I ever talked to Jose about that," Hargrove said.

Following the hit by Johnson, Nagy started warming up in the Indians' bullpen, and Mesa continued to leak oil. Counsell ripped a 1-1 pitch to deep right field, where it was caught by Ramirez, but Alou scored the tying run. Mesa finally got the third out when Jim Eisenreich grounded out to second, and Game 7 of the 1997 World Series staggered into extra innings.

"When they tied the game, it felt like we lost," said Anderson, in "The Dynasty That Almost Was."

Nen stayed on to pitch the 10th inning, where he rendered a single by Fernandez meaningless by striking out the side. Mesa, who threw 20 pitches in that disastrous ninth inning, came back out for the 10th. He retired the first hitter, but the next two, Renteria and Sheffield, both singled, putting runners at first and second with one out. John Cangelosi, pinch hitting for Nen, struck out for the second out. Nagy then relieved Mesa and retired Alou on a flyout, sending Game 7 into the 11th inning.

Jay Powell, the Marlins' fifth reliever of the game, retired the Indians on 10 pitches in the top of the 11th inning. There would be no 12th inning.

Bonilla led off the bottom of the 11th with a single to center on an 0-2 pitch from Nagy.

"Our pen was gassed. Charlie had no business being out there, frankly. It wasn't his role," Hart told the MLB Network.

Gregg Zaun, trying to lay down a sacrifice bunt, hit a soft popup to the mound that Nagy caught, and nearly doubled off Bonilla at first. Nagy hesitated before throwing to Fernandez, the second baseman covering first. Without the hesitation, it might have been a double play, and the inning might have ended differently.

But it wasn't, and history marched on.

"You were nervous with every pitch, because you knew how important everything was," said Sharon Hargrove. "I had all our kids with me and I was a little bit concerned with how they were feeling. And, of course, I couldn't see Mike, because we were sitting in the stands behind our dugout, so I couldn't see into it."

The pesky and pest-y Counsell then hit a ground ball into the hole between first and second. Fernandez closed on the ball, but whiffed on it, and the ball went bouncing into right field on what was ruled an error by Fernandez, whose two-run single in the third inning gave the Indians a 2-0 lead. Bonilla went to third on the play, and the Marlins had runners at the corners with one out.

"The ball took a funny little hop. It wouldn't have been a double play, but we would have gotten one out," Hargrove said.

The Indians intentionally walked Eisenreich to load the bases, and it seemed to work. The next batter, Devon White, swung at the first pitch and hit another grounder to Fernandez, who fielded it and threw home for the force out. The bases remained loaded, but now there were two outs.

There would be no third out.

Renteria took a called strike on Nagy's first pitch. On Nagy's second pitch, Renteria hit a soft liner up the middle, off the top of Nagy's glove, through the Indians' infield, and into Shangri-La. Counsell—who else?—gleefully skipped home from third with the winning run of the 1997 World Series.

And that, for the Indians—excruciatingly beyond belief—was that. The final scene in the final act of the deplorable drama.

*   *   *

Despite all the overwhelming previous postseason evidence, all the jaw-dropping plays, breathtaking moments and implausible endings, all of which surely seemed to portend a grand and glorious finish, the Indians, in the end, were *not* destined to win it all. They were destined to have the protective plastic champagne curtains frantically torn down from the players' lockers, the presentation stage speedily dismantled and lugged away, and the championship trophy hastily carried down the hall from the visitors' clubhouse to the home team's clubhouse. The Indians, in the end, were destined to be handed a lump of coal by the baseball gods, and to be told to go sit on it.

Could anyone concoct a more devastating loss?

"To this day I haven't watched a tape of that game, and I won't," said Hart.

"It was like a knife just went through your heart," said Omar Vizquel, in "The Dynasty That Almost Was."

It was the first time in history that a team went into the ninth inning of Game 7 of the World Series with the lead, and didn't win the World Series.

"Heartbreaking," said Thome, over 20 years later. "We were so fortunate to be put in that situation, but not to accomplish it, for the city, that was hard. That was so tough. That was hard. It still is. I don't watch any videos or clips of that game, because it's just one of those moments where you look and go, 'OK, that was us, and unfortunately we didn't accomplish it.'"

As her baseball world, and that of her husband's—on his birthday, no less—collapsed around her, Sharon Hargrove stood, watched and fumed.

"They made us stay in the stands," she said of the wives and families of the Indians players. "The ushers and police wouldn't let us go down. So we had to stand there and watch the Marlins celebrate, and all that crap. It was at least 30 minutes before they took us down to the clubhouse. I wanted really bad to get our family together. The kids were really sad, and they were worried about how Mike was going to feel. I honestly can't remember much about that night. It was so late, and so emotional."

While his family was grimly forced to watch the Marlins celebrate the World Series victory the Indians felt would be theirs, Hargrove walked into the clubhouse and was immediately met by one of the clubhouse attendants, who told him he had an important phone call in his office.

Hargrove looked at the attendant, incredulous, and said, "What?"

"I went in there, but I wasn't in a real mood to talk to anybody," Hargrove said. "So, I pick up the phone and said, 'Hello?' And this woman said, 'Mr. Hargrove, please hold for the President of the United States.' The president came on the phone and said, 'Hey man, I'm really sorry.' And I'm thinking, 'Hey man'? It was like when Eric Plunk called me 'Dude' on the mound one day. But I could tell President Clinton was sincere. He really empathized with what had happened, and I appreciated that. He said, 'I'm really sorry. I feel for you.' After that I don't remember much of what he said. I mean, I wasn't expecting a phone call five minutes after I got my heart ripped out."

After his brief conversation with the most powerful man in the world, it was somewhere around 1 a.m. Hargrove—it was technically no longer his birthday—walked down the hall and into the clubhouse to address his players.

"I just remember how quiet it was. How deathly quiet it was," he said. "I stood in the middle of the clubhouse and talked to the players. I'm sure what I had to say they didn't necessarily want to hear. I told them how proud of them I was and that even though things didn't turn out the way we wanted them to, they had nothing to feel ashamed about. We were not picked to be anywhere close to that. I was proud of them how professional they had been and how they were good people. It wasn't a long meeting. I'm sure they didn't want to hear it any more than I wanted to talk to the president."

After talking to the players, Hargrove returned to his office. It was empty. He sat in the chair behind his desk, ran his fingers through his hair, and, for the first time since all hell broke loose in the biggest baseball game of his life, he had that one moment, alone with his thoughts, to process everything.

"I did," he said. "And I was like, 'What the fuck just happened?'"

Everyone knew that this one was going to take a while to get over, to digest, and recover from. This wasn't just another garden variety loss. This was Game 7 of the World Series. With one out in the ninth inning the Indians were leading 2-1. They thought they were two outs away from winning it all, when in reality, they were two innings away from losing it all.

Indians owner Dick Jacobs was fond of saying, "There are two things in America men think they can do better than anyone else: cook a steak and manage a baseball team." The second guessing of Hargrove's decisions in Game 7 began immediately.

"Some people look at me funny when I say this, but I can't think of anything I would have done differently," Hargrove said, over 20 years later. "I felt we made the right moves. I'm at peace with that. It just didn't work out for us. I'm at peace with Mesa throwing that slider (on Johnson's ninth-inning single). If that's what he believed in, that's good enough for me. I believed differently. But I'm at peace with it. I wish we would have won it. I really do wish we would have won it. For the city, the organization, for all of us personally, I wish it had been different."

The most obvious second guess was Hargrove's decision to not let Jackson, who got two outs on six pitches in the eighth inning, pitch the ninth. Jackson and Mesa were co-closers in 1997. Mesa started the season as the closer, then experienced a prolonged mid-season slump, during which Jackson assumed the closer's role. When Mesa finally got straightened out late in the season, he returned to the closer's role, and at the start of the postseason Mesa was the closer again. In September, he was almost untouchable. In 13 appearances he had seven saves, no blown saves, a 0.69 ERA and opposing teams hit .163 against him.

But once the postseason began, Mesa began to wobble. In the Division Series vs. the Yankees and the ALCS vs. the Orioles, he made six appearances, had three saves, two blown saves, a 3.12 ERA and opposing teams hit .278 against him. In five appearances against the Marlins in the World Series, including his cataclysmic Game 7 appearance, he had one save, one blown save for the ages, and the Marlins hit .417 against him.

Hargrove's defense for using Mesa as the closer throughout the playoffs, including the World Series, is that Mesa was the team's closer the last two months of the season. So, naturally, he would stay in that role in the postseason. For Hargrove to do anything differently would invite legitimate second-guessing.

"One thing I always tried to do was not to manage to cover my ass. If I managed to cover my ass, I never would have put the wheel play on in Baltimore. So I'm at peace with (letting Mesa pitch the ninth), I really am," said Hargrove. "Us losing was not Jose's fault. We all had chances. Jose happened to be in there at the time, and didn't close the game. But he closed the game in extra innings in Baltimore to get us to the World Series, striking out one of the best hitters in the game (Roberto Alomar) for the last out."

Hargrove wasn't going to leave his closer twisting in the wind. However, one of Mesa's teammates would. In his autobiography written six years later, Vizquel pulled no punches in discussing Mesa's Game 7 blown save:

"The eyes of the world were focused on every move we made. Unfortunately, Jose's own eyes were vacant. Completely empty. Nobody home. You could almost see right through him. Not long after I looked into his eyes, he blew the save and the Marlins tied the game."

The second guessers among the crushed Indians faithful wondered why Mesa, and not Jackson, pitched the ninth inning.

"What if I had let Jackson go back out for the ninth inning? Well, that wasn't his role. That was Jose's job," said Hargrove. "Was I disappointed or mad at Jose? No. I'm not. I wasn't then and I'm not now. I wished the outcome had been different, but I felt like we all did our jobs. Me, the coaches, and certainly the players."

Hargrove's feelings in that regard got a little boost the day after Game 7, when he received a phone call from St. Louis Cardinals manager Tony La Russa.

"Mike, between you and Jimmy (Leyland), I felt like that was the best-managed Series I've ever watched," said La Russa.

"I appreciated that because I felt like we did do a good job," Hargrove said. "We got the right people in the right spots, and that's all you can do."

In the days and weeks following the World Series, the temperature of those who participated in it, or were emotionally invested in it, eventually cooled. What sometimes gets lost in the discussion was that for much of the 1997 regular season there seemed to be nothing special about that Indians team. The manager nearly got fired. The pitching staff was ninth in the league in ERA, 13th in complete games and 13th in shutouts. The Indians had losing records against seven teams that year. Against the Orioles, Angels, Red Sox, Reds, Yankees, Mariners and Rangers the Indians were a combined 14 games under .500: 28-42.

But it was a team that caught fire late in the season and rode it through the postseason, piecing together some outrageously dramatic wins, to the point that, with a modest 86 regular-season wins, it came within two outs of winning the World Series. Once the anguish of that agonizing loss in Game 7 finally wore off, the contextualizing of that team could begin.

Hargrove called it the least-talented, yet grittiest, scrappiest, toughest team of his five division winners in Cleveland.

"The least-talented team we had, and yet we were two outs away from winning the World Series," said Dan O'Dowd, the Indians' assistant general manager at the time. "But it was probably fundamentally the best team we had. Marquis Grissom was a really, really good fundamental player. He and Matt Williams had a toughness about them. We had underachieved in 1996. Too many players were thinking about their future that year. But the '97 team really came together. With that team, the whole was greater than the sum of its parts."

"Did they overachieve? Yeah, probably," said Hargrove. "But you look at the individual talents, and you've got Sandy and Matt Williams, and Omar, Justice, Grissom, Thome and Manny. Pretty good parts. They overachieved in some instances, but their talent really shone through, too."

The 1997 Marlins were in some ways counterfeit champs. Ownership impulsively bulked up the roster that year to try to win it all. They won it all, then immediately began a roster purge, with the intent of eventually selling the team. Within six weeks of the end of the World Series the Marlins traded Alou, Nen, Leiter, White and Conine. The dismantling continued into 1998, when Sheffield, Bonilla, Johnson and Eisenreich were all traded to the Dodgers for Mike Piazza, whom the Marlins traded eight days later, and Todd Zeile, whom the Marlins traded two months later. By the time the Marlins visited the White House as World Series champions, only 14 players remained from their World Series roster. The other 11 had been traded or released or had left as free agents.

After winning the World Series in 1997, the stripped-down Marlins in 1998 went 54-108, the worst record in the majors. They finished 52 games behind the AL East champion Braves. The crass roster dump trivialized and cheapened the World Series victory, and it didn't sit very well with the team the Marlins beat.

"That really pissed me off. It still pisses me off today. They had talent on that team, but they blew it up and said, 'Let's try something different.' Why not try and do it again?" said Hargrove.

"They had a chance to cement a legitimate major league franchise, but I still think today that they are feeling the effects of breaking up that team," O'Dowd said. "It's been a really challenging franchise through the years, to build a consistent fan base. I think if they could have figured out a way to keep that group together, even if they hadn't won, I think they would have established a foundation of having a legitimate purpose within the community. But by breaking it up, I don't think they ever recovered from that.

"So they may have won the World Series, and the Indians may have lost. But I do think winning the World Series and then disbanding the team, that they lost a baseball community for years and years. Or maybe I'm just rationalizing it because I was so pissed off."

The Indians' frustration over losing the World Series to this particular team in this particular way was understandable. The Marlins' victory was almost a case of organizational taunting. The Marlins bulked up for one go-for-broke attempt to win it all, and it worked. They won it all, and then they immediately tore the thing down.

The Indians, after wandering for decades in the wilderness before, in 1991, beginning a patient, systematic rebuild that they religiously adhered to, finally saw it pay off with two trips to the World Series in three years. They built their team the right way, and just as they were about to cash in on all that hard work towards creating the right plan, and executing it the right way, the ninth inning of Game 7 happened. The team that was painstakingly crafted and constructed over the previous six years lost baseball's biggest prize to a team created on nothing more than a whim.

Then the Marlins rubbed further salt into the wound by winning the World Series again in 2003. The Marlins, starting from scratch, as an expansion franchise, won two World Series in their first 11 years of existence. The Indians, through 2018, won two World Series in 118 years, none in the last 70 years.

Losing Game 7 of the 1997 World Series is arguably the most painful loss in the tortured history of professional sports in Cleveland. But it wasn't just that the Indians lost that Game 7, it was how they lost. With one out in the bottom of the ninth inning, they were winning. With two outs in the bottom of the 11th inning, they had lost. They were that close. It was that painful. The wounds have never healed.

In spring training in 1998, a reporter asked Hargrove how long it took him to get over that brutal Game 7 loss.

Said Hargrove: "I'll let you know when it happens."

To this day, Hargrove has not flushed from his memory the

events in South Florida in a game that began on the night of his 48th birthday.

"For a long time I thought of it at least once a week," he said of that haunting Game 7. "You run different scenarios through your head. I believed then, and I believe now that we did everything right. There is nothing that I would change. Sometimes you just lose. Sometimes it's your turn to be in the barrel."

Hargrove admits he will carry that Game 7 loss with him forever. His jewelry will make sure of it.

"Every time I put that American League championship ring on," Hargrove said, "I wish it was a little bigger."

CHAPTER 14

Trying to Forget the Unforgettable

"If you put a red onion on the table and say, 'Don't look at the red onion,' that's all you look at the rest of the day."

Freddy Cinram is a golfing buddy of Mike Hargrove, and a huge Indians fan. Cinram did not handle the Indians' loss in Game 7 of the World Series very well. For two or three years after that Series, every time Cinram and Hargrove played golf together, Cinram would ask Hargrove why he brought Mesa in to pitch the ninth inning of Game 7.

"I'd explain it to him," Hargrove said. "I told him I brought Brian Anderson in to get Daulton out of the lineup, and that worked, because Brian wanted to face a right-handed hitter, and I knew they would pinch hit a right-handed hitter for Daulton, which they did. Mike Jackson, who we had used more than anyone else in our bullpen that postseason, said he had one hitter in his arm, and that worked. And Mesa came in to close the game, because that's his job."

For two or three years, every time the two men played golf, Cinram would ask why Hargrove brought in Mesa, and Hargrove would explain the whole scenario to him. If they played golf today and then played again tomorrow, Cinram would ask that same question both days.

"Finally," said Hargrove, "I told him, 'Freddy, I've explained this to you for four years. Four years, Freddy. If you ask me one more time, I'm going to drop you like soft shit in the rain. Do you understand what I'm saying?'"

Cinram never mentioned it again.

Jose Mesa never got over his Game 7 meltdown. At least not in Cleveland. He went on to pitch 10 more years in the major leagues, for a total of 19, and had some decent seasons as a closer after leaving Cleveland. But his best year, by far, was his 1995 masterpiece in which he made 62 appearances and went 3-0 with a 1.13 ERA and a career high and franchise record 46 saves. He was selected to the American League All-Star team, finished second in the Cy Young Award voting and fourth in the MVP voting.

He made the All-Star team again in 1996—the '95 and '96 seasons were the only seasons in his 19-year career that he made the All-Star team—but by 1997 there were already signs of slippage, even before the World Series.

As Mesa's performance curve started to decline, so, too, did his accountability. In 1995, when he was Mr. Automatic out of the bullpen—46 saves and only two blown saves—Mesa was waiting at his locker for the media after every game he pitched. In 1996, when he had 39 saves and five blown saves, he became less available. In 1997, he had 16 saves and five blown saves in the regular season, and talked to reporters even less.

At the start of the 1998 season Hargrove made the switch. He made Mike Jackson the closer, and relegated Mesa to middle relief, or a setup role. It did not go well. In 44 appearances with the Indians in 1998, Mesa was 3-4 with a 5.17 ERA.

In 1995, Mesa averaged 8.2 strikeouts per nine innings. In 1998, he averaged 5.8. In 1995 he averaged 2.4 walks per nine innings. In 1998, he averaged 3.3. In 1995, he gave up an average of 6.9 hits per nine innings. In 1998, he averaged 10.2.

In his last 12 appearances for the Indians, from July 10 to July 21 in 1998, Mesa was 0-3 with an 8.27 ERA, and opposing teams hit .328 against him. On July 23, almost nine months to the day that he couldn't get the final two outs that would have given Cleveland its first World Series title in 49 years, the Indians traded Mesa to the San Francisco Giants. At the time of the trade he held the Indians' franchise record for career saves with 104.

"The light turns out quickly on closers," Hargrove said. "With

Jose, I know he has gotten hammered over the years by a lot of people for the '97 deal. My personal opinion is that he wasn't the same person after the '97 World Series. His stuff was just as good. It just wasn't working for him anymore.

"Closers have to have a short memory, and I'm not sure Jose did. I never talked to him about Game 7. Given the chance to do it over, I still wouldn't. Certain things you can talk to players about, and certain things, no amount of talk is going to make a difference. I think Jose just never got over that, and was never going to get over that in Cleveland.

"It's a lot like what happened with Kevin Wickander after the boating accident. Kevin felt so guilty about not being there for Steve Olin, that we finally realized that was never going to change for him in Cleveland. He needed a change of scenery, and I think the same thing pretty much happened with Jose. You're not comparing the gravity of the situations with Jose as opposed to Kevin, but it's along the same lines. With Jose, his stuff was still good, he just couldn't get over that hump mentally. I remember, when he got to the Giants, he said, 'I can start throwing my curveball again.' He was still a productive pitcher after he left us, but nothing like the one who saved 46 games for us."

After leaving Cleveland, Mesa was eventually moved back into the closer's role, and he did have some good years. In a five-year span between 2001 and 2005, three years with the Phillies and two with the Pirates, Mesa averaged 36 saves per year, with a 3.83 ERA. His last career save came on Aug. 5, 2007, for the Phillies, at age 41. It was his 321st career save, which, through 2018, ranks 20th on baseball's all-time list. Mesa's 1,022 career appearances rank 12th in major league history.

But by far the game in his career that everyone most remembers came on Oct. 26, 1997, when his blown save on the biggest stage changed the course of history for two different franchises.

*   *   *

In the trade with the Giants, the Indians sent Mesa, infielder Shawon Dunston and reliever Alvin Morman to San Francisco for reliever Steve Reed and outfielder Jacob Cruz. That was one of many transactions made by the Indians in the wake of that calamitous Game 7, as the organization continued to furiously shuffle the deck, hoping to come up with a winning hand. Winning the division was no longer enough. Winning the last game of the postseason was the only goal.

In the span of one week in December 1997, the Indians made one blockbuster trade and one blockbuster signing. The trade, on December 1, was a forced trade. The Indians sent Matt Williams to the new National League expansion team, the Arizona Diamondbacks. In return, the Indians got Travis Fryman. It was an All-Star third baseman for All-Star third baseman deal. It was also at the behest of Williams himself, prompted by his divorce.

"His wife told him she was leaving him during spring training, before the 1997 season," said Hargrove. "So, it was going on during the season. He wrestled with that all year long. He had a tough year. At the end of the season he came in to talk to John Hart and said he wanted to be traded to Arizona, where he lived, and if we couldn't accommodate him, he was going to retire.

"My heart went out to him because I really realized what a struggle he was having," said Hargrove.

Given all that was going on in his personal life, it made Williams' 32-homer, 105-RBI season more impressive still.

"Matt was a tough guy. Physically he was tough, but mentally he was very tough. That club needed that sort of an attitude and that sort of a guy," said Hargrove. "He did a great job for us. I felt really bad for him that he was going through what he was going through, especially with his kids."

Seven days after trading Williams for Fryman, Hart really went into overdrive. On Dec. 8 he signed two free agents, Kenny Lofton and Dwight Gooden, and he traded Marquis Grissom and Jeff Juden to Milwaukee for pitchers Ben McDonald, Mike Fetters and Ron Villone. Then Hart completed his frenetic day at the office by trading Fetters to Oakland for pitcher Steve Karsay. That's four transactions involving eight players and three teams in one day. Fetters was traded twice in a matter of hours. He was the property of the Indians for less than one sunset.

Like Williams, Grissom spent only one year in Cleveland. Also like Williams, Grissom had a personal issue that weighed on him heavily throughout the 1997 season.

"During the playoffs, Marquis' sister was real sick. So, he went home a few times during that period to see her, and take care of things," said Hargrove. "Fans don't realize. They see a player at the ballpark—and we have a good life, I'm not saying we don't—but sometimes fans don't realize that the players have the same problems and the same feelings that they have. With Matt Williams, with his situation with his kids. And with Marquis, with his sister. That kind of stuff. But those guys played well. They were mentally tough guys. Marquis was a very important player for us."

Lofton returned to Cleveland nine months after the Indians traded him to Atlanta during spring training. Incredibly, in 1996 the Indians, with Lofton and Belle, failed to get out of the first round of the playoffs. In 1997, without Lofton and Belle, they nearly won the World Series.

The Indians traded Lofton because he turned down a five-year, $44 million contract extension from the Indians. He returned and signed a three-year, $24 million deal.

"It was good getting Kenny back. It felt right," Hargrove said.

The Indians were rolling the dice on Gooden, who broke into the major leagues with the Mets in 1984, at age 19, and by age 20 had already won the National League Rookie of the Year and Cy Young Awards. But his drug addiction derailed his career and resulted in a 60-day suspension by Major League Baseball in 1987. He had relapses throughout his career including in 1995, when he was suspended for the entire season. He spent 1996 and 1997 with the Yankees, and then signed a two-year, $5.3 million deal with the Indians. Hart said at the time the Indians were confident Gooden's problems were behind him.

"We went through an extensive interview process involving Doc," Hart told reporters. "We absolutely saw no red flags. In fact, we did not even see any caution flags . . . We are sold on Doc Gooden, the human being."

Gooden came with a handler named Ray Negron, a drug consultant with the Yankees, who became Gooden's personal "minder," as Hargrove called him. Negron was with Gooden virtually every minute of every day. He attended all the Indians' games, traveled with the team, and basically kept an eye on Gooden. The arrangement seemed to work.

"Dwight was good when he was with us," Hargrove said. "He showed up. He pitched when he was asked to. And he competed well. I had a special feeling for Dwight. I really did. Obviously, he had some inner demons that he was dealing with. But when we had him, he handled them very well."

Everything proceeded encouragingly through spring training with Gooden, until his last start of training camp, when he walked off the mound with a sore shoulder. He was placed on the disabled list, and, with opening day less than a week away, Hart whipped into action again, trading first baseman Sean Casey, the Indians' top minor league prospect, to Cincinnati for veteran pitcher Dave Burba, an innings-eater who would win 56 games for Cleveland over the next four years.

"We feel very strongly that Burba is going to help us continue the run we've been on over the last four years," Hart said at the time. "He's going to be much more valuable to us over the next two years than Sean Casey would."

In 1997 Casey hit .380 between Triple-A and Double-A in the Indians' minor league system. He would finish his minor league career with a .348 batting average and would go on to hit .302 in his 12-year major league career, spent mostly with the Reds.

"I think he's the best hitting prospect in the minor leagues, but I don't see where Sean Casey is going to play for us this year, next year, or the year after that," said Hargrove on the day of the trade.

In Cleveland, Casey was stuck behind Jim Thome at first base, and David Justice and Brian Giles at designated hitter. Later in 1998, the Indians would trade Giles to the Pirates.

"We knew Sean was going to be a player," said Hargrove, looking back on the trade 20 years later. "We also knew that Thome was a player, too. Sean Casey, Brian Giles. You hate to trade them because they are good, and you know they're going to get better. But we had needs, and Burba was awfully good for us."

This was a period of time when the Indians' major league roster was loaded, and their minor league pipeline was bursting with even more talent, waiting its turn. For example, right behind Casey was first baseman Richie Sexson, who hit 31 homers at Triple-A Buffalo in 1997. The Indians would eventually trade Sexson as well, and, in over five seasons starting in 2001, he averaged 38 home runs and 116 RBI per year for Milwaukee and Seattle.

"A player is scouted and drafted for one reason: to help the big-league club eventually," Hargrove said. "There's one or two ways they do that. One is they develop into a player you eventually slot into your club somewhere. The other way is you trade them for somebody that fills a hole. Sean, Brian and Richie fit that bill, they brought us players who filled a hole. Trades like that are never easy to make, because you know what you're giving up. But in Burba's case, we knew what we were getting back, too. He won some big games for us."

The flurry of trades and free-agent signings following the 1997 season were made by Hart, but not without first checking with Hargrove. There was never a move made on which both men didn't sign off.

"I can't remember any time where he proposed something, and I said, 'No, I wouldn't do that,' and he went ahead and did it anyway," Hargrove said. "We had some arguments about certain things. But they were healthy. There were times when he came in to discuss something, and the first thing that crossed my mind was, 'Are you fucking crazy?' The Baerga trade was one. John came into my office and started talking about that and my first thought was, 'Are you fucking nuts?' And then all of a sudden, the more we talked about it, and the more I thought about it, I realized he had a good handle on it."

*   *   *

It didn't take long for the irony horse to rear its head in the 1998 season. On opening day in Seattle, the Indians won a wild four-hour-plus, 10-9 decision over the Mariners. It was the Indians' first game that counted after the Mesa meltdown in Game 7 of the World Series. The Indians' opening day winning pitcher? Mesa, naturally.

With the Indians trailing 9-6, Mesa, in relief of Paul Shuey, retired the Mariners in order in the bottom of the seventh inning. The Indians then scored four times in the top of the eighth inning to take a 10-9 lead. Mesa retired the side in order again in the bottom of the eighth, and retired the first batter in the top of the ninth before Jackson came in to get the final out and the save. Mesa faced seven batters and retired them all in probably his best outing prior to being traded four months later.

However, two days before opening day Hargrove told Mesa he was no longer the closer.

"They told me they were going to put Mike (Jackson) in as closer because of the way I pitched in spring training. That's fine with me. I got to go with the flow. I'll do whatever it takes to help us win," Mesa said.

In 10 appearances in exhibition games Mesa had a 5.23 ERA, while Jackson had a 4.50 ERA in 10 appearances.

But spring training performance wasn't the only reason for Mesa's demotion.

"We want to get Jose out of the spotlight," said Hargrove at the time. "We want him to have a chance to step back and catch his breath."

The elephant in the room, as the 1998 season started, was whether the Indians' players could put behind them the painful way the 1997 World Series ended. Hargrove believes there was some negative emotional carryover from '97 to '98, but he chose not to address the subject on the eve of the 1998 season.

"If you bring up the obvious," he said, "like if you put a red onion on the table and say, 'Don't look at the red onion,' that's all you look at the rest of the day. I think each of the players handled it in their own way."

The Indians won their first six games, and eight of their first nine games in 1998. So much for any Game 7 hangover. They also won their first six games in the month of May. But that was followed immediately by a six-game losing streak, which was immediately followed by a streak in which they won seven out of eight. Later they lost seven out of nine. Then they won six in a row. It was classic roller coaster stuff.

It was also around this time that the Indians decided to retire the uniform number of Hall of Fame pitcher Bob Lemon, a third base-man-turned-pitcher who in his 13-year major league career, all of it spent with the Indians, won 207 games, third most in franchise history.

Lemon's number was 21.

In 1998, so was Hargrove's.

As a rookie with the Texas Rangers in 1974 Hargrove was given the number 56. But just before the start of the season, a pitcher got injured. His number was 21, but when he didn't make the club because of the injury, 21 was given to Hargrove, who wore the same number when he was with San Diego. When Hargrove was traded to the Indians in 1979, shortstop Tom Veryzer had 21, but he gave it to Hargrove. When Hargrove became first-base coach of the Indians in 1990, pitcher Greg Swindell had number 21, so Hargrove took number 12. When Hargrove became manager in 1991, Swindell came into his office the first day and said, "Here, this your number," and he gave 21 to Hargrove.

"It meant a lot to me for him to do that, because he didn't have to do it. I wasn't expecting it, and wouldn't have asked him to do it," Hargrove said.

Hargrove had worn number 21 as the Indians' manager since that day. But at some point in the first half of the 1998 season, Dennis Lehman, the Indians' vice president of business, came into Hargrove's office before a game and told him the club wanted to retire Bob Lemon's number 21, and would Hargrove mind giving it up? Hargrove told Lehman that he would be happy to give it up.

"But then I started giving Dennis a hard time, just for the fun of it," Hargrove said. "I said, 'I don't know why I should give up this number for Bob Lemon. I wore it longer than he did.' Just being stupid and giving Dennis a hard time. We continued to talk, and before I had a chance to say, 'Sure, Dennis, I'll give it up. I appreciate you asking,' somebody came into my office, I got distracted and never told Dennis I was joking."

A week later, a friend of Hargrove's in Los Angeles called and told him there was a story in one of the papers by a Cleveland columnist saying that Hargrove wouldn't give up his number for Lemon, to be retired.

"That's when I went to Dennis and said I was just joking, but the damage had been done," Hargrove said. "I was busting Dennis' chops, but it went the wrong way. I had a real problem with the writer about that, and I talked to him a couple times about it. My problem was, instead of him coming to me and saying, 'Is this true?' he ran with the story and it became a mountain out of a molehill.

"If it was true, I understand," said Hargrove. "Who the hell am I to not give up my number so they could retire it for Bob Lemon? I always felt bad about that."

Hargrove called a member of Lemon's family to explain and apologize for what had happened, and Hargrove and the columnist eventually talked it out and came to an understanding. Hargrove did relinquish the number, and it was retired by the Indians in a ceremony at Jacobs Field on June 20. Hargrove switched to number 30, which was his number in college.

The 1998 Indians finished near the middle of the pack in the American League in most of the team hitting and pitching statistical categories. They didn't spend a day out of first place, even though they finished with a good-but-not-great record of 89-73. They were the only team in the Central Division with a winning record. They won the division by nine games over the White Sox.

Manny Ramirez had a monster year, hitting .294, with 45 home runs and 145 RBI. The 45 home runs were, at the time, the third most in Indians' history (it's now fifth all-time), and the 145 RBI also ranked third in the history of the franchise. Fryman, in his first year with the team, and trying to fill the huge shoes of Williams, was outstanding, hitting .287 with 96 RBI and a career-high 28 home runs.

"I remember feeling good about Travis being there. He was the ultimate professional. Respectful. We didn't really miss a beat with Travis. In physical ability, he was similar to Williams," said Hargrove.

Charles Nagy (15), Burba (15), Bartolo Colon (14) and Jaret Wright (12) all won 12 or more games that year, and Gooden, after returning in mid-season from his shoulder woes, had a respectable season out of the No. 5 spot in the rotation: 8-6, with a 3.76 ERA. Jackson made everyone forget about Mesa, saving 40 games, third most in Indians history at the time, with a 1.55 ERA.

*   *   *

The Indians didn't exactly go barreling into the postseason. They were outscored by their opponents over the last three months of the regular season, and in late September, with their fourth consecutive division title clinched, they lost six of their last seven games.

In the Division Series the Indians faced Boston, the team they had swept in three games in the 1995 Division Series. But these were different teams on both sides. The Indians, naturally, lost Game 1 of the series, at home, no less, where they got pummeled 11-3. The Indians were trailing 8-0 before they scored their first runs, in the bottom of the sixth inning. Indians hitters couldn't do much with Pedro Martinez, while Boston hitters had their way with Wright, who was walloped for six runs on seven hits, two of them home runs, in just 4⅓ innings.

Already down 1-0, with all but one of the remaining games of the five-game series to be played in Boston, the Indians were on edge going into Game 2. It didn't take long for that to show.

Hargrove got thrown out of the game after the third pitch of the game. The issue was home plate umpire Joe Brinkman.

"Joe was a good umpire. He was a tough guy," Hargrove said. "I don't ever remember having trouble with him, even when I played. But that day, he didn't have a bad day. He had a terrible day."

Gooden's first three pitches to Boston leadoff hitter Darren Lewis in the first inning were all called balls. Gooden thought the last two were strikes, and showed his displeasure. Brinkman immediately took off his mask and started yelling at Gooden, who responded by giving Brinkman the "calm down" sign with his hands. Instead, Brinkman calmed up, to the point that Hargrove—remember, this is just three pitches into the game—went to the mound to try to lower Gooden's temperature.

"Dwight looked like he was throwing good pitches. Good, solid low strikes that Joe kept calling balls," Hargrove said. "I remember thinking we need Dwight in the game, but the way he was being squeezed, I was worried Dwight would do something and get kicked out of the game."

On the way back to the dugout, Hargrove said something to Brinkman and was ejected.

Lewis eventually walked, and so did the next hitter, John Valentin. Gooden struck out Mo Vaughn for the first out, but Nomar

Garciaparra doubled off the left field wall, scoring Lewis and Valentin, although TV replays showed catcher Sandy Alomar tagged Valentin before he slid across the plate. Gooden, who was backing up the play at the plate, lost it again, and, according to Brinkman, "Screamed an expletive right in my ear." Brinkman tossed Gooden out of the game. So at that point in the proceedings, there were more Indians thrown out of the game than there were outs.

Sometime between the twin ejections, Indians general manager John Hart showed up at the bottom of the stairs that lead from the dugout to the ramp leading to the clubhouse.

"After I got thrown out, I walked down the steps out of the dugout, and John is down there," Hargrove said. "John never, ever came down there during a game. And his face was beet red. He was screaming and highly agitated. I mean screaming. It was a wonder Brinkman didn't kick him out from home plate, because he could have heard him from there, John was screaming so loud. He was pissed."

Managers getting thrown out of games for sticking up for their players is as old as the game itself.

"Sometimes you don't necessarily want to get kicked out of the game, but sometimes you almost have to, just to keep the players in the game," Hargrove said. "As a manager there are certain ways you can let the players know you are in it as much as they are, and that you are backing them as much as you can. You do that by going out and arguing, and sometimes getting kicked out of the game."

Hargrove recalled a game when he was playing for the Indians, against the White Sox. The Indians' catcher was Ron Hassey and the hitter was White Sox second baseman Tony Bernazard.

"Tony was pissing and moaning the whole game, and in one of his at-bats the count got to 0-2, and the umpire leaned up to Hassey and said, 'Just get it close to the plate,'" said Hargrove. "Hassey said the next pitch was a foot outside, and the umpire yells, 'Strike three! You're gone!' You don't see that anymore, but there were umpires who did that."

In Hargrove's rookie season with Texas, there was an umpire named George Maloney, who was umpiring first base in a game between the Rangers and Angels. Doyle Alexander was pitching for the Rangers.

"George hated Alexander, for whatever reason," Hargrove said. "So, Bobby Bonds is on first base, and Doyle throws over. I catch the ball on the corner of the bag, and before I could close my glove, Bobby stepped in my glove. So now I've got the ball, and Bobby's foot IN my glove, and George says, 'Safe!' I said, 'George, he can't be safe. He's standing on the ball in my glove.' George says, 'No, he's safe. He got his toe in.' So, I just said, 'OK.'"

Nestor Chylak was another umpire in that era. He was the home plate umpire during the beer night riot in Cleveland in 1974. That same year, Hargrove's rookie year, but in a different game, "I argued a play with Nestor at first base, and he cussed me out for the next three innings. Just wore me out. 'You no-good, cocksucker, fucking rookie. Who do you think you are? You fucking little greenhorn rookie.' This went on for three innings. Finally, I just said, 'Mr. Chylak, I get it. I understand.'"

One of the moodiest, yet gregarious—if that's possible—umpires was Ken Kaiser, a former professional wrestler, who was built like a former professional wrestler.

"He put the sleeper hold on me one day in the tunnel, before a game," Hargrove said. "He had been a professional wrestler, and I was talking to him about wrestling, and he said, 'My favorite hold was the sleeper hold. Here, I'll show you.' He got me in the sleeper hold, and that little button on the top of your baseball cap? It felt like it was two inches down in my skull."

Back at Jacobs Field, in the top of the first inning of the 1998 Division Series between the Indians and Red Sox, Boston was leading 2-0, with one out, a runner at second, and the Indians' starting pitcher and manager had already been thrown out of the game.

"We could have gone one of two ways," Fryman told reporters after the game. "We could have said the umpires and everyone else are against us. Or we could say, in spite of all that's gone on, we've still got eight innings left to win this game."

So, the Indians did. Burba relieved Gooden and pitched 5⅓ innings of relief, allowing the Indians to hit their way back into the game. Knuckleballer Tim Wakefield, Boston's starting pitcher, never got out of the second inning. The Indians scored a run in the first, five in the second and one in the third to take a 7-3 lead, in route to a 9-5 victory that evened the series at 1-1.

"Today was a crash course in character building, so to speak," said Fryman. "I think a game like this will elevate our play a little bit."

Apparently, it did. The Indians followed it up with two one-run victories to eliminate the Red Sox, and to advance to the ALCS for the third time in four years. In Game 3, as the series shifted to Boston, Nagy was brilliant, needing just 88 pitches to get through eight innings, allowing just four hits and one run, which came in the fourth inning and gave the Red Sox a 1-0 lead. But the Indians countered by hitting solo home runs in each of the next three innings off Red Sox starter Bret Saberhagen, who had held the Indians hitless in the first four innings. Thome homered in the fifth inning, Lofton did in the sixth, and Ramirez did in the seventh, giving Cleveland a 3-1 lead. Ramirez hit another solo home run in the ninth inning, off 43-year-old Dennis Eckersley, to make it 4-1.

Ramirez's two home runs came off two veteran pitchers who would combine to win three Cy Young and one Most Valuable Player Awards in their careers. The home run off Saberhagen was Ramirez's only career hit against the 1985 Cy Young winner. In the regular and postseason, Ramirez's career batting average against Saberhagen was .077 (1-for-13).

Conversely, in the regular season and postseason, Ramirez had three career at-bats against Eckersley, and all three were home runs.

"Every time I watched Manny play, the phrase, 'Water off a duck's back' came into my mind. It seemed like nothing ever affected him," Hargrove said.

Ramirez was like that right from the start of his career, probably because it's hard to stress or worry about anything when you have a nearly perfect swing. After the Indians drafted Ramirez, and Indians hitting coach Charlie Manuel got a look at his new hitting machine, it was love at first swing.

"Leave this kid alone. Don't change anything," Manuel told the minor league hitting instructors.

"Charlie was a great hitting coach, and the guys believed in him, which was a big hurdle to get over," said Hargrove. "I don't think that Charlie tinkered with Manny at all. I don't think anyone did."

The ninth inning homer off Eckersley in Game 3 in 1998 was important, because it pushed the Indians' lead to 4-1. In the bottom of the ninth, Jackson struggled, giving up a single to Vaughn, and then a two-run home run by Garciaparra. That cut the Cleveland lead to 4-3, with still only one out in the ninth. But Jackson retired Mike Stanley and Troy O'Leary on groundouts to preserve the 4-3 victory, giving the Indians a 2-1 series lead.

Game 4 was tense. Garciaparra's home run leading off the fourth inning against Colon gave Boston a 1-0 lead. Red Sox starter Pete Schourek and reliever Derek Lowe nursed that lead through the seventh. Tom Gordon relieved Lowe to start the eighth, when singles by Vizquel and Lofton, plus a stolen base by Lofton, put runners at second and third with one out. Justice then doubled to center field, scoring Vizquel and Lofton, giving Cleveland a 2-1 lead.

The Red Sox threatened in the bottom of the eighth. Vaughn doubled with one out, and with two outs the Red Sox had runners at first and third. But reliever Paul Shuey retired O'Leary on a flyout to end the inning.

In the ninth, Jackson rebounded from his bumpy Game 3 appearance by retiring the side in order, giving the Indians a 2-1 victory. The Indians' bullpen was the collective star of the game. Colon gave up one run in 5⅔ innings. Then five Indians relievers, Jim Poole, Steve Reed, Paul Assenmacher, Shuey and Jackson, combined to pitch 3⅓ scoreless innings on one hit. Starting with that wild ejection-fest in Game 2, the Indians won three games in a row to eliminate the Red Sox and advance to the ALCS, where one of the most powerful Yankee teams ever was waiting.

During the regular season the Yankees had won 114 games, 25 more than the Indians and 22 more than the Red Sox, who finished in second place in the AL East. In the Division Series the Yankees overwhelmed Texas, sweeping the Rangers in three games, and outscoring them 9-1.

"We respect the Yankees. But the realization is that we're the defending American League champions. In reality, New York is in our way. We can't look at it any other way," Hart told reporters prior to the series.

Justice was asked if he felt the Indians had an edge over the Yankees in any category.

"I don't think so," he said.

The 1998 Yankees are considered one of the greatest teams ever. They won 114 games in the regular season, then went 11-2 in the postseason, giving them an overall record of 125-50 (.714). Nevertheless, prior to Game 1 of the ALCS, Hart expressed surprise that the Indians were considered such massive underdogs against the mighty Yankee winning machine.

"You can understand it because of their record," said Hart. "But I think people are missing the boat if they think we're the Washington Generals getting ready to play the Harlem Globetrotters."

The Yankees played three postseason series in 1998, and the Indians were the only team they didn't sweep. They swept the Rangers 3-0 in the Division Series and they swept the Braves 4-0 in the World Series. Through the first three games of the ALCS, however, the Indians led the Yankees 2-1. The Yankees won Game 1 as Wright never made it out of the first inning. He gave up five runs on five hits and a walk, faced eight batters, threw 36 pitches and only got two outs. The Indians' only runs came with one out in the ninth inning, when they were losing 7-0. Ramirez hit a two-run home run off David Wells, and the Indians lost 7-2. Nothing new there. Going back to the 1995 ALCS vs. Seattle, the Indians' record in Game 1 of postseason series was 0-8.

In Game 2, the Indians pushed across three runs in the 12th inning to win 4-1, as Nagy and six relievers held the Yankees' powerful lineup to just one run on seven hits. The series then moved to Cleveland, where the Indians got a sensational effort from Colon, who pitched a four-hit complete game in a 6-1 Cleveland victory. The Indians belted four home runs, two by Thome and one each by Ramirez and Mark Whiten. In the fifth inning, Ramirez, Thome and Whiten all homered in the span of four batters, off Yankee starter Andy Pettitte.

"That's an awesome lineup. They've got a lot of power. They can really beat you up," said Yankees manager Joe Torre. In winning Games 2 and 3, the Indians outscored New York by a combined score of 10-2, and all of a sudden, the Indians were just two wins away from advancing to the World Series for the third time in four years.

But Cleveland never won another game. Orlando Hernandez and two relievers combined on a four-hit shutout in a 4-0 Yankee win in Game 4. In Game 5, Indians starter Chad Ogea gave up four runs in less than two innings in a 5-3 New York victory. In Game 6, back at Yankee Stadium, the Yankees took a 6-0 lead into the fifth inning. In the top of the fifth, Thome belted a grand slam off David Cone in a five-run rally that cut the Yankees' lead to 6-5. But a two-run triple by Derek Jeter in a three-run New York sixth inning made it 9-5, and that was the final score, a loss made even more painful by the fact that five of New York's nine runs were unearned, thanks to three Indians errors. "We played with fire all night with our defense and got burned by it," said Hargrove after the game. Yankees relievers Ramiro Mendoza and Mariano Rivera combined to pitch four scoreless innings on one hit in closing out the victory that sent the Yankees to the World Series and the Indians home.

"It hurts," said Hart, when it was over. "This clubhouse is filled with championship players. At the beginning of spring training, our goal was to get two more outs. It was to win the World Series. We didn't get it done. And I'll tell you, I believe this team is more talented than last year's. At the end of the day, we'll look back and say it was another good season. In the short term, it's just another bitter pill to swallow."

The Indians were becoming experts at learning how to swallow a bitter pill. The degrees of bitterness varied, but at the end of the ride, the pill was always there, waiting for them. After getting to within two outs of winning the World Series in 1997, the Indians in 1998 got to within two wins of returning to the World Series, but they came up short again. That made it four consecutive trips to the postseason, but no World Series title. During the 1998 postseason, the inevitable rumors about Hargrove's job security surfaced again. Did the team need a new voice for it to get over the postseason hump?

One ESPN report said that should the Indians falter in the 1998 postseason they would have an interest in hiring Jim Leyland to replace Hargrove as manager. Leyland left the Marlins, through an out clause in his contract, after their disastrous 1998 season.

"That's ridiculous," said Hart of the report. "I've got my manager. We're in the postseason. Why would I do something like that?"

CHAPTER 15

The Boston Massacre

"OK kids, look around, because this isn't
going to be Dad's office anymore."

As the Indians began decompressing from the 1998 season, Mike Hargrove realized that 1999 would be a pivotal year for him personally. As manager, he had taken the team to the postseason four consecutive years, but his teams had failed to win the World Series. That did not go unnoticed.

"John Hart was a good general manager. He was also a very impatient man. I think everybody sensed that," Hargrove said. "We hadn't gotten back to the World Series in '98. So, yeah, I did think about that, although every year it sort of felt that way."

By this point, Hargrove had resigned himself to the fact that, until the Indians won a World Series, his job security would be a continuing source of speculation both inside and outside the organization. The 1999 season would be his ninth season as Indians manager. The team had gone from being a 105-loss disaster in 1991, the year he replaced John McNamara as manager at mid-season, to one of the most consistently elite teams in the majors. One, however, that had failed to end the franchise's long drought without a World Series title. The 1998 season was the 50th anniversary of the last time the Indians won the World Series.

Optimism still abounded in 1999. The fans were still invested. The streak of consecutive sellouts at Jacobs Field, which would eventually reach 455 games, was still going strong. But the elephant in the ballpark was the Indians' inability to win it all.

Until that happened, Hargrove's job status would remain a topic of conjecture, even within his own family. Sharon Hargrove told a local columnist that during the 1996 season she was so sure her husband was going to get fired that she started packing boxes.

When it came to her husband's job, Sharon was always tuned in to the prevailing winds. This is a woman, for example, who, when there were rumors that her husband was going to be traded by the Texas Rangers, simply called general manager Dan O'Brien and, point blank, asked, "Is Mike going to be traded?"

As the wife of a manager, Sharon knew and respected the ground rules of her position, but was also keenly sensitive to all the vibes and machinations that swirled around her husband, perhaps more so than the wives of most major league managers.

"She never asked questions about what was going on internally, and I never shared that with her," Hargrove said. "It wasn't any of her business, and she understood that. She never questioned me on things like that. I think, as a manager, you have to be so totally focused on what your job is, and that's how I was. It wasn't necessarily tunnel vision, because you have to know what's going on, what the media is saying, and what the people are saying. Because that's public perception, and that old saying that perception is 90 percent of reality.

"So, you're aware of that (speculation on the possibility of being fired), but I never managed a certain way to keep my job. My job was to get the club to play as well as we could, and win ballgames. So that's what I focused on. Not the other stuff. The only time I can remember feeling like there was a chance something could happen was in 1997. In 1999, not until the very end of the playoffs, when we got beat, and how we got beat, that was the first time I started to think, uh-oh, something might happen now."

One of Hart's pet peeves with the team at that time was that it didn't win enough games in the regular season. Hart thought the team should aspire to win 100 games every year, though he never said so publicly. But he and Hargrove would talk about it a lot, both to each other and to the ballclub, in order to try to challenge the players. It didn't always work.

When it didn't work, Hargrove would tell Hart, "They know they're good, and in their hearts they know they are going to get to the postseason. So, in their minds, it doesn't matter whether we win 85 games or 105 games, as long as you get to the postseason."

But in spring training in 1999, Hargrove decided to go public with Hart's yearly yearning. He told reporters in spring training that the team's goal was to win 100 games. Hargrove hadn't done that in the past because he felt it put unnecessary pressure on the players. But now Hargrove threw the 100-wins goal out there for public consumption.

"John was pissed. Oh, he was pissed," Hargrove said. "He said to me, 'What are you doing?' I said, 'I've tried everything in the world. Let's try this, and see what happens.' He was upset with me, that I came out publicly and stated that."

Hart let it be known that he was really bearing down on the '99 season. Before the season he made multiple changes to Hargrove's coaching staff, and a flurry of roster moves. During that season a total of 51 different players appeared in at least one game in an Indians uniform, including 40-year-old Harold Baines and former Indians retreads such as Carlos Baerga, Jim Poole and 41-year-old knuckleballer Tom Candiotti, who had last pitched for Cleveland in 1991. None of the retreads contributed much.

Just before the start of the season Hart signed pitcher Mark Langston, formerly one of the best pitchers in the American League. He broke in with Seattle in 1984 and led the league in strikeouts in three of his first four years in the league, was a four-time All-Star and a seven-time Gold Glove winner. But by 1999 Langston was 38, and out of gas.

A month after the Indians were eliminated from the ALCS by the Yankees in 1998, Hart overpaid for a left-handed reliever, getting Ricardo Rincon from Pittsburgh in exchange for outfielder Brian Giles, who over the next four years would average 37 home runs and 109 RBI for the Pirates.

Hart's biggest move of the offseason, however, was signing future Hall of Famer Roberto Alomar as a free agent.

"You always have a wish list, and the top of ours was that somehow, some way we could get Robbie on our ballclub. Obviously, because he was a talented player, but also because we felt like it rounded out our ballclub. Robbie was awfully, awfully good," said Hargrove.

From 1990 through 2001, the last three years with Cleveland, Alomar was selected to 12 consecutive All-Star teams, won 10 Gold

Gloves, and finished in the top six in the MVP voting five times. Coupled with shortstop Omar Vizquel, Alomar gave the Indians arguably the greatest defensive middle infield in major league history. During their careers they combined to win 21 Gold Gloves. In 2000, three of the American League's four Gold Glove infielders were Indians: Alomar, Vizquel and third baseman Travis Fryman.

"People always talked about how Robbie and Omar didn't like each other. I never saw any evidence of that," Hargrove said. "They didn't pal around, but they worked well together."

In 1999 Alomar would have one of the greatest seasons in Indians history, hitting .323, with 24 home runs, 120 RBI, an American League-leading 138 runs, 40 doubles, 37 stolen bases, a .422 on-base percentage, more walks (99) than strikeouts (96), and a league-leading 13 sacrifice flies.

The 1999 Indians were one of the greatest offensive teams in history. They scored 1,009 runs, the fifth most in major league history, since 1901. Only seven teams in history have scored 1,000 runs in a season. The 1999 Indians averaged 6.23 runs per game (13th most in history). By contrast, the powerhouse 100-win 1995 Indians averaged 5.83 runs per game.

The 1999 Indians had five players with over 20 home runs: Manny Ramirez (44), Jim Thome (33), Richie Sexson (31), Robbie Alomar (24) and David Justice (21). Four Indians that year had over 100 RBI: Ramirez (165), Robbie Alomar (120), Sexson (116) and Thome (108).

Alomar and Ramirez both had the greatest years of their careers, as judged by bWAR: Alomar 7.4, Ramirez 7.3. Ramirez's 165 RBI broke the Indians' record for RBI in a season, which had stood for 63 years. Hal Trosky had 162 in 1936. Ramirez in 1999 led the league in slugging percentage (.663) and OPS (1.105). Alomar led the league with 138 runs, second most in Indians' history behind Earl Averill's 140 in 1931, and Thome led the league with an Indians' record 127 walks.

Alomar and Ramirez finished tied for third in the extremely close American League Most Valuable Player Award voting. Alomar and Ramirez had 226 points, Pedro Martinez had 239, and Ivan Rodriguez, who had a lower WAR (6.4) than Martinez, Alomar or Ramirez, won the award with 252 points.

The Indians in 1999 had one of the most talented and prolific lineups in history—when the lineup was filled out correctly.

That was not the case at Jacobs Field for the game between Toronto and Cleveland on the night of July 22, 1999. It was not a good day in the relationship between Hart and Hargrove.

"John didn't talk to me for four or five days after that," Hargrove said.

The gist of what happened is that the lineup card Hargrove sent to home plate umpire Rocky Roe prior to the start of the game was incorrectly filled out. Ramirez was listed as the DH, but Ramirez thought he was the right fielder. He wasn't. But since he was listed as the DH, after he played right field in the top of the first inning, it meant the Indians lost their DH, meaning pitcher Charles Nagy had to bat for himself, and the Indians had no DH in the entire game.

That's the gist of it. The sub-gist is even better—or worse, if you're Hargrove.

Prior to the game Hargrove told Ramirez that he was going to give him a semi-day off, but he would stay in the lineup as the DH. Ramirez said that was fine with him. Hargrove made out the lineup card, the one that would go to the umpire, with Alex Ramirez playing right field and Manny Ramirez as the DH. As he did before every game, Hargrove then gave the lineup card to third-base coach Jeff Newman, who would make out the big lineup card that would be taped to the dugout wall. Newman then gave the big lineup card to Hargrove to check again, and then first-base coach Brian Graham was the fourth check.

After all that happened, Manny Ramirez came into Hargrove's office and told him he preferred to play right instead of DH. Hargrove said OK, and made out another lineup card with that correction, Manny Ramirez in right field, Alex Ramirez as the DH. Hargrove put the new lineup card on the chair in front of Newman's locker, so Newman could make the change on the big (dugout) lineup card. The replacement lineup card reached Graham, but he thought there was a mistake on it, so he changed it to match what he took to be the correct card.

"Normally, the last thing I do is check the lineup card I made out with the one posted on the dugout, to make sure they match," Hargrove said. "But I didn't have time to do it that night, because the umpires were at home plate waiting for me. So I rushed out there, and the lineup card had scribbles all over it. Things scratched out and put back in."

So, the lineup card Hargrove gave to the umpires had Alex Ramirez playing right field and Manny Ramirez as the DH. But in the top of the first inning Manny went out to play right field. Hargrove knew he was in trouble when Toronto manager Jim Fregosi approached umpire Roe after the top of the first.

"When Fregosi came out to challenge it, I thought, 'What's he doing?'" Hargrove said. "Then I looked at the posted lineup card in our dugout (with Alex, not Manny Ramirez in right field) and I said, 'Holy shit!'"

The upshot of the blunder was that for the rest of the game, the Indians pitchers had to bat in the DH spot, which was the No. 7 spot in the order, where Alex Ramirez, as the right fielder, was supposed to hit. It also caused the Indians to have to use pinch hitters for Nagy and reliever Ricardo Rincon.

"It was a mess," said Hargrove. "I couldn't hardly explain it without throwing Brian under the bus, and I didn't want to do that because ultimately it's my responsibility. We left for a road trip after the game, and when I got on the plane, John was standing in the aisle in first class. I said, 'Hi John,' and he just kept staring straight ahead, like he wished I was dead. 'If I'm lucky, maybe you'll die before we land.' That's the kind of look John had on his face."

The fact that the Indians lost the game, 4-3, didn't help.

To this day, Hart and Hargrove have never discussed that incident.

"He never asked me what happened," said Hargrove. "I never had a chance to explain, and I didn't go to him to explain. I figured if he's that pissed, I don't want to make it worse."

Fortunately for Hargrove, even with the loss that night, the Indians still had a record of 58-37 and were in first place in the division, 12 games ahead of their closest pursuer. The Indians came roaring out of the gate that season, winning eight of their first nine games and going 16-6 in April. They moved into first place on April 8, and they stayed there for the rest of the season.

Their only losing month was July, when they went 13-14. Nobody noticed because, for the second year in a row, and the third time in five years, the Indians had six players selected for the All-Star team: Roberto Alomar, Kenny Lofton, Nagy, Manny Ramirez, Thome and Vizquel. Also, nobody noticed that 13-14 record in July because the Indians went a combined 34-20 in May and June, and a combined 34-22 in August and September.

Midway through September, the Indians led the division by 25½ games, raising the possibility of breaking their major league record set by the 1995 team, which won the division by 30 games. The '99 team failed to break that record, finishing with a record of 97-65, and winning the division by 21½ games.

Those 97 wins matched the 1948 world champion Indians for the fifth-most wins by any team in franchise history up to that time. The 1999 Indians did lose the last three games of the regular season, which didn't seem to bother anyone, because, hey, this was a 97-win team that had scored a nearly unheard-of 1,009 runs and virtually lapped the field in winning its division by 21½ games. Dave Burba (15-9), Bartolo Colon (18-5) and Nagy (17-11) had combined to win 50 games.

*   *   *

This seemed like the most powerful Indians team since the 1995 battering ram. But then came the Division Series with Boston. For the Indians, it was no tea party.

But it couldn't have started out better. The Indians, who hadn't won Game 1 of a playoff series in their last eight tries, won this one, 3-2, on a walkoff RBI single by Fryman with one out in the bottom of the ninth. Colon pitched eight dominating innings, striking out 11 and allowing just two runs.

Boston's Pedro Martinez, who went 23-4 with a 2.07 ERA and would win the second of his three career Cy Young Awards, had to leave the game after the fourth inning with a strained muscle in his back. The Red Sox were leading 2-0 at the time, but Colon and Paul Shuey would hold the Red Sox scoreless on one hit over the last five innings.

In Game 2, the Indians rolled to an 11-1 win. Thome's grand slam in a five-run fourth inning, which followed a six-run third inning, blew the doors off the game early. The Indians were only one win away from winning the Division Series, which moved to Boston for Game 3.

"I remember us landing at Logan Airport for Game 3," said Hargrove. "A cell phone rang, and somebody said, 'It's probably Boston calling, saying they give up.' And I thought, 'Oh, you didn't say that, did you?'"

The wheels started to come off in Game 3. Early in Game 3. Burba started and pitched four scoreless innings on one hit, but then had to leave the game with a sore arm. That's when the roof caved in. Jaret Wright gave up five runs in two innings, Rincon had more runs allowed (3) than outs recorded (2), and the rout was on. The final score was 9-3 as the Red Sox had stopped the bleeding on their side, and started some on the other side.

Then, for the Indians, it went from bad to cataclysmic.

In Game 4, the Red Sox failed to score in only one inning. Colon, who was nearly untouchable in Game 1, was not just touchable, but maul-able in Game 4. The Red Sox sent 10 men to the plate in the second inning. Six of them got hits. Five of them scored. Colon never saw the third inning, and the Indians never saw the truck that hit them. The final, flabbergasting score was 23-7.

"It's embarrassing. Humiliating," said Sandy Alomar after the game.

"Everything we threw up there, they hit. When it came down, we weren't standing there," said Hargrove.

Just like that, the Indians' 2-0 lead in the series was gone. Their 2-1 lead in the series was gone. The series was tied 2-2, with the fifth and deciding game to be played at Jacobs Field. Nobody knew it at the time, but it would be Mike Hargrove's last game as manager of the Cleveland Indians.

"Those five-game series were always a worry to him," said Sharon.

"On the off day in Boston, we went to dinner, me, the coaches and our wives," Hargrove said. "Joe Carrigan, the Red Sox pitching coach, was there with his wife. We finished eating, and on our way out we stopped to say hello. I asked Joe how he was doing, and he said, 'I'm OK, but Martinez is out. He won't be able to pitch the rest of the series.' That was news to me."

Turned out it was fake news, "And I wanted to go over there and punch Carrigan in the nose," joked Hargrove.

The legend of Pedro Martinez didn't begin with Game 5 of the 1999 ALCS, but it did get some serious polishing. He came into the game as a reliever, starting the bottom of the fourth. By then it was a steel cage match between the Boston hitters and the Cleveland hitters. In the first three innings there were five home runs hit, two by Thome and one by Fryman on the Indians side, and one each by Nomar Garciaparra and Troy O'Leary on the Red Sox side. The Indians scored three runs off Bret Saberhagen in the first inning, and five runs in the second and third innings off Saberhagen and Derek Lowe. The Red Sox scored eight runs off Nagy in three innings. Going into the bottom of the fourth inning, the score was tied 8-8.

Enter Martinez. Exit Cleveland Indians.

Martinez pitched six scoreless and hitless innings. He struck out eight. In six innings the Indians only hit one ball out of the infield. It was complete and utter domination of a lineup that had scored 1,009 runs during the regular season. In the five-game Division Series with Boston the Indians averaged 6.4 runs per game, which was more than their per-game average in their 1,009-runs regular season. But for the final six innings of the last game of the Division Series, Martinez held the highest scoring team in the majors to no runs.

"That was as good as I'd ever seen Pedro," Hargrove said. "He's one of the only pitchers I ever saw who would throw almost exclusively one pitch, the first time around the order. Like he'd throw breaking balls to every hitter, every pitch. Then he'd come back the second time and throw all fastballs. Then he'd start mixing them up. He's a guy who had great command and a lot of confidence. As an opposing player, you didn't much care for him because of the way he was, the way he carried himself on the mound, and everything."

O'Leary broke the 8-8 tie with a three-run home run off Shuey in the seventh inning.

"Once that ball left the ballpark, and with Pedro pitching the way he was, it was a real helpless feeling," Hargrove said.

Garciaparra added an RBI double off Mike Jackson in the ninth. Over the last six innings, Jacobs Field was as quiet as the Indians' bats. In the bottom of the ninth, Martinez completed his masterpiece by retiring the side in order. Final score: Boston 12, Cleveland 8. The Indians had scored 15 runs in the last two games but lost them both because the Red Sox scored 35.

*   *   *

After the Indians got Pedro-ized in Game 5, Sharon Hargrove was sure her husband was going to be fired, not just because the team lost in the first round of the playoffs, but how they lost. Leading the series 2-0, then getting outscored 44-18 in losing three in a row. In situations like that, somebody usually loses their job.

"I knew that John had tried several times to get rid of Mike, so I knew (the loss to Boston in the Division Series) would be a tough one to survive," Sharon said. "After the last game, I went down to the Boston family room to congratulate their wives, because for us it was horrible to have it end so abruptly like that. We all came to the park with our bags packed, expecting to go on to the next city of the team we would play in the ALCS."

On her way back from congratulating the Boston wives, Sharon passed John Hart.

"He was coming from Mike's office," she said. "I don't know if he saw me. But I looked at him, and he didn't look at me."

Sharon then got her family, and they went to the Indians' clubhouse.

"We walked into Mike's office. He was showering, so I said to the kids, 'OK kids, look around, because this isn't going to be Dad's office anymore,'" said Sharon. "We were all upset. It was just such a shock, the way it ended. And our kids loved what he was doing. It was hard in some ways. When we lost the '95 World Series, our son Andy was at St. Ignatius High School, and different guys would come up to him and say, 'Your dad is so stupid. Why would he make that move?' We had to talk to the kids all the time about how to handle stuff like that."

Mike and Sharon would frequently tell their kids' teachers that when new kids came into class, to introduce them to the Hargrove kids as simply "Kim" or "Missy."

"We told them not to say their last name because then it's either they think our kids are too good for them and the kids won't speak to them because they think their dad is so cool, or they try to be nice with them, just to get in with them. To go to games with them," Sharon said.

For two days after the loss to Boston, Hargrove was numb. Not over fear that he was going to get fired, but over the way the Indians lost, getting outscored by 26 runs in the last three games, after leading the series 2-0.

"Two days later, Sharon said, 'Have you thought about what's going to happen?' And I said, 'No, what do you mean?'" Hargrove said. "I was totally unaware. I never concerned myself about stuff like that, other than that one day at the golf tournament in '97. But when Sharon said that, I got to thinking and said, 'You know, you may be right. We were up two games to none. We've been to two World Series and hadn't won one. She may be right.'"

A couple of days later Hargrove got a call from Hart's secretary, telling him to come in to the office for a 2 p.m. meeting.

Hargrove called Sharon at 2:15 p.m.

"You got fired, didn't you?" Sharon said.

"How did you know?" said Hargrove.

"Your meeting was at 2. It's 2:15. It doesn't take long to say, 'You're fired.' It takes a long time to say, 'This is what we're going to do,'" said Sharon.

"You're right," Hargrove said.

"Then he got choked up," said Sharon, over 20 years later. "He asked me to call his parents, and tell the kids, because he was too embarrassed to tell them he got fired. Then he said he was going to drive around for a while and think."

Hargrove drove around for three hours.

"When I got the call from John's office telling me to come in, that's when I thought, 'OK, this is going to happen,'" said Hargrove, speaking 20 years after the fact. "I didn't agree with it. When you lose your job and somebody tells you they're going to go in another direction, nobody agrees with that. I didn't. But it didn't surprise me. We were up 2-0 and got beat, especially the 23-7 game. All those little deals that make the meter go up more."

In hindsight, Hargrove views his firing differently than he did at the time it happened.

"Looking back on it now, it was the logical time to do it, although

I didn't think so at the time. Back then, I thought I was bullet-proof," he said. "But it was probably one of the best things that ever happened to me."

Dan O'Dowd left his position as assistant general manager of the Indians following the 1998 season, when he was hired as the general manager of the Colorado Rockies. So he was gone when Hart made the decision to fire Hargrove. Gone, but not necessarily surprised.

"The positions that John and Grover had, they come with a shelf life," O'Dowd said. "I don't think there's anything wrong with that, but they do. You put so much of every fiber of your being into the job that it's physically exhausting, emotionally exhausting and spiritually exhausting. You just get to a point in time where, you don't even realize it, but you've given all you can possibly give. Maybe that was the case there. But that's speculation by me."

Hart declined to speak, for this book, about the decision to fire Hargrove.

On the day of the press conference to announce the firing, Hart said, "This is a difficult decision for all of us. I spent some sleepless nights. Mike has made some major contributions to the rebuilding of this franchise. As difficult as it was to make this decision, it was made in the best interest of the club. It was time for a change. I want to make it perfectly clear that it was not a specific event or managerial move that led to this decision. We feel there is a need for a new energy, a new voice in the clubhouse . . . This is not something we enjoy doing. If anything, it sends a message that this club is serious about going to the next level. I have the utmost respect for Mike. He understands that I have a job to do. Under Mike, we went from an organization that was not very good, to one that was very good. His greatest quality is his loyalty."

When he replaced John McNamara in the middle of the 1991 season, Hargrove inherited a team on its way to a franchise-record 105 losses. He managed the team through a couple of difficult rebuilding years, a horrific spring-training boating accident, a strike-shortened season that probably denied the Indians a trip to the postseason, a tacky yet comical replacement-player spring training, then five consecutive AL Central Division titles, two pennants, two World Series appearances, both losses, one of epic proportions, all the while managing some of the biggest stars and biggest egos of that or any era.

In his 8½ years as manager he had a record of 721-591, and was only eight wins away from passing Lou Boudreau (728-649) for the most wins by any manager in Indians history.

"I felt real good about the job I did when I was in Cleveland," Hargrove says now. "I felt I kept the team on track and focused. And given the diverse personalities in the clubhouse, that could have been a different story."

When a manager is let go after a long run with one team, it's frequently attributed to the need for the players to hear a new voice. That they had tuned out the manager.

"I think there is some validity to that," Hargrove said. "I don't think it had gotten to that point with me in '99. The players still reacted well. Stating a goal to win 100 games, and we won 97. That's pretty much accomplishing the goal. I don't think any of us were too comfortable. We were still pushing. But it (being tuned out) can happen. Did it happen to me in '99? I don't think so. But it may have. John may have bought into the idea that it had, or was going to happen. And John had a pretty good handle on stuff like that. Like with the Baerga trade. He certainly may have been more right about that than I was."

The only thing that upset Hargrove about the way Hart handled the firing was when Hart basically said the team needed someone who could take it to the next level.

"That was the only thing that upset me, and it really, really upset me," Hargrove said. "What's the next level? That just absolutely flew all over me."

Over 20 years later, Hart and Hargrove remain good friends, which is impressive, and historically appropriate. They were the two most important figures in the Indians' glory years of the 1990s, the most successful run of excellence in franchise history. They didn't always get along, but they got along when it mattered most, and both men knew and respected the value of the other.

"It was two different personalities," Hargrove said. "John was Type A, getting up at night and writing down ideas he had, and walking in the fog of the dawn with the birds chirping. John and I came at things from different directions, but we made some good decisions, based on the fact that we both saw different angles on whatever we were talking about, and then came to an agreement.

"But we got along. John is a friend of mine. Was then, still is. I don't hold any grudges. John did his job, and that (firing Hargrove) was his job. I don't have any resentment. There were things John did and said that I didn't agree with, but I'm sure, on the other side of it, there were things that I did and said that John didn't agree with. But we're still friends."

Both men eventually went on to work for other organizations, but there's no question where they experienced their most success, their most gratifying achievements and most enduring memories.

"It was the best time of my life as a professional," Hart said. "I've been around a lot of baseball people and I have not seen one guy, not one, who managed a clubhouse better than Mike Hargrove. In the clubhouse, he was the best I ever saw. I never worried about the clubhouse. Never. Here's why: He was authentic. He is exactly who he is. From the minute he wakes up in the morning until the minute his head hits the pillow at night, he is authentic. Mike is a good man. It came across. He had no ego. He was a good player, so he had a certain level of respect (among the players), and he paid his dues.

"He wasn't a guy who was up today and down tomorrow. He was very steady. Always an even keel. He competed like crazy. He was pissed after a loss. But in the end, his greatest quality was he kept his club alive."

On Oct. 15, 1999, however, after the two men met for just 15 tense minutes in Hart's office, Hargrove left as the ex-manager of the Cleveland Indians, and he needed some time.

"That was hard, even though we knew it was coming," said Sharon.

"I was upset when I left the meeting, so I drove around in my pickup for two or three hours to gather my thoughts," Hargrove said. "Because I was sure people were going to start showing up and asking questions. And I didn't want to do or say anything that blew up 20 years of being in a Cleveland Indians uniform."

Sharon, meanwhile, was already shifting into "life goes on" mode.

"I was totally prepared for him to lose his job. It didn't shock me at all, given what had happened in the series with Boston," she said. "I had to go down to the end of our street to pick up (daughter) Shelly, who was 10, at the bus stop. She got in the car and I said, 'Shell, I've got to tell you something. Do you know what fired means?' And she said, 'Yeah, like what happened to Mike Fratello?' I said yeah, and then I said, 'Dad got fired today from the Indians.' She said, 'Oh, Mom. You could have at least waited until I have my snack before you told me.' "

Sharon conceded that her daughter had a point.

"That changed the way I felt about (the firing)," Sharon said. "I thought, you know what, our family is still going to be together. Life's still going to go on. We're still going to go home and have a snack."

After three hours of soul-searching while driving his truck, Hargrove returned home. He was greeted by multiple TV satellite trucks in his driveway. And not long after that, another truck showed up. A TV truck, to do a live report from the Hargrove's driveway. Mike and Sharon walked out to the end of the driveway and did the interview.

"I broke down right at the end of it. So, I just turned away and walked off. It was the last question. I don't necessarily regret doing that, but I wish it hadn't gotten to that point," Hargrove said.

"He did real good until they mentioned John's comment that they wanted to hire a manager that could take them to the next level," Sharon said. "Then on the news that night they had a picture of Mike that said, 'Mike Hargrove, 1979-99.' And I thought, 'Well, he didn't die.' "

Getting fired as manager of the Indians was the one acutely personal moment in Hargrove's baseball career that nothing he previously experienced had prepared him for. These were uncharted, lonely, emotional waters.

"Whatever I've tried to do, and whatever I've done, I've always been successful. Varying degrees of success," he said. "But this was the first time I ever had to consider that I had failed. That was hard to face."

CHAPTER 16

A Huge Raise, a Bad Team, a Tantalizing Phone Call

"Do you understand what I'm saying?"

The three-hour drive in his pickup truck, and the emotional walk away from the end-of-the-driveway TV interview helped Hargrove put his firing in his rearview mirror. The fog lifted relatively quickly. "I don't remember being in a funk," he said of the next few days. "I remember thinking I've got a son going to St. Ignatius, and that's not cheap for him to go to school there. I've got a daughter going to college who needs tuition. So, I've got to have a job. I made decent money with the Indians. I made a lot more money with Baltimore and Seattle. But I remember thinking I needed to find something in the game that I could do that paid."

Fortunately, Sharon didn't have to start packing boxes again, because when he was fired by the Indians, Hargrove still had one year remaining on his contract.

"So, I had a little wiggle room," he said, "but I'm sure John was on the phone with other general managers saying, 'Will you please hire this guy, so we don't have to pay him?'"

In hindsight, Hargrove felt that getting fired in Cleveland was in some ways the best thing that ever happened to him.

Why?

"Because it allowed me to command a better salary," he said. "I'm not sure I would have ever made the money in Cleveland that I made in Baltimore and Seattle. I got a real hefty raise from Baltimore from what I was making with the Indians."

But it was more than just financial. It was environmental.

"I think we all, at certain times, become real comfortable in our circumstances. Not complacent. Comfortable," he said. "I think that was happening for me in Cleveland. I still had my edge. I still loved the Indians and loved working for the Indians. I loved doing what I was doing, and didn't want to leave. But I think it was probably the right time. Because things started to go in a different direction (after 1999). So, I probably got out at the right time, when people still had a decent opinion of me."

Indeed, the arrival of a new century meant the arrival of a new owner for the Indians. On Nov. 4, 1999, Richard Jacobs announced he had signed an agreement to sell his baseball team to Lawrence Dolan and family trusts. Major league owners unanimously approved the sale on Jan. 19, 2000. On Feb. 15, 2000, the Dolan family assumed ownership of the Indians. That was a seismic shift for the franchise, and so was another headline-grabbing announcement.

At the start of the 2001 season, John Hart announced that it would be his last as general manager of the Indians. He left after the season to become the general manager of the Texas Rangers. Mark Shapiro, who had become Hart's assistant general manager after Dan O'Dowd left for Colorado following the 1998 season, became the Indians' new general manager on Nov. 1, 2001. So, in a 24-month span, the owner, the general manager and the manager of a team that won five consecutive division titles and two American League pennants were all gone.

Hargrove's 8½-year tenure as manager is the second-longest in Indians' history, exceeded only by Lou Boudreau's nine-year run from 1942-50. As impressive as Hargrove's longevity in Cleveland was, it pales in comparison to two of Hargrove's contemporaries, Bobby Cox and Tony La Russa, who managed the Braves and the Cardinals for 25 and 16 years, respectively.

"It's really rare for that to happen," said Hargrove of Cox and La Russa. "Because a lot of things—a LOT of things—have to go right for that to happen. The ballclub has to be successful, and the people you're working for have to really, really, really believe in you. I'm not saying John didn't really believe in me. But it may have been three 'really's' instead of five 'really's.'"

Once the dust had settled from that 15-minute, franchise-rocking meeting with Hart, the wait for the next chapter in Hargrove's career began.

It was a short wait.

Five days later, the Orioles called and asked Hargrove to interview for their manager's job. At about the same time, the Angels' managing job came open, and that was one in which Hargrove had a serious interest. He kept waiting and hoping for a call from Angels general manager Bill Stoneman, but it never came. So, Hargrove interviewed with the Orioles, and got the job.

"I saw Bill Stoneman at the winter meetings that year," said Hargrove. "He said, 'I really wish you would have waited a little longer,' and I said, 'I really wish you would have called a little sooner.'"

But it would have taken a lot for Hargrove to say no to the Orioles. There's landing on your feet and there's landing on your feet with a hefty raise. Nineteen days after he was fired by the Indians, Hargrove was hired by the Orioles.

"It's good to be back in the big leagues, even though I was gone only a couple of weeks," Hargrove said at his introductory news conference.

Getting another job was exciting in itself. Getting another job almost immediately was better still. Getting another job, almost immediately, at well over double your previous salary was best of all.

"It made you feel validated. That somebody else was interested," said Hargrove.

The next step was out of Hargrove's comfort zone. He'd been a member of the Indians' organization, as a player, a minor league coach and manager, a major league coach and manager, for the past 20 years. During that time, he'd formed friendships and relationships with countless players, front office personnel, ballpark employees and other employees of the organization. Now he was going into Baltimore cold.

"I knew the players," he said. "It was an old ballclub. Mike Bordick, B.J. Surhoff, Brady Anderson, Mike Mussina. All these guys were veteran players. Really good players. But they were getting older. I knew them. But as far as the people in the front office, I had no clue."

It was a time in baseball when the digital age, the computer age and the analytics age were all starting to become integrated into the sport. Not all the teams made that transition on the same timeline.

"In Cleveland, everything was so computerized," Hargrove said. "You'd go to the winter meetings and you'd have computers and boxes of scouting reports. You'd have three or four guys on computers saying, 'Hey, what about Joe Blow from Toronto? What are his numbers the last five years?' And they'd check their computers, and, almost immediately, here it is. With Baltimore, when I got there, it wasn't like that. They were in the process of doing it, but it wasn't done yet. That was hard to get used to."

The first order of business for Hargrove was to hire a coaching staff, and, unfortunately for all involved, owner Peter Angelos got involved with it.

"Peter called Mike and told him he wanted me to be on the staff," said former Orioles catcher Rick Dempsey, writing in his book, "If These Walls Could Talk: Stories from the Baltimore Orioles Dugout, Locker Room and Press Box."

"Hargrove really took offense to that," said Dempsey in his book. "He didn't want anyone telling him who his coaches are. He wanted to pick his own guys."

According to Dempsey, Hargrove called him and said that Dempsey had criticized him in the past, and Hargrove didn't want him on his staff.

"I was shocked, because I never talked to Mike in my life and had never even mentioned his name in a sentence," said Dempsey.

The two men continued to talk, and Hargrove eventually relented, telling Dempsey, "Don't worry about it" and that Hargrove's belief that Dempsey had criticized him in the past "was third-hand information, anyway." Hargrove eventually did hire Dempsey as his first-base coach.

"I was really happy to coach for Mike, because he had turned things around with the Cleveland organization and made the Indians a winner," Dempsey said.

But the Hargrove-Dempsey association did not get off to a good start.

"He didn't get to pick me, so there was some friction there. It was almost like it was a college hazing deal from the very beginning," Dempsey writes.

During spring training, there would be a coach's meeting every morning, in which they would vote on which coach had screwed up or done something wrong the day before.

"It was supposed to be a fun thing, but it wasn't. Not for me," said Dempsey, in his book. "Whoever got picked received a Mule Dick, which was something long and wrapped in a towel. You had to carry the Mule Dick through the clubhouse. I got it every single day. Every day they voted me the Mule Dick. I laugh about it now because it was almost funny how much Mike did not like me. To this day, I really don't know why. I guess it was that Peter put me in that job, and Mike thought Peter was eventually going to make me the manager. Mike wasn't a bad guy. I just think he didn't want me there because he perceived me to be a threat to his job, which I never would have gotten, anyway."

Hargrove's recollection differs from Dempsey's.

"I don't remember how the hiring of Rick came about, but I never was against it," Hargrove said. "He's right. I don't ever remember speaking to him, other than to say hello. When I got the job, I hired Jeff Newman, Brian Graham and Mark Wiley. The rest of the coaches, Sam Perlozzo, Terry Crowley and Tom Trebelhorn, all those guys were guys that were Baltimore guys, and I didn't have a problem with any of them. I liked them all, including Rick. So if there was any friction or tension between Rick and me, it was all on his part, not mine. I enjoyed having Rick on the staff, and I thought he did a good job."

When teams change managers, it's almost always because the team isn't very good. That was the case with the Orioles. Hargrove was replacing Ray Miller, who in his two years as manager had nearly identical mediocre records of 79-83 and 78-84.

There were some familiar faces on Hargrove's new team, not all of them smiling. Chief among those was Albert Belle, who used an out clause in his contract to flee the White Sox after two years. Belle signed a five-year, $65 million deal with Baltimore, and in 1999 had another big year, hitting .297 and leading the Orioles in home runs (37) and RBI (117) while also stealing 17 bases, the second-highest total of his career. Other players on the 2000 Orioles that Hargrove managed for varying lengths of time in Cleveland included Harold Baines, Mark Lewis, Trent Hubbard and Tim Worrell.

Overall, however, it was an aging group that Hargrove inherited. Eight of the nine regulars were over 30, five of the nine were over 35, and one of those was over 40, that being the 41-year-old Baines. In 2000, Hargrove's first year as manager, Sports Illustrated sent a reporter to the Orioles' spring training camp in Fort Lauderdale, Florida, and he came away unimpressed:

"Baltimore has problems, not the least of which is a thoroughly unlikable, dysfunctional clubhouse. Albert Belle snarls (and) rants . . . Will Clark . . . never shuts up. Delino DeShields sulks. Scott Erickson bitches . . . At best Baltimore is an old, ornery team," reported Sports Illustrated in its March 27 issue.

Back in Cleveland, Hart wasted no time in hiring popular hitting coach Charlie Manuel as the Indians' new manager. Meanwhile, the American League schedule maker wasted no time in sandwiching Hargrove between his past and his future. On opening day in 2000, at Camden Yards, the Orioles hosted the Cleveland Indians.

"I remember thinking somebody with horns made out this schedule," Hargrove said. Opening day was April 3. When the Indians and Orioles played that day, it was the 1,365th major league game that Hargrove managed. It was the first major league game that Charlie Manuel managed.

It did not seem to be a coincidence that the American League office would milk the promotional potential of that managerial subplot for all it was worth by having the two teams play each other in that season-opening series. "It was an uncomfortable feeling, because I had been, for so many years, so close to all those players," Hargrove said of the Indians. "So, it was very uncomfortable the first day, but it got better after that."

It never got better for Hargrove's wife.

"On opening day, I had to tell myself, 'Jim Thome just got a hit. Don't clap. Manny Ramirez just got a hit. Don't cheer.' That was tough," said Sharon. "Then after the game, I got on the elevator, and John and Sandy Hart were on it. So that was a little awkward."

The Orioles lost Hargrove's debut as manager, 4-1. But they won the next two games, beating Cleveland 11-7 and 6-2, as the over-amped Manuel got thrown out of both of games. "I'm going to have to learn how to present myself better to the umpires," said Manuel after his second ejection.

"Charlie didn't last real long in both games. But he was a new manager, trying to put his stamp on the ballclub, so I kind of understood it, and the gripes he had (both on the umpire's version of the strike zone) were legitimate gripes," Hargrove said.

Those two wins over Cleveland were the first two of a five-game winning streak by the Orioles, who followed that by losing four in a row, and followed that by winning six in a row. Then the bottom fell out. From May 3-21, they lost seven in a row, 11 of 12 and 15 of 17. In June they had a season-long nine-game losing streak. After a 14-10 April they had losing records in every month the rest of the season.

It was the kind of season Hargrove hadn't experienced as a manager since his under-construction 1993 Indians team went 76-86. The 2000 Orioles finished with a record of 71-91, in fourth place in the AL East. Baltimore's winning percentage of .457 was the worst by a Hargrove-managed team since 1991, the year he replaced John McNamara in Cleveland, when the Indians staggered to a franchise-record 105 losses and a .352 winning percentage.

The last game of the Orioles' 2000 season was on October 1, a 7-3 win over the Yankees at Camden Yards. With one out in the bottom of the eighth inning, in what would be—though nobody knew it at the time—the last at bat of his major league career, Belle hit a home run off Yankees' pitcher Denny Neagle.

It was career homer No. 381 for Belle. He hit 242 of them with Cleveland, which ranks second on the Indians' all-time list, behind Jim Thome (337).

When Hargrove became manager of the Orioles in 2000, it had been four years since he last managed Belle, and he noticed that Belle had changed. "He still had the intensity, but he wasn't nearly as confrontational as he had been. Obviously, he had matured," Hargrove said.

Belle was 34 years old when he went to spring training with the Orioles in 2001. For the last year or so he had been bothered by what would later be diagnosed as a congenital hip condition.

"In spring training in 2001, it was real obvious that his hip was bad," Hargrove said. "He would hit a ball, and his first three or four steps, he couldn't hardly get going at all. Once he got going, he was fine."

Prior to the Orioles' first exhibition game of that spring, Hargrove talked to Belle and asked him if he was able to play in the game.

"Not today. Let's talk tomorrow," said Belle. Hargrove talked to Belle the next day and got the same answer.

That went on for about three or four days in a row. On the fifth day, prior to the game Hargrove found Belle riding the exercise bike in the weight room. He wasn't in the lineup, but he was trying to get his hip loose. Just before Hargrove made out the lineup card, he asked Belle, "Do you want to try it today?"

"Oh," said Belle. "I'm thinking about hanging it up."

Slightly taken aback by so casual a retirement announcement, Hargrove asked Belle to come talk to him before he made a final decision. Belle said he would.

"I never saw him again," said Hargrove. "It didn't bother me that he didn't come by and say something to me. I don't think he said anything to anybody. He just decided he couldn't go any further, and it didn't surprise any of us, because he struggled so much. I respected him a lot for the effort that he gave trying to get through that. I admired how hard he worked to get through that. But it was kind of obvious it wasn't going to happen."

That was it. One of the noisiest sluggers of any generation retired in relative quiet. There was no ceremony, no press conference, no formal announcement, no TV cameras or farewell tour. There was merely a four-paragraph press release distributed by the Orioles on March 9, stating that Belle's career was over, that he was "totally disabled and unable to perform as a major league baseball player."

Two Orioles doctors examined Belle and the diagnosis was a severe case of degenerative arthritis in his right hip. "Belle has agreed that he is physically incapable of performing as a player and concurs with the findings of the doctors," the Orioles' statement said.

Belle still had three years and $39 million left on his contract with the Orioles, 70% of which was reimbursed to the team, per the insurance coverage included in his contract.

Belle's retirement was handled in typical Belle fashion. Orioles general manager Syd Thrift said he had no idea where Belle was. Orioles public relations director Bill Stetka was unable to locate him.

"He's somewhere in the area," Thrift told the Associated Press.

Hargrove knew where Belle was. Belle and his twin brother Terry lived in the same apartment building as Hargrove in Fort Lauderdale.

"He and Terry were on one floor, and me and my family were on another. I saw Terry two or three times, but I never saw Albert," said Hargrove, who didn't speak to Belle for years after that.

The two men had first met in Kinston, North Carolina, in the summer of 1987, when Hargrove was managing the Indians' Class-A affiliate. Belle, after a protracted negotiating period following the June Draft, had finally signed, and was ready to begin his professional career. His first professional manager would be Mike Hargrove.

Fourteen years later, in the spring of 2001, in Fort Lauderdale, Florida, Hargrove was Belle's last professional manager. It had been a long, historic, bumpy, magical, controversial ride, but it ended quietly in a weight room in spring training. A very brief exchange between the two men, and then it was over. A career, and a professional relationship. Hargrove saw, and benefited from, the best of Belle. Hargrove also saw, and had to endure, the worst of Belle. There was plenty of both.

"You play with the bull, you've got to deal with the horns," Hargrove said. "But I want to make sure I say this. I really liked Albert. He was a good guy. He did some crazy things. Some stupid things. And I'm not excusing them at all. But on the whole, I enjoyed Albert playing for me, because I knew that he would play."

For all the controversy that surrounded Belle in his 12-year career in the major leagues, he also produced at a borderline Hall of Fame level. He was arguably the most feared slugger of his era. Had the hip condition not prematurely ended his career, had he played, say three or four more years at that same level, he would have been hard to ignore by objective Hall of Fame voters. As it was, the numbers speak for themselves.

In his last five seasons in Cleveland (1992-96), all under Hargrove, Belle hit .303, averaged 41 home runs and 123 RBI per season, had a .989 OPS and a 154 wRC+. He averaged a home run every 13.2 at bats and an RBI every 4.4 at bats.

Clearly, Jeff Scott, the man who scouted, drafted and signed

Belle for the Indians in 1987, was right when he said, "Albert was really lucky that Mike was his guy, so to speak, for most of his career. Because not many people would have the temperament to handle everything with Albert that you had to handle."

Hargrove actually presided over the end of two careers in 2001, two players whose personalities and reputations couldn't have been further apart. In spring training of 2001, Belle retired. At the end of the 2001 season, so did Cal Ripken Jr.

"Cal was one of the most knowledgeable players, as far as the game's concerned, that I've ever been around," Hargrove said. "He was absolutely totally prepared. Great competitor. Pleasant to be around. Easy to talk to. Very accommodating."

The only problem for Ripken's manager was that everyone wanted Ripken's autograph—including Ripken's manager.

"I had a close friend who asked me if I could get Cal's autograph," said Hargrove. "I said I'd try, but I hated doing stuff like that. Just hated it. So, I asked Cal into my office, and I said, 'I hate doing this, but if you don't mind, I have a very dear friend who would love to have your autograph. Could you sign this ball for me real quick?' He said, 'I'll do better than that.' He went to his locker and came back an hour later with two dozen balls he had signed. He gave them to me and said, 'Here. More people are going to ask. This will save both of us time.'"

Ripken was right. More people did ask.

"Those two dozen balls were gone in about a month," Hargrove said.

Ripken's major league-record streak of playing in 2,632 consecutive games was over by the time Hargrove became the manager of the Orioles. Hargrove's second year in Baltimore (2001) was Ripken's last. So that was the year Ripken made his farewell tour. He was honored in every city the Orioles played, and Cal-mania got so intense that Ripken would not stay in the Orioles' team hotel. He would stay, under an assumed name, in a different hotel.

"But he was never late. Absolutely a leader by example," said Hargrove. "You could tell he was raised right by his dad (former Orioles coach and manager Cal Ripken Sr.)."

During that season a company loaned Ripken a plane, so the last time the Orioles would go into each city, Ripken and his family would use that company plane to fly into the city while the rest of the Orioles flew in on their charter. Some opposing teams even had parades for Ripken, and, of course, the ballparks were packed for the last chance to see the future Hall of Famer.

Ripken's back was bothering him at the time, so he needed a day off every third or fourth day. He and Hargrove would periodically sit down and map out Ripken's playing schedule for the next couple of weeks.

"We were in Anaheim one day, a day we decided Cal wasn't going to play," Hargrove recalled. "I had three or four fans come down to the dugout and scream at me, 'Hargrove! You asshole! We came 300 miles. This is our only time here and you're not playing Ripken? You son of a bitch, you!' They were screaming at me, seriously pissed. I wanted to turn around and say, 'Hey, yell at Ripken, he's the one who picked this day.'"

Fortunately for Hargrove, Ripken, who was born to be a star, knew and accepted everything that being a star entailed.

"Cal handled it all really well," Hargrove said. "He would fly ahead of the ballclub, but he was always in the clubhouse on time, laughing and joking with the other players. He wasn't an aloof player. A lot of guys who get to his stature can become really aloof. But he wasn't. Cal was Cal. A good guy from the start to the end."

In Hargrove's first two years in Baltimore, his roster was filled with mostly veteran players. One of those was first baseman Jeff Conine.

"He was one of my all-time favorite players, a really good guy. But gosh did he have a temper," Hargrove said. "He'd make an out at the plate, and as he was coming back to the dugout, everyone scattered, worrying about what he was going to do."

Answer: everything.

"He wouldn't throw things in the dugout, but he'd go down the steps to the swing area, and he would scream and holler and hit this one part of the wall. There would be wood chips flying up into the dugout from the runway. You could tell when he was steaming. But when he was done, he'd come back up into the dugout, sit down and act like nothing happened."

Hargrove may have earned a Ph.D. in crisis management during his time managing Belle, but that didn't make managing four bad

Baltimore teams from 2000 to 2003 any easier. In Hargrove's four years as manager, the Orioles had four consecutive losing seasons, finishing in fourth place all four years, anywhere between 13½ to 36½ games out of first place in the highly competitive AL East. The "best" of Hargrove's four teams in Baltimore was his first one, in 2000. That team went 74-88 (.457). The 2001 Orioles lost 98 games, but the most frustrating of Hargrove's four Baltimore teams was the 2002 edition. That team lost six of its first seven games, and then ended the season on a 12-game losing streak.

Following an 11-7 win over Toronto on Aug. 23, the Orioles were 63-63. But then, incredibly, they went 4-32 over the rest of the season, getting outscored in those 36 games 210-103. During that stretch it was not a question of whether the Orioles would score enough runs to win. It was a question of whether they'd get enough hits—one—to avoid being no-hit. They finished with a record of 67-95, in fourth place again, 36½ games behind the division-winning Yankees.

"It seemed like almost every day we'd go into the fifth or sixth innings with no hits, and you're wondering if you're going to get no-hit. It was not a fun month," Hargrove said.

The following year, 2003, the last year of Hargrove's contract, it was more of the same: 71-91, another fourth-place finish, this time 30 games behind the Yankees. Loss No. 91 came on the last day of the season, a 3-1 loss to New York, at Yankee Stadium.

"It was obvious they weren't going to renew my contract," Hargrove said. "So, I'm sitting in my office after the game, packing my bag and getting ready to take a shower, and the clubhouse guy says to me, 'GMS is on the phone, and he wants to talk to you.' I said, 'GMS? Who is that?' He said, 'The Boss. George Steinbrenner. He wants to talk to you.'"

Through the years Hargrove had seen Steinbrenner enough to say hello, but he really didn't know the Yankees' owner well at all. Hargrove picked up the phone and said hello.

"Mike, I understand Baltimore's probably not going to renew your contract," Steinbrenner said.

"Yeah, that's the rumor I'm hearing," Hargrove said.

"I want you to hear what I'm saying now," Steinbrenner said. "Don't jump at the first job offer you get. Be patient. Wait a little bit."

"What?" said Hargrove.

"Read between the lines here. Do you understand what I'm saying?" said Steinbrenner.

"Yes. I do. I appreciate it," Hargrove said.

Hargrove put down the phone and tried to digest what he'd just heard. What he did know was that Steinbrenner at the time was trying to negotiate an extension with Yankees manager Joe Torre. Apparently, those negotiations at that time were not going well. Clearly, Steinbrenner was lining up Hargrove as his Plan B, should the Yankees and Torre part ways.

"Two weeks later I heard Joe signed the extension and I was like, 'Motherfuck!' But I was happy for Joe. Happy that he got the extension. I never saw Steinbrenner again, or never talked to him again," said Hargrove.

Still, Hargrove's mind was racing after that dizzying conversation with Steinbrenner. Could a kid from tiny Perryton, Texas, grow up to become the manager of the New York Yankees? Who wouldn't be enraptured by the thought of that?

"I did think about it a little bit," Hargrove said. "But I kept coming back to the fact that I wasn't sure I wanted to be the guy who replaces Joe Torre. It was one of those interesting stories. I never had that happen before. I appreciated the phone call. But I was glad it worked out for Joe."

Hargrove was much more certain about his immediate future. He had none. Not in Baltimore, at least. Early one morning, a couple of days after the end of the season, Hargrove got a call from Orioles vice presidents Jim Beattie and Mike Flanagan, asking Hargrove to come to their office at 1 p.m. Hargrove couldn't because he and Sharon had a 1 p.m. flight to Texas, where Sharon's father had died. So, Beattie and Flanagan asked Hargrove to come to the office immediately.

Hargrove did, and was told by the two men that he was no longer the manager of the Baltimore Orioles.

"It took 30 minutes. But I knew it was going to happen," Hargrove said. "It wasn't a surprise at all. I would have been surprised if they hadn't done it. I had been there four years and we had not really done anything."

Beattie and Flanagan chose not to give their reasons for making the change. Beattie told the Baltimore Sun the reasons were "private." Flanagan said, "Different direction, different voice."

After being let go by one major league team after 8½ years as manager, Hargrove had now been let go by a second team after four years.

"I was the same manager in Baltimore as I was in Cleveland. The talent was just different. Good players make you look smart," said Hargrove.

His two managerial stints couldn't have had a greater contrast. One was ultra-successful, with five consecutive division titles and two trips to the World Series. The other was four consecutive losing seasons.

Nevertheless, his Baltimore experience didn't diminish Hargrove's desire to continue managing somewhere.

"I still wanted to do it," he said. "I didn't know if it would happen or not, but I wanted to do it."

Indians general manager Mark Shapiro offered Hargrove a job as a special assistant to the general manager, and Hargrove accepted. He spent the 2004 season observing spring training, and, once the season began, visiting the minor league affiliates and evaluating players. He also offered advice and opinions on major league matters.

After the season, Hargrove and a friend were playing golf one day, when Hargrove's phone rang. It was Bill Bavasi, general manager of the Seattle Mariners.

"He asked me if I would be interested in coming in for an interview," said Hargrove. "I said, 'You bet.'"

CHAPTER 17

The Long Drive Home

"You need to quit, or you're going to die."

To interview for the Seattle Mariners managing job, Hargrove flew to Phoenix, because that's where Seattle general manager Bill Bavasi was in early October 2004. The interview took place in a high-end steak restaurant. Hargrove showed up wearing a sport coat and tie.

"Bill and a couple of the guys said, 'What are you doing?'" Hargrove said. "I said, 'I'm here to interview.' They said, 'You don't have to dress like that. Go up and take your coat and tie off and roll up your sleeves.'"

Hargrove did that, and when he came back down to go to dinner, most of the Seattle officials were in slacks, some in shorts. Six or seven guys, most of whom Hargrove did not know.

"We ate dinner, and it was a good interview. An interesting interview," Hargrove said. "I don't know if it was orchestrated or not, but you'd eat and be talking baseball, or talking about something, and all of a sudden one of them would ask me a question. We'd talk 10 minutes more, then another one would ask me a question. Just out of the blue, one of them would ambush you with a question. But it didn't bother me. 'Ambush' was probably not the right word. But it wasn't an A-B-C-D-type interview. It was talk, ask a question, talk, ask a question. I enjoyed it."

Hargrove flew home the next morning, and four or five days later Bavasi called and said they wanted Hargrove to come back for another interview, and to meet Mariners president Chuck Armstrong and CEO Howard Lincoln. This time the interview was in

Seattle, and this time nobody was wearing shorts. It was just the four men: Hargrove, Bavasi, Armstrong and Lincoln.

"We had dinner in a private room in the hotel, and everybody was in coats and ties. We had dinner and talked," Hargrove said.

When it was time to order drinks, Hargrove's mind flashed back to the time, while managing the Indians, he interviewed a candidate for a coaching position.

"We talked in my office for two or three hours. Then it was lunchtime, so we went upstairs to the Terrace Club, and he ordered a beer for lunch," Hargrove said. "I drink beer, but for whatever reason, that really flipped my switch. And so I didn't hire him, because of that. That's how stupid I was. I felt good about the interview, but then that happened, and I thought, 'I don't know.'"

In the interview in Seattle, they were taking drink orders at the table, "In this little private setting. Really, kind of formal. The kind that makes your butt clinch up," Hargrove said. "You're a little on edge, because you know how important the interview is, and the thought slammed into my mind, 'Don't order a beer.'"

Hargrove was the first one asked for his drink order. "I'm not really sure," he said. The other men all ordered, and they all ordered wine. So did Hargrove.

"I'm not much of a wine drinker, but if they're drinking wine, so am I. I'm not going to give them any reason not to like me."

Hargrove felt the interview went well. When it was over, Bavasi told him to wait in his room the next day, and that if Hargrove knew anybody in Seattle, not to call them and tell them he was in town. Hargrove had checked into the hotel under an assumed name.

"By noon tomorrow," Bavasi told Hargrove, "I'll give you a call or come by and see you and I'll let you know what's going on."

"The next day, I'm sitting in my room, and noon came and went, 12:30 went by, and 1:00, then 1:30, and I'm thinking, 'Eh,'" said Hargrove.

Then Sharon called to tell Hargrove that Kim, their oldest daughter, who was pregnant, had gone into labor and had been taken to the hospital. Sharon then asked what was going on with the Mariners.

"I don't know, but I don't think it looks real good. It's 1:30," said Hargrove.

"I was sitting there sweating, and I had come to the conclusion that it wasn't going to happen, because it had been so long," he said. "Then there was a knock on the door. Bill came in and offered me a deal. I said I appreciated it. We negotiated for about 15 to 20 minutes, and he said, 'Let me make a couple phone calls and see what I can do.' So he went outside and made the phone calls and came in and said, 'OK, we'll do that.' So I signed the contract, and told Bill, 'I'd love to stick around, but my daughter is in labor with my second grandchild.' So I flew home, and Drew was born, and that was it."

Hargrove was introduced as the Mariners' new manager on Oct. 21, 2004.

"He's battle-tested and he's got a lot of postseason experience," Bavasi told the Kitsap Sun. "The recommendations come far and wide on his behalf. People like playing for him, they like working for him."

The Mariners at that time were at what seemed to be a pivotal point in their history. They were just three years removed from their epic 2001 season, in which they won 116 games, tying the 1908 Chicago Cubs' major league record for most wins in a season. The Mariners then beat the Indians in five games in the Division Series, even though Cleveland outscored Seattle by 10 runs in the five games. In the ALCS, the Mariners lost to the Yankees in five games. That season marked the fourth time in seven years that Seattle reached the postseason, a streak that started in 1995, when Hargrove's best Indians team eliminated the Mariners in six games in the ALCS.

After winning 116 games in 2001, the Mariners won 93 games in each of the next two years, but failed to reach the postseason in either year. However, in 2004, under second-year manager Bob Melvin, the roof caved in. Seattle's win total plunged 30 games from the previous year—from 93 to 63—and Melvin was fired after the season.

As was the case in his first year with the Orioles, Hargrove inherited a Seattle team loaded with veterans. All nine regulars on the 2004 team were 30 or older, and DH Edgar Martinez was 41. The pitching staff included 41-year-old soft-tossing Jamie Moyer, who in 2003, at age 40, went 21-7, made the All-Star team for the only time in his 25-year career, and finished fifth in the Cy Young Award voting.

But Moyer, who would throw his last pitch in the major leagues for the Colorado Rockies in 2012, at the age of 49, slipped to 7-13 with a 5.21 ERA in 2004. Fortunately for Seattle, Hargrove, in his first spring training with the Mariners, saw a right-hander from Venezuela who was half Moyer's age, but was ready to burst upon the big-league scene. His name was Felix Hernandez. He would turn 19 on April 8.

"Oh, my goodness, yeah," said Hargrove. "We knew we had something real special with him. I'd seen him in spring training. That was his first year, and Bill and his people had come up with a formula for protecting Felix. The formula was, you take 10 innings times his age, which came out to 190. So his limit for the year was 190 innings, and spring training counted. So, there's probably 25-30 innings before you even start the season."

This was one of Hargrove's first exposures to baseball through analytics.

"I talked to Bill and said, 'To do this, to limit Felix to 190 innings, there are going to be times where he is going to be out there with a one-hit shutout and we're up 6-0 in the fifth inning, and I'm going to have to take him out of the game to get him through the season. If he's going to be our horse, horses pitch anywhere from 200 to 225 innings a year.'"

Bavasi told Hargrove there was no flexibility to the plan. It was a firm 190 innings, and not one pitch more.

"So I said, 'OK,'" Hargrove said. "We tried to make it public so people wouldn't be in an uproar when we took Felix out of games; so they wouldn't say, 'What's that idiot doing?' or 'What are the Mariners doing?' So we did that the whole year."

Hernandez split the season between Seattle and Triple-A Tacoma. In a combined 26 starts he was 13-8 with a 2.45 ERA, and he pitched 172⅓ innings. Throw in his spring training appearances, and he finished right round his prescribed 190-innings limit.

"He was fun to watch pitch. He was just a fun kid," Hargrove said.

During his rookie season Hernandez was quoted as saying that there was one major league pitcher who was his idol. Hargrove cringed when he read the quote.

"That pitcher was a drunk," Hargrove said. "I mean, he was. He had a history of not taking care of himself."

So Hargrove called Hernandez into his office for a talk.

"I said, 'Felix, there are other people you can pattern yourself after who are a better role model than this guy. I understand that you like him, and personally, I do, too. But he's a guy who hasn't taken care of himself. If you do the same, you may not last as long as he has, because of that. I'm not telling you not to look up to him, but just to realize maybe you don't want to pattern yourself after him.' Felix said, 'I didn't think about that.'"

There were a handful of former Indians on Hargrove's 2005 Mariners roster, including Pat Borders, who, in the last year of his 17-year major league career, started 37 games at catcher, at age 42. The 2005 Mariners were all over the place at the catching position. Seven different players started games at catcher, and none of them started more than 45 games. In addition to Borders, there was Miguel Olivo, Yorvit Torrealba, Wiki Gonzalez, Rene Rivera, Miguel Ojeda and Dan Wilson.

In addition to Borders, other former Indians on that Mariners team were reliever Ron Villone, who pitched for Hargrove in Cleveland in 1998, and Richie Sexson, who signed with Seattle as a free agent shortly after Hargrove was hired.

Sexson had two big years for Hargrove in Seattle. In 2005 he belted 39 home runs, with 121 RBI, and the next year he had 34 homers and 107 RBI. The free-swinging 6-foot-7 slugger also struck out 321 times in those two years.

"Richie was a little ahead of his time," Hargrove said. "He'd be a superstar now, because nobody would care that he struck out a lot."

In Seattle, some people did care that Sexson struck out a lot. General manager Bill Bavasi, for one.

"Richie's strikeouts were driving the front office nuts, and Bill came into my office once to talk about it," Hargrove said. "During my career as a manager, I never had a general manager tell me who to play or who not to play. But Bill came down and said, 'Mike, you don't HAVE to play Richie.' They had signed Richie to a big contract. He was making a lot of money. But Bill said, 'You don't *have* to play him. I don't care how much money he's making, you don't have to play him.'

"I told Bill I understood that, and I understood the strikeouts. But it's kind of a give-some-to-get-some thing. We all remember Richie's strikeouts as he's going through them. But at the end of the year, he's going to hit 30 home runs and drive in 100 runs. That's what his track record says. If we want him to do that, we have to give him the at-bats to do that. I'm willing to do that. And Bill said, 'OK, that's good enough for me.'"

Another player on Hargrove's Seattle teams was third baseman Adrian Beltre, who after leading the National League with 48 home runs for the Dodgers in 2004, signed with the Mariners as a free agent.

"Adrian was one of my all-time favorites," Hargrove said. "He was really good. We had two middle infielders, Yuniesky Betancourt and Jose Lopez, good players, but really young kids, and they liked to have a good time. Goof around and joke around. Nothing nasty or bad, but at times it was hard to keep them focused. So I had a meeting with Adrian and I said, 'I'm going to put you in charge of these two. Just keep them in line. I'm not talking about off the field. But between the lines, during the game, keep them in line and be a leader for them. And Adrian did that. No complaints, and he wasn't overbearing about it."

*   *   *

Hargrove's Seattle teams were extraordinarily diverse culturally.

"One day our pitcher was in trouble, so the catcher went to the mound, and Adrian came in from third, and I looked at my bench coach, Ron Hassey, and said, 'What can they be talking about? I've got a Chinese pitcher on the mound who doesn't speak English or Japanese. I've got a Japanese catcher who doesn't speak anything but Japanese. I've got a Dominican third baseman who speaks English and Spanish, and I've got an American first baseman who speaks only English. What the hell can they be saying?' And they all had their gloves over their face. There's not an interpreter alive who could have picked up on that conversation."

During a game in Kansas City, Beltre slid hard into a base and sprained his ankle. He was limping around and having a tough time. At the start of the next inning, Beltre was trying to play through it, but was really struggling. So between innings Hargrove sent Willie Bloomquist out to replace Beltre, who was already on the field.

"I look out there and Willie is standing on third base while Adrian is taking ground balls and throwing them to first," Hargrove said. "I'm wondering what's going on out there."

Hargrove went out on the field to talk to Beltre.

"A.B., you're out of the game," Hargrove said.

"I don't want to come out of the game," Beltre said.

"Well, you're out of the game."

"I don't want to come out of the game."

"You're out of the game. Willie's here to take your spot. Come on, let's go in the dugout."

"I don't want to."

"I know you don't want to, and I really appreciate that, but you're out of the game. Let's go."

Only then did Beltre leave the field.

"I wasn't mad. He was very respectful about it, but he didn't want to come out," Hargrove said.

The conversation continued in the dugout, but it was more monologue than conversation.

"I got him down in the runway and said, 'Look, I'm not pissed at you. I understand, and I appreciate you trying to play. But when I do something, you're really kind of disrespecting me as a manager when you do something like that. I don't do it lightly. I understand you want to play, and I really want you to play. But you know you aren't even 60 percent. So respect my decisions enough so you don't do something that causes me to have to come out onto the field like that in front of all the fans, and take you out of the game. Because the writers are going to blow that up for more than it probably is, and rightfully so."

"I never thought about that. I'm really sorry. That won't happen again," said Beltre.

"That's just the kind of guy Adrian was. Respectful of the game. He wasn't a suck ass. But defensively, I don't think I've ever seen a better third baseman, especially going back down the line for a foul ball—he was better than anyone I've ever seen."

The biggest star on Hargrove's Seattle teams was Ichiro Suzuki. In 2004, Suzuki had the greatest year of his career, leading the

American League in hitting with a .372 average, 32 points higher than any other hitter in the league. He set a major league record with 262 hits, 46 more than anyone in the league. In 2005, his first year under Hargrove, Suzuki's batting average plunged nearly 70 points, to .303, the lowest of his first 10 years in the majors. In Hargrove's first year as manager, he and Ichiro reportedly had a tough time adjusting to one another, and according to the Seattle Post-Intelligencer, there were unconfirmed reports that Ichiro didn't like playing for Hargrove.

"At the beginning, there were complications between us," Ichiro told the Post-Intelligencer. Some of those complications were serious, some were frivolous. Ichiro, for example, didn't like it that Hargrove wore a pullover warm-up during games instead of a traditional game jersey. "It's safe to say that some of the baseball values Ichiro favors were not found in abundance with Hargrove," wrote a columnist in the Post-Intelligencer.

"The coolness between the two men seemed too real," wrote another. However, Hargrove and Ichiro met toward the end of the 2005 season and seemed to iron out their communication problems.

Those problems probably stemmed from an early scouting report on Ichiro, given by Hargrove, while Ichiro was still playing in Japan. This was a year or two before his sensational rookie season in 2001, when he led the league in hitting, hits and stolen bases, and won the Most Valuable Player and Rookie of the Year awards.

"I took an all-star team to Japan, and there were hundreds and hundreds of Japanese reporters at the game, every day," said Hargrove. "It was towards the end of the tour, and I was fed up with everything. I was ready to go home.

"The Japanese reporters asked me about Ichiro, and whether he could play in the big leagues. For whatever reason, it just ticked me off, and I said, 'No, I don't think he can. He's a slap hitter who runs well. I think he'd be a fourth or fifth outfielder in the big leagues—if he makes it.'"

Ichiro saw Hargrove's comments about him at the time, and still hadn't forgotten about them several years later, when Hargrove became his manager.

"I think it was kind of a bone of contention between us. I know we did talk about that," Hargrove said. "Obviously, I wouldn't have made a very good scout. He played against our all-star team on that tour, and it was the first time I'd seen him or heard of him. He was a good-looking player, but the contrary side of me just decided to vent. Obviously, I picked the wrong time, the wrong player and the wrong country."

The 2005 Mariners under Hargrove looked a lot like the 2004 Mariners under Melvin. Hargrove's team went 69-93, six games better than Melvin's 63-99 bunch. Both teams finished in fourth place in the AL West, Hargrove's 26 games out of first, Melvin's 29 games out of first. The 2005 Mariners played .500 ball in April (12-12). They lost their first game in May, and had a losing record the rest of the season.

The 2006 Mariners were better, going 78-84. The 2007 team was better still, although it took a while to get going—literally. The Mariners were scheduled to be the opponents for Cleveland's home opener in early April, which would be the first game of a four-game series. But all four games got snowed out. As a result, because that was Seattle's only scheduled trip to Cleveland that year, three games had to be made up by the Mariners flying to Cleveland for single games during three different road trips later in the season. They would play one game against the Indians, then leave and resume their road trip. That just added to the grueling travel schedule for the Mariners, who fly more air miles every year any team in the majors.

After starting 10-10 in the month of April, the Mariners went 16-14 in May and 18-9 in June. But it was a roller coaster. Starting on June 2, the Mariners won nine of 10 games, then immediately lost six in a row.

"We were really inconsistent," said Hargrove. "We'd play really well for four or five games, then we'd play two really bad games."

In an interleague game on June 22, Cincinnati clobbered the Mariners, 16-1. The next day the Mariners clobbered the Reds, 9-1. That was the first win in what would become an eight-game winning streak. But as that winning streak grew, so too did, unbeknownst to everyone but his wife, Hargrove's anxiety. Slowly at first, but steadily. Inexorably. Regardless of the scores or the outcomes, the games ceased to be satisfying. The job seemed more like work than ever. Sleep did not come as easily as it should. Morning came too fast. Not even the winning during the winning streak could change any of it.

The more Hargrove became sure of what he needed to do, the more the team won. Five in a row, six in a row, seven in a row.

None of it mattered. Hargrove had made up his mind, and prior to a Sunday game, at home against Toronto, on July 1, he called a team meeting, where he stunned his players by announcing he had resigned as manager.

"When I made the announcement, I had just handed J.J. Putz his All-Star invitation, the official notice that you've been named to the All-Star team," Hargrove said. "I happened to look at J.J. when I made the announcement, and he dropped the envelope and had this look on his face like, 'What did you just say?'"

*   *   *

It was not a knee-jerk decision.

About 12 days before the announcement Hargrove told general manager Bill Bavasi what he was going to do. Bavasi talked Hargrove into waiting. To give it some time and think about it some more, to make sure that was really what he wanted to do.

Every night for the previous two weeks, Hargrove would talk to Sharon about the decision.

"This wasn't something that I just flew off the handle and did," he said. "It was something that I thought about a lot. I called people and talked to people that I respected."

It was during this time that Sharon, their daughter Shelly Hargrove and her boyfriend, after attending a Mariners game at Safeco Field, came home with Mike, who was having trouble putting the game behind him.

After they arrived at home, "Mike was pacing and pacing and swearing and was really upset," said Sharon. "He had never done that before. It was totally out of character for him. He was always even keel after every game. Finally, I asked Shelly and her boyfriend to leave the room until Mike cooled down."

When they did, Sharon told her husband to sit down. Hargrove sat down, and Sharon sat on the floor in front of him.

"You need to quit," she said.

"I've never quit anything in my life," Hargrove said.

"Well, you need to quit, or you're going to die. You're going to have a heart attack. This is enough. You don't have to do this anymore. Your health is more important."

Sharon saw this situation building because she lived it. They both had.

"We were both just tired of trying to fit family into baseball," she said. "It had caught up with us, because our lives kept expanding. We had kids getting married. We had grandkids. We had a daughter get married on a Sunday. Mike flew to Seattle for a second interview on Monday. He was named manager the same day our grandchild Drew was born. Mike flew home, came straight to the hospital.

"So, over the years, you do that and do that and do that. He had missed everything. I look back and wonder how we did it. People don't understand. He never, in 35 years of baseball, called in sick. You didn't do that. You just didn't miss. You didn't say, 'Hey, I don't feel like going in today.' You may not feel like going, but you went. What man or person can say they never called in sick in 35 years? It's just not acceptable. He was sick of the travel, especially to Seattle, because it was so far away (from their home in Cleveland). He quit because he was exhausted. He was just exhausted."

He also no longer enjoyed the job, and that, in itself, was a deal breaker for Hargrove, as he demonstrated in college. At the time, basketball was his No. 1 sport, and he went to Northwestern Oklahoma State on a basketball scholarship. But when basketball, for a variety of reasons, stopped being fun, he walked away from it and concentrated on baseball and football. That situation, in many ways, paralleled the one in Seattle, and he reacted to it identically. He followed his heart.

One day after Hargrove had made the decision, but before it was announced, Mariners president Chuck Armstrong cornered Sharon in the parking lot at the ballpark.

"Sharon, there are only 30 jobs like this in the whole world. You've got to talk him into not leaving," Armstrong said.

"I don't think I can, Chuck," said Sharon.

Meanwhile the Mariners' winning streak kept growing. Once the streak reached seven games, their record was 44-33. They were in second place in the AL West, four games out of first, and squarely in the wild card race. The next day was Sunday, July 1.

"I told Bill that morning that I was going to do it," Hargrove said. "The hardest part was telling the players."

The second hardest part was the realization that by resigning from a team in the middle of the season, in the middle of a long winning streak, with a team that appeared to be good enough to reach the postseason, this was probably going to be the end of Hargrove's managerial career.

"Yeah, that was tough, because I still wanted to manage. But it was to the point where I was getting no joy out of what I was doing," he said.

"We both just felt like the timing was right. The only thing is, we probably should have stuck out the season," said Sharon.

After the pre-game meeting with the players in which Hargrove told them of his decision, a pitcher came up to him and said, "I know there's something more going on with this, and I'm going to find out."

"No you won't," said Hargrove. "Because there's nothing there."

Following that bombshell meeting, the Mariners somehow went out and played one of their best games of the year. They beat Toronto 2-1 on a walk-off RBI single by Jose Guillen, scoring Hargrove-favorite Beltre, who crossed home plate with the winning run, then raced to the dugout to jump into the arms of his now ex-manager. The victory extended Seattle's winning streak to eight games.

"After the game, I had to walk through the players' area to get to my office. When I came in, the players were all at their lockers and they stood and gave me a standing ovation. That really, really broke my heart," Hargrove said.

"Everyone's still in shock," veteran outfielder Raul Ibanez told the Post-Intelligencer. "Blown away . . . definitely a weird day. Strange, sad, shocking, whatever adjective you want."

Hargrove then went into his office, and a succession of Seattle front office personnel came in to say goodbye.

Prior to the game, the Mariners held a hastily called news conference to announce that Hargrove was stepping down. The reporters at the press conference were no less astonished by the news than were the players in the clubhouse.

"Hargrove managed one last game, then handed over his position to bench coach John McLaren, whose stunned expression at a morning news conference spoke to the shock reverberating throughout the Mariners' clubhouse and the baseball world," wrote Larry Stone in the Seattle Times.

Bavasi said at the news conference that his shock when Hargrove told him he intended to step down was, on a scale of one to 10, "probably 10 or 11. This was not something we were prepared for, or that we wanted."

Hargrove said at the news conference that he and Bavasi "agreed we would wait and give it some time, thinking it would pass. No matter what you do, you go through spells like this. But I'd never felt it at the depth I felt it . . . The highs weren't high enough, and the lows were too low."

Bavasi, quoted in the Seattle Times, called Hargrove's resignation "an important, hurtful move for us . . . We're not happy about it . . . It's very upsetting to us because he's done such a great job. But again, he's one of the best guys any of us have ever run across. It's hard not to be happy for him if he's convinced you he's truly doing what he wants to do . . . So I'm happy for him, and selfishly upset for us."

One Seattle columnist wrote, "Let's face it, he never seemed happy here. He wasn't embraced by the fans, who wanted more emotion from him. Regular calls for his firing started midway through his first season. He suffered, as did his predecessor Bob Melvin, from all the unfair comparisons to Lou Piniella."

At the end of the press conference, Hargrove told the Seattle Times, "I won the first game I ever managed and I won the last game. Pretty good bookends."

In his first game as a major league manager, Hargrove's Indians beat Milwaukee 2-0, on July 6, 1991. It was one of only 57 wins by that 105-loss Indians team.

In his last game as a major league manager, Hargrove's Mariners beat Toronto 2-1, on July 1, 2007.

At his final news conference as a major league manager, Hargrove bristled at the notion that he had lost his passion for his job, or that this was a case of burnout. But those might have been the words of a career warrior, who had to fight to prove himself every step of the way through his career as a player and a manager. There may or may not have been some element of burnout, or him feeling he was losing his edge, which partially explained his decision to resign. But both then and now, he prefers to assign a more ethereal, than concrete, explanation for his Seattle mic drop moment: Sometimes it's just time.

"That didn't surprise me at all. I could identify with that," said Dan O'Dowd, of Hargrove's decision to walk away from the Mariners. O'Dowd was Cleveland's assistant general manager during most of Hargrove's 8½ years as manager, and later became the general manager of the Colorado Rockies for 15 years.

"When I left the Rockies, I was done," said O'Dowd. "The owner offered me a five-year extension but that place had worn me down. I was exhausted. I knew I was going to miss it, but I also knew I had given all I could for 15 years, and I was tired. It was 30 years overall of non-stop, 200 days a year on the road, the cumulative effects of the job itself."

That, in truth, seems more to the heart of what drove Hargrove to his decision. Sharon Hargrove is sure of it.

"We just needed family time. It was always a balance," she said. "I always said baseball was Mike's livelihood. It wasn't his life. It's the way he made his living. Luckily, it was in baseball, and it was a great life. And we met some wonderful people.

"But even though you don't say it's your life, it's your life. Baseball dictated eight months out of our lives as a player, but year-round as a manager—and 35 years of missing birthdays and July 4, then Father's Day and Mother's Day. He saw (son) Andy play baseball three times in high school. Three games! And he'd go and watch maybe two innings, then have to go to the ballpark. Andy had a great run in high school, and Mike never got to see him play.

"Who's going to sign on for that? Who's going to sign on for (major league) teams getting every 19th day off, and that day is going to be a travel day? Who would look at a contract like that and say, 'Oh yeah, that sounds good!'"

After that emotion-drenched Sunday ordeal, that at least ended with a rousing Seattle victory, the Mariners' eighth in a row, the team boarded its buses for a trip to the airport and a flight to Kansas City. They lost the next day, 3-2, a walk off victory in the 11th inning by the Royals. Seattle's winning streak was over, but the season wasn't. The Mariners survived a seven-game losing streak in late July, and actually climbed to within one game of first place in the AL West five different times in the next six weeks. But they faded slightly coming down the stretch, finishing with a record of 88-74, in second place, six games behind the division champion Angels. The 2007 Mariners were 45-33 under Hargrove and 43-41 under McLaren.

"It was real sad leaving Seattle because we both loved it. It was beautiful there," said Sharon. "I really think if Mike had stayed there, they could have had teams as good as we had in Cleveland. He had a bunch of good guys and the chemistry was coming together. One of Mike's regrets is that he let those guys down. Every one of them came into the office after the game that day and hugged him. I think everybody thought he was sick."

After the goodbyes and the hugs and shrugs were over, after the awkward conversations with their uncomfortable pauses had run their course, after the buses taking the team, and its new manager, to the airport had left, after all the fans had departed and the ballpark cleaning crews had arrived, when the sunlight started to fade, and the early-evening quiet had descended on one of the most emotionally noisy days of their 36-year marriage, Mike and Sharon Hargrove exhaled.

They sighed. Together.

*   *   *

"It was the first time in our married life that we got to make adult decisions without having to look at one of those little baseball pocket schedules," said Sharon. "And we didn't know what to do. Do we want to go back to Perryton? No. Do we want to do this? No. Do we want to do that? No. So we laughed and said, 'It's a good thing somebody has told us what we had to do our whole lives, because we obviously can't make a decision.'"

Better yet, in that moment, they didn't *have* to make any decisions. That in itself was refreshing. But when the time came for decisions to be made, they would be made by the two of them, not by baseball.

The first major decision was how to get home. They decided to drive. It turned out to be a three-week baseball decompression tour, slowly winding their way across the country, back to their home in Ohio. With no particular place to go, and all the time in the world to get there, the ex-manager of the Seattle Mariners and his wife rode off into the sunset, following no particular schedule at all.

The Mariners offered them the use of the vehicle they provided for Mike during the season, a brand-new Tahoe. They could drive it home, and then the Mariners would have it shipped back to Seattle.

"But we ended up buying a red Ford truck from a dealer in Puyallup," said Hargrove.

They packed up their baseball lives and they drove south on Highway 101, along the Pacific coast, from Washington, through Oregon, then into northern California.

"We'd drive along and we'd stay in these little motels right on the coast," Hargrove said. "Right on the beach. We'd get up in the morning at 11 and start driving, maybe an hour or two hours down the road, and we'd see a place that looked neat, so we'd stop and check in there for the night. There were days when we drove 10 hours and days when we drove one hour. We just took our time."

It was a nomadic journey for a couple that, for 35 years, had lived a nomadic baseball life. Sharon has the canceled checks to prove it. In their home in Richfield, Ohio, Sharon has framed and hanging on a wall off the kitchen, a display featuring a canceled check from every home they lived in from 1970 to 1995. The final tally: 23 houses in 25 years.

They drove into southern California to watch son Andy play a few games for Seattle's Class-A affiliate in the California League. The Hargroves have five children. Mike had told the kids in advance that he was going to resign. "But they didn't know exactly when it happened until they heard the announcement," he said.

They drove through Arizona, then went up through New Mexico and into the Texas Panhandle for a stop in Perryton, where they were born and raised. They spent a day or two visiting relatives there, then it was on to Liberal, Kansas, which is about 45 miles north of Perryton. Hargrove had played in a college summer league in Liberal the year he got drafted by the Rangers. He became friends with Bob Carlisle, who helped run the team. By 2007 Carlisle had become the general manager of the team, the Liberal Bee Jays.

The team had fallen on hard times, so Sharon talked Mike into accepting the job as manager of the team to hopefully get the program back on its feet.

"I went back and worked for a dollar a year for two years, 2008 and 2009. Sharon got 75 cents of the dollar, for being my agent," Hargrove joked. "We were second in the nation one year and third the next."

Liberal, Kansas, in the summer can get a little toasty.

"You'd dress at home, then took batting practice in your shorts," said Hargrove. "Then you sat in your truck and turned on the air conditioning so you could cool off. Then you'd change into your uniform." One of the players on that Liberal team was Torrey Jacoby, the son of former Indians third baseman Brook Jacoby, who had been a teammate of Hargrove's on the Indians in 1984-85.

Their drive from Seattle to Ohio was loosely mapped out, "But Sharon is the queen of side trips," Hargrove said.

One of those was to El Dorado, Kansas.

"We stayed at this motel called The Great American Motel, or something," Hargrove said. "We checked in, and if they charged you $20 a night for that room, they were over-charging you. But it was the only place we could find. The Mariners at that time were in Texas, and we were in this hotel room with a bed that, when you pulled back the bedding, all the sheets and blankets slid onto the floor. It was just terrible."

That night, Sharon asked her husband, "Mike, do you remember, when you were managing, that suite you had in Texas?"

"Yeah," said Hargrove. "It was a nice suite. The Byron Nelson Suite. It looked out over everything. It had a grand piano in it. You couldn't have gotten anything better."

"Well, John McLaren is sitting in that suite tonight, and here we are in this thing," said Sharon with a laugh.

Three weeks after they left Seattle, the Hargroves rolled into Ohio, where they had lived since 1995. Over the next few weeks

Hargrove would occasionally get phone calls from baseball people, wanting to know how he was doing.

"Jim Leyland called. Joe Torre called. John Hart called," Hargrove said. "When I resigned from Seattle, I had psychologists deduce that I was in a depressed state, or that I had cancer and was going to die. Stuff like that."

Perhaps the most sobering aspect of walking away from his job in the middle of the season was the realization for Hargrove that the decision was probably going to mark the end of his career as a manager.

"I tried to get a job for the next two or three years, but people shied away from me, which I understood," he said. "It hurt a little bit, but I understood that, by doing this, there was a real good chance that being hired to manage another team wasn't going to happen."

The temptation to second-guess his decision to walk away from the job in Seattle lingered in the back of Hargrove's mind for the next couple of years, but he never gave in to it.

"I think it's a normal human reaction to do that," he said. "Did I do the right thing? Slowly but surely, I've come to terms with it. There are times when I'd think 'Would I still be managing if I hadn't done that?' But I'm at peace with it."

CHAPTER 18

Life Without Dugouts

*"I don't miss having to constantly be on
guard about what I say and how I say it."*

When Hargrove returned home in the summer of 2007, it was
the first summer in over 40 years that he wasn't playing for, coaching or managing a baseball team. He was 57 years old. But not once
did the thought enter his mind, "Now what do I do?"

"I didn't need to do anything—and I didn't, for a while," he said.

Well, actually he did. He managed the Liberal Bee Jays, at a
salary of $1 per year, in 2008 and 2009.

He also rode his motorcycle a lot. For a few years, every Memorial Day he trailered his motorcycle out to Perryton, from which he
and four or five buddies would ride their motorcycles to a rally in
Red River, New Mexico.

"It was a seven-hour ride. That was a good time," he said.

Early in 2010, Indians president Mark Shapiro called and asked
Hargrove to lunch, where he offered Hargrove the job of special
advisor to the president, a job he holds to this day. Part of it is ceremonial; he hosts guests in his suite at most of the Indians' home
games. But part of it is baseball. He goes to spring training for a
couple of weeks each year, and periodically talks to manager Terry
Francona and the coaches, helping out wherever he can.

"The thing I miss most is being around the players. I miss the
interaction with the players. I miss the competition of the game,"
he said. "I don't miss talking to the media. I don't miss talking to
general managers. I don't miss the traveling. I don't miss having to
constantly be on guard about what I say and how I say it."

Depending on their audience, major league managers sometimes have to finesse or massage the truth.

"I never lied to the media, but there were times when I talked around the truth," Hargrove said.

Talking to players was completely different than talking to the media. Hargrove learned that lesson as a player, and it stuck with him when he became a manager.

"I played for 11 different managers in 12 years in the majors, and I tried to think back on all those guys I played for, and what I appreciated, and what I didn't appreciate from all of them," he said. "And the one thing I came away with was, I appreciated honesty. I appreciated it when managers wouldn't tell me something I wanted to hear just to get me out of their office. I can take the truth. I may not like it, but at least I know what's in front of me. So, I tried to be that way with my players. I probably could have explained myself better in certain situations than I did. Taken more time.

"But I always tried to be truthful with the players. I always told them if they wanted to come in and talk to me, I was always willing to talk to them. But I was going to tell them the truth, so they have to make sure they want to hear the truth. They must also realize that in baseball, what is true today might not be what is true two days from now. That's where you kind of get into a bind."

There are dozens of reasons why so many managers get fired. But the main one is this: It's a really hard job.

"You've got a lot of balls you're juggling, and if you get shaky juggling them, it can really hurt you," said Hargrove.

Managers, of course, also have to do their jobs in front of 30,000 people.

"When I was playing for Texas, there was this dentist who sat right behind home plate, and he would give Billy Martin hell every time Billy stuck his head out of the dugout. Give him hell, and scream at the players," Hargrove said. "So, one day, Billy walked to the backstop and said to the guy, 'I know who you are. I know where you work, and I'm coming down to your office tomorrow when you're drilling someone's tooth, and I'm going to stand right over your shoulder and scream and holler and tell you how horseshit you are while you're doing your job. See how you like it.'"

Hargrove's best managing job may have come off the field, not on it. The spring-training boating accident in 1993 tested the resolve of everyone in the organization, but as Hargrove said, "Somebody has to drive the bus," and he drove it expertly. There is no manual for how to handle the death of two players in spring training, but Hargrove trusted his heart and his faith to get him through those difficult days, holding together the team in the face of an unspeakable tragedy that could have broken it emotionally.

He also didn't, doesn't and probably won't in the future get enough credit for managing the '95 Indians juggernaut, whose collective abilities were exceeded only by their collective egos. That clubhouse was loaded with arrogance, swagger and, most of all, egos, the kind that can devour a lesser manager.

Sometimes, however, it comes with the turf.

"First of all, you have to have a big ego just to get to the big leagues," said Hargrove. "Some guys have big egos, but they don't let it get in the way. Some guys, they do let it get in the way."

For Hargrove, on that 1995 Muscle Beach version of the Indians, ego management was as important as game management.

"Mike's personality was perfect for that team," said Dan O'Dowd. "He was patient. He knew when to pull the reins in. Mike's whole way about him was just a really good fit for that team. Those personalities that Grover had to manage in Cleveland were very challenging and unique. I'm not sure anybody without his personality would have been able to handle that situation."

Jim Thome, whose lack of ego stood out as much on that ego-swollen '95 team as his bat did on its wrecking ball lineup, said Hargrove had an inherent knack for handling all the disparate personalities on that team, egos and all.

"When you're on a great team like we had, everybody wants to be the star, and that's a good thing, not a bad thing," Thome said. "To have an Albert Belle motivating you, or a Manny Ramirez, Carlos Baerga, Sandy Alomar, Omar Vizquel, Kenny Lofton. We had great personalities, but we all wanted to be the guy, which was to our credit. But Mike knew how to work each of those personalities, and get us all on the same page."

"What made Grover so good with that team," said O'Dowd, "was they competed with one another, but their sense of their own abilities, their cockiness, their arrogance towards the game—that was hard to manage. But it also was fun to watch, come 7 o'clock."

Hargrove said his ability to handle big-ego players was helped by the fact that he had been a major league player himself, and a pretty good one.

"If the players respect what you'd done in the game, you get instant respect," he said. "You can't rely only on that, because if you don't do your job right, they'll think, 'This guy's a flaming idiot.'

"But every player has a hook. Something that they care about. If you can figure that out, then you can use that so they'll start listening to what you're saying. I always tried to be real honest with players. I'd tell them, if there's something you want to talk about or ask me about, be real sure you want to hear the answer. Because I'm not going to tell you what I think you want to hear. I think they respected that. And I would listen to them. There'd be guys come in and talk and they would say stuff in my office about the game, and I'd say to myself, 'Are you serious? Is that how you saw it?' Then I tried to turn it so that I calmed his ego.

"There's not a formula for handling big-ego guys. It's just case by case, what feels like the right thing to do or say. And I would listen. I might not always agree with them, but I listened to their point of view."

Albert Belle's hook was his obsession with his career statistics.

"He knew all of the offensive records for the Indians, and from our conversations I could tell it was really important to him to break some of them," Hargrove said. "So, when Albert would go off the reservation, I'd bring him in and we'd talk, and I'd say, 'To be able to accomplish all these goals you have, you have to play. But if you keep doing this (loafing, throwing tantrums or whatever the crisis du jour was), you'll never reach these goals, because I won't play you. I'll sit you down. So, it's up to you. If you want to play, and I want you to play, you've got to let these things slide.'

"He'd be OK for a while, then we'd have to have that meeting again."

Although the use of analytics began to creep into the game in the mid to late '90s, baseball today is more analytics-driven than any time in its history. Major league teams now have entire departments devoted to analytics. Hargrove was done managing by the time analytics took over, and it sounds as if he's glad he was.

"You hear rumors that front offices are, at the very least, suggesting lineups, based on analytics. I don't know if that happens," he said. "I'd be shocked if it happened to Terry (Francona). But I think I could handle it. As long as they let you do your job.

"With analytics—and I'm probably over-simplifying it—you can get numbers to read what it is you want them to read. It's like the guy who drowned in a river whose average depth was 2 inches. How do you drown in a 2-inch deep river? Well, he stepped into a 20-foot hole. The rest of the river is only an inch deep.

"I think sometimes there is too much reliance on it. I think the infield shift has come from that, and it looks like it works nine times out of 10. But I think it's taken away from the game. Everybody's talking about launch angle. They aren't going to hit the ball the other way because you're not going to make a lot of money hitting the ball the other way, unless you've got Jim Thome power. So, everyone is trying to hit it so hard that you hit it past the shift, or over their heads and out of the ballpark."

During a recent spring training, Indians president of baseball operations Chris Antonetti and general manager Mike Chernoff held a meeting with the team's analytics staff, in which they made their case for the shift. Hargrove was asked to sit in on the meeting.

"You try to defend 75% of the field. That's the best you can do," Hargrove said. "But with the shift, they're defending 100% of the field for a left-handed pull hitter, and 20% of the left side of the field. So, I think it's been bad for baseball. But in that meeting, they gave all their reasons and all their numbers for doing it, and they made a compelling case."

After that case was made, the group asked Hargrove what he thought.

"I said for me, this is one of those things where if you're going to buy into it, you really have to buy into it. It's not like we'll do it 80% of the time and not do it 20% of the time.

"So, if you're going to buy into it, the question you have to ask yourself is, it's the seventh game of the World Series. The tying run is on third, the winning run is on second, and you've got two outs, and a left-handed pull hitter at the plate. Are you going to buy into it so that you're going to shift everybody over and you've got the third baseman playing shortstop? Or not?

"Because if you do that, you're assuming the hitter won't lay down a bunt, trying to get the tying run in. Or hit the ball to the left side, to win the ballgame. For me, that would be a real hard thing to do. In the seventh game of the World Series, ninth inning, one-run lead, the tying and winning runs are in scoring position, and you're going to vacate one entire side of the infield? As a manager, that would be a hard thing to do, but if you're going to do this, if you're going to commit to the shift, that's what you've got to do, because the numbers say that's what happens if he swings the bat.

"But for me, that would make it tough to do. Because if you don't shift, and he hits the ball to the right side and gets the hit, where you don't have a guy shifted, as a manager, you'll get hammered for that. Just like if you shifted, and he hits the ball to the left side of the infield, you'll get hammered for that. So, it's a no-win situation. So, everyone's got to buy into it, or not."

With the proliferation of the shift, and the concurrent proliferation of the absence of action in baseball games, those in the old-school camp suggest the shift should be banned.

"I would like to see it banned, because it would pure-up the game," Hargrove said. "It will make the game a little more honest. You've seen shifts in the past, but nothing as dramatic as they are now, where you've got the shortstop playing second base and the second baseman 40 feet into the outfield. So now the really good hitters are hitting .280 and the average hitters are hitting .230.

"It's just my opinion, but I think a lot of the beauty of the game, the athleticism of the game, has been slowly eroded because of different regulations and rules changes. I don't blame them, because the numbers say let's do it. That's taking advantage of a tool. But somebody in charge needs to start taking a look at that.

"How about in the minor leagues, where they start the extra innings by putting a runner at second base? What in the hell is that? Gosh damn! Come on! I might stop going to (major league) games if they do that."

The old skipper was gaining momentum on an old-school roll. Ask him what he thinks about the game today, and you can either ignore what comes next, or sit back and enjoy the scenery:

"It's changed. Players still play hard. They still want to win. They still love the game. But I think in certain instances we are legislating out of the game what makes the game beautiful. What makes the game what it is.

"You can't break up a double play anymore. The catcher can't block the plate. You've got instant replays to the point where you watch infielders, when a runner slides into second base, they keep the tag on the runner the whole time, and if the runner lifts his foot a half inch off the bag, he's out. Technically, he is out, but that's not the spirit of the rule.

"I never liked the neighborhood double play, but I like the beauty and the athleticism of turning a double play, coming across the bag. And a lot of times now it's not as fluid. I think instant replay, while it's good in a lot of instances, it's taken away the ability of the manager to go out and argue. I think a lot of people enjoy that part of the game. But arguing takes time, and they are trying to cut down on the time of games."

The price of which means we all miss transcendent theater such as this:

"There were a lot of times when I would go out to argue even when I knew the umpire made the right call. But I would go out to argue because the player was arguing, and I wanted to let him know I was there.

"We're in Toronto. Manny is playing right field and Thome is at third base. One out, man at first, and we're up by one run. A real close game, and the SkyDome was jam-packed. It was so loud you couldn't hear anything. A ball was hit to right field on one hop to Manny. Manny had a strong arm, a quick release, and he was pretty accurate. So, Manny makes the throw and it's a one-hop strike to Jimmy at third, and Jimmy catches the ball, and the runner is 5 feet from the bag when Jimmy catches it, and makes a beautiful swipe tag. Beautiful swipe tag.

"There was just one problem. The runner wasn't there yet. It was swipe tag, slide, safe! At that time in baseball, if the ball beat you, you were out. But this time he was called safe. So, the umpire, Larry Young, called him safe, and he was right. The runner was safe.

"My bench jumps up, everyone is screaming and hollering, and I'm thinking, 'I hate going out there because he made the right call.

But if I don't go out there, he's going to kick somebody out of the game, and we don't need that.' So, I run out there and get up to Larry, and we're walking down the left field line and I say, 'Larry, you didn't miss the call. Jimmy made a great tag, the guy just wasn't there yet. You made the right call. But I came out here because you're going to kick somebody out of the game. I don't want that, and you don't want that, because then you've got to write it up. So just let me stay here and let's talk, and we'll let everyone settle down. And Larry says, 'OK, no problem.'

"So, we're walking back towards the bag, side by side, and Buddy Bell gets up off the bench, says something and throws his hands up in the air. You can't hear a word he says. And Larry says, 'Bell! You're out of here!' And I said to Larry, 'Now, why did you go and do that? Why did you kick him out of the game? You can't hear shit. I'm 3 feet away from you and you can barely hear what I'm saying to you. We had this whole thing handled. Everything was fine. And now you did this. I don't understand this.' And Larry said, 'He yelled at me.' And I said, 'Oh, bullshit! You couldn't hear him. Now you're going to have to kick me out of the game.' He said, 'Well, you haven't done anything yet.' And I said, 'How about, you're a no-good dirty cocksucker? Will that do it?'

"Larry said, 'Oh yeah, that'll do it. You're gone!'"

Postscript

His full name is Dudley Michael Hargrove, but nobody ever calls him Dudley.

"His dad's name was Dudley. He was always Mike or Michael, or Saint Michael to his mother," joked Sharon.

Sharon is as much a part of her husband's story—and far more important in the big picture—as was any team, player or front office executive. Married in Perryton, Texas, in 1970, they remain, as their 50th wedding anniversary approaches with five grown children and 14 grandchildren, as devoted to each other as they both were to baseball. She was the quintessential baseball wife; Mike played, coached and managed it. Sharon got it. She understood the rhythm, the nuances and the heartbeat of the game and its participants better than many of his players.

She was a tower of strength, faith and understanding that heartbreaking night, and the days that followed the tragedy on Little Lake Nellie. She instinctively knows what to do and say in any and all situations, and, when Mike became a manager, she was closer to the day-to-day execution of her husband's job than anyone knew.

"The only thing I asked Mike to do," she said, "was if he knew a player was getting sent down or traded after a game, just tell me. I won't tell the wife or act like I know anything. But I'll watch them, to be sure somebody's there. So, if a player was going to be sent down or traded after the game, Mike would tell me, so I could be there in the family room when the wife got the call. The call would come, and whoever answered it said to the wife, 'Your husband wants to talk to you.'

"I would stand in the back and watch the wife react. Then I'd go to the wife and say, 'What happened? Is everything all right? Is everything OK?' even though I already knew what it was. Then they'd tell me, and I'd say, 'OK, here's a shoulder. You've got about 15 to 20 minutes to cuss, cry or kick. Whatever you want to do. But when he comes through that door, you're going to have to knock it off. Because he's the one that has to go through it.'"

Sharon knew, because she went through it, too. In 1979, when Mike got traded from San Diego to Cleveland, it was Sharon who "sat on the floor with our three little girls and bawled, and bawled, and bawled."

After Eric Wedge was fired as the Indians' manager following the 2009 season, Hargrove, then 2½ years removed from his Seattle swan song, was starting to get the itch again. He let it be known that he'd be interested in coming back as the Indians' manager, and for a time it looked like a possibility.

"Mike thought and hoped he'd get an interview," Sharon said. "It wasn't a pride thing. It was just that Mike loved the Indians, and was available again. And he kind of wanted another chance at it."

But then Hargrove got a call one morning from Indians president Mark Shapiro, who told him they weren't going to interview him, and that they were going to name the manager that day. The new manager was Manny Acta.

"Mike was kind of bummed out," said Sharon. "We went to an Our Lady of the Wayside (charity) function, and a radio guy was there and interviewed Mike. He asked Mike if he'd be interested in the Indians' manager's job, and Mike said, 'Oh yeah, I would,' even though he knew it wasn't going to happen."

It was a cold, rainy, dreary morning, and the Hargroves then went to breakfast at an IHOP. The manager recognized them and gave them a table in the back, so nobody would bother them.

"So, we're sitting back there by ourselves, talking about things, how we were frustrated and everything," said Sharon. "Then this older man walked by. He had on a white jacket, with a white hat, and he walked past Mike, patted him on the shoulder and said, 'Hiya, Mike.' And just kept going. Mike kind of teared up and looked at me and said, 'Gosh, I feel like God just walked by and patted me on the shoulder and said everything is going to be OK.'

"I could hardly stand not being able to go talk to that gentleman and tell him how much he helped Mike. But we were kind of talking, and I was involved with that also. So, I was almost hoping

Mike would go to the bathroom so I could go tell that man how much it meant to Mike, but he didn't."

The Hargroves finished their meal without saying anything to the man. But on their way out they paid for his breakfast. About a week later, one of the Hargroves' daughters brought home a letter, from a co-worker, who happened to be the granddaughter of that man. The letter thanked the Hargroves for the gesture. The granddaughter wrote that her 81-year-old grandfather, John Yuhas, had died suddenly, just a couple of days after their paths crossed at IHOP. She wrote that her grandfather intended to write a thank-you note to the Hargroves, but she believed he died before he could send it. Sharon called the granddaughter to tell her how much her grandfather patting Mike on the shoulder had lifted Hargrove's spirits.

As it turned out, John Yuhas did send that letter. But not knowing the Hargroves' address, he sent it to the Indians, asking them to forward it to Mike and Sharon. John Yuhas died a couple of days later. A couple of days after that, the following hand-written letter arrived in the Hargroves' mailbox:

> Mike and Mrs. Hargrove:
> It's just great how surprise gestures by others can make the sun shine on a rainy day in Cleveland. Your generous action to pick up my tab at the IHOP impressed me and awoke many great memories of Indians baseball. You gave us many good seasons and you would certainly look good again in the Indians dugout. Lots of luck in that respect and many thanks to you both for my pancakes and berries.
> (Signed)
> John Yuhas

The letter was dated Oct. 15, 2009, which was 10 years to the day that Hargrove got fired by the Indians.

"It kind of makes you think," said Sharon, "that no matter what you're going through, God's hands are in all of it. Sometimes you don't have to look for it. Sometimes he just pats you on the shoulder."

OTHER BOOKS OF INTEREST . . .

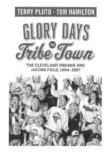

Glory Days in Tribe Town
The Cleveland Indians and Jacobs Field 1994–1997

Terry Pluto, Tom Hamilton

Relive the most thrilling seasons of Indians baseball in recent memory! Cleveland's top sportswriter teams up with the Tribe's veteran radio announcer and fans to share favorite stories from the first years of Jacobs Field, when a star-studded roster (Belle, Thome, Vizquel, Ramirez, Alomar, Nagy) and a sparkling ballpark captivated an entire city.

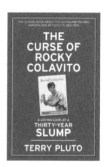

The Curse of Rocky Colavito
A Loving Look at a Thirty-Year Slump

Terry Pluto

A baseball classic. No sports fans suffered more miserable teams for more seasons than Indians fans of the 1960s, '70s, and '80s. Here's a fond and often humorous look back at "the bad old days" of the Tribe. The definitive book about the Indians of that generation, and a great piece of sports history writing.

"The year's funniest and most insightful baseball book." – *Chicago Tribune*

The Making of Major League
A Juuuust a Bit Inside Look at the Classic Baseball Comedy

Jonathan Knight

A behind-the-scenes look at one of the greatest baseball movies ever. Based on interviews with all the major actors, plus crew and producers, it tells how writer/director David S. Ward battled the Hollywood system to turn his love of the underdog Cleveland Indians into a classic screwball comedy. Full of little-known facts and personal stories.

"Jonathan Knight has done something I never thought possible: uncover things about 'Major League' that I didn't even know." – *David S. Ward*

More at **www.grayco.com**